In the Service of the Emperor

STUDIES IN WAR, SOCIETY, AND THE MILITARY

IN THE SERVICE OF THE EMPEROR

Essays on the Imperial Japanese Army

Edward J. Drea

UNIVERSITY
OF
NEBRASKA PRESS

Lincoln
and
London

Chapter 3, which originally appeared as "Strategy Split for Aggression," is reprinted from 9 pages of the September 1987 issue of *World War II* magazine with the permission of PRIMEDIA Special Interest Publications (History Group). Copyright World War II magazine.

Chapter 6, which originally appeared as "In the Army Barracks of Imperial Japan," is reprinted by permission of Transaction Publishers from *Armed Forces and Society* 15:3 (1989). Copyright 1989 by Inter-University Seminar on Armed Forces & Society.

Chapter 11, which originally appeared as "Previews of Hell," is reprinted by permission of MHQ: *The Quarterly Journal of Military History*.

© 1998 by the University of Nebraska Press
All rights reserved
Manufactured in the United States of America

⊚

First Nebraska paperback printing: 2003

Library of Congress Cataloging-in-Publication Data
Drea, Edward J., 1944–
In the service of the Emperor: essays on the Imperial Japanese Army / Edward J. Drea.
p. cm.—(Studies in war, society, and the military)
Includes bibliographical references and index.
ISBN 0-8032-1708-0 (cloth: alk. paper)
ISBN 0-8032-6638-3 (paper: alk. paper)
1. Japan—History, Military—1868–1945. 2. Japan. Rikugun—History—20th century. I. Title. II. Series.
DS839.7.D73 1998
952.03—dc21   97-40180
CIP

CONTENTS

	List of Illustrations	vii
	Preface	ix
	List of Abbreviations	xix
ONE	Tradition and Circumstances: *The Imperial Japanese Army's Tactical Response to Khalkhin-Gol, 1939*	1
TWO	The Development of Imperial Japanese Army Amphibious Warfare Doctrine	14
THREE	Imperial Japanese Army Strategy and the Pacific War (1941–1945)	26
FOUR	An Allied Interpretation of the Pacific War	42
FIVE	U.S. Army and Imperial Japanese Army Doctrine during World War II	60
SIX	"Trained in the Hardest School"	75
SEVEN	Adachi Hatazo: *A Soldier of His Emperor*	91

EIGHT	A Signals Intercept Site at War	110
NINE	Leyte: Unanswered Questions	127
TEN	Japanese Preparations for the Defense of the Homeland	145
ELEVEN	Intelligence Forecasting for the Invasion of Japan: *Previews of Hell*	154
TWELVE	Chasing a Decisive Victory: *Emperor Hirohito and Japan's War with the West (1941–1945)*	169
	Notes	217
	List of Personalities and Terms	265
	Bibliographic Essay	271
	Index	285

ILLUSTRATIONS

Figures

1. Lacking effective antitank weapons, individual infantrymen were left to destroy Soviet tanks 6
2. Fifth Infantry Division landing operations at Bias Bay, 22 October 1938 23
3. Roll call 78
4. Marching troops of the Guards Division parade in barracks area 88
5. Adachi in command of Thirty-seventh Infantry Division on China front 101
6. Adachi at Bay: Wom, New Guinea, August 1945 109
7. D/F operator in grass shack, New Guinea, October 1942 115
8. Fifty-five Wireless Section log entry for 1 December 1942 identifying the Japanese Eighteenth Army 121
9. Listening to and recording the enemy at Vint Hill Farms, Virginia 159
10. Japanese ground order of battle in Kyushu 163
11. Hirohito, on his favorite horse, reviews his troops in May 1941 176
12. Meeting of the Supreme Council for the Direction of the War, September 1941 181
13. The emperor visits the Yasukuni Shrine in Tokyo to pray for Japan's war dead 212

Maps

1. Soviet plan to encircle Japanese forces, 20 August 1939 4
2. The Pacific and adjacent theaters, 1942 35
3. The Pacific areas, 1 August 1942 36
4. Battle for Leyte Gulf, Phase II 134

PREFACE

The war Japan waged between 1937 and 1945—the pivotal event of the twentieth century in Asia—fatally undermined and discredited Western colonial empires throughout Asia; destabilized China, leaving chaos, destruction, and civil war in its wake; spread untold suffering through Asia and the Pacific; left its former colony of Korea divided, with ominous implications; eliminated the military as a meaningful institution in Japan; and left a power vacuum throughout Asia that the United States chose to fill and continues to fill to the present. Newly available documents and supporting materials appearing on both sides of the Pacific make it possible to reevaluate Japan's war, and in so doing, to better understand the historic and cultural traditions shaping late-twentieth-century Japan and its relationships to Asia and the West.

Over the past fifteen years I have written and lectured extensively about the Imperial Japanese Army. In researching these projects, it became apparent that Japanese military historians were exploiting newly discovered or recovered records to interpret not only the field operations of the emperor's army but also its inner dynamics as an institution in prewar Japanese society. Japanese historians were not simply writing about what happened but were trying to explain why things had happened as they did. Such an effort involved sophisticated analysis of the evolution of Japanese army strategy, tactics, doctrine, operations, and leadership, including the role of the army's titular commander, the

Shōwa Emperor, known to the world as Hirohito, in whose name so many Japanese suffered and died. This historical scholarship, a natural development as a new generation of Japanese historians worked from different assumptions and posed questions different from those of their predecessors of the 1950s and early 1960s, revised and reinterpreted Japanese military history. The result was a spectrum of scholarship with viewpoints ranging from ultraconservative to neo-Marxist. Regrettably, most of this rich literature remains confined to Japan, unavailable to the wider community of military historians with an interest in Japanese military operations in Asia.

More than half a century after Japan's surrender marked the end of World War II in Asia, English-language historiography of Japan's war, with few notable exceptions, remains firmly entrenched in the 1960s. For the most part, Japanese army doctrine, training, tactics, leadership, strategy, and motivation continue to be areas little known or appreciated in American accounts of the war in Asia. To be sure, part of the deficiency is that many answers to important questions reside in an extremely difficult language. Another reason is that the current generation of U.S. scholars on Japan seems not much interested in developing military history, which must include military operations, in a systematic fashion to analyze Japan's wartime past. Consequently, these decades of Japanese scholarship about the war are unavailable to the Western reader. Excellent works in English on the army as an institution or the army in a specific campaign do exist, but they are rare. For that reason, the essays in this collection rely heavily on Japanese-language descriptions of their operations in Asia.

My own curiosity about the Imperial Army led me to examine subjects insufficiently covered in English or in need of updating because of newly available documentation in Japan and elsewhere. In the former category are topics such as Japanese amphibious warfare doctrine, enlisted training in the Imperial Army, the career of Lieutenant General Adachi Hatazo, and the evolution of Imperial Army doctrine. In the latter are such subjects as the operations of the Australian Fifty-five Wireless Section field intercept site in 1942–43 and the revived debate about Hirohito's wartime responsibility. A final group of essays compares Japanese and American perspectives on wartime strategy, Leyte operations of 1944, and homeland defense in 1945. In gathering these essays into published form, I have incorporated the latest Japanese scholarship and archival releases of previously classified documents into a single volume. The result, I hope, is to update and expand our knowledge of the war Japan fought against Asia. Although the essays focus mainly on the period between 1941 and 1945, several carry the story back to the 1920s and 1930s, formative decades that witnessed the creation of the new doctrines, tactics, and strategy the imperial forces used to fight World War II. Training, education, and indoctrination of the previous two decades created a well disciplined, professionally led emperor's army whose willingness to fight to the last man became an enduring legacy of the global conflict. Describing how the Imperial Army functioned, ranging from basic training and minor tactics at the worm's-eye view of the enlisted soldier to grand strategy at the rarefied level of the throne, helps explain why the army acted as it did.

A second objective is to discuss the war in Asia as it appeared to the nations involved in the great conflict. The war in Asia was fought between Japan and several Allied nations—Australia, China, Great Britain, the Netherlands, New Zealand, the Soviet Union, and the United States, among others—over the course of almost four years. Despite being a total war across half the globe, Japan's war against Asia remains compartmentalized as though events in China bore no relation to those on New Britain, or the Japanese invasion of India to battlefield setbacks in New Guinea and the central Pacific. Such mistaken notions about the history of the war happened because of the nature of the Allied war effort against Japan. China endured the war against Japan on the Asian continent; the United States carried the war in the Pacific, the naval and amphibious assault war; Australia and the United States fought the war in the southwest Pacific, MacArthur's war; Great Britain led the war in Southeast Asia; and the Soviet Union conducted operations in Northeast Asia. That the war was fought in distinct operational theaters where one Allied nation dominated the struggle against Japan reinforced the natural proclivity to describe the war in national terms, resulting in an Australian, a British, an American, a Soviet, and two Chinese interpretations—Kuomintang and Communist—of the war.

Paradoxically, only the Japanese have published an official history of the conflict covering all aspects of their war against the Allies in Asia. The Japan Defense Agency's 102-volume official history allows one to compare Japanese with Allied official histories and to write a more rounded narrative of what happened and why. Drawing on the Japanese official account, in spite of its shortcomings, enables the historian to offer the reader a more complete assessment of what happened in Asia.

Because character always influences decision making, I have also written and lectured about Japanese leaders not well known to the Western reader. Our stock image of Japanese leadership as faceless robots ruthlessly stamping out strategic decisions in an assembly-line fashion is simplistic to say the least. We need to know how a field commander motivated his troops and what techniques of leadership he used and why. We might well imagine a Japanese general briefing the emperor in a scene of great solemnity and authority. The more likely reality is that the general was so nervous during the imperial audience that he would sweat through his uniform, mumble and stumble over words and phrases, and appear overwhelmed by the occasion. If we know this, we might consider asking how seriously the emperor listened to this officer's advice. And, regarding the emperor himself, how did his character influence decision making?

In examining these topics, the essays make use of fresh documentary evidence in archival and published form, to revise existing accounts of the war. At war's end the Imperial Army did its best to destroy or conceal incriminating evidence about its atrocious conduct during the war. Much documentation did go up in smoke, but much was also entrusted to former officers and officials for safekeeping. As these contemporary diaries and memoirs continue to surface in Japan, as participants on both sides continue to reveal heretofore arcane information, and as governments continue to release documents, more and more new facts about Japan's war will come under scrutiny.

It is fashionable to write that Japan was defeated the day it attacked the Western powers, and, to a degree, this is true. Still, had the Allies been content to implement a straightforward steamroller approach to the war casualty lists would have been longer, as would have been the war itself. It does a disservice to the Allies, and gives far too much credit to the Japanese, to believe the material power of the West simply overwhelmed the Japanese. The essays herein show time and again that Allied commanders outthought and outmaneuvered their Japanese opponents, and Allied troops outfought them. They also show that Japanese commanders did not think through the consequences of their actions. Desperation in the Japanese leadership conjured up such appeals to irrationality as the kamikaze but also rational changes in counter-amphibious doctrine and tactics to enable the Japanese to inflict as many casualties as possible on the counterattacking Allied forces.

The war in Asia, in which the Pacific front was the decisive theater of operations, was waged by Japan against an Allied coalition. In studying Pacific front operations, I have matched the Japanese official history account with those in their American and Australian counterparts. This avoids overrelying on or uncritically accepting Japanese interpretations while establishing a series of checks to evaluate and to analyze the respective national military histories. The synthesis provides a fuller picture of what happened at several critical junctures in the war. At Leyte, for example, it now seems clear that on two occasions during the naval and ground fighting, commanders on both sides had absolutely no notion of their opponent's capabilities or intentions. Such confusion caused indecision, vacillation, and ultimately untimely withdrawal by Admiral Ozawa, and uncertainty, tentativeness, and a tardy advance by General Krueger.

The selections for this volume are grouped according to themes. Two chapters inquire into Japanese army minor tactics; two examine the belligerents' grand strategy; two analyze Japanese army enlisted and officer training and education; two evaluate Allied military intelligence directed against Japan; and two explore events in the summer of 1945. The two remaining selections are wider ranging—one discusses tactical doctrine during the Pacific war; the other, the emperor's role in that phase of Japan's war.

Chapter 1, "Tradition and Circumstances: The Imperial Japanese Army's Tactical Response to Khalkhin-Gol, 1939," was originally presented at the 1982 International Military History Symposium held at Carlisle Barracks, Pennsylvania, whose theme was the impact of unsuccessful military campaigns on military institutions. It describes the Japanese reaction to their humiliating defeat at the hands of the Soviets and attempts to relate Japanese tactical doctrine to battlefield performance as well as the larger issue of cultural response of armed institutions to defeat. In the second chapter, I deal with the development of Japanese amphibious doctrine, concluding that based on their doctrine, Japanese actions were rational, consistent, and effective. I presented a slightly abbreviated form of the paper at the April 1992 meeting of the Society for Military History held in Fredericksburg, Virginia.

Chapters 3 and 4 offer evaluations of Japanese and American strategy, respectively, during the Pacific phase of the war in Asia. The first appeared in *World War II* magazine with the title "Strategy Split for Aggression." It evaluates Japanese strategic concepts for waging a naval and continental war simultaneously and finds them wanting for lack of coordination, leadership, and resources. Juxtaposed against Japanese strategy, in chapter 4 I discuss the U.S. plan for Pacific warfare, developing the general strategies of the southwest and central Pacific theaters against the backdrop of technology, changing not only the initial plans but ultimately, with atomic bombs, the very nature of warfare. This essay originated in a lecture presented in October 1991 to the U.S. Marine Corps Command and Staff College at Quantico, Virginia.

Chapter 5 compares and contrasts U.S. Army and Imperial Japanese Army tactical doctrine during the Pacific war, continuing and expanding themes of the first two chapters and refining explanations of why the Japanese fought as they did. It was first presented in March 1989 at the U.S. Army Command and Staff College, Fort Leavenworth, Kansas.

Chapters 6 and 7 inquire into how the Imperial Army trained and educated its enlisted and officer ranks. Enlisted training is the subject of "Trained in the Hardest School," which appeared in the spring 1989 issue of *Armed Forces and Society*. By following Japanese recruits through a typical training cycle, it explains their tenacity in battle, rock-ribbed courage, and willingness to fight to the death. The complementary piece focuses on Lieutenant General Adachi Hatazo to investigate officer education in the imperial forces. A fascinating character, Adachi had long perplexed me. As commander of Eighteenth Army on New Guinea, he lost at least 110,000 of the 130,000 soldiers and sailors under his command. Yet today's Japanese Ground Self Defense Forces regard Adachi with awe and reverence. I chose Adachi as my subject for a March 1994 lecture at the U.S. Army War College and thus was able to study the man's career much more closely. The essay, although highlighting Adachi, is also about Japanese officer education. As such it should make clearer the means officers used to motivate their soldiers and to understand why Japanese commanders so stubbornly resisted surrender.

The selection on Number Fifty-five Wireless was delivered at the April 1996 meeting of the Society for Military History held in Arlington, Virginia. One happy result of the recent declassification of archival materials in Australia was the opening of Fifty-five Wireless's journal and log for the August 1942–February 1943 period. This critical time, early in the Asia war, witnessed the operational baptism of Fifty-five Wireless, whose daily records are now the only openly available and comprehensive documentation in any language on the formative period of a field intercept site. Comparing these sources to Japanese operational accounts enables us to assess the effectiveness of the Allied intelligence effort as well as to cross-check published Japanese versions of events.

The piece on Leyte was presented at the October 1994 MacArthur Memorial Bureau of Archives, Norfolk, Virginia, conference marking the fiftieth anniversary of General Douglas MacArthur's triumphal return to the Philippines. In preparing the essay, I assumed the recently declassified

American intelligence reports and documents would answer puzzling questions about contentious questions lingering over the conduct of the fighting on both sides. On the contrary, they did not. The process reaffirmed that documents alone cannot resolve all thorny issues. Some historical conundrums will remain unanswered if the personalities involved fail to leave an honest record of their motivations.

Chapters 10 and 11 are controversial. Each addresses events in Japan and the United States during the summer of 1945. In chapter 10 I describe Japanese feverish preparations for defense of the homeland calling into question the conclusions of some historians who insist that Japan's leaders wanted to end the war in April 1945. The paper was presented at the Admiral Nimitz Museum Conference held in March 1995 in San Antonio, Texas. While chapter 10 deals with the Japanese buildup, chapter 11 describes how Allied intelligence uncovered and tracked the progress of the Japanese reinforcement effort. This essay originally appeared in the spring 1995 issue of MHQ: *The Quarterly Journal of Military History*. It is reprinted here with its supporting notes.

The final essay is also the longest. It developed from my presentation at the May 1995 annual meeting of the Society for Military History held in Gettysburg, Pennsylvania. Relying mainly on Japanese language sources, many of which have come to light only lately, the essay describes and analyzes Hirohito's interaction with his military chieftains as a way to evaluate the emperor's personal role during the Pacific war. During the 1990s in Japan there has been an unprecedented outpouring of books, articles, and published documents about the role of the Shōwa Emperor in the war. Much of the new information is controversial; all is stimulating. And the debate over the late emperor rages on in Japan. Because much more work will be done on this subject by historians in Japan and the United States over the next decade, my interpretation of Hirohito raises more questions than it answers, but that was my intention.

To conclude, these newly available materials do not "change" the well-known general outlines of the war in Asia and the Pacific. Instead they do offer us greater insight about the "whys" and "hows" of that great catastrophe, in turn opening the way to new explanations.

A Note on Names

The names of Japanese nationals are rendered in English according to Japanese usage, surname first. I have taken the liberty of omitting macrons in the case of well-known Japanese loan words, such as *judo*, or places such as Tokyo and Kyushu. See the list of personalities and terms at the end of the book for more details.

ACKNOWLEDGMENTS

In preparing these essays over the years I am indebted to many people. In Australia, Desmond Ball, Geoffrey Ballard, Lieutenant General (Ret.) John M. Coates, Peter Dennis, Jeffrey Grey, David Horner, Stewart Lone, David Sissons, David Stevens, and Jozef H. Straczek all shared information and insights about Japan and the war in the Pacific. I am especially grateful to the History Department, Australian Defence Forces Academy, for a generous grant in the summer of 1996 that aided my research. In Japan, Aizawa Kiyoshi, Akagi Kanji, Asada Sadao, Hata Ikuhiko, Miwa Kimitada, and Takahashi Hisashi provided me with primary and secondary materials distilled in these essays. In the United States, Jeffrey Acosta, Edward J. Boone, now retired, and James Zobel always made research visits to the MacArthur Memorial Bureau of Archives a true pleasure. Thomas E. Camden helped me at the George C. Marshall Center, and David Hatch and Thomas Johnson did the same at the National Security Agency. Richard Boylan, Timothy Nenninger, and John Taylor at the National Archives and Records Administration unfailingly steered me to the precise source materials I needed. At the U.S. Army Military History Institute, Lieutenant Colonel (Ret.) Martin Andresen, Louise Arnold-Friend, Pam Cheney, Nancy Gilbert, Randy Hackenburg, David Keough, John Slonaker, Richard Sommers, Dennis Vetock, and Michael Winey assisted my research in archival, photographic, and library collections. Sherry Dowdy, Steve Hardyman, James Knight, Robert Wright, and Roger Wright at the U.S. Army Center of Military History were always helpful. I also owe thanks to Robert H. Berlin, Carl Boyd, Raymond Callahan, John Carland, Eugene Carvalho, Stanley L. Falk, Roger B. Jeans, Steve Rabson, Joseph E. Richards, W. Glenn Robertson, and Roger J. Spiller on whom I inflicted one or more of these essays during an earlier stage of the draft. I am especially indebted to Robert J. C. Butow for his insightful criticisms. Robert Cowley, Editor, MHQ, and Marlena Davidian, Permissions Manager, *transaction*, are owed special thanks for their kind permission to reprint "Previews of Hell" and "In the Army Barracks of Imperial Japan," respectively. I am indebted to the

Mainichi shimbun for its permission to reproduce several photographs that appear in the book. Special thanks are due to my editor Colby Stong for bringing clarity and consistency to these diverse essays written over a number of years. Lastly I once again thank my wife Kazuko and daughter Rika for putting up with my interest in Japanese military history.

ABBREVIATIONS

AR	army regulation
ASWG	Australian Special Wireless Group
D/F	direction finding
FDC	fire direction centers
FECB	Far East Combined Bureau
FSR	Field Service Regulations
GHQ	General Headquarters
IDP	Imperial Defense Policy
IGHQ	Imperial General Headquarters
IJA	Imperial Japanese Army
IJN	Imperial Japanese Navy
IMB	Independent Mixed Brigade
JCS	Joint Chiefs of Staff
LOC	lines of communication
NCO	noncommissioned officer
RAAF	Royal Australian Air Force
RAN	Royal Australian Navy
RCT	Regimental Combat Team
SCAP	Supreme Commander of the Allied Powers
SWPA	Southwest Pacific Area
TO&E	tables of organization & equipment
TOT	time on target
USAEUR	U.S. Army, Europe

In the Service of the Emperor

CHAPTER ONE

TRADITION AND CIRCUMSTANCES
The Imperial Japanese Army's Tactical Response to Khalkhin-Gol, 1939

This chapter emphasizes the tactical realm and examines in detail the impact of military defeat on small unit organization, equipment, and doctrine: in short, it looks in microcosm at the reaction to defeat.

Such an approach is illuminating provided one has access to military documents that candidly acknowledge the deficiencies responsible for defeat and prescribe the remedies for future victory. My method is to describe a single example of how a large and modern army tactically analyzed a grave military defeat. I also discuss what that army did to implement tactical reform based on the lessons of defeat. I have selected the Imperial Japanese Army's reaction to its disastrous defeat by the Soviet Red Army at Khalkhin-Gol (Japanese name, Nomonhan) in the summer of 1939.

The IJA regarded Khalkhin-Gol as their first exposure to modern, combined arms warfare.[1] Khalkhin-Gol was the culmination of almost two decades of Japanese tactical innovation, alterations in force structure, and doctrinal development designed specifically to fight the Soviets. When applied, however, these improvements were deficient. As a consequence, Japanese staff officers carefully and meticulously studied the tactics of their battlefield operations in search of lessons applicable to future combined arms warfare. Before discussing their findings, however, a brief review of the military operations around Khalkhin-Gol is needed to convey the magnitude of the disaster that befell the IJA.

The campaign began innocently enough in May 1939 when more than fifty Outer Mongolian cavalrymen crossed the Khalkhin-Gol (river) into a disputed zone between the river and the village of Nomonhan. The Japanese Kwantung Army Headquarters had recently issued operational guidance for dealing with such incursions. Following these rules of engagement, the commander of the Twenty-third Infantry Division, Lieutenant General Komatsubara Michitarō, ordered his 220-man reconnaissance unit to evict the intruders. The commander of the overconfident Japanese unit believed that only weak Outer Mongolian cavalry were nearby and that the mere sight of Japanese regulars would frighten away the trespassers.

As the Japanese approached their objective, however, they came under sustained heavy artillery fire from the west bank of the Khalkhin-Gol. When Soviet light tanks and infantry attacked the exposed Japanese flank, it became clear that regular Red Army troops were opposing the Japanese. In a sharp, two-day battle, the Japanese lost nearly 140 men, about 63 percent casualties, before they could break the Soviet encirclement and withdraw from the area.

After the engagement, Soviet forces remained in the disputed zone and fortified their positions. In response, the entire Twenty-third Division, two tank regiments (seventy-three tanks total), and one infantry battalion detached from the Seventh Infantry Division tried to drive out the Soviets. The Japanese offensive commenced on 2 July when, in a flanking maneuver, the Twenty-third Division crossed the Khalkhin-Gol north of the original battle area while the two tank regiments, supported by the infantry battalion, drove straight into the original Soviet positions. Both attacks failed, though only after intense fighting. Soviet tanks and armored cars counterattacked the flanks of the northern Japanese pincer. Japanese infantrymen, lacking antitank guns and thus unable to defend themselves against the concerted armor onslaught, retreated. To the south, Soviet antitank guns and entrenched infantry stopped the Japanese attack. Instead of attacking en masse, Japanese tankers made piecemeal attacks because of poor command and control procedures and overconfidence in their tanks' capabilities on the battlefield. They tried to exploit any opportunity, no matter how slight, and to press forward regardless of losses.[2] Soviet gunners riddled Japanese tanks, leaving half of them smoldering wrecks.

Both sides then reinforced, and in mid-July the Japanese again attempted to dislodge the Soviets. For that offensive the Japanese greatly strengthened their artillery support and fully expected their concentrated artillery fire to destroy Soviet entrenchments, thus preparing the way for a subsequent infantry frontal assault. Japanese artillery, compared to the Soviets', was outdated, because Japanese tacticians had not kept pace with changing weapons technology.[3] Even though the Japanese fired what was, for them, an unprecedented 15,000 artillery rounds, the Soviets withstood the barrage and repulsed all Japanese infantry attacks. The combatants then settled down to a month of daily artillery exchanges, infantry probes, raids, and patrols—a classic battle of attrition. Japanese tactical doctrine had envisioned a war of rapid offensive maneuver; their officers and men were unprepared for such a defensive struggle, and their higher commanders seemed uncertain of the conduct of the battle. Meanwhile the Soviet commander, Lieutenant General Georgi Zhukov, marshaled his forces and launched a massive surprise offensive on 20 August 1939, catching the Japanese off guard. Soviet armored formations raced around or smashed through the Japanese flanks and surrounded the Twenty-third Division. A primary reason the Soviets attained surprise was that the Japanese underestimated Soviet logistics capabilities. Japanese logisticians maintained that major military operations could be conducted only within a zone 200 to 250 kilometers from a major supply base. The extreme difficulty the Japanese had in keeping their forces replenished from their Hailaerh base, about 220 kilometers from the battle zone, reinforced this conviction. Yet Khalkhin-Gol was more than 600 kilometers from the nearest Soviet base.

Although the Japanese fought with the fanaticism characteristic of the later Pacific campaigns, the Soviets overwhelmed them. After smashing through the infantry front line, Soviet tanks overran several Japanese artillery batteries with comparative ease, because artillerymen had no antitank or antiaircraft weapons for self-defense. The Japanese forces suffered 73 percent casualties, over 17,000 total, including 8500 fatalities. Soviet losses were officially announced as slightly over 9200, but an authoritative Soviet military journal (*Voyenno-Istoricheskiy Zhurnal*) puts the figure for the entire campaign at over 18,000.[4]

The Soviets had bested the Japanese in offensive and defensive operations, although the IJA had been preparing for nearly two decades to fight the Soviet Union. Such a stunning reversal, in spite of all the doctrinal and organizational preparations, demanded a comprehensive review of the engagement to determine what went wrong and why.

Even before the 16 September 1939 cease-fire at Khalkhin-Gol, the Japanese army began studying, analyzing, and evaluating its recent bitter exposure to modern combined arms warfare.[5] On 13 and 14 September,

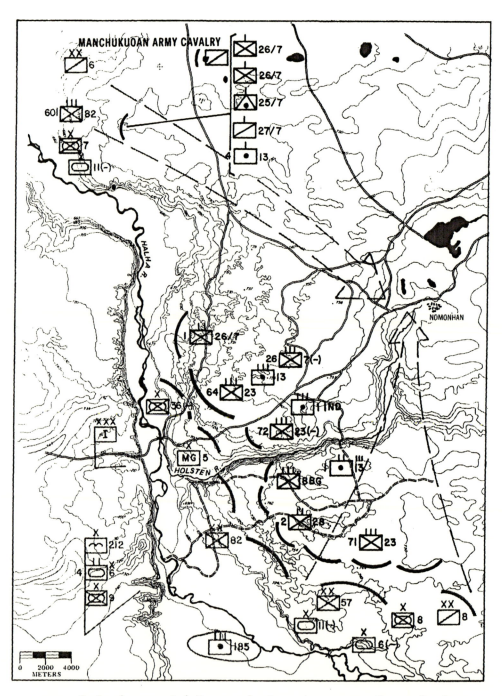

MAP 1. Soviet plan to encircle Japanese forces, 20 August 1939. Source: Combat Studies Institute, Fort Leavenworth KS

for example, ordnance experts issued their findings and evaluations of Japanese and Soviet weaponry in the battle. A seventy-four-page assessment of the tactical use of Japanese combat forces at Khalkhin-Gol appeared on 30 September. A series of officers' impressions and preliminary recommendations followed about two weeks later. The Investigating Committee of the Kwantung Army issued its postmortem on 27 November, and Imperial General Headquarters' (IGHQ's) 262-page final report was distributed on 10 January 1940. The following month Lieutenant Colonel Konuma Haruo, a staff officer who helped to prepare the IGHQ report, presented to the Kwantung Army chief of staff his analysis of the Japanese need to complement their infantry tactics with increased firepower to meet the demands of modern warfare.[6]

All these reports were classified and not for public consumption. Their veracity is of the highest order, because they were intended for the use of staff officers who would be charged with implementing the recommendations. The documents are candid, and although one may disagree with specific interpretations or conclusions, there can be no doubt that these materials accurately reflect the Japanese army's realistic assessment of its defeat at Khalkhin-Gol. Taken together, these documents provide a striking example of an army's ability to criticize itself. Throughout these materials, Japanese staff officers freely acknowledged marked deficiencies and offered recommendations for improvement. The description below of the army's deficiencies and the recommendations of staff officers are based on those documents. Following this description, I examine the army's force structure in the 1940s to determine if the recommendations were acted upon. This is not a discussion of grand strategy but is instead a "nuts and bolts" examination of how one army applied "lessons learned" after a military debacle. In other words, I examine the impact of an unsuccessful campaign on a military institution at its tactical level.

For the sake of convenience, the themes that appear throughout these documents may be divided into specific categories by branch of service, infantry, armor, artillery, and three general groups, motorization, logistics, and doctrine. These categories are not exhaustive, because the after-action narratives and analyses contain hundreds of recommendations and mention dozens of areas for possible improvement.

Perhaps the salient complaint voiced by the Japanese infantry at Khalkhin-Gol was their lack of sufficient antitank weapons. Without such weapons, one report noted, the troops would be annihilated.[7] The same observer suggested attaching four 37 mm antitank guns to each infantry battalion, whereas previously such a unit would have been organic only at

FIGURE 1. Lacking effective antitank weapons, individual infantrymen were left to destroy Soviet tanks. Courtesy of National Archives 111-SC-301096

the regimental level. Another officer recommended that the light antitank gun, rather than the light machine gun, should become the heart of the infantry fighting formation. He reasoned that the antitank gun could be used in attack as well as defense, because its ability to destroy enemy tanks would allow the attacker to continue to press forward.[8] The exhaustive report on weaponry not only recommended one 37 mm gun per infantry company (thereby more than doubling the standard regimental total) but also endorsed research to design a more powerful antitank gun that would, these experts believed, be necessary to defeat heavier armor likely to appear in the future. The 37 mm gun itself required improvements, particularly to upgrade its ability to hit targets at longer ranges. It also needed a new motorized vehicle to transport the weapon and give it battlefield mobility.[9]

The findings in the Nomonhan Research Report also endorsed the concept of making the antitank weapon the nucleus of the infantry formation and suggested increasing the number of antitank guns to eighteen per division along with production of a new 47 mm gun. The Kwantung Army seconded that recommendation and planned to assign 47 mm guns to its motorized infantry divisions. The report also advised that each infantry battalion should have six 37 mm guns and its parent division an antitank battalion composed of eighteen 47 mm guns. In short, the consensus was that more and better antitank guns were needed at company level.

In 1941 the Japanese army fielded a new 47 mm antitank gun but never uniformly distributed these weapons to its infantry divisions. By August 1945, a cursory examination of the intact Japanese infantry divisions revealed that even units such as the Eleventh, Twenty-fifth, or Fifty-seventh divisions, which had been stationed in Manchuria throughout most of the war, were still equipped with the 37 mm weapon.[10] The Fifth Division conversely had towed 47 mm guns for its operations in Malaya during 1941–42. The Seventh-seventh and Eightieth divisions, organized in 1944, had 37 mm weapons at regimental level and twelve 47 mm guns at the divisional echelon. Other infantry divisions, such as the 201st, 202d, 203d, 209th, and 214th, were specially mobilized in April 1945 as mobile strike forces to destroy enemy amphibious assaults. These units lacked regimental antitank guns but had twelve 47 mm weapons added at the divisional level in June 1945.[11] Other 200 and 300 series divisions, such as the 225th or 303d, completely lacked antitank guns.

The only standardized issue of 47 mm guns was apparently to the infantry divisions assigned to the three Japanese tank divisions organized in June 1942. The motorized infantry regiment of these tank divisions had twenty-seven towed 47 mm antitank guns in addition to an organic antitank battalion with eighteen of the same model. Nevertheless, the remaining Japanese tank division, the Fourth, organized in July 1944, had no organic antitank weapons. The need for such a weapon was apparent, the distribution haphazard.

Regarding armor, let us examine the Japanese appreciation of the tank. In 1939 Japan had no tank divisions, although it did have tank regiments. Two Japanese tank regiments fared poorly at Khalkhin-Gol, and higher headquarters ordered their survivors to withdraw after the early July fighting. On the organizational level, staff officers recommended that one tank and one armored car company be attached to each infantry battalion, probably because Soviet tanks and armored cars were so instrumental in encircling the Japanese infantry.[12] After Khalkhin-Gol the Japanese concluded that the design of their tanks was inferior. One general officer recommended that the tank silhouettes be lowered by reducing height, the armor plating be thickened, and the muzzle velocity of the tank cannon be improved.[13] Ordnance specialists also recognized the requirement for improved armor plating on the Type 89, 95, and 97 tanks. They planned to increase muzzle velocity of the tank's main gun to allow Japanese gunners to engage enemy tanks at mid-ranges. Other significant changes would lower the silhouette and substitute a higher-velocity main gun of 45- to 50 mm caliber for the 37 mm or 57 mm gun then in service on the Type 95 light tank and the Type 97 medium tank.[14] Tanks needed the capability of speeds in excess of 25 kilometers per hour and the ability to cover 200 to 300 kilometers per day. Furthermore, ordnance officers insisted on radio communications between and among tank crews because of the increased range requirements and the confusion that marred tank operations at Khalkhin-Gol. The research committee also wanted a self-propelled gun unit attached to tank regiments. In sum, a variety of specific recommendations were made to improve Japanese armor. How then did Japanese armor develop in the 1940s?

The Type 95 light tank had seen action at Khalkhin-Gol. Its main armament was a 37 mm gun, and it had 12 mm thick armor on its turret and front. It could attain a speed of 40 kilometers per hour and had an operational range of 250 kilometers. The subsequent design, the Type 98 light tank appearing in 1942, retained the 37 mm gun, although it had improved armor, speed, and range. Only about 100 of these tanks were produced by Mitsubishi Heavy Industries. It is uncertain whether any of these models with a 47 mm gun were ever produced.[15] At any rate such a weapon was never distributed to combat units despite favorable test reviews.

The Type 97 medium tank changed significantly. From February 1940 to November 1942 Hitachi's tank factory in the Kameari district of Tokyo built about 350 of these improved models, which mounted a 47 mm main gun versus the earlier model's 57 mm gun. Armor thickness remained the same, although the high-velocity 47 mm gun demanded a redesigned turret cupola, which actually increased cupola width and overall height by nearly 5 inches. Production amounted to 355 tanks compared to the 1120 older models produced by Mitsubishi.[16] As for the Type 89 medium tank, only its range was improved, from 140 to 170 kilometers. In 1941 a Type 1 medium tank appeared that fulfilled the requirements envisioned by the ordnance officers in 1939, but only about 600 were ever built. A modified version manufactured in 1943 mounted a 75 mm main gun, but only about 60 of these models were completed. Once again the recommendations were followed in a piecemeal fashion.

Every investigatory committee commented about the Japanese artillery's performance deficiencies at Khalkhin-Gol. There were four basic problems: a shortage of weapons, a shortage of shells, insufficient mobility, and a lack of organic antitank and antiaircraft weapons to defend the artillery guns. Several officers recommended increasing organic divisional artillery batteries, in one case doubling the number of artillery batteries from the standard nine to eighteen and augmenting their firepower with heavier 150 mm guns and 105 mm howitzers.[17] As for the artillery weapons themselves, ordnance experts noted that the standard 75 mm field artillery gun was ill suited for a counter-battery role, and recommended an improved version. The Kwantung Army, in turn, wanted a new, longer-range, heavy artillery weapon.[18] Several observers suggested the need for a self-propelled gun, and everyone agreed that the artillery's mobility had to be improved mainly by replacing its standard horse-drawn transport with motorization. As before, we discover a specific list of recommendations based on lessons learned in the defeat at Khalkhin-Gol.

By 1945 the organic artillery of Japanese infantry divisions seemed so bewildering as to defy the notion of standardization. Some units that had been stationed in Manchuria, such as the Eleventh and Twenty-fifth divisions, adopted the 75 mm mountain gun but retained the nine artillery batteries per division. The Fifty-seventh Division, also of Manchurian vintage, retained a battalion of the obsolete 75 mm field artillery pieces but added two battalions of 105 mm howitzers, for a total of nine firing batteries. In other divisions artillery assets depended on the unit's mission, and there was wide variation. Two important facts: First, the Japanese developed no new artillery weapon after 1939; and second, there was no organic protection for the artillery.

Self-propelled guns, however, did begin to appear in Japanese units in early 1942. There were two main types: the 150 mm howitzer (self-propelled) and the 75 mm gun Type 1, the so-called gun-tank.[19] Both were hybrids that used a Type 97 medium tank chassis to carry a standard artillery gun or howitzer tube. Both models appeared at Luzon in 1945, probably as units of the Japanese Second Tank Division, which fought American forces there. The self-propelled guns, as in the case of the 47 mm antitank guns, were assigned primarily to the motorized artillery regiments of the tank divisions. Self-propelled guns also appeared in the tables of organization and equipment of infantry divisions stationed in Manchuria. Nevertheless, the majority of infantry divisions never fielded such weapons, because production never reached a level permitting universal distribution.

The lack of self-propelled artillery was symptomatic of a larger problem also visible at Khalkhin-Gol, namely a general deficiency of battlefield mobility caused by insufficient motorization. There was an obvious problem, an acute shortage of trucks, identified by all officers. They linked that shortcoming to their logistical difficulties because the shortage of trucks handicapped logistics efforts, particularly the movement of reinforcements and material at Khalkhin-Gol.[20] The solution was evident. More trucks, motorized transport for artillery, antitank guns and artillery, and a motorized logistics regiment were needed.[21] Ordnance men even recommended a small, four-wheel drive vehicle capable of moving over poor roads or in areas where roads were nonexistent.[22] These improvements, in turn, would allow Japanese operations to move farther away from the railheads that had heretofore determined the operational radius of units. Beyond that the Kwantung Army report noted, instead of adhering to the traditional practice of lines of communication following in the wake of operational movement, the most pressing problem was to calculate the replenishment capacity required to fight a protracted battle and have the capability to transport the necessary men and supplies to the operational units.[23]

From January 1941 motorization of selected Japanese infantry divisions occurred, but only three operational units ever appeared, the Fifth, Eighteenth, and Guards divisions. I submit that it was not coincidence that these divisions participated in the Malayan operation of 1941–42. The Fifth and Eighteenth divisions were, it is true, specially trained amphibious assault units with extensive combat experience from the China fighting. And all three divisions had participated in a series of amphibious assaults on the south China coast earlier in 1941. But IGHQ tabbed the Fifth and Guards divisions for a consciously designed, fast-moving operation, because they were two of Japan's three motorized divisions.

The Fifth Division was an enormous formation. A square division (composed of two brigades of two regiments each), it boasted 25,000 officers and men organized in two brigades. Motorization began in early 1941, and the division conducted operational maneuvers in south China that April. It had about 860 trucks echeloned at 91 per infantry regiment, 149 to its artillery regiment, and 124 to a motorized transport regiment. The Guards had fewer troops, 18,000, and fewer trucks, 663, and was a triangular formation having a single brigade with three regiments subordinate to it. The Eighteenth was also a square division but had only 17,000 men available for Malayan operations, a brigade headquarters and regiment being detached for Borneo operations. It also relied more on horse-drawn transport than the two motorized divisions.[24] In that sense, the Eighteenth was representative of the majority of the Japanese divisions as horse-drawn carts and artillery remained the rule in the army throughout the war years. Even in the motorized divisions, however, the number of trucks only reached about one-quarter to one-third that of the European forces then fighting in North Africa.[25] As late as 1945, the Fifty-seventh Division had 119 trucks in its transport regiment, the Eleventh Division but 39.

Despite the lessons of Khalkhin-Gol, Japanese logistics never really improved. Operations were repeatedly conducted on a logistics shoestring.

The successful Malayan campaign, for instance, saw Japanese lines of communication stretched to the breaking point.[26] The replenishment capability was never present, because Japanese operations officers refused to invest their time and energy in logistical matters. The army placed a premium on fighters, not coolies. When such grand tactics worked, as in the Philippines, Burma, or Malaya, their weak logistics support could be glossed over. But when disaster struck the deadly folly was all too obvious. Ill-fated schemes, such as Lieutenant General Mutaguchi Renya's Fifteenth Army Imphal operation in 1944, underlined with Japanese corpses the folly of launching a major offensive without adequate lines of communications. Other examples are the disastrous Japanese battles in Burma in 1945 or the Ichigo Operation in China from 1944 to 1945 when unarmed troops were sent forward with instructions to retrieve the weapons of their fallen comrades. So, despite many lessons learned, few substantive changes appeared. I believe that the failure of the Japanese to respond to the lessons of Khalkhin-Gol can be traced to Japanese tactical doctrine.

Japanese doctrine presupposed an early decisive battle and rapid cessation of hostilities. Officers carried that notion to Khalkhin-Gol, and, despite the Kwantung Army's after-the-fact warning, Japanese officers carried the concept in their kitbags throughout the war. Underpinning the doctrine was an unquestioning faith in the inevitable victory of Japanese arms. This intangible, or to the Japanese "spiritual," side of combat was the propellant for infantry tactics predicated on rapid maneuver designed to encircle and destroy their opponent quickly. These were the tactics at Khalkhin-Gol, and they did not work. But every Japanese analysis of the defeat paid at least lip service to the intangibles of battle. Colonel Terada Masao regarded the "magnificent fighting by the Twenty-third Division as a serious blow to Soviet aggressive ambitions in the Far East."[27] IGHQ merely endorsed existing tactical concepts when it recommended that Japanese forces could still take advantage of the Soviets' lack of "spiritual power" to exploit the greatest Soviet weakness, because "our belief in inevitable victory will overcome the Soviets."[28] Other observers were more cautious. They endorsed "spiritual power" and the tactic of hand-to-hand combat, but recommended additional firepower be given to infantry divisions.[29] "The greatest lesson of Nomonhan," wrote a staff officer, "is that we must quickly raise our heretofore low level of firepower to the high standards of our army's traditional spiritual power."[30]

The solution then was to augment spiritual power with material power. This was never done in a systematic fashion. Instead subtle shifts in tactical doctrine emerged, because officers on the general staff began to doubt the shibboleth "Faith in Inevitable Victory." That slogan was quietly dropped from Japanese training manuals in 1942 and replaced with a more innocuous admonition, "Accomplish One's Duty."[31] The concept became further distorted when border guard detachments in Manchuria during the final days of World War II were instructed to hold their positions to the last man against overwhelming Soviet forces, because "this spirit is the culmination of the army's tradition of attack."[32] Such convoluted thinking only revealed the paucity of tactical innovation. Why did significant tactical reform come to a dead end?

The obvious answer is that the Japanese were preoccupied with other wars, the war in China from 1937 and later the Pacific War. These "completely changed conditions" caused the general staff to shift its interest to the South Pacific theaters, so the lessons of Khalkhin-Gol were not applied in a practical manner with any zeal.[33] As one Japanese historian has pointed out, high-level Japanese officers hoped that Khalkhin-Gol was a minor episode in relation to Japanese operations in China and the worsening European situation.[34] Yet the lessons became the basis for the December 1939 Revised Armaments Replenishment Plan, whose goal was to reequip the soldiery within five years for a possible war against the Soviet Union.[35] The lessons also seem to have been applied in Malaya operations, in the TO&E of Manchurian divisions, and in some newly created divisions. Moreover IGHQ created special ocean operations divisions, such as the Fourteenth, Twenty-ninth, Thirty-sixth, and Fifty-second. These triangular (composed of one brigade and three regiments) divisions had two regiments assigned to defensive operations against enemy amphibious attacks, and the third regiment, with an organic tank company and heavy weapons company, served as a mobile counterattack force.[36] Although the evidence is circumstantial, it at least suggests that Japanese military planners tried to implement lessons of modern warfare they first learned at Khalkhin-Gol.

Two hindrances account for the lack of systematic change, one material and one "spiritual." The Japanese military machine lacked the industrial base and natural resources to convert an infantry force into a motorized one while engaged in a full-scale war. Within these constraints some attempts were made at meaningful reform, but the crux was the "spiritual" aspect of Japanese tactics.

Traditional values of Japanese "spirit" in warfare reinforced the natural tendency of subordinates not to voice suggestions to higher-ranking officers that they did not want to hear.[37] Besides, the Twenty-third

Division was newly activated on 11 July 1938, so staff officers could rationalize its defeat on the grounds that it needed more unit training before its first battle. To reorganize a superb infantry force into heavy units flew in the face of the historical process of the development of tactical doctrine in Japan. Battlefield intangibles were important, and any staff officer who tried to ignore their powerful influence could soon find himself in an awkward position. Lieutenant Colonel Konuma, for instance, told the deputy chief of staff of the Kwantung Army that instead of bragging about victories in China based on fighting spirit, the IJA hereafter would need equal or superior weaponry to fight foreign armies. His frankness earned him a stinging rebuke from Major General Endō Saburō, who roared, "You imbecile! What you say insults the Imperial Army."[38]

Similar attitudes were not a so-called post Khalkhin-Gol syndrome. Eleven years earlier Colonel Kobayashi Jun'ichirō's pamphlet, *The Reformation of the Japanese Army* (Nihon rikugun kaizōron), warned that an excessive reliance on "material goods" would corrupt the soul of the Japanese army.[39] Such views stressing reliance on Japanese spirit might be considered eccentric, but Kobayashi had been the leading proponent of artillery as the decisive weapon of future warfare. Also, Kobayashi was hardly a voice calling in the wilderness. Words such as "surrender," "retreat," and "defense" were removed from the language of the revised 1928 Field Service Regulations because their negative connotations might adversely influence morale.[40] This deeper cultural resistance to change manifested itself as the cluster of uniquely Japanese values found in expressions such as *bushidō* (the way of the warrior) or *Yamato damashii* (Japanese spirit). In short, powerful natural and historical forces worked against sweeping military renovation in Japan during World War II.

It seems commonplace that military defeat can be salutary in nature, because it forces out incompetents and promotes innovative reforms. The popular historian Barbara Tuchman wrote, "Whereas defeat in war galvanizes military development, nothing contributes to military desuetude like total victory."[41] Like most generalizations it overstates the case. The way an army interprets defeat in relation to its military tradition, and not the defeat itself, will determine, in large measure, the impact an unsuccessful military campaign will have on that armed institution.

CHAPTER TWO

THE DEVELOPMENT OF IMPERIAL JAPANESE ARMY AMPHIBIOUS WARFARE DOCTRINE

I aim to outline the evolution of amphibious warfare doctrine in the IJA from the 1890s to 1941. This chapter elaborates and clarifies other treatments of the subject by relying on specific examples to illustrate the changing doctrine.[1]

IJA amphibious operations proceeded through three general stages.[2] The first occurred from about 1890 to the opening days of World War I. During this period Japan conducted landing operations in three major conflicts against Ch'ing China (1894–95), Czarist Russia (1904–5), and Imperial Germany (1914–18)—as well as punitive expeditions to seize Taiwan (1895) and to North China to suppress the Boxer Rebellion (1900). At most these landings met fleeting resistance. During the Sino-Japanese War, for instance, Japan's First Army (First Division and Twelfth Brigade) conducted an unopposed landing on the Liaotung Peninsula about 100 miles north of Port Arthur then turned south to seize the key installation. Likewise the Second Army's (Second and Sixth divisions excluding the Twelfth Brigade) landing on the eastern tip of the Shantung Peninsula met scant Chinese resistance. The invaders seized their objective, the port of Weihaiwei, about 35 miles from their landing area, within two weeks.[3]

Operational doctrine mandated ship-to-shore landings and subsequent development of the landing site to handle the unloading of additional troops and cargo. Success depended, in turn, on the Japanese navy's ability to control the seas. The Liaotung and Shantung landings, for example, followed the Battle of the Yellow Sea in which the Japanese fleet sunk or forced aground five of fourteen Chinese warships, heavily damaged several others, and left the demoralized Chinese fleet at one-third effectiveness and unable to sortie against the Japanese forces.

Tactical landing doctrine proceeded from operational success. Under cover of the warships, naval special landing parties preceded army forces ashore. Once ashore the sailors organized the beachhead and established a perimeter from which to screen the main landings from hostile eyes. Next, army troops climbed down rope ladders while horses and equipment were sling loaded into wooden barges. These were of two sorts, each having one smaller variation. There was a 5-ton, 42-by-11-by-4-foot-deep wooden barge capable of carrying seventy troops, or ten horses, or three artillery and a smaller version (forty troops, or six horses, or two artillery guns). The other type, partially armored but mainly wooden, was much larger—150 by 28 by 30 feet and able to lift 500 men or 104 horses. It took an 18-ton steam-powered motor launch to tow these barges, which weighed about 40 tons fully loaded, to shore.[4] Technological limitations then made debarkation a slow and cumbersome process that was inadvisable under enemy fire. Operationally it dictated that one land one's forces away from, not close to, the main enemy concentrations. Tactically it meant that the shuttling of troops, horses, supplies, and equipment to shore had to wait until the initial waves had secured the beachhead. How did the Japanese establish a secure beachhead?

An example from the Russo-Japanese War provides an excellent illustration that typifies Japanese amphibious doctrine into the 1920s. The Japanese navy's surprise attack on the Russian naval base at Port Arthur in February 1904 had given Japan local superiority on the seas, the prerequisite for a landing. With this advantage, in May the IJA's Second Army (First, Third, and Fourth divisions) went ashore unopposed on the Liaotung Peninsula about 40 miles north of the Russian fortress at Port Arthur.

On the morning of 5 May a naval landing party composed of two battalions of sailors with two light artillery pieces went ashore at the designated site. A general staff officer assigned to the Third Department (foreign military affairs and terrain studies, statistical office), Sixth Section (transportation) accompanied the sailors to reconnoiter the anchorage to ensure its suitability for a major landing. Next a battalion of army engineers landed to prepare for the main landings scheduled for the next day.[5]

Meanwhile the naval landing party had occupied the high ground overlooking the anchorage to cover the landings. The 5-ton barges carried the Third Division in the first wave. Debarking from the barges at 0730, the division immediately proceeded to relieve the sailors. Lead units of the division's Seventeenth Brigade conducted a passage of lines and occupied the high ground within thirty minutes of going ashore. Now they looked down on the second-echelon landings, which commenced at 0830. Three hours after the first soldier waded to the beach, the entire Seventeenth Brigade (about 6000 men and 450 horses) had landed in a combination of large and small barges, had relieved the naval landing party, and had fanned out to control nearby key terrain. By midafternoon, the sailors were back aboard their ships, although the two artillery pieces remained with the ground troops.[6] Japanese forces consolidated their anchorage over the next several days, and on 15 May the three divisions moved south on the first leg of their painful advance to Port Arthur.

This landing highlights the tenets of Japanese amphibious doctrine for this early period. First, gain control of the sea lanes to ensure the safe transport of infantryman. Second, select a landing area well beyond enemy strongpoints and thus likely to be undefended. Third, dispatch a naval landing force with appropriate engineer and technical support to secure the beachhead and prepare for the main landings. Fourth, sacrifice speed to consolidate the landing area, thereby transforming it into a staging area for future land operations. This pattern reappears during the Japanese invasion of Sakhaklin Island (7 July 1904), the two landings on the Shantung Peninsula (September 1914) that led to the siege of the German naval base at Tsingtao, and the Siberian Expedition (22 April 1920).

The second stage of amphibious development lasted from 1918 to 1937. After World War I, the Japanese army found itself in a situation similar to the one the American military confronts today. The disintegration of Imperial Russia, similar to the collapse of the former Soviet Union, left both armies without a major threat. In 1918 the Japanese cabinet approved and the emperor sanctioned a revised national defense policy that replaced Russia with the United States as the main hypothetical threat. The new strategy mandated joint operations far from continental Asia. Now the army had to commit one division to a joint operation directed against Luzon, Philippine Islands. Subsequent revisions of defense policy in 1923 and again in 1926 expanded the army's role to include seizing Guam and allotting three divisions to the reduction of Luzon.[7]

Already aware of the technological revolution during World War I, the Japanese army reexamined its forces and equipment with an eye toward modernization. Between 1918 and 1937 (the outbreak of the Sino-Japanese War), the army developed motorized landing craft to enable troops to move directly from ship to shore without naval landing parties interceding. Despite the emphasis on joint operations, the army also moved toward conducting independent landing operations and organized special engineer and landing craft groups to carry its infantrymen to shore.

Yet it did not earmark specific divisions for amphibious training, apparently assuming that each and every division could play an amphibious role. As in the earlier phase, amphibious operations depended on control of the sea, but the general staff recognized the growing aerial threat to shipping. The army tested its emerging doctrine and amphibious tactics in numerous joint exercises beginning in the early 1920s.

In July 1918 the Fifth Division conducted the first independent direct landing of army troops from ship to landing craft to shore. Army Chief of Staff Uehara Masasaku's exposure to the 1920 amphibious exercises convinced him that landings conducted from towed wooden barges were obsolete, and he directed studies to design a steel, self-propelled landing craft.[8] The following year, high waves in Sagami Bay swamped towed barges carrying men of the Sixth Division, thereby underlining the need for a modern landing craft. While awaiting delivery of the new vessel, the army ran numerous amphibious exercises in 1922 involving the Fifth, Sixth, and Eighteenth divisions as it continued to test its concepts of independent army landings directly from ship to shore.

The first field tests in joint operations of the newly produced steel-plated, self-propelled landing craft occurred in 1925 and proved inauspicious. High waves and rough seas swamped vessels and washed several men of the Third Division overboard to their deaths. Following this debacle, Lieutenant General Inoue Kitarō, the division commander, somberly reported to the annual conference of army division commanders that "in the present circumstances, the army lacks the materiel to renovate existing landing equipment for modern amphibious operations."[9] He recommended that the general staff nominate specific divisions for amphibious missions and concentrate necessary resources, equipment, and training on those units thereby conserving scarce yen and manpower in times of fiscal and personnel austerity.

The general staff tabbed the Fifth, Eleventh, and Twelfth divisions for the amphibious mission. Contrary to Edward Behr's fatuous statement that the Fifth Division was chosen because its men came from Hiroshima and knew how to swim, the general staff selected these three divisions (from a force structure of seventeen divisions) for two sound military reasons.[10] First, the three divisions were clustered around Ujina, which had served as Japan's premier logistics base for overseas expeditions since 1894. Located in Hiroshima Bay, Ujina was Hiroshima's port and headquarters for the army's transport and shipping command. In other words, operationally the division camps were ideally positioned for rapid deployment from a major military port. Second, in the strategic sense, the proximity of these "western divisions" to the Asian mainland and to the Philippines made them the most likely to be involved in future amphibious operations.[11]

Their selection coincided with the appearance of the new landing craft, the familiar daihatsu and kōhatsu, which served throughout World War II. The daihatsu, completed in 1929, was a metal-hulled, diesel-powered craft 41 to 49 feet long capable of traveling 8.5 knots. Crewed by seven men of the army's Water Transport Command, it weighed 10 tons and could carry seventy men, or ten horses, or one tank, or 12 tons of cargo. A smaller version, the kōhatsu with a five-man crew, completed in 1927, carried roughly half as much.[12]

In 1927 and again in 1930, the western divisions conducted amphibious assault exercises in concert with the navy. Special engineer exercises held in October 1929 tested disembarkation training and doctrine. In 1930 training for selected engineer units stressed removal of beach obstacles in preparation for assault landings. Meanwhile amphibious training for the western divisions proceeded. All trends indicated that the army was intent on developing an amphibious capability for a forced assault landing. Although no one could know it at the time, the 1930 exercises were to be the high point of pre–World War II Japanese amphibious training.[13]

Doctrine and training did receive a practical application during the Shanghai Incident of 1932. On 15 February the general staff dispatched the Ninth Division to Shanghai complemented by provisional engineer units from the Fifth Division as well as an infantry regiment, an artillery battery, and two tank companies from the Twelfth Division. They debarked in a sleet storm without incident and then were thrown into the city fighting. Two weeks later, the Eleventh Division made a dawn landing 25 miles north of Shanghai against negligible Chinese resistance. In danger of encirclement, the Chinese withdrew from the city.

Despite the success of a rapid deployment amphibious force to Shanghai and the subsequent division-size landings to outflank the enemy, interest in amphibious operations was waning. Over the next eight years, only two landing exercises were conducted, the Fifth Division's in October 1932 and the Eleventh's in 1934. International events dictated shifts in the national military strategy that deemphasized landing operations in general and against American targets in specific.

The revived Soviet Union reemerged as a menace to Japan's north. For reasons discussed elsewhere, Japanese officers precipitated the Manchurian Incident in September 1931. Although they quickly achieved their immediate goal of conquering Manchuria, the long-term result was to set Japanese and Soviet troops eyeball to eyeball across a vaguely defined frontier. The United States slipped to a weak second as a hypothetical opponent for the Imperial Army, and throughout the 1930s the general staff showed little interest in even updating basic planning for a war with America. Instead, training and doctrine focused on an anticipated war against the USSR. In short, the army was not simultaneously considering a land war on the continent and one in the Pacific Ocean.[14] The Imperial Army was looking to the northeast Asian land mass, so it no longer needed to emphasize a deep water amphibious capability having already had a forward presence in Manchuria and developed ports, harbors, railroads, and so forth in its adjoining colony of Korea.

Makeshift arrangements compensated for a force structure that was inadequate for its new missions. Unable for budgetary reasons to expand the number of divisions in the standing army, staff officers devised war plans in 1936 that designated the Fifth and Eleventh divisions, already matched against the Philippine Islands, as a contingency force mission in Manchuria. Furthermore, in April 1936 the Twelfth Division was ordered to Manchuria to augment Japanese units there in the face of the Red Army's buildup in the Soviet Far East. The outbreak of an unanticipated full-scale war in China in 1937 further complicated the force structure issue.

The Japanese general staff ordered initial mobilization following the Marco Polo Bridge Incident of July 1937 on the assumption that the fighting would remain localized. They wanted to marshal sufficient force to intimidate the Chinese and bring hostilities to a quick conclusion. But only three standing divisions, including the Fifth and Eleventh, were available in Japan for immediate deployment to north China. Thus the Fifth Division found itself fighting on the north China plain. As a division trained for amphibious operations, the Fifth had pack horses, not the sturdier, more powerful draft horses needed to pull heavy artillery. It ended up using three packhorses to do the work of one draft animal. This naturally lengthened supply columns, reduced the division's mobility, and is one of the reasons that Lin Piao's Eighth Route Army annihilated the Fifth Division's transport at Tai-er-chuang in April 1938.[15]

Meanwhile the Eleventh Division was ordered to Shanghai where fighting had spread in August. The Eleventh made an unopposed landing, but then had to fight its way through well-sited and well-defended Chinese fortifications. The division was not properly trained for this type of combat, and of the 12,795 officers and men deployed, 2293 were killed in action and another 6084 wounded, a casualty rate of almost 66 percent. Its first battle proved to be its last because the division never fought again.[16]

Subsequent mobilizations to keep pace with the escalating China War also disrupted prewar plans. By the summer of 1938, the army had doubled from seventeen to thirty-four divisions. Such a rapid expansion was possible only by mobilizing the reserve. The effects of a mass mobilization altered the character of the standing army. In August 1938 the army was composed of 11.3 percent regulars; 22.6 percent from the First Reserve (30–34 years old); 45.2 percent from the Second Reserve (20–29 years old); and 20.9 percent from the depot reserves (25–37 years old).[17] Regular divisions provided cadre for the newly mobilized ones. For example, to replace the deployed Fifth and Twelfth divisions and to maintain an amphibious capability, the general staff mobilized the Eighteenth Division in September 1937. A cadre from the Twelfth Division trained and organized the recalled reservists and conscripts who filled out the Eighteenth Division. Just two months later the Eighteenth Division conducted its first landings near Shanghai.

Moreover, the army's constant concern that the Soviets might take advantage of the China fighting to launch a preemptive attack in Manchuria forced it to station more units in that theater. Thus in 1938 the Eleventh Division, still reconstituting after Shanghai, had joined the Twelfth in eastern Manchuria. Both divisions remained there into 1945, at which time IGHQ ordered the Eleventh to Japan and the Twelfth to Taiwan as part of its plans for homeland defense. Neither division fired a shot in anger during the Pacific War (1941–45). From 1937 to 1939 the other amphibiously trained division, the Fifth, was fighting in north China. In brief the general staff did not use the western divisions initially in battle according to their specialized training and roles.

Nonetheless the China theater did afford numerous opportunities for the Japanese to validate their amphibious doctrine in operations. This third stage of doctrinal evolution lasted from 1937 to 1945. Refining their amphibious unit organizations and handling of troops and cargo, along with adapting the daihatsu and shipboard cranes to lower and raise the landing craft, soldiers conducted amphibious operations in the traditional, time-tested manner. In other words, core doctrine never varied. The Japanese army paid increased attention to the threat that enemy aircraft posed to troop transports and gave correspondingly greater attention to aspects of naval and air cover during landing operations. It is, however, important to note that the primary Japanese concern was about air or surface attacks on troop transports, not on overcoming enemy resistance on a landing beach. In part Japan's experience during the China War explains its soldiers' attitude.

Between August 1937 and March 1941, IJA forces conducted sixteen amphibious landings on hostile shores. In 1937 there were three landings near Shanghai, China, and one in the neighborhood of Tsingtao on the Shantung Peninsula. The Tsingtao landing was unopposed. A naval landing force preceded the Third and Eleventh divisions ashore at Shanghai in August 1937 and, supported by naval gunfire, covered their main landings. It was, in effect, an unopposed landing and one that a staff officer from the Russo-Japanese War era would have felt comfortable planning.

Subsequent division-sized landings in November occurred when the 6th and 18th divisions landed 40 miles south of Shanghai in Hangchow Bay on the exposed Chinese flank well beyond the range of the main enemy forces. These unopposed landings met greater resistance from the swampy terrain than from the Chinese armies.[18] A later landing by the 114th Division was similarly unopposed. Nearer Shanghai, the Shanghai Expeditionary Army ordered the 16th Division to land at Paimou Inlet after it was clear that the Chinese were in retreat.

This pattern of landing soldiers away from concentrations of enemy forces and then moving quickly inland to engage the opponent is reminiscent of the Russo-Japanese War and reoccurs in October 1938 at Chingtao and Canton when Japanese units went ashore against almost no opposition. These night landings east of Hong Kong achieved total surprise, enabling the Eighteenth Division to reform and move quickly inland toward Canton. The Fifth Division conducted amphibious assaults against the forts guarding the mouth of Canton's Pearl River the same month. Under cover of naval gunfire and naval aircraft bombing Chinese positions, Japanese daihatsu forced their way past the outermost casemates and landed soldiers on the fortress flanks. Infantrymen then reduced the forts by overland attacks.[19] The joint operation against Hainan Island in 1939 again featured nighttime landings and encountered either weak or no enemy opposition. So did the five landings of the "C" Operation of February and March 1941. They involved separate battalions from the Fifth, Eighteenth, and Guards divisions and were designed to isolate Hong Kong from mainland China by a series of landings on the south China coast.

The Japanese army displayed a sophisticated ability to conduct simultaneous multibattalion landings at widely disparate points; an ability to conduct night landings, which it favored; and an ability to coordinate forces once ashore. Yet it did not advance to large-scale assault landings into prepared enemy positions. Thus on the eve of the Pacific War the Japanese army relied more on surprise than suppressive firepower to achieve its lodgment. It preferred night amphibious landings to cloak its forces in darkness and opted to land at points distant from the enemy main forces.

In October 1940 the Fifth Division, a veteran of Shanghai, Canton, and "C" Operation landings, drew the assignment to begin extensive training for amphibious operations against a yet unannounced opponent. Two months later the Guards and Eighteenth divisions received similar orders. Three newer divisions, the Forty-eighth, Fifty-fifth, and Fifty-sixth, all mobilized in 1940, also began specialized amphibious training in 1941. The Fifty-fifth and Fifty-sixth, incidentally, were western divisions, the former a depot division of the Eleventh and the latter of the Twelfth.

Nevertheless, the continuity of planning and of doctrinal development for amphibious operations in the Pacific had long since been broken. No concrete preparations occurred for such contingencies from 1930 to 1939, and the Japanese army frankly did not display much interest in its American counterpart.[20] Indeed, of the seven major exercises that the army conducted in 1940, not one dealt with amphibious warfare. The following year, as IGHQ seriously considered moving south, there was a burst of activity. Seven of thirteen exercises emphasized amphibious operations ranging from debarkation of motorized equipment and supplies to a beachhead, assault landings, use of smoke to conceal landing areas, and small-boat operations to landing exercises on Hainan Island. Other units engaged in exercises having no connection to the southern advance, such as combined arms training, corps and division logistics' exercises, river crossing operations, or methods for the employment of armored forces. Because the Japanese army had spent the previous decade always looking over its shoulder at the Soviets, the scenario announced for the annual Fuji Maneuvers set for November 1941 was one of offensive operations against Soviet-fortified positions.[21] Initial plans for war against the United

FIGURE 2. The Fifth Infantry Division landing operations at Bias Bay, about 50 miles east of Hong Kong, 22 October 1938. Courtesy of Mainichi shimbunsha

States, Great Britain, and the Netherlands allocated just eleven divisions and three brigades to the task. Furthermore, the army's timetable laid out a 150-day schedule of operations after which half the divisions on the southern front were to be withdrawn for operations against the Soviet Union the following spring.

In comparing Japanese amphibious doctrine to that developed by the U.S. Marine Corps for the comparable period, perhaps the most striking distinction is that the notion of a Marine Expeditionary Force became inextricably tied to a specific war plan, Orange. In other words, the marines linked doctrine to a real mission.[22] Without a "realistic" mission, the general staff could easily shift the three amphibiously trained divisions to protracted land campaigns. In theory the Japanese did have a "realistic mission," a hypothetical invasion of the Philippines. Yet as one critic has observed, these were desktop plans, carefully stored and dusted off as the occasion demanded and not what was taught at the Imperial War College.[23] In contrast, from 1935 to 1943 the Marine Corps schools at Quantico sent to the Naval War College solutions to amphibious problems that entailed working out detailed plans for the capture of various advanced bases, such as Truk (1935), Palau (1936), Guam (1939), and Saipan (1940–43).[24]

Although amphibious landings were a necessary but preliminary element of the Imperial Army's campaign, the establishment of the Fleet Marine Force in 1933 and the doctrine espoused in the *Tentative Landing Manual* the following year regarding base defense and amphibious assaults became the marines' first priorities. As the Fleet Marine Force was resuming landing exercises in 1934, the Imperial Army was abandoning such maneuvers.

Likewise, the Japanese were world leaders in the design of landing craft in 1929, but then, satisfied with the daihatsu models, innovation stopped. The U.S. Marines spent the decade of the 1930s searching for the right combination of landing craft that would translate doctrine into reality.

Finally, the IJA went its own way in developing amphibious doctrine. The American Army was in charge of continental defense, so it was not well represented in amphibious maneuvers until the revision of war plans in the late 1930s. After a series of fits and starts, in February 1941 the First Infantry Division Task Force (two battalions) and the First Marine Division (three battalions) tested existing amphibious assault doctrine and trained army and navy officers in joint command and staff procedures.[25] The American military then was conducting joint training for its mission. The Imperial Army, however, had developed and crewed its independent transport and landing craft and depended on the navy to control the seas and to cover landings. Perhaps this resulted because amphibious operations were not the primary mission of either Japanese service. We do know that the Japanese army continually honed its armor, infantry, artillery, and engineer doctrine during the 1930s and that its capstone manual, the revised Field Service Regulations (Sakusen yōmurei), appeared in September 1938. The 1938 regulations, however, were the culmination of doctrinal thought about how to fight the Soviets, that is, continental not amphibious warfare.

Certainly the Japanese army developed the technique of amphibious landings, but I wonder about the claim that by 1941 its "guidelines [read doctrine] for amphibious warfare were unquestionably the most thoroughly developed from a technical viewpoint and the best tested in practical application."[26] Doctrinal development peaked in the 1930 maneuvers' emphasis on amphibious operations. From then on, the Japanese army was preoccupied with the Soviet menace, which caused them to change permanently the mission of two of their three divisions trained in the techniques of amphibious warfare. The China War did afford numerous occasions for landing operations, but badly misused two of the three western divisions. Moreover, however skillfully these amphibious attacks were executed, they were conducted according to a doctrine of the late 1920s, not one of the early 1940s. In other words, did the Japanese army learn and adapt, or did it overlook deficiencies, thereby reinforcing mistakes? I do not know, but it surely is a question worthy of further study.

CHAPTER THREE

IMPERIAL JAPANESE ARMY STRATEGY AND THE PACIFIC WAR (1941–1945)

The Japanese surprise attack on Pearl Harbor on 7 December 1941 began a string of victories that culminated with the American surrender in the Philippines in May 1942. The shock of Imperial Japan's devastating and ruthless defeat of the Western powers convinced Americans of a long-standing and detailed Japanese timetable for world conquest. The Imperial Japanese Navy (IJN) actually had long planned for a war with the U.S. Navy, but the IJA had no long-range strategic concept for a war with the United States, because, for the army, the Pacific War was the wrong war at the wrong place at the wrong time and with the wrong enemy.

"Strategy," according to Carl von Clausewitz, "is the use of the engagement for the purpose of the war. The strategist must therefore define an aim for the entire operational side of the war that will be in accordance with its purpose. In other words, he will draft the plan of the war, and the aim will determine the series of actions intended to achieve it: he will, in fact, shape the individual campaigns and, within these, decide on the individual engagements."[1] Based on this definition, the IJA leaders had no strategy for their war against the Western powers, nor did they develop a strategy during the course of the entire war. As a result, the leaders of the Japanese army failed to devise a strategy for the Pacific War and, more often than not, had to follow the lead of Japanese naval planners and operations officers.

Several factors were instrumental in the Japanese army's failure to develop a strategic approach to the Pacific War. Interservice rivalry with the Imperial Navy was a significant one. The ineffectiveness of the Japanese command and control system at IGHQ was another. A third was the tendency of Japanese army officers to think in tactical and operational terms, not in the strategic realm. Perhaps the Japanese army's preoccupation from 1905 until 1941 with devising a continental strategy against Imperial Russia and later the Soviet Union was the major factor that affected the IJA's conception about any future war with America.[2]

Even as late as 14 August 1941, the day the IJN planners notified their army counterparts that the schedule for preparations for war against the United States and Great Britain was to be completed by 15 October, the army staffers were taken by surprise, because they were not fully prepared for such a war.[3] Mesmerized by their traditional enemy, the Soviet Union to the strategic north, the Japanese army commanders gave little consideration to a war on its strategic southern flank. In short, they did not consider the United States a serious opponent until the very moment of hostilities. As a consequence, the army chieftains lacked a comprehensive plan for war with the West in the Pacific theater.

Japanese victory in the Russo-Japanese War (1904–5) cost the army 118,000 casualties, as nineteenth-century tactics met twentieth-century technology, which included machine guns, barbed wire, improved artillery, and hardened fortifications. The IJA won supremacy in Korea and the right to station troops in Manchuria. After the costly triumph, however, the Japanese general staff worried that the Russians, wanting revenge, would never accept the Japanese presence in Manchuria and Korea, and their main concern was the possibility of another war with Imperial Russia over Manchuria. Therefore Japan's armed forces had to be prepared to repel the inevitable Russian strategic counteroffensive in the Far East.

Concern over the Russian bear appeared in Imperial Defense Policy authored by the Supreme Command composed of the army and navy chiefs of staff, who formulated strategy, processed planning, and conducted operations. The Army general staff functions were distinct from those of the war ministry, whose minister, an active duty general officer, was a member of the cabinet. The war ministry was in charge of administration, personnel, and related matters. The Naval general staff was responsible for operations and the navy minister, policy making. In time of war or emergency the respective army and navy general staffs became the army and navy departments of IGHQ. IGHQ's purpose was to serve as the central directing and coordinating organ of the army and navy high commands. Membership included the chiefs of both general staffs and their selected subordinates as well as staff officers from the more important bureaus and sections in the war and navy ministries. The IGHQ-Government Liaison Conference (attended by the prime minister and war, navy, and foreign ministers, plus the chiefs of both staffs) decided policy, which, in turn, the responsible military or government agency implemented. Major decisions—such as war with America—received the emperor's sanction at an imperial conference and were then implemented. In theory IGHQ executed the joint strategy formulated by the chiefs of the general staffs. The army's main threat was Russia, and the navy's was the United States, and interservice rivalry, not cooperation, was the hallmark of the Japanese military.

Such thinking persisted even through the First World War (1914–18). The revised "Imperial Defense Policy (IDP)" of 1918 listed Japan's hypothetical enemies in a future war as Russia, America, and China. The post–World War I naval arms race between Japan and the United States forced Japanese army leaders to acknowledge that in case of a war between Japan and America, it would cooperate with the Imperial Navy and attack the American bases in the Philippine Islands. The army's acquiescence was, however, mere lip service to interservice cooperation, because it neither pursued concrete research nor developed specific operational plans for a ground campaign in the Philippines.

The Japanese general staff revised IDP again in 1923 and assumed that the United States would be Japan's most likely future foe. In part this was by default, because the Bolshevik Revolution of 1917 had overthrown the Czarist monarchy and had thrown the newly created Union of Soviet Socialistic Republics into a state of apparent chronic instability. With the Soviet preoccupation over domestic problems, Japanese leaders no longer needed to fear a strategic ground threat from the north, and the army could turn its attention to its southern flank.

In 1924 the Committee for the Research of Military Preparations Against the United States was established within the general staff, and within a year the committee produced an operational concept outlining plans for the occupation of Guam and the Philippine Islands. According to this outline, immediately before the opening of hostilities, an emergency mobilization order would activate one and one-half army divisions for amphibious operations against Lingayen Gulf and Lamon Bay on Luzon Island.[4] Plans called for the occupation of Manila and the completion of Japanese operations in the Philippines before the American main battle fleet could steam to its rescue.

The defense of the Philippines for the U.S. Army was a dilemma, because its forces were too weak to hold all the islands. Accordingly the U.S. Army designed its defense plans for the Philippines to preclude a rapid Japanese conquest of the islands. The 1914 war plans specified that the army hold Corregidor Island in Manila Bay for sixty days until the navy arrived with reinforcements. Ten years later American joint planners decided the army should hold all of Manila Bay as a future operating base for the U.S. Navy. By 1932 the U.S. Army was back to defending only the entrance to Manila Bay in case of hostilities. General Douglas MacArthur's ambitious decision in 1941 to hold all of Luzon was a marked departure from prewar army planning.

In the meantime, Japanese plans also changed. The planners of the 1936 revision of IDP assumed Japan's likely opponents would be the United States, the Soviet Union, China, and Great Britain. In the American war scenario, the Japanese army would occupy Luzon as well as fortresses in Manila Bay and Guam. Having concurred in this strategy, the following year, however, the army placed its Fifth and Eleventh divisions, both trained in amphibious operations and earmarked for operations against the Philippines, in the strategic reserve for possible future operations against the Soviet Union.[5]

Japanese troops had seized Manchuria in 1931 and created various autonomous buffer zones in North China from 1932 to 1936 thereby expanding their presence on the Asian continent. In July 1937 the unplanned and unexpected military escalation of a minor incident outside Peking resulted in a major undeclared war. The Japanese army leadership, with certain exceptions, believed that any concessions to the Chinese would only further weaken Japan's position in China.

High-ranking officers such as War Minister, General Sugiyama Hajime; Kwantung Army Chief of Staff, Lieutenant General Tōjō Hideki; and general staff, Operations Branch Chief, Colonel Mutō Akira favored a military solution to the China Incident, which they assumed incorrectly would require but a few months. Other influential officers, such as general staff, Operations Department Director, Major General Ishiwara Kanji, regarded the use of Japanese troops in China as wasteful, because all Japanese soldiers were needed for the wars Ishiwara foresaw first with the Soviet Union and the final apocalyptic war he envisioned with the United States. The former group of officers also believed a war with the Soviets was inevitable, but they saw the opportunity to secure Japan's open eastern flank in such a war by subjugating China.[6] The Japanese learned, as others before and after, that however undeclared wars start, they sometimes prove very difficult to stop.

For the Japanese army, the China War (1937–45) became a meatgrinder. By the end of 1937 the IJA had 700,000 troops in China, approximately four times its total prewar standing army. Japanese casualties were extremely heavy. In operations from August to November 1937 to force Chinese defenders from Shanghai and advance up the Yangtze River to capture the Chinese Nationalist capital at Nanking, the Japanese suffered 40,000 casualties. In July 1938 the Japanese army had twenty-three divisions fighting in China, only nine in Korea and Manchuria poised against the traditional enemy from the north, and but two in strategic reserve at home. Even before Japan's attack on Pearl Harbor, Japanese casualties in the China War amounted to more than 600,000, mostly army personnel. Moreover the unplanned China War disrupted all Japanese army plans to reorganize and reequip itself to fight the Soviet Union. While the war ministry and general staff officers may have differed over the conduct of the war in China, they remained in agreement that the Soviet Union was the primary enemy. Thus if Japan could end the China War it could free its ground forces from a quagmire that seemed to offer nothing save endless attrition.

Furthermore the Japanese army's presence on the USSR's far eastern borders and expanded war in China prompted a massive Soviet buildup in the Soviet Far East, adjacent to the Japanese puppet state of Manchukuo. The increase from eight Soviet divisions in 1932 to thirty in 1939 alarmed Japanese general staff officers enough that they reallocated forces to meet the reinvigorated threat from the north.[7] The United States may have been high on a list of Japan's hypothetical enemies, but army planners continued to treat an American threat abstractly and failed to produce specific operational plans as the basis for strategic wartime preparations.[8] Even with the worsening of U.S.-Japanese relations after 1940, the Japanese army neglected thorough plans or preparations for a war with the West and instead remained preoccupied with the Soviet threat. Moreover the army's main interest in the southern region was the occupation of the Netherlands East Indies. Although army leaders rather casually assumed a move against the East Indies would mean war with America and Great Britain, the Japanese army never defined as a strategic objective the defeat of those two powers. Rather the Japanese army's objective was to seize the natural resources of Southeast Asia.

At the end of May 1940 the Japanese army arrived at a crossroads. Japan's ally, Nazi Germany, had overrun Western Europe, and the triumph seemed to presage the imminent capitulation of Great Britain. European colonies in East Asia stood almost defenseless as German troops occupied the Netherlands and France, while Great Britain gathered its scarce resources to oppose the impending German onslaught. It appeared Germany's victories had given Japan the opportunity to advance unhindered into the European colonial empires of Asia. Meanwhile IJA leadership still did not regard war with the United States as inevitable and indeed did not give it excessive attention. The Japanese army was more interested in concluding its involvement in the stalemated war in China so that it might again focus all its attention on the Soviet threat.

One strategic means to end the China War, Japanese army leaders believed, was to isolate China from the rest of the world. Amphibious operations in 1939 and 1940 sealed China's ports, but the nettlesome overland supply route running through French Indochina into southern China remained. If, thought Japan's generals, they could sever that last link, then surely the Chinese would cease fighting. In the meantime, the United States intensified its economic and military pressure to show its displeasure at Japanese aggression in China. The U.S. termination of the thirty-year-old commercial treaty with Japan in July 1939 and the indefinite stationing of the U.S. Pacific fleet at Hawaii in April 1940 signaled a tougher American policy toward Japan. The Japanese reacted by concluding the Tripartite Pact with Nazi Germany and Fascist Italy in 1940, both militantly anti-communist and anti-Soviet states. That decision and the Japanese presence in China caused the continued deterioration of American and Japanese relations through 1941. Nevertheless the Japanese general staff determined to continue preparations for an advance to the south into French Indochina to cut the overland supply routes to China, but prepared no strategy for a war with America.

Then came the exciting news of Germany's invasion of the Soviet Union. Preoccupied by this seemingly golden opportunity to vanquish its mortal Soviet enemy, the army leadership decided to wait for a favorable opportunity to intervene decisively against the Soviet Union while the Soviets were fighting Germany.

An Imperial conference on 2 July 1941 determined that Japan would not enter the war unless a Soviet collapse seemed possible or rebellion erupted in the Soviet Far East, nonetheless army preparations for operations against the Soviet Union for such an eventuality had to commence almost immediately if Japan wanted to be in strategic position to take advantage of the imminent Soviet collapse. Based on long-standing contingency plans for war with the USSR, the Army general staff prepared a timetable of operations commencing mobilization orders on 28 June 1941. They assumed that operations against the USSR would begin on 29 August and conclude in mid-October before the onset of the brutal Siberian winter. Ultimately nearly 700,000 Japanese troops in sixteen divisions and 600 aircraft assembled in Manchuria under the guise of the Kwantung Army Special Maneuver. The Soviets, though, failed to play their assigned role in Japanese assumptions, because they neither collapsed before the German offensive nor withdrew the twenty divisions from the Soviet Far East that the Japanese war planners expected. Instead twenty Soviet divisions remained in the Soviet Far East throughout the war and provided sufficient deterrent to their Japanese counterparts.[9] By 5 August 1941 the Japanese army had abandoned plans for an attack on the Soviet Union. In terms of strategy against America, the diversion of effort and manpower to the north detracted from the army's formulation of war plans against the West and accounted for the army planners' surprise when presented with the navy's operational schedule just nine days later on 14 August.

Meanwhile war with the United States was growing nearer. The American oil embargo against Japan imposed in July 1941 backed Japan into a corner, especially the navy, which was more dependent on oil for fleet operations than was the army, which was an infantry and horse-drawn force. The Japanese could meet U.S. demands and thereby forsake their gains in China. They could continue diplomatic efforts to effect a favorable compromise with America, or they could go to war. And here the Japanese army leaders could not contribute meaningfully to the highest level decisions for war, because they were woefully ignorant of the overall potential of the American armed forces.

Japanese army intelligence had traditionally targeted the Soviet Union, not the United States. Most army attachés went to the Soviet Union or to Poland. There were few "experts" on America at the general staff offices at Ichigaya. Instead, opinion replaced fact as the Japanese army leaders viewed Americans as products of liberalism and individualism and incapable of fighting a protracted war and viewed Japanese soldiers as far superior to their American foes.[10] Perhaps such stereotyping and underestimation of one's likely enemies is commonplace, but when an army acquiesces to resort to war as a national policy, it does help for an army to have a strategy for such a war.

Japanese army officers thought only in terms of offensive operations to open hostilities with Britain and the United States, the first stage of the war. No thought was given to how to conclude the war or what might constitute victory for Japan. Certainly they never considered the annihilation of the United States, but they remained hazy about operations other than the seizure of the natural resources of Southeast Asia and converting those raw materials for use by the Japanese war machine. Moreover the continental bias of army planners showed in the first draft of plans for operations in the southern region when they insisted that the army's operational area be in the region closest to the Asian mainland and the navy's extend into the Pacific. Consequently the army assumed initial responsibility for the Philippines, North Borneo, Malaya, Sumatra, and Java. The navy's zone extended, among other places, to New Guinea and the Bismarck Archipelago in the western Pacific, two areas that would cost the army staggering casualties and aircraft losses in the Solomon Islands and New Guinea fighting of 1942–44.[11] The evolution of the army's strategic commitment to the southwest Pacific demonstrated that its planners originally gave no thought to even occupying the areas let alone to formulating a strategy to define the role and scope of operations on extended lines of communications.

On 5 November 1941 Army Chief of Staff Sugiyama Hajime, at the Imperial Liaison Conference held at the palace, indicated that if sea lines of communication could be maintained, the army could establish an invincible posture in the southern areas. Neither Sugiyama nor his naval counterpart chief, Naval general staff Admiral Nagano Osami, however, forecast with confidence the probability of strategic victory or defeat in the impending war. At root was a basic difference between the army and the navy in strategic conception of the Pacific as an area of operations. Army planners simply had no means, and could discover none, to inflict a decisive defeat or subjugate the enemy in the Pacific. Naval theorists, however, traditionally conceived of the western Pacific as the theater for the decisive main battle fleet engagement that its planners had dreamed about and that its officers had studied about for a generation. The army opted to acquire sufficient strategic basis to engage in a protracted war with America and then envisioned a protracted war of attrition and exhaustion. The navy proposed active offensive operations designed to produce the decisive battle of the war. Moreover the development of island air bases convinced the Japanese navy to extend the distance of the decisive fleet engagement from the prewar Marianas line to a more advanced line running from Wake through the Marshalls to the

Bismarck Archipelago. The army viewed Rabaul as a forward base covering the Japanese naval base at Truk in the Caroline Islands, and the navy considered it an advance base for offensive operations.

Similarly, early in 1942, while the navy expanded its frontage in the Pacific, the army wanted to reduce the number of its ground units in the southern areas. The army plan called for the reduction of 450,000 troops in eleven divisions and seventy-seven aerial squadrons to 250,000 men in seven divisions with fifty squadrons by the end of 1942. The 200,000 troops withdrawn from the area would be reequipped and reorganized and then used to strengthen Japanese army preparations against the Soviet Union. This strategic redeployment to the north was but part of the general staff's replenishment plan decided in March 1942. According to this plan, Japan's existing fifty-one ground divisions and 150 air squadrons would be increased by 1950 to 100 divisions and 1000 squadrons that the general staff now believed necessary for the conduct of a ten-year conflict with America.[12] Still Japan's original strategy for the southern regions did not exceed a five-month operational plan.

To compound the shortsighted planning, the Japanese army high command estimated that any serious Allied counterattack in the Pacific would not commence until the latter half of 1943. By then Japan would have used the time to withdraw selected units from the South Pacific, reconstitute them, and simultaneously develop an invincible defensive perimeter from which to repel the anticipated Allied counteroffensive. The army thought in terms of a strategic defensive, but the navy continued to press for more aggressive operations.[13]

The navy's ambitious March 1942 plan called for the occupation of Port Moresby, Papua New Guinea, on 7 May 1942, Midway a month later, and the Aleutian Islands by the end of June. By early July the Japanese would occupy New Caledonia, by 1 August Fiji, and twenty days later Samoa. Basic assumptions that underpinned such grandiose undertakings had little connection with Japan's main opponent, the United States. The Japanese high command assumed, for instance, that the German 1942 spring offensive would defeat the Soviet Union and thereby eliminate the threat to Japan from the north. Japanese thrusts into the Indian Ocean and against Australia would isolate Great Britain from its colonies and likely cause Britain's collapse. The war itself would reduce the heretofore high standard of living of both Britain and the United States, and, if neither nation nourished hope of victory, civilian morale would plummet, adversely affecting their war effort. Great Britain's defeat, however, would have tremendous psychological repercussions in

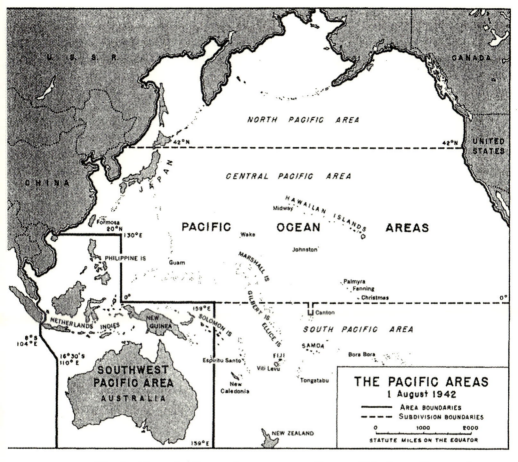

MAP 2. The Pacific and adjacent theaters, 1942. Source: U.S. Army Center of Military History

the United States, possibly causing the Americans to negotiate peace with Japan. These misplaced notions provided the hothouse for the germination of the FS (Fiji-Samoa) Operation.

As early as August 1941 Army Vice Chief of Staff Lieutenant General Tsukada Osamu had opposed the use of army troops for a Bismarck operation, reasoning that, "If we send small numbers of troops to faraway isolated islands, command and control as well as resupply will be extremely difficult. It's like sowing salt in the sea."[14] Tsukada's frankness perhaps resulted in his transfer on 6 November 1941. The IGHQ Confidential War Diary entry for that day described him as a first-rate theoretician but not much of a politician.[15]

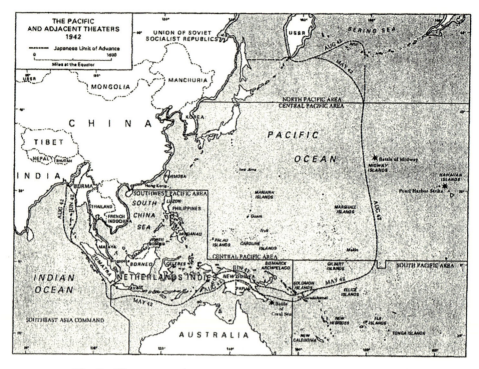

MAP 3. The Pacific areas, 1 August 1942. Source: U.S. Army Center of Military History

The Japanese navy dominated the seas during the opening months of the Pacific War, and these victories expanded naval operations into the Bismarck Archipelago and toward Australia to the south and Midway to the east. The navy's victories also placed it in the driver's seat, and by March 1942 the Imperial Army found its objectives took second place to the Imperial Navy's insistence on the decisive battle. Naval proposals for the second stage of operations elicited lukewarm reactions, at best, from the army. The combined fleet and the navy ministry favored attacking Australia to eliminate potential bases for an Allied counterattack and to ensure the collapse of Great Britain by isolating it from its allies. The army leaders demurred that the plan exceeded the limits of national power, particularly in terms of shipping and available military manpower. Similarly the army was unenthusiastic over navy plans for the occupation of Ceylon because of the potential air threat the Japanese army garrison on Ceylon would face from India. As for the navy's Hawaii operation, projected in October 1942, the army withheld any comment. The sweeping MI (Midway and Aleutian Islands) Operation received left-handed endorsement as the army agreed to cooperate if the navy was confident of success. Criticized after Lieutenant Colonel James Doolittle's B-25 raids against Japanese cities on 18 April 1942 of Japan's inability to defend the skies over the homeland, embarrassed army leaders "recognized the necessity to dispatch troops" to occupy Midway to extend Japan's defensive perimeter and destroy the U.S. carrier forces thereby precluding future air threats to the home islands.[16]

The army remained unaware of the magnitude of the navy's reverse at Midway. On 6 June 1942 the confidential war diary recorded, "No report on offensive operations against the Aleutians and Midway. There seems to have been a decisive naval surface engagement near Midway. According to Naval Captain Onoda [Sujirō], the situation does not permit optimism."[17] Nevertheless, based on incomplete strategic information, the army did dispatch battalion-size landing parties to Rabaul and then to the northern New Guinea coast to provide flank security for the burgeoning Japanese naval base at Rabaul.

After Midway, however, the American Joint Chiefs of Staff (JCS) directed Allied forces in the South and Southwest Pacific to commence operations to seize Rabaul and reestablish Allied control of the Bismarck Archipelago. General MacArthur's forces in the Southwest Pacific would advance along the north New Guinea coast, while those of Vice Admiral Robert L. Ghormley, replaced in November 1942 by Admiral William F. Halsey, pushed up the Solomon chain toward Rabaul. Guadalcanal was the first step.

The Japanese navy's construction of an advanced air base on Guadalcanal provoked an unexpectedly quick reaction from the United States when on 7 August 1942 the First Marine Division landed on Guadalcanal and began a grinding battle of attrition on land, sea, and in the air. The Japanese general staff's original estimates indicated that the American landings represented nothing more than a reconnaissance in force. The army confidently dispatched a battalion-size force to evict the impudent Americans.[18] Six months and twenty-five thousand Japanese army casualties later, the Americans remained in possession of the island. Moreover the serious naval air losses at Midway and the Solomons forced the navy in August 1942 to request that the army provide aerial reinforcements to the Southwest Pacific front. Reluctantly the army agreed to send its air units and the accompanying ground forces required to guarantee airfield security. The newly formed Eighth Area Army on Rabaul oversaw operations on New Guinea, and the Seventeenth Army was responsible for the Solomons front. Overextended lines of communications and a shortage of shipping made resupply of these far-flung army garrisons in the Southwest Pacific the nightmare prewar army officers had feared. In addition, no clear strategic concept of operations existed for the army, and it lost the strategic initiative following its repulses on Guadalcanal and the defeat of its Port Morseby expedition, culminating in the reduction of the Japanese garrison at Buna, Papua New Guinea.

By mid-1942 the JCS envisioned ultimate Allied landings in China to control the South China Sea and cut Japanese lines of communications to their southern resource areas. Furthermore, from Chinese bases American aircraft could launch strategic bombing raids against the Japanese homeland as well as implement a naval blockade against the island empire.

By early 1943 Japanese army planners were searching for ways to reduce the commitments to the southwestern Pacific and contract the overextended defensive perimeter. Behind the shorter and seemingly more easily defensible perimeter, the army expected to replace its aircraft losses and reequip ground units for an eventual counterattack against the Allies. At the end of September 1943, IGHQ's new operational policy envisioned holding the "absolute zone of national defense" while completing preparations for a new, stronger primary line of resistance further to the rear, where the army could reconstitute its battered air and ground units. The execution of this conception, however, required that the Japanese army hold the September line for twelve months.

The Americans did not allow the Japanese the time they needed to restore their fortunes. The Sextant Conference of late 1943 directed that the main Allied effort be concentrated in the Pacific along twin axes of advance through the Central Pacific—Gilberts, Marshalls, Marianas, Carolines, Palaus—toward the Philippines and along the New Guinea coast to the southern Philippines. Sensing Japanese weakness evidenced by the virtual abandonment of the Truk naval base in early 1944, Admiral Chester Nimitz advanced his timetable to strike the Marshalls and Carolines. Similarly MacArthur accelerated the tempo of his operations in March 1944. These converging attacks penetrated the Japanese "absolute zone of national defense," and by late May 1944 elements of the U.S. Forty-first Infantry Division had invaded Biak Island, while U.S. Marine and Army units had assaulted the Japanese-held Marianas in June 1944.

Constant U.S. pressure against Japanese strategic outposts hindered Japanese army leaders' attempts to reconstruct their shattered air and ground units. Replacements were rushed to the fighting fronts at the expense of strengthening the rear areas. Even if Japan had sufficient reserves to deflect American advances in the Southwest and Central Pacific, Japanese industry lacked the resource base and technological capability to mass-produce annually the 55,000 aircraft the Japanese army and navy demanded for successful prosecution of the war effort. In 1944 alone Japan lost 7000 front-line aircraft in combat and 12,000 total aircraft from all causes, yet actual aircraft production was 17,000–18,000, which barely replaced losses.[19] Experienced pilots could never be replaced.

By mid-1944 Japan had been at war for seven full years, had more than 1 million troops holding strategic rail lines and cities in China, and had begun to conscript previously deferred university students. The magnitude of Japan's manpower shortages was apparent. Furthermore, Japan in 1944 was a labor-intensive, not machine-intensive, war economy. Although the United States was able to replace men with machines, especially for construction of island bases and airfields, the Japanese never had this advantage. Instead they had to use valuable trained soldiers to assist in the construction of an inner defense perimeter. In certain cases, notably Iwo Jima and Okinawa, the Imperial Army prepared formidable defenses that inflicted heavy losses on the American attackers. These bastions, however, were the exception, not the rule, because the Japanese army lacked the manpower and resources to build an inner defensive perimeter in only twelve months.

The fall of Saipan in July 1944 forced the Japanese high command once again to react to American strategic initiatives and redesign its basic strategic policies. Significantly, for the first time in the thirty-two-month course of the Pacific War, both the Imperial Army and Navy concurred on the Pacific theater as the decisive battleground of the war. While this chimera had long provided the navy the stuff of illusions, now the army concluded that it, too, had to concentrate its forces for a decisive land engagement with the Americans. The results of Japanese planning appeared as the "Shō-go" Operation.

"Shō-go" identified four areas where the decisive battle might occur: "Shō-1," the Philippine Islands; "Shō-2," Formosa and the Ryukyu Islands; "Shō-3," Japanese home islands, except Hokkaido; and "Shō-4," Hokkaido. In August 1944 the Imperial Army activated the Fourteenth Area Army in the Philippines with the Thirty-fifth Army under its control. Dissatisfied with Lieutenant General Kuroda Shigenori's seemingly lackadaisical approach to training and preparations for the impending clash, the army high command appointed General Yamashita Tomoyuki, the Tiger of Malaya, commander of the Fourteenth Army in late September.

A combination of Japanese reinforcements from Manchuria—such as the Eighth Infantry and Second Armored divisions—and the upgrading of independent mixed brigades—such as the 103d and 105th—to divisions augmented defensive preparations in the islands.

Despite these major redeployments, the IJA remained undecided about the locus of the strategic defense of the Philippines. Yamashita favored a main defense fought on Luzon to conserve his forces and to shorten his lines of communication. The commander-in-chief of the Southern Army, Field Marshal Count Terauchi Hisaichi, however, ordered Yamashita's main defensive effort at Leyte, thereby extending resupply lines and siphoning troops from the Luzon garrison. Yamashita protested, but he followed orders and reinforced Leyte, transforming that island into the decisive battleground. Thus Japanese army strategy now reached the stage at which the army was prepared to risk everything on one decisive land battle in the Pacific, a major change from the army's original notion of a protracted war of attrition. Now the Japanese army aimed to destroy, not exhaust, its American foes.

While the decision to reinforce and fight the main battle on Leyte extended the duration of that operation, it cost the Japanese perhaps 75,000 soldiers, 2500 aircraft, and 26 warships. After Japan's decisive defeat on Leyte, Yamashita could do little except mastermind a tenacious defense of Luzon that cost the American forces more than 60,000 casualties to liberate. Yamashita's forces were still operational when the Pacific War ended, but cornered and isolated in northern Luzon they posed no threat to American plans to use the Philippines as a staging area for the greatest invasion of all, the Japanese home islands.

Having lost the decisive battle, in the final stages of the war Japanese Army strategy reverted to inflicting the maximum number of American casualties to convince the United States that a negotiated peace was preferable to continued severe losses as the Americans fought their way closer to the Japanese home islands. The army planners' problem was that they no longer fought the war from a faraway perimeter whose distances from the home islands provided security. War had come to Japan's doorstep with daily air raids, naval gunfire bombardment, and American troops ashore in Okinawa, a prefecture of Japan itself.

The army, which had introduced suicide aircraft during the Philippines campaign, now expanded that tactic of desperation to create scores of aerial suicide units and used them extensively at Okinawa. Army units also continued to shift from Manchuria to the Japanese home islands to strengthen homeland defenses for the anticipated Allied invasion.

Denuding ground forces in Manchuria exposed the strategic salient to Soviet attack. The Kwantung Army, in command of Japanese forces in Manchuria, conducted a mass mobilization in July 1945 and, on paper, organized twenty-four divisions and fourteen brigades with 700,000 men. These men were for the most part ill equipped and usually untrained, although several did fight well when the Soviets invaded Manchuria in August 1945. When the war with Japan's primary prewar hypothetical opponent, the USSR, finally began, the Imperial Army defending Manchuria was merely a shadow of its once powerful self. Its original units lay broken on Pacific islands stretching from Guadalcanal to Okinawa.

The course of the Pacific War unmasked the deficiency in the Japanese army's strategic concept of the direction of the war. The army was capable of brilliant individual operations, such as the conquest of Malaya in 1941–42 or the Philippines, but it formulated no comprehensive framework in which to translate these operational successes into strategic victory. Instead, pulled along by the Japanese navy, the army first overextended itself in the South Pacific and then had to reinforce failure, thereby reacting to American strategic offensives. Without a clear grasp of the overall aim of the Pacific War, the Japanese Army ultimately self-destructed, literally with its suicide tactics and figuratively as it collapsed overnight, similar to a punctured balloon, following Emperor Hirohito's announcement of Japan's defeat.

CHAPTER FOUR

AN ALLIED INTERPRETATION OF THE PACIFIC WAR

Americans think in terms of the war in the Pacific, Australians mull over the war in the Southwest Pacific, the British tend to reflect on the war in Southwest Asia—Malaya, Burma, and India—the Chinese, and some Japanese, the cataclysmic campaigning on the China fronts that extended thousands of miles, and the Soviets on Manchuria, northeast China. In other words, one must visualize Allied military operations against a common opponent that stretched from the borders of Burma and India south to Australia, north to the Aleutian Islands, and east to Hawaii. Simultaneously one must understand naval warfare (because the Pacific phase was a naval war), airpower (because the quest for air bases from which to bombard Japan into submission was a driving element in strategy and one that made China seem so attractive), amphibious operations (in the Central and Southwest Pacific to secure bases), and army-level and army group operations on the Asian mainland in Burma and China. In the latter two cases, the United States had little military involvement.

I arbitrarily use 7 December 1941 as the beginning of the World War in Asia. This is capricious, because Japan and China had been engaged in a full-scale war since July 1937. For Japan the China War was the wrong war, at the wrong place, against the wrong opponent, at the wrong time. IJA strategic thinking was predicated on a war against the Soviet Union fought on the plains of Manchuria, which bordered on north China. In

1937 certain Japanese officers saw a chance to eliminate quickly any possibility of a Chinese threat to an open Japanese strategic flank if Japan went to war with the Soviet Union. These officers believed the Chinese would crumble before Japanese military might. The Chinese, however, refused to play the role the Japanese warlords assigned to them. Japan suffered 40,000 casualties while capturing Shanghai and advancing up the Yangtze River to Nanking, the Nationalist Chinese capital. Japanese brutality, exemplified by the rape of Nanking in December 1937, encouraged Chinese resistance, especially among the Communist Eighth Route Army led by Mao Tse-tung. The Nationalist leader, Chiang Kai-shek, moved the recognized Chinese government 1000 miles inland to Chungking where, safe behind the gorges of the Yangtze River, he held court.

Japan's military leaders then embarked on vast encirclement campaigns designed to annihilate the Chinese field armies. By July 1938, twenty-three Japanese divisions were fighting in China, and nine others were in Manchuria or Korea waiting to fight the Soviets. Ultimately Japan's military plans to subdue China failed, but even before Japan's attack on Pearl Harbor, Japanese casualties in China amounted to 180,000 dead and 425,000 sick or wounded.[1] Plans for a war against the Soviets were disrupted, and, when the Japanese did fight the Soviets, at Changkufeng in 1938 and Khalkhin Gol in 1939, the results were disastrous. In short, Japan's army was bogged down in China. The strategic implications were great, because the United States, in particular, reacted harshly to each new Japanese escalation.

Japan, for instance, tried to isolate China from the Western powers by seizing all the main Chinese ports, except Hong Kong. America reacted by terminating its commercial treaty with Japan and moving the U.S. fleet from the West Coast to Hawaii in 1940. Meanwhile, Hitler had conquered Poland in 1939 and in the spring of 1940 had overrun France and the low countries. The British Expeditionary Force was in ruins, evacuated by sea from Dunkirk, and Germany appeared invincible. At odds with the Western powers, Japan felt a natural affinity for Germany as a fellow "have-not" nation whose just ambitions were quashed by the status quo powers such as Britain and the United States. For his part, Hitler seems to have thought highly of the Japanese navy, and cared little about the Imperial Army. Obviously when dealing with the Nazis, race was a problem. Imagine a Nazi eugenicist having to prove to Hitler that his Japanese allies were really descended from a tribe of lost Aryans. In any event, Japan, Germany, and Italy initialed the Tripartite Pact in September 1940 forming the Axis alliance. This polarized relations between Japan and the United States, and, in effect, set the strategic alliance for World War II in Asia. The Allies were Britain (and its Australian and New Zealand dominions), China, and the United States against Japan.

The defeat of British arms on the European continent by Nazi Germany left the British alone in 1940 to fight on against Hitler. The British were facing a life-and-death struggle for their island; naturally the fate of Britain's colonies, with the exception of India, received little attention. The British prime minister, Winston Churchill, insisted that Singapore, the British naval base on the tip of Malaya, was a fortress and refused to believe that the Japanese were deranged enough to undertake what he described as the "mad enterprise" of attacking it. The British realistically wrote off Hong Kong, and never dreamed that the Japanese would invade Burma. As late as April 1941, Churchill thought that Japan would not attack British colonies in Asia until Hitler had invaded Britain.[2] It was also painfully clear that Britain alone could not sustain its position in Asia. Everything depended on Washington, where, as revealed in 1989, the British ran an extensive covert campaign designed to bend American policy to such ends.[3] However, the American political strategic leadership, expressed by President Franklin D. Roosevelt and echoed by American public opinion, was hostile toward colonial structures. Simply put, the notion of going to war with Japan to preserve the British Empire was repugnant to most Americans.

American interests in Asia were commercial and colonial, although the major American colony, the Philippine Islands, was scheduled to receive its independence in 1946. By 1913 the United States saw the Philippines as Japan's first objective in any war against America in the Pacific. American prewar strategy rested on the notion of the battle fleet moving across the Pacific, securing its line of communication as it advanced, and relieving the army garrison in the Philippines. The army had to hold Manila Bay until the navy arrived, otherwise the navy had no base from which to operate in Asian waters. The U.S. Army thought in terms of a strategic defensive triangle stretching from Alaska to Hawaii to Panama, while the navy thought in terms of offensive fleet operations west of Hawaii.

This was the American Pacific strategy when World War II erupted in Europe in 1939. The United States, however, could not afford to witness passively the collapse of the British Empire. As the chief of naval operations, Admiral Harold Stark, said "If Britain wins decisively against Germany, we could win everywhere; but if she loses, the problems confronting us could be very great; and while we might not lose everywhere, we might possibly not win anywhere."[4] So in 1940–41 American army and navy planners developed the strategy to defeat the Axis. The Allies rightly regarded Germany as the most dangerous member of the Axis coalition and the one that had to be defeated. Italy and Japan, in theory at least, would be handled as opportunities and forces became available.[5] This was the famous "Germany First" strategy.

Axis nations shared only the common totalitarian trait of obsessive secrecy. They rarely exchanged planning information, intelligence, and military technology, or coordinated their operations. Germany and Japan were, in the words of one historian, a "Hollow Alliance."[6] For example, Hitler's attack on the Soviet Union was as much a surprise to the Japanese as to the Soviets. Muttering about "inscrutable Europeans," the Japanese cabinet resigned in mortification.[7] Similarly, the Japanese did not make Germany privy to the secret of Pearl Harbor. Hitler did try to convince the Japanese to attack Singapore, which the Japanese ultimately did, but for their own reasons, not the German dictator's.

In July 1941 the Imperial Army had mobilized 700,000 troops in sixteen divisions in Manchuria for possible operations against the Soviet Union. The Soviets neither totally collapsed before the German onslaught nor denuded their far eastern defenses where twenty Soviet divisions remained throughout the war. With the festering war in China, the Japanese army abandoned plans for a war against the Soviet Union by 5 August.[8] Instead the army would join the navy and strike south against the Western colonial empires. Japan's initial strategy, decided on 15 November, was as follows:

Quickly destroy American, British, and Dutch bases in East Asia.
Hasten the fall of the Chiang Kai-shek regime in China.
Work for the surrender of Great Britain in cooperation with Germany and Italy, with the idea that if Britain surrendered, the Americans would lose their will to fight.

Japanese military minds assumed that by conquering the southern region (Southeast Asia), Japan could be self-sufficient and able to prosecute the war successfully. By controlling the Indian Ocean, Japan could cut Britain's line of communication, making it possible for Germany to invade Britain. Britain's fall would cause the United States to lose its will to fight. From this position of strength, Japan would negotiate an advantageous peace settlement. In short, Japan went to war on the strength of a five-month plan of operations: an exceptional operational strategy premised on first achieving local air and naval superiority before landing troops. Generally Japanese infantrymen avoided direct assaults on fortified areas in favor of flanking maneuvers. Their initial objectives were always airfields, and airpower (carrier and land-based) dominated their operations.[9] In effect the Japanese operational level of war was a prototype of the American way of war in the Pacific. The great strategic paradox of all this was that Japan's sneak attack on Pearl Harbor in December 1941 had accomplished its aim. The American fleet was immobilized and the Japanese flank in Southeast Asia secured. But while the Japanese spread almost unchecked throughout Southeast Asia and the Pacific, American passions unleashed at Pearl Harbor were already eyeing Japan's destruction.

First of all, the Germany First strategy did not mean Germany only.[10] The American JCS, and especially the new chief of naval operations, Admiral Ernest King, stressed an offensive campaign, largely naval and air, to destroy Japanese armed forces, to sever Japan from its sources of raw materials, and to force unconditional surrender through some combination of economic blockade, strategic bombardment, and invasion. King wanted to avenge Pearl Harbor without being encumbered with inter-Allied command and consultation.[11] He reflected the American public's inflamed reaction to the Japanese attack. The U.S. Navy sought every opportunity to strike at the Japanese whenever and wherever possible. In part this early attention to Japan instead of Germany was forced on the United States, because the Japanese advance, not the Allied strategy, dictated what had to be done in April, May, and June 1942. After all, the real and imminent danger to America at that time was in the Central, South, and Southwest Pacific. It was natural then that resources and manpower went to the Pacific.

The U.S. Navy thwarted Japanese ambitions in April 1942 in the Coral Sea battle thus blocking a Japanese thrust at Australia. The decisive battle of Midway in June that year wrested the strategic initiative from the Japanese as four of their first-line carriers and hundreds of elite naval aviators were sunk. But Japan was still powerful in the South and Southwest Pacific, where General Douglas MacArthur had withdrawn following his humiliating defeat in the Philippines. MacArthur's base in Australia was initially part of an independent American strategy to use Australia as a supply route for the beleaguered American and Filipino forces in Philippines. After MacArthur's exit from the islands, Australia served as his fallback position and base for an eventual advance against the Japanese in the Southwest Pacific.

At the peak of Japanese success, March 1942, Japanese military strategy foresaw the surrender of Great Britain as pivotal to the outcome of the war in Asia and the Pacific. Army leaders believed that the time had come to consolidate initial gains and to establish a defensive perimeter encompassing the vast treasure house of recently acquired resources. They estimated that a major Anglo-American counteroffensive could begin not sooner than the latter half of 1943 and that the interval should be used to prepare strong defenses in the Southwest Pacific and Indian Ocean fronts. Eternal optimists regarding China, they believed that Chiang Kaishek would be discouraged by Japan's military success against the West and see the wisdom of a negotiated settlement with Japan. Chiang and Churchill shared only one strategic concept, namely that the entry of America into the war made Japan's defeat inevitable. Rather than being discouraged, the Kuomintang government in Chungking was jubilant, because Japanese defeat had now become a foregone conclusion.[12] One also needs to keep in mind the one-sided nature of China's effort.

With little but moral support from its Allies, China had suffered enormously under Japanese attack and cruel occupation. China also stayed in the war, which tied down 1 million Japanese soldiers who had settled in central and south China as an occupying army guarding strong points and lines of communications, including railroads and bridges. In north China the Japanese engaged in rapacious bandit suppression campaigns against Mao's forces, but elsewhere in China by 1942 the fighting fronts had reached a stalemate. Also, in early 1942 Britain and the Soviet Union were locked in a life-and-death struggle with Germany and were unable to divert resources to China. The Kuomintang, battered by the Japanese, the communists, and its own internal corruption, was unable to carry the war to the enemy. Only the United States had the authority to do anything in China, and here Roosevelt's romantic notions of what the Chinese could do conflicted sadly with what they did do. China, however, could not be ignored in 1942, because it did divert Japanese ground troops, and it might in the future serve as the location for the dreamed-about air bases from which retribution would be rained from the skies on Japan.

At a White House meeting on 7–9 March 1942 the president suggested a three-way division of the Allied world to carry out the war effort. The Pacific Ocean would be the American sphere; Singapore to the Mediterranean, the British; and Europe and the Atlantic jointly administered.

This was agreed to, and from it stem basic strategic questions that arose repeatedly throughout World War II. The British consistently objected to the American diversion of men and material to the Pacific, which they regarded as a drain, similar to the Americans dismissing the British Mediterranean strategy as a swamp. In addition, the British, except for those unlucky enough to fight there, were not much interested in Burma and India. The fall of Singapore with 130,000 Allied prisoners of war raised eyebrows about military incompetence, but otherwise the British directed their overwhelming effort at Hitler, which opened the route to India for the Japanese.

As the British expected, the Japanese seized Hong Kong immediately after their attack on Pearl Harbor. As they did not expect, Singapore capitulated just seventy days later, opening the resource-rich Malaya and Netherlands East Indies to the Japanese conqueror. Neither did the British expect a Japanese thrust into Burma, but it too materialized in such force as to drive the British imperial forces and a few Americans, such as General Joseph Stilwell, to the safer havens of India. Despite the presence of one of the great World War II commanders, Field Marshal Sir William Slim, the British high command was reluctant to commit itself to any sustained operations against the Japanese in Burma. British strategy aimed at the retaking of Rangoon and Singapore from the sea. But Stilwell's strategic goal was opening a route to China through northern Burma. The objectives were not only irreconcilable but also geographically divergent. As long as neither the British nor the Americans tried to execute such strategies, the absence of any Allied strategy for Burma could be papered over.

The Cairo Conference of November 1943 endorsed this Fabian strategy by stamping the approval of the Combined Chiefs on the major Allied effort against Japan in Asia to consist of a two-pronged attack on Japan through the Central Pacific and along the New Guinea–Philippines axis.[13] This reduced Slim's efforts, at least in 1942–43, to diversionary ones, and even these were failures similar to the ill-considered Arakan offensives of 1943–44. Brigadier Ord Wingate's daring, and some would argue foolhardy, Chindit operations deep behind Japanese lines in February and April 1943 were about the only sign of British initiative in Burma. Churchill seized on Wingate's exploits, as a drowning man grabs a leaky life preserver, to demonstrate British commitment to fight the Japanese. Wingate's newfound fame elevated this brooding mystic to the status of jungle fighter guru and enabled him to form what amounted to his own private army.

Aside from Slim, whose memoir incidentally contains paragraph after paragraph starting, "My next mistake was . . . ," there were few willing to learn from their mistakes. Stilwell's abrasive personality soured relations, and he was as uncritical in his admiration of the Chinese soldier as he was outspoken in his contempt for Chiang Kai-shek. Also, he was a noted Anglophobe who loudly proclaimed British incompetence in Asia to anyone willing to listen. Because his venom contained large doses of truth, Stilwell also had difficulty with the newly appointed commander of Southeast Asia command, Lord Louis Mountbatten, whom he served as deputy. Mountbatten dismissed Chiang's claim to be a full-fledged ally and with it the strategic concept of Allied positions in China threatening the Japanese flank or home islands. British strategy in 1943 pointed south to Rangoon and Malaya to clear those colonies from Japanese domain. After all, Churchill had announced that he had not become prime minister to oversee the dismemberment of the British Empire. Because Stilwell's ambitions pointed north along the Ledo Road to resupply China and equip its splendid fighting men to crush the Japanese, friction between the British and Americans was inevitable. Perhaps it was so splenetic in 1942–43, because they did little else. Slim's moment was yet to come.

These Allied disagreements, however, pale beside the conflict between the IJA and IJN. While the army wanted to consolidate gains, the navy wanted to push forward to cut Allied LOCs to Australia. They aimed to seize Port Moresby, Papua New Guinea, as well as to establish forward air bases on Guadalcanal and Tulagi. The former would isolate Australia from the north, while the latter would sever its supply line from the American West Coast. The result was the grinding battle in the air, sea, and land for Guadalcanal accompanied by MacArthur's successful defense of Port Moresby and offensive against Buna. The rugged six months of fighting permanently crippled Japan's offensive capabilities and consigned the Japanese to react to attacks at the time and place the Americans chose. Victory was not cheap in this war of attrition and in the subsequent campaigning in the Solomon Islands and New Guinea until early 1944.

Japan now revised its Pacific strategy, pulling back to prepared positions or strengthening new ones, but not attempting to recover reconquered territory. For the navy everything depended on forcing the American fleet into a decisive battle. Behind a strategic barrier, Japan would marshal huge numbers of aircraft that would be used to blunt the enemy's counteroffensive. This inner defensive zone included the Kurile Islands, Ogasawaras, western Pacific, and Western New Guinea,

Sumatra, and Burma. Clearly the Japanese recognized that they were on the strategic and operational defensive. Their main goal was to protect the lines of communications between the Empire and resource-rich Southeast Asia. Aside from a network of supporting bases, the Japanese hurried to adopt antisubmarine warfare techniques that they heretofore had ignored. Naval doctrine presumed a decisive fleet engagement would decide the course of the war, and not much attention had been given to convoy and antisubmarine tactics. Now American submarines, notably assisted by deciphered Japanese army and navy messages, embarked on the destruction of the Japanese merchant marine. This undersea interdiction campaign threatened to economically isolate Japan and limited or hindered the redeployment of Japanese ground forces from Asia to the Pacific. It ultimately sunk the Japanese merchant fleet.

By early 1943 the Australians and Americans had blunted the Japanese advance into the South and Southwest Pacific, had seized the operational initiative from the enemy, and were slowly working their way toward the major Japanese air and naval bastion at Rabaul. Pacific geography shaped future American strategy in a couple of ways. First of all the enormous ocean distances in the Pacific made it almost completely dependent on water transportation, which, in turn, created an insatiable demand for ships, which were in short supply because of the competing requirements for shipping to support a cross-channel attack against Germany.[14] Second, the network of Japanese bases effectively blocked any Allied advance toward the Philippines. Rabaul defended the Bismarck Sea and New Guinea approach from the southwest. If Allied operations swung northeast of Rabaul, they could be victimized by flank attacks from Rabaul to the southeast and the great prewar Japanese naval base at Truk to the northwest. Such a strategy promised bitter fighting for minimal gains in restricted waters that did not allow the U.S. Navy to exploit its growing mobile carrier forces. Alternatives were a drive through the Aleutians, which was not seriously considered, or a Central Pacific advance.

That Admiral King advocated an advance across the Central Pacific is not surprising, because it basically resurrected the prewar Orange plan that a generation of future naval strategists and commanders had studied. King, however, envisioned the Central Pacific drive occurring simultaneously with those in the South and Southwest Pacific. Those ongoing operations, he believed, were essential for the security of Australia and protection of the Allied line of communications. A two-pronged attack aimed at the Philippines would whipsaw the Japanese, who would be prevented from concentrating their forces in one area.¹⁵ A Central Pacific drive would also outflank Truk, and was a shorter and more direct route to the Philippines than an approach from the south. Seizing the Philippines would sever Japanese communications to the southern areas and plug the flow of oil and natural resources to the Japanese homeland. The Philippines could also serve as a springboard for Allied landings in China designed to secure a major port that, in turn, would be the entry point for a massive logistics effort to create an infrastructure in China to support aerial operations against Japan.

Obviously this was more than a diversion, and the British complained bitterly about the American resources deposited in the Pacific area. By the end of 1943, for example, 1.791 million American troops were engaged against Japan versus 1.849 million against Germany. About 7800 aircraft were allocated to the war against Japan, and 8800 were directed at Germany; and, as might be expected, 713 U.S. Navy ships were operating in the Pacific as opposed to 515 in the Atlantic and Mediterranean theaters.¹⁶ King in particular took perverse glee in the British refusal to commit themselves to a cross-channel attack in 1943, because any delay in the invasion of France improved his prospects for a larger war effort against Japan.¹⁷ In fairness to the British, they had been fighting for four years, often alone, against the might of the German Reich. While the United States had enough resources and reserves to recover if the invasion of Europe should fail, the British did not. For them, it was a one-shot chance that must not fail. They were cautious, because they realized that the combined might of the Soviet Union and the United States would crush Hitler, but unless Britain were involved, any notions of preserving its place in the world balance and its empire were illusory. Thus the British vacillated and talked about a Mediterranean strategy, the soft underbelly of Europe approach, an indirect approach, and a bomber offensive; in short about every direction of attack on Germany except the one the American JCS wanted—a direct, cross-channel attack aimed at bringing German arms to decisive battle in northwest Europe.

This indecisiveness about a second front enabled Admiral King and the JCS to go forward with their Central Pacific drive against Japan, grudgingly approved by the combined chiefs at Cairo in 1943. But even after this highest approval, an insurmountable problem remained. MacArthur, the Southwest Pacific commander, adamantly opposed a Central Pacific thrust, in large part because it detracted from his own theater's exploits. It became a question of command, and, although King favored unified command under a naval officer, given personalities such as MacArthur's to contend with, the prospects for this were dim. King finally gave up his dreams of navy control of Pacific operations in favor of preserving his good working relationship with the army chief of staff, General George C. Marshall. Marshall supported MacArthur's position, and King, rather than risk damaging his rapport with Marshall, acquiesced to a divided command.[18] It worked as one drive in the Pacific supported another and kept the Japanese off balance, but the inherent dangers in divided command imperiled MacArthur's operations at Biak Island in June 1944 and again at Leyte in October 1944.

The Central Pacific drive commenced in November 1943 with the assault on the Gilbert Islands. Joint planners agreed that the first operation could not fail, so they demanded amphibiously trained, battle-tested "shock troops," in other words U.S. Marines, for the attack.[19] As terrible as Tarawa proved, it might have been worse had the Japanese not diverted proposed reinforcements from the Gilberts to Rabaul to stem the South Pacific advance. There probably was no way to bypass Tarawa, because its airfield and the other Gilbert Islands were needed as staging and support bases for the planned jump into the Marshall Islands set for February 1944. Henceforth the Central Pacific thrust was characterized by assault forces venturing far beyond the range of land-based air cover, exposing themselves to Japanese air and surface attack, to seize strongly held atolls too small for maneuver or mass assault. Swiftness was the key to such operations as American air and naval forces had to establish local superiority and even take on the Japanese combined fleet if it ventured into the contested area.[20]

In the Southwest Pacific, by contrast, MacArthur staged his operations until April 1944 within range of friendly land-based airpower. Aircraft carriers were not available to him, because they would have to sail in restricted waters still contested by Japanese airpower. Consequently MacArthur's operations through 1943 had reconquered about one-third of the long, 900-mile New Guinea coastline. He had made progress, but had yet to crack the Bismarck barrier, though he stood poised to do so in early 1944.

Japan's losses on these Pacific fronts were crippling, but Japan was far from defeated. Military planners now looked to the creation of an invincible inner defensive zone (24 September 1943) that reached from Kuriles, Ogasawaras, and midwest Pacific and from western New Guinea, Sumatra, and Burma. Behind this strategic barrier the Japanese army would marshal its air and sea forces to beat back any future Allied advances in the Pacific. Japanese planners expected to concentrate vast numbers of newly produced aircraft in the Pacific to wrest control of the air, and thus the sea, from the Americans. Japanese industrial capacity could not produce the 55,000 aircraft the military chieftains demanded, and actual production barely sufficed to keep pace with aircraft losses. For its part, the Imperial Navy would seek the opportune moment for a decisive fleet engagement that would turn the fortunes of war in their favor.

IGHQ had not abandoned the idea of driving to India or knocking China out of the war. If either, or better, both, plans worked, Japan's military might in those theaters could be shifted to its Pacific front. Since autumn of 1942, Tokyo had talked about an advance to India, but nothing concrete had materialized. In Burma, Japan aimed to secure a line east of the Chin Hills bordering India and the Aykab region on the Bay of Bengal, thereby protecting Rangoon to the south and simultaneously blockading China to the north. Wingate's daring penetrations, however, dramatically affected Lieutenant General Mutaguchi Renya, commander of the Fifteenth Army. Mutaguchi believed that if Wingate could live in the jungle, so could the Japanese and their Indian National Army allies. Though a controversial plan that engendered much debate in high army circles, on 7 January 1944, IGHQ ordered an advance into India.

Mutaguchi, in charge of the offensive, was one of those larger-than-life characters whose passionate belief in Japanese spirit convinced him that willpower could overcome the rugged jungle terrain of northeastern Burma. He had once read that Genghis Khan, whom he greatly admired, had driven cattle alongside his mounted nomad army to ensure a steady food supply. Inspired, Mutaguchi launched what can only be termed a Southeast Asian version of *Rawhide*. Japanese soldiers loaded supplies on 20,000 head of cattle and drove them into the rain forests, across rivers, and over two mountain ranges dividing Burma from India. Because Mutaguchi had no air cover, his staff purposely selected the most remote, and consequently the most arduous, tracks for their approach march. Naturally the cattle died in droves leaving Mutaguchi without food or transport.[21] Nonetheless the Fifteenth Army's 85,000 Japanese and Indians pushed on and reached the Indian frontier in April, where they commenced a three-month siege of Imphal under appalling conditions.

Here Slim displayed the resourcefulness of a great commander. He maintained the combat effectiveness of his British and Indian units through extensive aerial resupply, which enabled his units to fight from hedgehog defenses, or the "administrative box" tactic. To isolate the British formations as they had in 1942 now required the Japanese to own the air above the battleground. It was beyond them. Japanese infantrymen suffered enormous casualties from forcing attack after attack against a position without flanks. Slim first defeated the Japanese diversionary attack in the Arakan and next at Imphal-Kohima. By July Tokyo had had enough and called a halt to Mutaguchi's quest for the grail. Overall 60,000 Japanese troops perished in the ill-conceived adventure. While this was transpiring, Stilwell was pushing north on Myitkyina and Wingate's columns, who, minus their leader killed in a plane crash, were fighting behind Japanese lines on missions of their own. Little strategic control of the operations existed. Their cumulative effects, however, and the startling Japanese losses left other points in Burma weakly defended and susceptible to Slim's planned counteroffensive.

Meanwhile the Imperial Army had reopened large-scale campaigning in China. In April 1944, the Ichigo Operation began. This massive fifteen-division offensive stretched the length of China. Its aim was to capture Chinese air bases in southwest China to prevent their use as B-29 bases and simultaneously reinforce the region against British or American counterattacks from Burma, to destroy the Chinese field army, and to construct a railway running across China to Saigon, French Indochina. The airfields were captured, but only after heavy fighting. Chiang's refusal to reinforce his besieged commander at Henyang in south central China soured foreign observers who took it as proof that he had no desire to fight the Japanese. In a sense they were right. Chiang judged the Japanese an external wound that could be healed. The Chinese communists, however, were a cancer that had to be eliminated. Thus the best Kuomintang troops were withheld from combat and kept ready for the showdown with Mao Tse-tung's communist armies that he knew awaited. Ichigo achieved its objectives, and the Japanese had opened a land route that ran from Saigon, French Indochina, to Pusan, Korea. It helped to somewhat relieve the incessant toll extracted by Allied submarines on Japanese shipping.

The outlook for Japan in the Pacific was much darker. The Quadrant Conference gave priority to Admiral Nimitz's Central Pacific advance and set a June date for the invasion of the Marianas. MacArthur, facing the possibility of being left in the navy's strategic backwash, promptly proposed an ambitious series of amphibious flanking operations. His planning was aided immeasurably by the newfound Allied ability to read the Japanese army's most secret cipher messages. MacArthur boldly seized the Admiralty Islands in February 1944 thereby encircling and isolating Rabaul. Next he leapfrogged to Hollandia and Aitape, some

400 miles up the New Guinea coastline. Three days of navy carrier support sufficed for the general to establish air bases to support his troops. The seaborne envelopment cut off 60,000 Japanese troops on New Guinea and rendered another 100,000 on Rabaul powerless. Following up this fast-paced tempo of operations MacArthur landed at Wakde/Sarmi and Biak in May. By August Japanese forces on New Guinea were cut off from the homeland. They did not surrender; instead Australian forces continued a bitter, unrelenting struggle in the primeval rain forests until war's end.

The Japanese First Mobile Fleet planned to strike MacArthur's smaller fleet off Biak, but Nimitz's landings on Saipan forced Admiral Ozawa Jisaburō to divert his main forces to the Central Pacific. Many of his newly minted pilots died during the great Marianas turkey shoot. Besides his airmen, Ozawa lost nine carriers, and Japanese naval airpower was broken beyond repair. Fighting on Saipan was grim for the Americans, but it was a death knell for the Japanese. The loss of Saipan meant that the Americans had broken Japan's inner defensive zone and now had an air base within range of the sacred home islands. Prime Minister General Tōjō Hideki's cabinet resigned, and the general staff prepared for a showdown.

Four plans, Shō 1–4, were devised to counter anticipated American landings against the Philippines, Formosa, and the Ryukyu Islands; southern Japan; and Hokkaido, respectively. Wherever the enemy struck in these areas, the full might of Japanese air, ground, and sea forces would be unleashed. The scene of Shō became Leyte Gulf in the central Philippines, although American strategists debated long and hard over their next objective.

The original notion was for the twin Allied drives to converge on the Philippines to cut Japanese lines of communication and secure a port on the Chinese coast. To accomplish this goal, the Allies had to control the South China Sea, which involved seizing and developing bases in a strategic triangle formed by the south China coast, Formosa, and Luzon. Washington planners and the U.S. Navy, especially Admiral King, saw Formosa as the most important objective. MacArthur violently disagreed, claiming that the United States had a moral obligation to liberate all of the Philippines. He was on firmer ground when he pointed out that unless Luzon was taken, Japanese aircraft threatened the navy's line of communication to Formosa. The argument went back and forth throughout the summer of 1944 as the JCS preferred vacillation to decision. Admiral William Halsey, in effect, made the decision for them.

In September 1944 Halsey's fast carriers launched a series of raids on Japanese bases in the Philippines. So weak was the Japanese reaction that Halsey recommended an immediate invasion of the central Philippines. Although strategic intelligence revealed clearly that the Japanese were strengthening, not withdrawing, from the islands, Nimitz was won over. MacArthur had been convinced all along, and on 15 September the JCS ordered the date for the invasion of Leyte be changed to 20 October. This did not, however, settle the Luzon question. Nimitz still favored an invasion of Formosa once Leyte was secured. But by this time the extended range of the new B-29 Superfortress made Formosa less attractive as a major air base complex. Luzon would serve as well. Furthermore, logistics difficulties involved in any assault on Formosa grew more complex with each passing day. On October 3 the JCS announced that Luzon would be taken and Formosa bypassed. Technology had overcome the initial strategic requirement for air bases in China and with it the need for a Chinese port. After Luzon the Allies could jump directly to Okinawa, which would serve as one of the major staging bases for the invasion of Japan.

Divided command again caused the Allies to flirt with disaster at Leyte Gulf. Halsey's decision to move north and strike Admiral Ozawa's decoy fleet left MacArthur's transports naked in Leyte Gulf. Only the courage of sailors on small destroyers and escort carriers sailing into the way of Japanese battleships deflected the enemy blow. Unwilling to push past this aggressive, if weak, screen, the Japanese admiral, for reasons that still remain vague today, broke off the action and retreated northward. The Battle for Leyte Gulf destroyed most of the remaining Japanese surface fleet, but still the Japanese did not give up. Japan's new prime minister declared that Leyte was the decisive battleground of the Pacific War. Ground reinforcements rushing from Luzon to Leyte were subjected to vicious Allied air and surface attacks. More than five Japanese divisions were ultimately lost, which left General Yamashita Tomoyuki's Luzon defenses unready to repel an invasion. A new Japanese weapon, the kamikaze, appeared in full force at Leyte and throughout the Philippines. The war in the Pacific now seemed to pit those determined to die against those who wanted to live. MacArthur's forces landed on Luzon on 9 January 1945 and were still digging out stubborn Japanese defenders in August.

These disasters in the Pacific made IGHQ realize that the decisive battle would now take place on Japan's shores. Defensive preparations went forward on Okinawa, a prefecture of Japan, and Iwo Jima, administratively part of Tokyo. Allied air attacks by B-29s on the homeland had begun, but their full effect, that is the rain of incendiary bombs aimed to destroy populated urban centers, was still two months away. As desperate as the Japanese situation was, there were bright spots.

Twenty-six divisions were in China at the end of 1944, and during the spring of 1945 several of them were on the move against American airfields in China. After capturing fields in west central China, the Japanese turned their attention to strengthening coastal defenses against a possible invasion. They also began to call up reserves and conscripts to flesh out new divisions, especially in Manchuria. The elite divisions of the Kwantung Army had been, or would shortly be, transferred to the Pacific front. Because the Soviet menace remained, new formations had to replace these losses. Simultaneous with a mobilization in Japan itself, 700,000 Japanese and Koreans were recalled or pressed into new units of the Kwantung Army. Lacking training, equipment, and leadership, there was little that they could do except sit in defensive positions throughout Manchuria and hope that the Soviets would not invade.

Disaster struck the Japanese in Burma. Forced on the defensive after the Imphal fiasco, Japan's Burma Army by January 1945 had fallen back to southern Burma. Its new mission was to hold that area to protect the flank of the vital Malaya, Sumatra, Indochina region. Tokyo then had given up cutting off Allied forces in China from those operating in India, and, not coincidentally, January 1945 marks the time that the first American truck convoy crossed the eastern borders of Burma en route to Kunming, China. In March 1945 Slim's XIV Army crossed the mighty, mile-wide Irrawady River south of Mandalay, isolating Japanese forces there. In a race against the spring monsoon (at which time the Americans would withdraw their airpower), Slim's Indian Army struck south for Rangoon, 350 miles distant, on the Bay of Bengal. The XIV Army, pressing forward in a 300-mile-long salient that was usually 1 to 2 miles wide, liberated the city in early May just as the first raindrops fell.[22] The Japanese in Burma were a shattered remnant, cut off from resupply and reinforcement. Of the 330,000 Japanese officers and men available at the outset of the Imphal madness, at least 200,000 had been killed in action or died from disease and starvation. Lord Mountbatten began plans for the reconquest of Malaya.

There was no letup to the Allied strategic pincers closing on Japan. Iwo Jima was taken at great cost in February 1945 and Okinawa invaded on 1 April 1945. One school of Japanese thought maintains that the high command intentionally sacrificed the people of Okinawa to the invaders' guns to make the point that Japan would fight to the bitter end.[23] Massed kamikaze attacks, suicide boats, defenders fanatically resisting to the last man, mass civilian suicides, and utter destruction were Okinawa's fate. The carnage on Okinawa was appalling, by any measurement of warfare. The enormity of the destruction is understated in casualty returns:

U.S. Casualties	Japanese Casualties
49,151 (plus another 31,000 nonbattle losses)	110,000
36 ships sunk, another 368 damaged	
763 aircraft lost	7830 aircraft lost
	(4155 in combat)[24]

The specter of Okinawa haunted the Joint Chiefs and new American President Harry S. Truman as they prepared for the invasion of the Japanese home islands.[25] Despite an aerial pounding of the homeland that since March 1945 had killed more than 200,000 Japanese and left more than 1.3 million homeless, Japan's military leaders were determined to fight until they could achieve an honorable end to the war. For the Allies, the end of the war against Japan might have been in sight in June 1945, but only after a showdown on the home islands. Since April the Japanese high command had been preparing for just such an eventuality. Hundreds of thousands of men were rushed to southern Kyushu, where the anticipated invaders were expected to land. By August at least 700,000 Japanese troops were crowded into fortress Kyushu.

The U.S. Army, in particular Generals Marshall and MacArthur, believed that an invasion of the home islands was necessary to end the war. From strategic intelligence the specific shape of the Japanese reinforcement effort on Kyushu was well-known.[26] Both Marshall and MacArthur also favored Soviet participation in the war to tie down Japanese troops in Manchuria. The U.S. Navy believed a combination of air and sea blockade would compel a Japanese surrender. The JCS opted for a direct invasion, OPERATION OLYMPIC, scheduled for 1 November 1945.

In mid-June the atomic age exploded in the New Mexico desert. The atomic bomb quickly convinced Secretary of War Henry Stimson that Soviet entry into the war against Japan was no longer needed, because the new weapon would win the war. Marshall was uncertain, and MacArthur was not informed until shortly before the bomb was scheduled to be dropped on Hiroshima on 6 August. Even after the first atomic attack, Marshall worried that an invasion would be necessary. The Japanese leadership was indecisive, unable to agree on a means to capitulate to the Allies. A second atomic attack on 9 August was delivered against Nagasaki. At dawn that same day, Soviet forces, as promised in February 1945 by Stalin at Yalta, entered the war against Japan. Eighty Soviet divisions, more than 1.7 million troops, launched a blitzkrieg against Japanese troops in Manchuria. With Japanese hopes gone Emperor Hirohito announced that his nation must surrender and "bear the unbearable." The Pacific War ended as suddenly as it began.

Elsewhere in Asia the war ended on a ragged note. In Southeast Asia, British and Indian troops accepted Japan's surrender. Colonial rule was reinstated temporarily, at least in French Indochina, Burma, Malaya, and the Netherlands East Indies. All would soon gain independence, in three cases by revolting against their colonial masters. The British had accomplished their immediate aim, securing the empire east of Suez, but the victory was ephemeral. China's victory also proved temporary. Within a few months of Japan's surrender, civil war again broke out between the communists and nationalists. Mao's triumph in 1949 marked the end of American presence in China until President Richard Nixon's historic visit over twenty years later. The Soviets withdrew from Manchuria and the northern half of Korea, but left behind well-trained, thoroughly indoctrinated, and equipped communist armies.

Thousands of miles to the south, Australian troops accepted the surrender of Japanese on New Guinea, Rabaul, and the Netherlands East Indies. They engaged in most of the early fighting against Japan, and then found themselves consigned to a thankless mop-up role. As a minor partner in the Allied coalition, perhaps it was inevitable that Australia was overwhelmed by the United States. In the Philippines, General Yamashita was escorted out of his mountain redoubt to surrender. America fought its Pacific War much in the fashion that the U.S. Navy always thought that it should be fought. It was, however, the unmatched and undamaged industrial reserve of America that spewed forth the resources to make the two-front war a success. By pushing against both major enemies simultaneously, the Allies allowed neither to consolidate gains fully. The great Allied victory stands as a tribute to a strategy that was broad enough to encompass theaters of enormous diversity; strong enough to withstand the inevitable coalition clashes of personality and objectives; flexible enough to seize and exploit opportunities; and farsighted enough to defeat a mighty Axis alliance in the greatest war the world has ever witnessed.

CHAPTER FIVE

U.S. ARMY AND IMPERIAL JAPANESE ARMY DOCTRINE DURING WORLD WAR II

Doctrine provides an insight into an army's concept of warfare, how an army thinks about itself. Links between doctrine and an army's force structure offer an appreciation of the army's tactical and operational methods of executing that doctrine. For instance, if an army understands warfare as primarily an affair decided by the infantry, a doctrine emphasizing infantry tactics, morale, and leadership qualities might emerge. Another army that understands warfare as a matter of combined arms may highlight weapons technology and machinery. No such clear-cut dichotomy exists in real armies, as the differences of emphasis are mainly those of degree, not exclusion. Nevertheless, armies do disregard unfeasible means of warfare, because they cannot afford to consider or invest seriously in doctrines and force structures that they lack the potential resources to implement.

It made no sense, for example, for the IJA of the 1920s and 1930s to ponder heavy divisions and armor units, because they lacked the industrial capacity and natural resources to augment such a force structure. It did, however, make sense for them to concentrate on infantry tactics and design a doctrine based on infantry spirit overcoming technological deficiencies. Similarly, for the Americans it made no sense to build 175 infantry divisions when a strategic air force, armored divisions, or Lieutenant General Lesley McNair's pooled artillery and tank concepts could be realized. In short the basic American strategic decision to out-produce the foe pushed the U.S. Army toward a technological, not a tactical, solution of ground combat in the Pacific theater. If our object was to win the war against Japan, which no one doubted was possible, at the lowest possible cost in human terms, which many believed would be difficult, then the strategy worked. But overlooked in victory was the nagging fact that American infantrymen were not the tactical equals of their Japanese counterparts. This is no inherent flaw in national character. The American GI in the Pacific was as tough, nasty, ruthless, and efficient as any infantryman once he mastered his craft. But his initial training emphasized machine solutions—firepower, truck-borne mobility, armor maneuver, airborne or amphibious surprise—that were trade-offs for a thorough training of the infantry. That is the major difference in the doctrine and practice of the major belligerents in the Pacific theater. Now I provide evidence to support these generalizations.

Pre–World War II U.S. Army doctrine stressed offensive action, describing a defensive attitude as a temporary expedient. It placed great emphasis on leadership and insisted, "Man is the fundamental instrument in war."[1] The 1939 Tentative Field Service Regulations (FSR) declared that when the situation does not favor an envelopment, the main attack, one of combined arms, must be one of penetration. What they are talking about is a massed infantry frontal attack. The FSR prescribed successive waves of infantry attacking on narrow zones of action (frontages) reinforced by artillery and heavy infantry weapons. Breakthrough was achieved by successive concentration of fire on critical objectives and by proper timing in the engagement of tanks and reserves.[2] This doctrine obviously reflects the American experience in World War I on the Western Front, and the planners' belief that the next European war would be waged under similar conditions. Consequently the American Army attached great importance to the infantry-artillery team.[3] Artillery's "special mission" was to open the way for the troops in the attacking echelon by engaging enemy elements that stood in the way of the advance. Direct artillery support was emphasized, and artillery units were assigned specifically to designated infantry or horse cavalry units.

The 1941 FSR "Operations" also recognized that against organized defensive positions the limited firepower of infantry must be adequately reinforced by the support of artillery, tanks, and so forth, but stated, "No one arm wins battles. The combined action of all arms and services is essential to success."[4] Nonetheless, the description of main attacks was unchanged, as was the injunction to execute frontal attacks. A new, two-page section did appear on jungle operations that recognized that close fighting characteristic of jungle combat "is performed largely by infantry." Terrain restrictions on observation precluded as extensive a role for artillery as in other theaters, but combat aviation, in particular, light bombardment aviation, "is used to compensate for lack of artillery."[5] This statement assumed a close-air-support doctrine that was nonexistent in 1941.

Throughout the interwar years, the American Army stressed the notion of the infantry-artillery team and trained accordingly. Though often overlooked, U.S. Army artillery innovations during the 1920s and 1930s bore fruit during World War II. I am referring to motorization of artillery batteries—61 batteries of 100 total of those in service in 1937 were motorized—and the development of fire direction centers (FDC).[6] The FDC's ability to control fires of all attached artillery batteries and those of nearby field artillery battalions allowed multiple artillery guns to coordinate their fire so that all their shells hit a target simultaneously at a predesignated time. This was the devastating TOT (time on target), whose lethal synchronization of artillery firepower so singularly impressed both friend and foe.[7]

The flip side, however, was that interwar emphasis on artillery-infantry cooperation, and later armor and air doctrine, naturally diluted "pure" infantry training and dragged potential infantrymen to these other branches. In 1936 the chief of infantry said the combat infantrymen made up fewer than 25 percent of the whole American Army under the expansion plans versus 50 percent in the German establishment. Furthermore, force structure alterations reduced the number of riflemen in an infantry regiment from 2500 (approximately 70 percent of the 3600-man establishment) to 970 (about 28 percent of the 3500-man establishment).[8] The reason was that more crew-served weapons entered the force; that meant more firepower.[9]

Other army manpower needs, especially for the fast-growing Army Air Corps, stripped away potential infantrymen. Those draftees who did well on army-administered aptitude tests more often than not found themselves assigned to noninfantry specialties. The army also gravely underestimated its wartime infantry replacement requirements. Infantry represented 14 percent of the U.S. Army's overseas strength, but suffered 70 percent of its cumulative casualties. To keep units up to strength, the army adopted a short, four-week course that converted personnel from other specialties to infantrymen. As a veteran of the Pacific fighting put it to a postwar army board, "You cannot train an infantryman overnight.... A soldier in any branch may have to fight as Infantry any time.... I believe all men should be basically Infantry and then if assigned to another branch or service, be kept aware at all times that he might be transferred back to duty as an infantryman."[10] In summary, the U.S. Army entered the war against Japan with an infantry force trained to conduct combined arms maneuvers in close cooperation with the artillery. The army was without a jungle warfare doctrine and had not fully considered the implications of modern infantry combat on its forces. In the Pacific this meant that at the lower tactical levels, regiment and below, fewer riflemen than ever before had to carry a heavier load of the fighting than doctrine or army planners anticipated.

For the IJA the Infantry Branch was the heart and soul of the force. Only the best officers were commissioned into the infantry. The bulk of the force structure remained predominantly infantry even as the army modernized in the 1920s and 1930s. In 1917, 68 percent of the force was infantry.[11] Twenty years later, a square Japanese infantry division still counted about 48 percent infantry rifle strength (5600 of 11,858), and its wartime rifle strength stood at 37 percent despite extensive augmentation of what we today term combat service and combat service support troops.[12] To meet the requirements of their China War, which began in July 1937, the army created triangular divisions. These units were 43 percent infantry (3780 of 8872) and many ended up in the Pacific fighting the U.S. Army.[13] Moreover, in the post–World War I military reductions between 1922 and 1925, the Japanese army opted for a large-scale reduction of artillery firepower, eliminating 115 artillery batteries in 1922 and twenty-four more in 1925. As one former Imperial Army staff officer and historian remarked, "Those thinking that the way to strengthen the division's fighting strength was by eliminating the field artillery brigade and independent mountain artillery regiment probably were influenced by the 1908 Infantry Manual."[14] The doctrine espoused in that particular manual, weighted heavily on the intangible factors of infantry in battle, marked the beginning of a consistent theme in Japanese military thought that infantry, properly led and motivated, can overcome the material advantages of the foe. The Japanese army then was diverging from machine and firepower solutions to tactical problems. Men, not machines and firepower, win wars.

One can, however, search in vain to discover a jungle warfare doctrine in pre–World War II Japanese FSRs. In the final chapter of the 1938 FSR, part 2, three pages explain operations in wooded terrain by lumping them together with operations in populated areas.[15] Simply put, in terms of doctrine, the Japanese were unprepared for operations in the South

Pacific as late as the summer of 1940. Japan did have contingency plans for an invasion of the Philippine Islands as early as 1907, but actual preparations amounted to little more than desktop plans carefully stored and dusted off annually or as required for a visiting staff officer overseeing a periodic revision of the plan.[16] Incidentally, the famous bicycles the Japanese used during their seventy-day advance to Singapore originated around 1924–25, when ideas of improving infantry mobility with bicycle troops were fashionable in all major armies. The Imperial Army remained woefully ignorant of its American counterpart, neither bothering to prepare any in-depth analyses of U.S. combat power, morale, and equipment, nor conducting specific studies against the United States as the hypothetical opponent, nor linking exercises to particular plans.[17] For example, the Fifth Division began actual planning for the Malayan Operation on 15 August 1940, while the Sixteenth Division, scheduled to invade the Philippines, learned it would not participate in Manchurian operations in June 1941. In brief, for the Japanese army the war in the South Pacific was one against an unknown enemy in an unstudied climate and unfamiliar terrain.[18]

If the Japanese were not writing or adapting doctrine for a war against America, then what was the focus of their doctrine? It was the Soviet Union. Just as U.S. Army doctrine envisioned its likely opponent in Western Europe deployed in defenses in-depth, so too the Imperial Army doctrine foresaw a war against the USSR on the plains of Manchuria. The previously mentioned 1938 FSR emphasized morale factors and tenacity of the will and stressed training designed to develop the command ability to recognize opportunities for attack and make quick decisions. The wide-open plains of Manchuria offered Japanese officers opportunity to envelop open Soviet flanks, encircle formations, and destroy numerically and technologically superior forces. Japanese infantry always probed for an open flank to exploit. Since 1908 the traditional Imperial Army emphasis on highly motivated infantry conducting night attacks pressed home with the bayonet had never varied and had served as the basic tactical doctrine of the Japanese Army to counter the superior firepower of the Red Army. Training then emphasized the unique role of the infantryman. He was expected to be tough and resolute and to fight without elaborate combined arms support. Such a doctrine, according to the FSR, while designed for operations against the USSR, "will not hinder our operations against other armies in other instances."[19]

Similar to their American counterparts, Japanese doctrine writers regarded one tactical doctrine, prepared against a specific, if hypothetical, enemy, as applicable in all cases to all opponents. Furthermore, if the American Army conducted the famous Louisiana Maneuvers of 1940 predicated on a war of maneuver in Europe, it perhaps is fitting that the largest annual exercise in the Japanese army scheduled for November 1941, the "Fuji Experimental Maneuvers," had for its theme operations against Soviet-fortified zones in Manchuria.[20] This scenario proved as remote for Imperial Army units such as the Fifty-fifth and Sixteenth Infantry divisions, which fought in Malaya and the Philippines, respectively, as for that of the Louisiana Maneuvers for several participating American units, including the Thirty-second and Thirty-seventh Infantry divisions, bloodied on New Guinea and the Philippines.[21]

The lack of a Japanese jungle warfare doctrine was evident on Bataan in 1941–42. When the Sixteenth Division met American units that were trained to fight in the jungle, such as the Philippine Scouts, the Forty-third and Fifty-seventh Infantry regiments, and the Fourth Marine Regiment, they were beaten back with heavy losses. The Japanese did not help their cause by blundering into the prewar maneuver areas on Bataan where the defenders knew the terrain and could call in preregistered artillery fires with deadly effect.[22] The Fifty-fifth fared better against the British Empire forces in Malaya by simply probing for the open flank, usually a few hundred meters into the jungle growth, hooking around the flank, and charging into rear areas. This was standard Japanese doctrine, and its successful execution gave rise to tall tales of Japanese jungle warfare. That stereotype, however, is dispelled when one examines the tactical effectiveness of the Japanese units fighting the U.S. Army in the Pacific.

I now shift to that brief examination of the tactical effectiveness of the Japanese and American lower-echelon units in the Pacific, particularly on New Guinea and the Philippine Islands, because those grueling campaigns consumed so many American and Japanese fighting men. Three campaigns—Buna (November 1942–January 1943); Aitape (April–August 1944); and Leyte (October–December 1944)—provide the framework for analysis. My chronological selection was deliberate, because I expected to find tactical evolution based on "lessons learned" in both armies during the course of the war. As for the U.S. Army, my summation of these three battles is: Buna, prewar doctrine without firepower; Aitape, evolving doctrine plus firepower; and Leyte, doctrine and firepower stalemated.

The U.S. Army, or at least the commander, I Corps, Lieutenant General Robert Eichelberger, concluded that American failures at Buna did not expose fundamental flaws of doctrine, and that "our training program is satisfactory but must be greatly intensified." In particular, combat "patrols were neither determined, aggressive nor resourceful. They were consistent in their over-estimate of enemy strength and prowess." This led to "hiding out" and "fairy stories."[23] "Enemy patrols," the report continued, "displayed commendable training in the use of cover, silence, fire control, camouflage, and patience, lying motionless for hours on end in order to achieve their missions. In one spectacular instance, after two members of a four-man Japanese patrol were killed, the survivors stayed in the area and, among other things, buried their dead undetected."[24] These anonymous Japanese were, I believe, infantrymen. The G-3 noted the Japanese worked at night and slept during the day, just the opposite of the GIs' routine. Among Japanese troops, fire discipline, defensive positions, and camouflage were especially good, just as they were noticeably absent in the U.S. units.[25]

The men of the Thirty-second Infantry Division, a National Guard unit, were unprepared mentally and physically for their first battle at Buna. They expected a walkover because of rumors that the Japanese were already whipped and planning to withdraw. Training suitable for World War I–style warfare was the sum of their theoretical military experience, and they fully expected to enjoy artillery support from the division's four artillery battalions. Actually, at Buna, the use of truck-drawn artillery was as the division historian noted, "out of the question, even if it could have been brought to the area." The division's organic artillery at Buna never exceeded eight guns, so the Red Arrow men lacked sufficient artillery support in a battle that became a frontal assault broken into "distinct small engagements to capture individual [Japanese] bunkers." When artillery support was available, the gunners discovered that the dense jungle foliage limited radius of burst, so that even accurately located targets required "more than the amount of ammunition normally thought adequate."[26]

Again staff officers lamented the GIs' lack of determination to press home attacks or, at times, even to engage the enemy. Their solution was "vigorous leadership" to revitalize shattered units. It was a stark bottom line. "All commanders, in training and in battle, must ruthlessly weed out incompetent leaders, and energetically seek out new leaders in their units. . . . The combat leader must use every means at his disposal to train his men properly before battle is joined, to bring his men into contact with the enemy in the best possible fighting trim and yet be tough minded enough to expend them unhesitatingly to achieve victory."[27] An officer in the Southwest Pacific recorded: "In too many instances, either due to lack of training or poor leadership, or to a combination of both, our troops did not have the will to close with and kill the enemy. Troops seemed to think they should be able to stand off at a distance and kill the enemy, or have our aircraft, tanks, artillery, mortars, or machine guns do the killing for them, and were reluctant to believe that it was their duty to personally go forward and kill the Japs themselves."[28] The Japanese shared these unblinking assessments. "The Americans depend on firepower, they are weak in hand-to-hand combat and exposed as a powerless army absolutely unable to resist our bayonet attacks."[29] Rather than a leadership problem, I suggest the U.S. Army had a doctrine problem. It trained men for open, mobile warfare emphasizing machines and then had to consign them to primeval jungle swamps to root out stubborn defenders in a manner more reminiscent of tenth- rather than twentieth-century warfare.

Nonetheless, the U.S. Army officially identified mistakes and learned lessons. Unofficially, however, tactical doctrine changed little. According to Brigadier General Julian W. Cunningham, commander, 112th Cavalry Regimental Combat Team, defending the Driniumor River line in 1944, the men exhibited similar tendencies to those noted at Buna. Yet Cunningham stated, off the record, that he doubted most of his patrols did what they said they did. The XI Corps Commander, Major General Charles P. Hall, concurred that most of the troops just hid out and then returned without doing anything.[30] In a 16 July 1944 letter to Sixth Army Commander Lieutenant General Walter Krueger, Hall complained that "it is too late here to teach the principles of patrolling, but we are still trying to do it." Charges of lack of aggressiveness also filled the air, as Krueger, at one point, threatened courts-martial for unaggressive troops and put tremendous pressure on Hall to conclude the campaign expeditiously.[31] These commanders were disparaging veteran units. By this time, July 1944, the 112th were blooded veterans of New Britain and the other unit, the Thirty-second Division, had won at Buna. American tactics were predictable, massive artillery shoots followed up by cautious infantry probes. There were three field artillery battalions (the 120th, 129th, 148th) at the start of the campaign. Four more, the 103d, 192d, 149th, 181st, plus the XI Corps Artillery Section, naval gunfire support, and close air support augmented firepower. Indeed artillery support was profligate, the largest expenditure to date in the Southwest Pacific theater.[32]

American soldiers, however, could negate the lavish artillery firepower by not making what Chief of Staff George C. Marshall termed a "continuity of effort."[33] Too often daylight gains faded away as American units "buttoned-up" after dark, conceding the night to the Japanese for movement, redeployment, and local counterattacks. This American trait played to the strengths of conventional Japanese doctrine. And the Thirty-second Division's G-3 after-action report stated, "The need for aggressive, active, and intelligent leaders of small units was again emphasized.... Commanders of companies, battalions, and higher units must be aggressive. They must be constantly on the alert, aware of the situation, and in control of their various organization commanders." The report added, "Close liaison between infantry and artillery was very effective in stopping enemy attacks."[34] In short, the GI relied on artillery firepower to kill the enemy, just as doctrine and prewar training had emphasized.

Leyte differed in scope from the previous two battles, being a multicorps operation ultimately involving eight-plus U.S. Army divisions (1st Cavalry, 7th, 11th Airborne, 24th, 32d, 38th, 77th, 96th, 112th Cavalry RCT) and fighting elements of six Japanese divisions (1st, 8th [minus], 16th, 26th, 30th, and 102d). Much of the fighting centered around Breakneck Ridge, a series of rugged hills barring American entry into the Ormoc Valley. For more than one month, American infantrymen, supported by tanks, aircraft, artillery, and naval gunfire, fought to dislodge the stubborn Japanese defenders. During the fighting, General Krueger, overall ground commander, analyzed the performance of his Sixth Army. American tactics, he observed, usually employed frontal attacks against enemy positions, and not enough use was made of envelopments. The infantryman had a "natural reluctance" to engage the enemy at close quarters, and patrols exhibited this trait by withdrawing from the enemy on contact. If more than minor resistance was encountered, larger units of troops "frequently fell back and called for fire from supporting weapons." Krueger believed that the infantry-artillery team again proved effective, but the infantryman had grown too dependent on the artillery and expected it to do the work of the infantry. This in turn had developed into a tendency for the Americans to telegraph their punches. Furthermore, the American soldiers were too road bound and reluctant to root out the Japanese defenders in rugged terrain. If this sounds familiar, so does the American praise for the Japanese infantry, whose firepower discipline was excellent as was an effective control of all arms. On the defensive, the Japanese used rear-slope positions skillfully and adapted the terrain to their defense. Their counterattacks came at night against the American front and flanks and often recaptured ground lost during the day. Japanese artillery support, however, was considered inferior, massed fires being nonexistent.[35] So in these three cases, American commanders evaluated their opponents higher than their own troops in terms of tactical infantry proficiency.

I am suggesting that a superior tactical infantry doctrine and commensurate emphasis on infantry training account, in part, for the superior performance of Japanese combat infantrymen. The basic Japanese field manual was the Infantry Manual, and all other arms revolved around that shining example. Furthermore the traditional Japanese emphasis on turning flanks, night attacks, and the bayonet was quickly adaptable to jungle fighting, which places a premium on small-unit infantry combat. The trade-off was that Japanese officers were imbued with the spirit of the offensive at the expense of sound campaign and logistic planning.

At the outbreak of the Pacific War, the Imperial Army viewed its opponents (United States, Great Britain, Holland) as colonial armies and either ignored them or exaggerated their deficiencies.[36] Underestimating a potential opponent may be commonplace, but to insist on that stereotype throughout an extended war is rather unusual. Consistently the Japanese army validated their own tactics, because they saw the American Army doctrine as a simplistic belief in weaponry and materiel superiority. Japanese spirit, such staff officers believed, could offset those tangible advantages. As late as September 1943 during the IJA's postmortems on the Bataan (a success) and Guadalcanal (a failure) operations, directed by the inspector general of military education, various school commandants complained, "It's unnecessary to conduct a study of the weak American Army. Better to spend our time studying the powerful Red Army"; or "We don't have any documents about the American Army, so it will make research difficult"; or "This year we are studying operations designed to breach Soviet border fortifications and cannot waste time to study American tactics."[37]

Despite the presence of Army Ground Forces Observer Teams, which were comparable to the U.S. Army, the Japanese refused to adapt their basic infantry doctrine to their opponent. For instance, the main Imperial Army concern during their 1941 invasion of Luzon, Philippine Islands, was the danger of an American air attack while the troops were still packed aboard ship. Enemy ground tactics were not discussed. In August 1942 Colonel Ichiki Kiyoano's 600-man detachment really did believe the U.S. Marines on Guadalcanal would flee when attacked, and were subsequently annihilated for their hubris. Tactical shifts from defense on the beaches—because the infantry manual decreed one defends a river line at the water's edge—to defense inland or to greater emphasis on defensive operations, such as Iwo Jima or Okinawa, did not fundamentally alter the basic infantry doctrine and emphasis on hand-to-hand combat. Nor did references to operations in the Southern region depart from basic tactical doctrinal principles.[38]

All too often Japanese troops acted more like simpletons than supermen in the jungle. The Fifty-third Infantry, Seventeenth Division's action on New Britain was not uncharacteristic. "The regiment," a battalion commander reminisced, "knew nothing of American tactics. We would attack them the same way we fought against the Chinese. Full of confidence, we moved forward to attack in a standard close-column. Next thing we heard from the jungle was violent gunfire and men started to drop everywhere. We pulled back."[39] Those unfortunate Japanese infantrymen on the receiving end of American combined arms also had a different point of view. A survivor of Buna wrote, "I was suffering from malaria and malnutrition, so weak I could only carry a pistol. . . . Soldiers sat like mummies in front line foxholes. . . . Because of malnutrition, after dark we had trouble seeing. . . . Enemy patrols freely penetrated our front lines. Everyone had malaria or amebic dysentery and there were many nervous breakdowns or shell shock. . . . The enemy attacks intensified and it seemed like we're bombed everyday as the seriously wounded begged the battalion surgeon to kill them."[40] Not all Japanese fought as tenaciously as the two aforementioned infantrymen who buried their dead companions and completed their missions. Japanese officers were quick to criticize "troops in support areas who refuse to fire at enemy planes for fear of being bombed."[41] Aside from demonstrating that perspective is relative, how could such tactical infantry proficiency be so poorly spent? For that answer, the respective prewar American and IJA officer education systems may hold the key.

Japanese commanders, with a few notable exceptions, were not proficient in the command of large units, or in what today is termed the operational level of warfare. If the Japanese infantry was tactically superior to its American enemy, then the American commander consistently displayed the ability to maneuver and sustain large units in combat. American corps and army-level commanders were very competent at formulating and executing an operational plan, although they seem to have lacked a strategic vision of the ultimate goal of the operations. Perhaps the best example is the American JCS's humiliation at the Casablanca Conference in 1942. British chieftains were able to outmaneuver their American cousins, because the latter had an operational plan—invade the continent of Europe immediately—but no accompanying strategic framework. General Douglas MacArthur may be an exception because of his megalomaniac insistence on returning to the Philippines. But my point remains that American generals were solid operational planners, and their Japanese counterparts were not. The Japanese overemphasis on infantry tactics was instrumental in this deficiency in the high command.

Tactics and tactical instruction—battle drills and so forth—are products of training designed to implement instinctive reaction. Command of large units cannot be accomplished by reflex. It requires years of education and experience to produce commanders capable of innovative thought and creativity on the battlefield. Yet in the IJA "the heart of the War College curriculum was tactics,"[42] although its mission was to prepare officers for high-level command.[43] A typical class for the two-year course between 1925 and 1938, whose graduates became the World War II leaders, had about fifty officers. They were normally captains and majors who were eligible for selection after eight years' service, including at least two with a unit. Subject matter, for the most part, relied on rote memorization of facts, which similar to training, can produce narrow, if effective, specialists.[44] Infantry branch officers accounted for at least half the enrollment and in the Twentieth Class for three-quarters of the student officers.

Instructional materials in the 1930s included the superb tactical histories of the Russo-Japanese War, as the course concentrated on tactics. Students spent fewer hours on military history, studies and lectures on logistics, intelligence, airpower, and communications. After their two years of study they participated in a staff ride to the battlefields of the Russo-Japanese War in Manchuria and Korea, because these were the hypothetical battlegrounds of the next war.

Missing, however, was the dimension of a common education because of the conscious decision to limit special courses dealing with the operational level of war to a select ten officers annually. For them, Colonel Tani Hisao convened a special seminar using sensitive classified documents unavailable to other army officers let alone other War College students. Only a few War College faculty and students, for example, even knew that the compilation on the Russo-Japanese War titled *Wartime Statistics* existed for planning purposes.[45] While the officially published version of the Russo-Japanese War stressed tactical fine points in illuminating detail, the crucial operational and administrative military history remained secret and hidden from most future staff officers. Thus most War College students argued tactics, and the ability to persevere in one's argument regardless of facts was highly valued. As one former instructor remembered, the ability, as the Japanese put it, to turn black into white was taken as a mark of confidence, because it displayed an officer's initiative and determination. Decibel levels became more important than knowledge in the classroom. Decisiveness and resolution were prized, perhaps because so much decision making in Japan requires a consensus that battlefield pressures did not permit.

Assertive staff officers, nurtured in this training hothouse, lacked, in the words of one of their contemporaries, "the ability to undertake an objective assessment of their own actions." Japanese officers had drummed into them from their cadet days that because the difference between victory and defeat was razor thin, the most tenacious side would be the victor.[46] The practical result was repeated decisions to reinforce failures or a singular lack of imagination when approaching operational problems. Resolute action, however unrealistic, under pressure or when faced with an unexpected crisis, usually carried the day. To exacerbate the problem, even if the "gung-ho" staff officer bungled, as more and more did as the war dragged on, the army leadership overlooked it.[47] In extreme cases, the results might appear as they do in the following anecdote. "On a rainy day in the middle of August 1943, the instructor stood behind the lectern to announce to his War College seminar, 'From now on the curriculum is changed. The main emphasis will be on countering U.S. tactics, and will become the "A" course.' He paused, then continued. 'If anyone can teach this course, go ahead because frankly I don't know a damn thing about it.'"[48] Yet this rote staff mentality fit in perfectly with a doctrine emphasizing inflexible infantry tactics—battle drills to imbue small-unit commanders to rush forward into battle. In short, the War College system almost guaranteed a rigid approach to operations, and the enlisted men and junior officers had to pay this butcher's bill with their blood.

Contrast this officer education system with that of the U.S. Army's Command and General Staff College in the 1920s and 1930s that groomed officers for the highest levels of command, including combined arms, command, and staff functions at division and corps level.[49] Education at Leavenworth emphasized a generalized professional competence across the spectrum of staff duties. It was, as one officer-historian said, "an education that qualified men to design, operate, and repair a military machine, but not to select its objectives."[50] Officers selected for the two-year Leavenworth course were more mature in age and experience than were their Japanese counterparts and understood the tactical underpinnings of army doctrine. With that advantage, they were in a position to capitalize on a demanding course of instruction that dismissed those unable to keep pace. In 1926, to eliminate the "unhealthy" concern of the students with their relative standing within the class, the designation honor and distinguished graduates disappeared, whereas this remained a keenly competitive award at the Imperial War College. Leavenworth, then, educated those officers to think, to analyze, and to decide realistic courses of action. Not all succeeded in the pressures of World War II, however, but those who did invariably graduated from Leavenworth, where they learned not only large-unit doctrine but also received an education that enabled them to apply this theory at the operational level to win the greatest war the United States ever fought.

In summary, both the American and Imperial Japanese armies fought the Pacific War pretty much in terms of their prewar doctrinal emphasis. The American soldier relied on artillery and later naval and air support, because the infantry-artillery team was the nexus of training. They fought the way they trained, and their training stressed quantity not quality. One bludgeoned the foe into submission.

The Japanese also went to war against America the way they trained. They relied on grueling, demanding training that produced quality infantry men to compensate for inferior materiel and technological support. On a one-to-one basis in the jungle, there probably was no better fighter than a hard-bitten, mercilessly trained Japanese infantryman who refused to surrender no matter how hopeless his condition.

Field Marshal Sir William Slim, who led the XIV Army to victory in Burma against similar Japanese tenacity and fanaticism, summed up his opponent. "He fought and marched," wrote Slim, "till he died. If five hundred Japanese were ordered to hold a position, we had to kill four hundred and ninety-five before it was ours—and then the last five killed themselves. It was this combination of obedience and ferocity that made the Japanese Army, whatever its condition, so formidable, and which would make any army formidable. It would make a European army invincible."[51] Aside from the racist implications of Slim's remark, the Japanese soldier was not invincible. His bones, scattered on battlefields from the Aleutians to India, only leave mute evidence to his unimaginative determination to die before giving up. And victory in twentieth-century warfare does not depend on a samurai-like, sword-swinging, one-against-one encounter. It is the ability to combine doctrine, arms, support, will, and leadership at the critical time and place that guarantees success. I mean that American material and technical superiority alone do not account for Japan's defeat. The American high command out thought its Japanese opponents.

After mid-1942, American skill and imagination at the operational and strategic level forced the Japanese to fight at times, places, and on terms of American choosing. The Japanese, in turn, had to react to American strengths, whereas Americans capitalized on Japanese weakness. The Japanese high command misused its men in a criminal fashion, because most officers lacked the intellectual framework to think beyond the present engagement. Action, not rigorous analysis and thought about alternatives and implications, was the hallmark of a Japanese staff officer. One can admire them as fighters, but not respect them as professional soldiers.

The only way that a professional officer learns the judicious application of doctrine is through experience, usually with units, and from education, because we are not in perpetual war. He needs the practical involvement to understand the tools and weapons of warfare. His profession demands the theoretical so that he may apply imagination, creativity, judgment, and intelligence to adapt a doctrine that makes full use of those warrior tools in future battle. Imperial Army officers well understood their weapons and their troops. Their doctrinal emphasis on these limited factors circumscribed their theoretical understanding of modern warfare and strategy.

CHAPTER SIX

"TRAINED IN THE HARDEST SCHOOL"

During its brief, violent history, the IJA grew from a handful of loyalist warriors in 1868 to 5.9 million officers and men by 1945. It achieved monumental triumphs over Manchu China (1894–95), Czarist Russia (1904–5), and Western colonial powers (1941–42). Yet it ended in ashes, stigmatized as an army of fanatics run amok.

Radical change characterized the early army. Although the slogan "Rich country, strong army" became a rallying cry for the newly constituted government headed by Emperor Meiji (1868–1912), the restoration displaced the societal role of the warrior-administrators, or samurai, by revoking their privileges and status.[1] The abolition of clan armies and the subsequent introduction of universal manhood conscription in 1873 offer the most striking examples of the assault on samurai privileges. Almost all the officers of the new Imperial Army were aristocrats or samurai,[2] but, in addition, the great Satsuma uprising of 1877 was inspired, fueled, led, and fought by disaffected samurai. Moreover the mutiny of an Imperial Guards artillery battalion the following year—the Takebashi Incident[3]—underscored that discontent in the ranks could erupt at any moment.

The army's problem then was twofold: first, how to guarantee the loyalty of the troops to the nation; and, second, how to capitalize on the highly esteemed warrior values—courage, loyalty, bravery, obedience, frugality, self-sacrifice, and so forth—to convert these traditional and romanticized ideals to national as well as Imperial Army standards. Meiji government leaders, such as Yamagata Aritomo, the father of the Japanese army, solved the former by linking all ranks to the emperor and institutionalized this relationship in the 1882 Imperial Rescript to Soldiers and Sailors.[4] The resolution of the latter required incorporating derivative samurai values as a part of the ethos of the Imperial Army. Even as the percentage of officers of samurai lineage on active duty steadily declined in the early twentieth century, the army leadership designed methods to inculcate traditional values associated with the warrior caste into its formal recruit training system.

Widespread agreement exists that basic military training is the keystone of battlefield performance, although exact correlations between training and combat performance prove elusive, more often in the eye of the beholder than in supporting empirical evidence. A rigorous analysis of the historical record of a foreign army, besides offering additional factual data about systems of training, provides a perspective for comparative study of military institutions. This chapter examines in detail the military training system of the IJA to identify correlations among training, combat performance, and unit cohesion. The pre–World War II Japanese army case provides general insights about recruit training as well as about the influence of cultural and national norms on group behavior and stability. It also suggests that military training capitalized on existing Japanese traditions, customs, and mores to mold a fighting man whose highest duty was to die an honorable death for his emperor.

Perhaps the most enduring image of the Japanese-American War (1941–45) is the fanaticism and willingness to fight, literally to the death, that characterized the emperor's officers and men.[5] The Japanese soldier's dogged resolution to resist even when all hope of survival, let alone victory, had long vanished was, in a terrifying sense, a realization of the ideal of "death before dishonor" that all armies attempt to inculcate into their recruits. This combination of rock-ribbed fighting qualities and persistence to fight to the death made the Japanese infantryman a most dangerous foe. The seeds of this tenacity were nurtured in the hothouse training cycle of the Imperial Army, but they were sown much earlier in Japanese society at large.

This chapter focuses not on the officer corps but on the enlisted troops and more exactly, on the conscripts—the first- and second-year soldiers who provided the underpinnings of the Imperial Army. Specifically it examines a conscript's life in the barracks in the quasi-peacetime army of the mid-1930s when the Japanese army was engaged in what it termed "bandit-suppression campaigns" in Manchuria. Nevertheless, the army still functioned according to its peacetime table of organization and equipment. Furthermore, many of the 1936 recruits reappeared as the recalled reservists of the Pacific War, where they put into deadly practice the lessons from basic training. Finally, during wartime the activities it describes persisted even among front-line units.

The method used here describes in detail the first year of a Japanese conscript's life in the Imperial Army, thereby providing a framework to analyze features of daily life for the enlisted troops in their barracks. Who were these soldiers? From where did they come? How did recruits transfer training into combat performance? Finally, and most importantly, what role did Japanese values have in the army? In other words, did the army adapt or let itself be adapted to the social and ethical values of Japan?

In the 1930s the army produced a series of illustrated postcards; the cards portrayed the self-image of life in the IJA.[6] Army camp canteens sold these postcards for a nominal fee to the recruits to send home to reassure everyone that all was well in the barracks. Certain themes were apparent. First, the recruit reported to active duty in a social ritual that included not only the draftee but also family, friends, and well-wishers in a typical Japanese *omi-okuri* (send-off), not unlike what one sees today among clusters of Japanese tourists at Tokyo Station or Narita Airport. Once in the army the recruit was well cared for, and he clearly enjoyed his new life as a soldier. Interestingly even on these one-sen postcards, solitary soldiers never appeared. Everything depicted was accomplished in group activity—a characteristic of any basic training camp in the world. The first-year soldiers—often shown doing favors for their senior second-year comrades—benefited from their association with such veterans. Officers and NCOs served as surrogate parents either tucking the recruit into his futon or patiently correcting rookie mistakes. One postcard showed parents assuring the recruit that everything was fine at home, and his sole duty was to become a good soldier. Two themes emerge from these self-admiring illustrations. First, the Imperial Army was the natural extension of the prewar Japanese family writ large with all the trappings of respect for hierarchy and group versus individual identification implied in that notion. Second, this was a highly positive and flattering image of the life of a common Japanese soldier. It was also misleading insofar as it idealized and romanticized the daily routine of the first-year soldier, while it concealed the less savory aspects and violence of life in the barracks.

In prewar Japan, recruiting districts—conscription districts—served as the administrative areas that managed the conscription process. Everyone

FIGURE 3. Roll call. The recruit reports "all present and accounted for" to the inspecting officer in the spotless barracks. Courtesy of Mainichi shimbunsha

entered the army through the draft. A few individuals applied for voluntary induction to active service, but the vast majority took their chances on being conscripted. Each year twenty-year-old Japanese males had to report for physical examinations, the basis for their subsequent classification according to fitness for service. In peacetime only Category "A"s—those taller than 1.55 meters and in top physical condition—were eligible for conscription. Even among those classified as "A" group, approximately 150,000 of 750,000 examined each year, the army needed perhaps 120,000 conscripts.[7] Consequently all the draft-eligible "A"s went into a pool, and a lottery determined which ones would indeed enter active service. In 1934, 28.9 percent of all those examined received induction notices. Even as late as January 1937, the last year of peacetime for the Japanese army, the Imperial Army inducted about 23 percent of the young men it examined.[8]

Chances of being drafted also depended on where in Japan one lived. Shizuoka Prefecture had the highest conscription rate in 1934, when 37 percent of those examined were conscripted; Kagoshima was the lowest with barely 25 percent accepted for service. Normally the poorer agricultural and backward areas, such as Kagoshima, and the cities provided the fewest eligible males able to pass to army's pre-induction physical.[9] Almost all those examined and not classified as "A" moved to the First

Conscript Reserve—which provided replacement fillers in wartime—or the Second Reserve—mainly for garrison replacements in wartime—or the National Militia—which was almost everyone else unable to meet the qualifications of the first three categories. These groups initially received a maximum of 120 days' training and thereafter limited mandatory training not to exceed thirty-five days per year. There were two other categories: "D" for the physically or mentally deficient or those regarded as unsuitable for soldiers, including criminals and dwarfs; and "E," a special category for those who were ill at the time of the annual physical. They had to report for reexamination and reclassification the following year.[10]

It was possible to beat the system by fasting to be underweight or to drink soy sauce to produce symptoms of heart trouble. These were, naturally, criminal offenses if detected, so most reluctant would-be conscripts attached their white prayer slip to a tree or post at a nearby Shinto shrine or invoked various Buddhas to relieve them of the burden of military service. According to the war ministry, the number of draft dodgers increased proportionate to the higher degree of formal education and was always higher in cities than in the farming villages. Nevertheless, because the Japanese army tended to idealize the farming communities as its best source of conscripts, even small numbers of draft evaders, such as the 176 total reported in Ibaraki Prefecture in 1931, were considered unacceptably high. Nationwide campaigns appealed to the public to "Report Persons Illegally Avoiding Military Service or Neglecting to Register" and reminded everyone that "One's Life Is Not a Privilege: Draft Dodgers Shame the Region," and similar slogans.[11]

This lengthy description of the induction system shows the Imperial Army's appeal to certain segments of Japanese society. The army accepted only the best physical specimens, and for the peasant lad, conscription was a mark of status.[12] It placed the recruit, particularly the peasant, in a hierarchical relationship to his peers. In short, it provided him a place within his group within the village community. He was acknowledged as one of the best physically, and the Japanese peasantry in the 1930s demanded physical ability to endure the backbreaking labor attendant to wet rice agriculture.

A recruit entering the Imperial Army in 1936 was one of 240,000 regular active duty soldiers and officers. By contrast, the U.S. Army had about 165,000 active duty soldiers at this time. The peacetime Japanese army, with its two-year conscripted tour of duty, annually turned over about 50 percent of the relatively small, seventeen-division army. Besides its smallness, it was an intimate army, because the recruiting districts inducted draftees into the barracks based on the area of their homes of record as did various European armies. Japanese infantry recruits joined infantry regiments in regimental districts affiliated with their homes of record. Other branches—artillery, signal, logistics, cavalry—entered divisional districts affiliated with their respective homes of record, except for members of the Guards Division, whom the army selected nationwide, and the Nineteenth and Twentieth divisions, permanently assigned to Korea, whose recruits the army gathered from other divisional districts. If the population of one district was small, other divisional districts supplemented its draft quotas. Other features of this army were that a majority of the soldiers were in the infantry branch, each infantry regiment had ties with a specific locality, and each had its respective hometown unit. In short, one did not escape one's peers and village by joining the army; they came along, and the consequent motivation not to disgrace one's family or village by delinquent military service was powerful. This was especially the case for the peasants—whom the army chieftains regarded as the backbone of the force. Joining the army provided first an elevated status and second a responsibility to meet expectations of family and village or town. "The young men of the village," wrote an observer in 1929, "consider it the greatest honor attainable, once they enter the army, to become a private superior class. . . . All the villagers share this view. As the young recruits leave the village, they all vow to come back as private superior class."[13] This metamorphosis from civilian to private superior class occurred in the following context: Recruits inducted into the army received a send-off from their neighbors and reported to their local unit on 10 January of the year following their physical. In peacetime they could look forward to discharge, depending on branch and previous military training, in eighteen months, or 9 July, or the normal two-year tour that expired 30 November.[14] The first thing the recruits received was a physical examination. Satisfied with their health, the regiment then assigned them to one of its three battalions and then to their respective companies. Each battalion had three companies, on paper numbered consecutively 1 through 12, but in peacetime omitting the Fourth, Eighth, and Twelfth companies for economy reasons. The total of 160 officers and men of an infantry company included 150 private soldiers, usually apportioned in about a fifty-fifty mixture of first- and second-year soldiers. The company commander, usually a captain, exercised command directly and individually over the lower ranks. The platoons that comprised the companies had about thirty men who shared a common barracks.

To inculcate the determination to go forward into battle, the Japanese army consciously molded the company on familial or paternalistic models. As in any army, the entire universe of the lower ranks—the NCOs and privates—was localized in their respective company. In the Japanese army, however, army regulations officially reinforced the place of the company as the soldier's home and family.

According to the 1908 revision to the *Guntai naimusho* (Army handbook for squad administration) regulations, "The barracks is the soldiers' family where together soldiers' share hardships and joys, life and death.... A family means that the company is one household in the one village of the regiment. The heads of the household are the father and the mother. The company commander is a strict father, and the NCO a loving mother. The lieutenants are relatives and in perfect accord with their company commander whom they loyally assist." To underline the NCO responsibilities, in 1934, the chief of military affairs bureau, war ministry, explained that, "The NCOs' birthplace is the company; his growth is also with the company; and his place of death should also be with the company."[15] No one was ever allowed to forget that the company was the echelon that directly engaged in combat, the primary purpose of an army.

When the new recruits first entered their company barracks, their NCOs lined them up for an inspection and address from the company commander. This standard talk emphasized that the company commander was the recruits' father and the sergeant their mother. The second-year soldiers were regarded as older brothers. In this traditional familial setting, if the recruit got into trouble, he had these relatives to fall back on for support. The master sergeant, section NCOs, and sergeant major had separate quarters, but everyone else lived in the barracks squad room, where about fifteen first-year soldiers normally found themselves paired with an equal number of second-year soldiers in two-man groups.[16] A few superior privates were scattered throughout the platoon and shared the same barracks. The recruits rarely again saw, or wanted to see, an officer for their first four months of intensive basic training.

All these little loyalties to higher authority, cultivated originally in one's own family, in this surrogate or substitute family added up to the one great loyalty due to His Imperial Majesty, the emperor of Japan.[17] For most conscripts it was a logical progression from the school curricula, which stressed the uniqueness of Japan because of the unbroken imperial line. The ministry of education went to great lengths to ensure that the six years of required schooling had a heavy tinge of nationalism and patriotism throughout the curriculum.[18] Virtues of *chukun aikoku* (loyalty to the emperor and love of country) were values most brought with them into the army as their intellectual baggage. The army, in turn, played on these concepts by claiming a special relationship to the emperor exemplified by the Imperial Rescript to Soldiers and Sailors, which the recruits had to study daily. This was a long, 2700-character document distinguished by such obscure *kanji* (Chinese characters) that it was difficult even for college graduates to read. Recruits also had to memorize and recite on command a shorter version of the rescript, "Five Principles of the Soldier." In certain units troops recited the principles in unison before being seated for breakfast. The entire Imperial Rescript was read to the troops on special occasions, such as National Foundation Day (11 February) or Army Day (10 March), but every morning the troops bowed toward the imperial palace to pay homage to the emperor before they began their arduous daily regimen of training.[19]

A second legitimacy provided by imperial sanction was mandatory respect for all superiors in one's chain of command to include anyone who had been in the service longer, irrespective of rank. Hierarchy in Japan, then, as today, was taken for granted. Status was very important. The pattern of hierarchy within groups was paralleled by a hierarchy between groups.[20] All military organizations have a clear hierarchical order, and the Japanese predisposition to such social arrangements made organization for training comprehensible for the recruit and easier for the drill master. The recruit had a place in a well-ordered military society and through hard work, loyalty, and proper attitude in the squad could advance in that closed, hierarchical society.

Besides emperor worship and the daily reading of rescripts to soldiers, the recruits learned that they had to take special care of their equipment, because it came to them from the emperor. The imperial crest on items of equipment, such as the breech of the standard Type 38 rifle, served as a constant reminder to even the most dim-witted recruit that the emperor had entrusted this precious equipment to a lowly and unworthy subject like himself. To further reinforce proper care and maintenance of uniforms and equipment, senior soldiers or NCOs would physically beat their subordinates for the slightest infractions—a spot of oil on a rifle, a blemish on a bayonet, a button askew, or dirt on white socks, and so forth.[21] All this was done in the name of the emperor, because the miscreant soldier had failed to take proper care of the items the emperor had so generously bestowed on him. Internal squad discipline was the cement for the army's training edifice.

The regulations governing squad training and administration stated that "The objective of daily life in the barracks is to perfect the self-discipline of the soldiers through military drill."[22] The cultivation of self-discipline for the Japanese tends to involve practices of mortification of the flesh designed to develop will power. They commonly make a fetish of self-discipline and the cultivation of willpower, and the popular belief is strong that sufficient willpower can overcome any obstacle if one tries hard enough.[23] This concept was coupled with the Japanese notion of sincerity, which means as long as one had the proper motives and acted sincerely, almost any act can be understood, if not fully appreciated.[24] Again these are popular, not military, values.

The young Japanese recruit moved into a rigorously controlled barracks. He was forbidden to read newspapers, magazines, or books unless his commander gave prior approval. The barracks became the place where the recruit would sleep, eat, stand inspection, stand guard, and cultivate self-discipline. He awoke to the bugle, stood morning inspection in rank in the aisle between the two rows of beds left free, ate by the third bugle, and ultimately turned out the lights with the final bugle. A bugle call normally announced reveille, inspection, meals, reports, sick call, sentry duty, roundup of horses, and lights out. The bugle started daily life and chased time in the new rhythm of military life.

Besides adjusting to the incessant bugle calls the recruits had to master the specialized vocabulary of military life. The Japanese army, as in other armed forces, consciously adopted an argot, including *kanji*, and usage beyond ordinary conversational Japanese. A recruit learned, for instance, that *uwagi* (jacket) really was *guni* (military clothing), *surippa* (slipper) was *jyoka* (upper leather), and even money transformed from 1 sen to 1 *senchi* (centimeter) or 1 yen was 1 *metoru* (meter).[25] Naturally the specialized vocabulary confused the recruits until they could master it. Such confusion was costly, because the senior soldiers looked for pretexts to inflict violence on the new soldiers in the name of instilling self-discipline into the newcomers. The emphasis was on discipline and obedience and for the lowest ranking soldiers this meant, in practical terms, constant abuse and beatings. The recruits were always being supervised, and petty harassment filled their days. The objective was to reform the personality by making unquestioning obedience second nature.

A few examples serve to illustrate the point. A new recruit might be ordered to stand at attention—all day. Forbidden to move, even to relieve himself, the young man would stand motionless for several hours. When the agony became too great, he would collapse and would promptly receive a beating, because he was still supposed to be at attention. His will power or self-discipline was at fault and needed cultivation.

The seniors always looked for indications of the recruit's attitude, speech, and bearing. Soldiers had to stand at attention and answer endless trivial questions, such as "You have time to eat in the Army. Don't you have time to care for your boots?" "Don't you sleep at night? Since you have time to sleep, can't you take care of your equipment?"[26] Even answering a question was no guarantee you could avoid being beaten for improper attitude. Seniors beat their subordinates for talking or for remaining silent. Most recruits soon learned the best thing to say was "yes, yes" and accept a few slaps in the face. It was standard practice to beat a soldier while simultaneously explaining the reason for beating him.

In spite of such harsh treatment, the number of soldiers officially convicted in court-martial proceedings was low, about 1.16 per thousand men.[27] Again life in the barracks played a significant role in holding court-martial proceedings to such a low number. Following the evening inspection, the NCOs withdrew, and the corporals, superior privates, and second-year soldiers took charge of their respective barracks. With the day's official duties and formal training completed, this was the ideal time to discipline the young soldiers, because nothing and no one would interfere with the enforcement of internal squad discipline.

Their predecessors who had served in the army and returned to the villages had told the first-year soldiers about this thirty- to sixty-minute period before "lights out," and warned them that "In the light of the full moon, the second year soldiers turn into demons."[28] This "time of the devils" occurred when the senior soldiers established their own informal tribunals to mete out appropriate punishments to their juniors, whose errors and mistakes had embarrassed the entire platoon. Although regulations officially forbid the use of violence, these kangaroo courts handed down verdicts of punishments ranging from slappings to beatings, and, if called for, gang assaults on an especially blatant offender. In other words the squads themselves internally handled discipline cases, and because they did it unofficially the official record bears no trace of their actions.

In this type of corporate, informal punishment, no one was responsible, and the culprit, though bruised and battered, was not totally humiliated, because his contemporaries were in the same condition. Besides he did not have to endure official censure and public humiliation for his actions. It was preventative violence, and a typical Japanese solution to a problem. In a sense the squad served as a *nakadachi* (go-between) negotiating the recruits' capabilities with the officers' and NCOs' demands in such a manner that recruits and NCOs need not interact directly, and therefore officially nothing ever happened. This is similar to the Japanese political parties' use of go-betweens to deal with unsavory elements that the politicians cannot officially have links with for reasons of avoiding confrontations and maintaining group solidarity.[29] Similarly the squad dealt with its internal problems privately beyond official eyes and thereby linked individual success or failure to the entire group and the coercion of group sanctions.

The recruits had plenty of reasons to anticipate with trepidation the evening hour when the squad area became the kingdom of the senior soldiers, because throughout the day the recruits had countless occasions to make mistakes. Beyond the normal training routines, guaranteed to produce mistakes, the recruits acted as servants for the second-year soldiers. It was the recruits who waited on the common squad room table, brewed tea, carried the platoon leader's settings to the NCOs, and distributed rice and soup from the huge pots brought in by kitchen workers, as everyone also ate in the barracks. Recruits washed the dishes after meals, swept and scrubbed barracks floors, shined or oiled boots, did the washing and did all the menial tasks for the older soldiers who shared the barracks with them and were thus always available to keep a watchful eye on the newcomers.

Furthermore, the extremely low monthly pay rates consigned most recruits' existence to the immediate world of the barracks. Recruit pay was a pittance, especially during their first four months of basic training when they received 2 yen 75 sen per month, the U.S. equivalent in 1936 of about 65 cents. By contrast, the lowest-paid basic recruit in the U.S. Army received $21.00 a month. Even a first- or second-year Japanese private soldier received 5 yen 50 sen a month, or about $1.20. Nor did private soldiers receive any family benefits. A PFC, for instance, received 42 yen 40 sen if living outside the barracks with a family. A sergeant major made 22 yen 50 sen a month and received another 55 yen 50 sen if living outside the barracks.[30]

To put these wages in perspective, a Japanese common laborer in 1927 made about 64 yen ($15–16) a month for twenty-five days' work. A peasant, however, averaged less than one yen per day for twelve hours of hard, physical labor. A rough estimate is that a twenty-year-old laborer made around 50 yen a month and a college graduate about 80 yen as a starting salary. Women made about one-third the wages of their male counterparts. Put differently, a subway ride cost 10 sen; a bottle of

Johnny Walker Red Scotch 5 yen—two months' wages for the recruit. In the depression year of 1931 at the Tokyo Municipal Restaurant one could buy breakfast for 8 sen and lunch and supper for 15 and 10 sen, respectively. A private soldier's monthly wages then were inadequate even to feed him outside the barracks let alone provide for lodging or clothes.[31] By any standards, conscript pay in Japan was extremely low. Furthermore, all disbursement of pay was done formally in the company commander's office, which gave the commander additional leverage to withhold a soldier's pay, meaning the soldier could not even buy cigarettes, postcards, or small delicacies at the camp store.

The army did, however, provide a conscript's family 30 sen a day in military relief pay. A 1930s newspaper human interest story illustrated that this too could be a mixed blessing. A superior private requested that his company commander not nominate him for discharge or early release from active duty. The enlisted soldier did not like military life, but without the supplemental relief pay and his previous civilian job filled by another worker, his family faced disintegration.[32] In brief there was no guarantee that after military service a veteran could return to his former work, unless he was a peasant, because there never was enough brute labor available for the bone-tiring, back-breaking work in the fields.

Another army solatium was the death benefit awarded to families of soldiers who died or were killed while on active duty. An episode related in Second Lieutenant Suematsu Taihei's elegant memoir sheds a different light on the payment. While serving with the Second Division in Manchuria in 1931, Suematsu was censoring mail to his troops when a subordinate asked the meaning of a letter to one of the soldiers in his company. The soldier's father had written to his son that on no account must the son return home alive. Suematsu answered that if the boy were killed in action in Manchuria the family would receive a death benefit of 150 yen.[33] Payment was proportional to rank, similar to the solatium paid to victims of automobile accidents in Japan today. Not incidentally, Suematsu became one of the "radical young officers," a uniformed political activist, and spent four years in prison for supporting the military mutiny in Tokyo on 26 February 1936.

The Japanese army trained its recruits and units in four-month segments. The first four months of service equated to basic training, and was keyed to developing individual proficiency of the recruit, unquestioning obedience to orders, and cultivation of self-discipline. After the first month of rigorous training, NCOs told recruits that the second month would be even harsher, to which most recruits probably felt, "If it's any worse than this, they'll probably kill us."[34] The second month toughened the recruit even more and, as with any basic training regimen, the NCOs assaulted them with verbal and physical abuse. The physical beatings seem more characteristic of Japanese military training techniques and must be understood as a means of instilling self-discipline, not, in most cases, permanently disabling recruits. Nonetheless, the immediate results could be nasty. Discolored, swollen faces marked the newcomers, as each mistake might cost them a slap or punch. Even sitting in a class learning about weapons and equipment, an inability to answer instructor's questions could get you slapped. One former artilleryman recalled being tapped gingerly in the face with a rifle cleaning rod if he could not answer his corporal's questions. "Everyone's face was black and blue and mine was the worst because I got hit the most. Only my eyes and teeth stood out because the rest of my face was black and blue."[35] Why did the Japanese recruits meekly submit to such indignities? Anyone who went through basic training immediately knows part of that answer. But in this case the fatalistic attitude deeply ingrained in the Japanese—as expressed by "shikata ga nai" (it can't be helped)—allowed them to accept such mistreatment with a more stoic resilience than an American counterpart.[36]

Next recruits moved into a four-month training cycle that emphasized small-unit training—squad, platoon, company-level training, and exercises. Both recruits and second-year soldiers participated in this phase, and competition among units, which permeated throughout the army, could become fierce, as each strove to be the best. Finally the third cycle stressed battalion or higher level training. Usually just preceding the grand maneuvers were exercises involving regiment- and brigade-size units designed to sharpen the troops for the major event. The last weeks of this cycle, around early November, saw the annual autumn maneuvers. These were usually division-level or higher echelon exercises involving maneuvers of the combined arms—artillery, cavalry, and so forth—and were the high point of the year.

Indeed the presence of His Imperial Majesty at the fall maneuvers imbued the exercises with special significance. Villagers and townspeople turned out, some attracted by a break in the routine monotony of their lives provided by army band concerts or the hustle and bustle of soldiers running about. Others were attracted by the commercial opportunities in selling commemorative postcards, cigarettes, or sundries to the troops. While there was a festival-like spirit surrounding the maneuvers, one should also remember that at this time the farming communities in Japan

FIGURE 4. Marching troops of the Guards Division parade in barracks area. Courtesy of U.S. Army Military History Institute (USAMHI), Japan Miscellaneous Collection

were enduring terrible poverty and having strangers tear up your fields or damage what few possessions you might have—even though entirely by accident—offset to some degree the attendant good will that the army wanted maneuvers to generate. The maneuvers did, however, get the recruits out of the barracks and gave them a chance to do what they had trained all year to do—play soldier. The ritualized warfare broke the monotony of barracks routine and the training cycle. It also marked the close of the active duty service for second-year soldiers and the elevation to the esteemed second-year status of the heretofore recruits. Their hazing completed, the new second-year soldiers, in turn, inflicted the punishments meted out previously on them on their successors.

One must, however, consider this military training system in its historical context. For most recruits army life was an acceptable change from the drudgery of their daily lives. Mikiso Hane cites a friend in the army who told a peasant, "his work in the army is easier than farm work. The food is good, and the second year soldiers have considerable free time. He is now worried about the hard work that is waiting for him on the farm after he is mustered out. At first, until one gets used to the regulations in the army camp, things are tougher than on the farm, but once one gets used to things army life is a lot better than farm life."[37] He probably accurately summed up the feelings of many young Japanese boys who entered the army from the poverty-stricken rural areas of Japan.

A natural question arises about the degree to which the recruits' training conditioned them to fight to the death. A 1939 Japanese Army Medical Corps study of the Twenty-third Infantry Division soldiers' reactions to battle dealt with this question.[38] A "new" division, it was organized in April 1938 and composed of first-year soldiers, recalled reservists, and volunteer company grade officers. Their training was still incomplete when they marched off to their first battle in May 1939. That summer the division suffered more than 70 percent casualties fighting the Soviets at Khalkin Gol.[39] The sketchy psychological profile of the survivors offers a Japanese insight into the relationship between training and battlefield performance.

Before the battle, troop morale was very high, and the soldiers believed that they would quickly defeat and rout the Soviets. While this trait is characteristic of green troops, innocent of the realities of combat, it does indicate that training had inculcated an aggressive spirit and a conviction that Japanese arms were invincible. Furthermore, the troops initially had confidence in their weapons, tactics, and supporting arms, all indications of thorough training. As the battle turned against the Japanese and casualties increased, the infantryman reacted according to his initial expectation of combat, meaning that the higher his initial belief in victory, the greater his corresponding sense of breech of faith by his higher officers when defeat loomed. Recruits trained to expect nothing but victory felt betrayed when they encountered only defeat. Japanese doctors characterized neurotic behavior as manifesting itself in: suicidal attacks to ensure an honorable death; individual and group aimlessness as well as disorientation; dispirited individuals and units daunted by failure; breakdown of unit cohesion; as well as unauthorized withdrawal from assigned positions, a court-martial offense in the IJA.[40]

The reactions just described seem to be universal responses of men in battle, which only means that the Japanese soldiers had the same human emotions as any other soldiers. Training success then was not contingent on creating robots or fighting insects as the British General Sir William Slim called them.[41] According to IJA doctors, success in battle depended on three criteria. Men in units fought well when their commanders were present; when the men believed that other units continued to support them, despite temporary isolation; and when closely knit emotional ties existed among soldiers in small units.[42] This is hardly surprising, because military theorists from Ardant du Picq to S. L. A. Marshall make similar claims about men in battle.[43]

Training methods of the Imperial army did instill those values, leadership, interdependence, and cohesion, so highly prized by military leaders. They did this by building on the existing values of the society, especially the creation of a surrogate family. This is not to deny that the prewar IJA certainly adopted Western forms of organization, uniform, rank structure, military education, and modern weaponry along with the associated modern tools of warfare. It did not, however, attempt to impose either a Western or a modern model on the social structure inside the barracks. Instead the army emphasized traditional Japanese values—not merely simplistic martial values summed up in clichés, such as *bushido* (way of the warrior) or *Yamato damashii* (Japanese spirit), but the values of a people conditioned over centuries to accept a hierarchical social structure, clearly defined ranks and status, informal sanctions to avoid public embarrassment and humiliation, and above all identifying allegiance to the unit as allegiance to the emperor and thereby giving official approval to the concept of the unique and superior Japanese race. By cultivating these values in a pseudo-family-like setting, the army joined and molded its recruits. Thus, despite being poorly led at the higher levels, the Japanese infantryman, according to one who fought against him, was "the bravest soldier I ever met. . . . It is the fashion to dismiss their courage as fanaticism, but this only begs the question. The Japanese soldier believed in something, and they were willing to die for it, for the smallest detail that would help achieve it."[44] The Japanese enlisted man's belief in those values was the result of the imposition of military training on the existing social and cultural mores of prewar Japan.

CHAPTER SEVEN

ADACHI HATAZO
A Soldier of His Emperor

Why talk about a general who is relatively obscure in Japan and virtually unknown elsewhere? We hear so much of either successful commanders or spectacular failures as generals that we often forget that there is a middle ground; the professional soldier (although Adachi Hatazo would have bridled at that description), whose steady yet unspectacular rise to important commands speaks volumes about the nature of the man as well as the army he serves. Perhaps by discussing a general officer who was neither a genius, such as Napoleon or MacArthur, nor a fool, such as McClellan or Mutaguchi, we gain a keener sense of what it meant to be an officer, a commander, and a leader in a major army. Moreover a preeminent Japanese military historian regards Adachi as one of only three general officers commanding troops who upheld Japan's military tradition by not disgracing the uniform.[1]

Adachi Hatazo was born in Tokyo in 1890, the fifth of a family of six brothers and seven sisters. The family descended from the samurai (or warrior class), and Adachi's father was a professional officer, although tuberculosis had caused his removal from the active list.[2] By all accounts the elder Adachi was a martinet, perhaps because illness beyond his control cut short his military career. He then turned his frustration into a quest for perfection narrowly focused on the traditional values of the Japanese warrior class, such as courage, loyalty, bravery, frugality, stoicism, and self-sacrifice. One sees the influence on the young Hatazo of this exceptionally strict father who dominated family life.

Adachi Hatazo was a big child and by prewar Japanese standards a big man at 5'10", 175 pounds. Being the third brother in a family that emphasized martial qualities obviously had its drawbacks, as his older and bigger brothers could physically best him and, as siblings do everywhere, tantalize and taunt him. What one sees in the child Adachi is the forging of a strong-willed, stoic man, capable of persevering in the face of hardships and enduring physical suffering in silence.[3] In other words, he endured his childhood trials like a good samurai.

Adachi originally leaned toward a naval career, but family finances precluded that road. The navy gathered its academy cadets from middle school graduates. The army had a two-track system that collected about one-third of its future officers from its own preparatory schools and two-thirds from its middle school graduates. Adachi's family could not afford to send him to middle school, so he took the demanding entrance examinations of the Tokyo Cadet Academy. Dreams of a naval career were put aside.[4]

In Adachi's day there were six cadet schools, each accepting fifty students annually. Reflecting the prestige of the officer corps, competition for the few slots was fierce with more than ten times the number of applicants versus available spaces.[5] Adachi ranked twenty-first among all applicants.

The purpose of the cadet academies was to inculcate military values into the cadets and beyond that to make them think of themselves as the emperor's servants. Living conditions during this era were intentionally spartan because of the emphasis on cultivating one's spirit. Hazing and corporal punishment for minor infractions, usually administered as repeated hard slaps to the face, were commonplace and accepted, although certainly not to the extremes permitted in the enlisted barracks. Simultaneous with physical toughening, however, the army demanded that the cadets acquire the traits associated with cultivated members of Japanese society; they were, after all, officers and gentlemen. Thus instructors educated the cadets in the nuances of verse, because a sign of learning was the ability to compose a short poem; calligraphy, because a fine hand with the brush was an acknowledgment of a refined man and social etiquette; and reading because of its educational value.

Study of these subjects opened another side of Adachi's personality. He became a skilled writer of short verse (*tanka*) and indeed would spend some of his darkest moments in the New Guinea jungles writing poetry.

He practiced calligraphy with the same intensity that he brought to all his projects. And, unusual for a Japanese officer whose service was primarily with units, not staffs, over the years he built up a personal library of several hundred volumes. He also developed a cultivated palate and, in later life, became a gourmet.[6]

Adachi took some interest in the martial arts, including judo and kendō, and also shared the worldwide officer passion for horseback riding with all the physical rough and tumble that was an expected part of an equestrian's pastime. Martin Blumenson has written about the numerous accidents resulting from George S. Patton's love of horses. For Adachi too the sport showed his bedrock personality. While a brigade commander on the China front, Adachi was thrown from his horse. Initially knocked senseless and with a deep gash in his forehead, he refused to report to the dispensary. He reasoned that if anyone saw him in the hospital it would be only a matter of time before word reached the enemy. Rather than embolden the foe to action, Adachi insisted on overcoming pain by ignoring it. It does remind one of Patton's method of dealing with aches and pains.

Obviously Adachi's cadet years were not all fun and games. He was, almost inevitably, a disciplined, spit-and-polish cadet capable of snapping off crisp salutes with the best of them. Moreover Adachi's years at the Tokyo Cadet Academy and the Military Academy spanned the Russo-Japanese War years (1904–5) and, more significantly, the immediate postwar ones.

Unlike the cadet schools, the Military Academy concentrated on military subjects and tactics. Between 1906 and 1910 discipline at the academy was especially harsh, because most of faculty were veterans of the Russo-Japanese War. These survivors constantly instilled in their charges the notion of deprivation at the front.[7] The effects of rigorous military training and spartan regimen, plus extensive and excessive hazing and corporal punishment, showed in the attrition rate of 15 percent. Adachi ranked sixty-sixth among the graduates, respectable but not eyepopping.

Adachi carried a dual legacy from his cadet days. The discipline, austerity, and hardship that were hallmarks of his cadet days reinforced his father's strictness to forge a stoic officer who accepted deprivation and hardship as necessary consequences of service to his emperor. On the other hand, the social skills, reading, verse, calligraphy, and so forth became integral parts of Adachi's kit bag, as he affixed one silver star to the yellow stripe on his red shoulder board, marking him as a second lieutenant of infantry.

Just as in the U.S. Army, where one's year group is crucial to career progression, in the Imperial Army one's graduating class at the Military Academy was critical to future advancement.[8] Adachi was one of 721 graduates in the Twenty-second Academy Class of 1910 (50 were still on active duty in August 1945). This was a typical class size between 1910 and 1915, because the army planned to expand to twenty-five divisions and had programmed its future officer needs accordingly. But between 1922 and 1925 reductions cut the twenty-one division force structure to seventeen, eliminating 80,000 personnel and creating a "hump" in these classes. It was common, just as in the interwar American Army, for Japanese officers to remain in grade as second lieutenants for nine or ten years with the bleak prospect of spending another eight or ten years as first lieutenants.[9]

Adachi's early career as a commissioned officer was not that dismal in terms of being locked in grade, but neither was it spectacular. Adachi was one of the herd of 513 other members of his class (71 percent) who opted for the infantry branch. Because he ranked in the top 15 percent (a respectable ninety-second) of his class, he received a choice billet with the First Guards Regiment, Imperial Guards Division, stationed in Tokyo. Unlike other Japanese divisions, the guards recruited nationwide and were always looking for big, sturdy officers and enlisted men to add to the symbols of power and strength surrounding the emperor. (The U.S. Army's practice of assigning tall, sturdy military police to Panmunjon, Korea, is somewhat similar.)

Adachi's imposing physical presence and military bearing surely helped get him the assignment. He spent the next eight years of his career with a hometown unit, making first lieutenant after three years' service, about the norm for young officers on a fast career track, and captain after seven years, about one year later than average. He faced another six years in grade before becoming a major.

What did he do in the First Guards Regiment? As with any decent subaltern in any army he learned how to soldier by serving as a platoon leader, company adjutant, or by working in the battalion or regimental headquarters. Mastering minor tactics, presiding over endless drills and training, engaging in the annual autumn field maneuvers, and participating in protocol ceremonies for the imperial household, that is, following the time-honored and usually dull routine of a very junior officer in a peacetime army devoured his time.

Unimaginative officers allow an army's routine and repetition to lull them into mediocrity. Adachi did not. He developed his command philosophy during these formative years with troops and cultivated a relationship with his soldiers premised on taking good care of the enlisted men. It may not sound like much, but this was an era when troop welfare received short shrift as exemplified by the common army saying, "Use up enlisted men as you please. They only cost the postage for their draft notices."[10] Adachi believed, and throughout his career displayed, that the one who gives the orders had to share firsthand the implications and hardships those orders cause his subordinates. Simply put, Adachi led by example and understood his officers and men at an emotional level. He brought this trait to combat operations. Adachi was conspicuous by his presence where the action was hottest and the enemy fire heaviest.

But Adachi did not spend all his time with troops in the field. He enjoyed a good time away from the barracks, being known for his ability to consume large quantities of sake (Japanese rice-wine). He was not, however, mean when he was drunk. If anything he became mellow when drinking and was a good drinking campanion.[11] Later, as a regimental and division commander, he often held after-action critiques with his officers over warm sake. Heated sake made for heated arguments, but the point of this most informal setting was that it enabled Adachi to correct subordinates' battlefield errors without causing them undue embarrassment.[12]

It would also be unfair to leave the impression that Adachi was just another Japanese version of the good old boy. He brought his habit of reading to the regiment, where he impressed his regimental commander and division headquarters staff as a studious officer deeply interested in his profession. Adachi read not for diversion but for education, and his personal library, heavily stocked with volumes on history, international relations, and philosophy was uncharacteristic of most Japanese army officers (as well as most American Army officers). Nevertheless, the impression of an officer who studied serious subjects was crucial because of the nature of the Imperial Army's officer education system.

The Army War College (*rikugun daigaku*) in Tokyo's Ichigaya section was the pinnacle of an officer's professional education. It was, just as the U.S. Army War College is, also the discriminator that marked officers for future senior command and staff positions. One major difference was that in Japan students for the War College were selected from the relatively junior ranks of company-grade officers. After recommendations by their battalion and regimental commanders, actual selection was based on a series of qualifying tests, written and verbal. Competition for the seventy-five or so slots was intense, as only 2 or 3 percent of those eligible ever saw the classrooms at Ichigaya.[13]

The War College's mission in its two-year course was to teach officers the art and science of large unit operations, that is division or higher echelon command and key positions on the general staff.[14] Subject matter, for the most part, relied on rote memorization of facts to produce narrow, if effective, specialists. Students concentrated on tactics at the expense of intensive study of logistics, intelligence, communications, and military history, although they did conclude their two years with a staff ride to the former battlefields of the Russo-Japanese War in Manchuria, because these were their hypothetical battleground of the next war. Japanese student officers had drummed into them from their cadet days that the difference between victory and defeat was so thin that the most tenacious fighters would win.[15] Resolute action, however unrealistic, under pressure or when faced with an unexpected crisis, usually carried the day.

Graduating twenty-first in a class of sixty-seven in November 1922 with the Thirty-fourth War College Class, Adachi returned to the First Guards as a company commander. As an aside, this class produced thirty-eight lieutenant generals and eighteen major generals.[16] (The least distinguished member of the class ended up in the Foreign Military History Branch, general staff).

After spending the mandatory year as a company commander, Adachi moved to the general staff, where he served in a variety of assignments that helped earn his promotion to major in 1926 and a concurrent staff job with the naval general staff. The next year Adachi received a coveted appointment as a special research fellow at the War College. He spent twelve months conducting in-depth research on the operation of railroad and railway facilities. This plunged him into the business of mobilization.[17] The Japanese army's attempt to incorporate the lessons of World War I made national mobilization, total war planning, and national defense states the hot and controversial issues for the Imperial Army during the 1920s and 1930s.

Tokyo in the early 1930s was a hotbed of army factionalism, but apparently Adachi avoided these internecine struggles. He focused on his work not on domestic politics. He also had recently married and, unlike many Japanese officers of that time, was monogamous. Adachi was not addicted to the geisha houses where officers often met to discuss politics, gossip, and national renovation before retiring with the hired help. He was deeply devoted to his wife and family despite the enforced separations that were a soldier's lot. Finally Adachi immersed himself in his work bringing to it that streak of perfectionism inculcated by his father.

After completing his year as a special research student, Adachi returned to the general staff with a concurrent assignment to the naval general staff (*gunreibu*) and for the next four years worked mobilization and joint deployment issues. His effort merited a promotion to lieutenant colonel in 1930, and in September 1932 he embarked on a six-month tour of Europe to study European railroad systems. As a sidelight, he also took up smoking around this time. As with everything else he was compulsive about his new habit, puffing through four packs of Golden Bat cigarettes daily.

In April 1933 Adachi was ensconced in Manchuria as the railway control officer, Kwantung Army, the Japanese equivalent in those days of USAEUR in the mid-1980s. This was an especially important posting, because the railway control officer had civil and military responsibilities.[18] Besides serving as the economic lifeline for Japan's exploitation of Manchuria, militarily the railway network was vital to Imperial Army's operational planning against the Soviet Union.

Adachi's challenge was fourfold: sustain army units moving into eastern, northern, and western border areas with the Soviet Union; maintain the LOCs for transport of raw materials and finished goods to Korea; combat anti-Japanese guerrillas; and sustain multidivision operations in north China. Even in the heady atmosphere of the Kwantung Army Headquarters, he never forgot why he and his staff were regulating the rail system. When troops rode to their operational areas in unheated troop trains, Adachi ordered all heating in the headquarters' building turned off, so that everyone on his staff understood what the front-line soldiers were going through. Perhaps this even managed to encourage a lackadaisical staff officer or two to find shortcuts to speed the freezing troop trains to their destinations.

Adachi's work was recognized with a promotion to colonel and reassignment as chief, railroad and shipping branch, general staff, in Tokyo. For the next two years he combined his previous staff experience with the navy and his practical work in Manchuria. About the middle of his tour, the February 26, 1936 Incident erupted, as 1400 officers and men of the First Division mutinied and occupied downtown Tokyo. The shock effect was comparable to the Old Guard mutinying and occupying the National Mall. Once the army leadership collected itself, it quickly quashed the rebellion and purged its sympathizers from the ranks.[19]

Adachi's noninvolvement in army factions was a plus when he came due for regimental command. In December 1936 he received command of the Twelfth Infantry Regiment, Eleventh Infantry Division, a unit trained for amphibious assaults, and one of three that composed Imperial Japan's rapid-reaction force. So far Adachi's career progression was typical of an officer marked for important staff positions in Japan's peacetime army. He could expect to retire as a colonel, perhaps with great luck as a major general. Then war erupted with China in July 1937, and Adachi discovered his calling—he was a combat commander who led from the front, always appearing where the bullets were thickest. In the street-fighting meat grinder of Shanghai where head-on assaults into fortified positions became the accepted tactics, this was no small feat.

As fighting spread to Shanghai in central China, the Twelfth Infantry went on alert. The regiment formed the shock element of an expeditionary task force. Adachi's mission was to secure the northern flank of the Twelfth's sister regiment, the Forty-fourth Infantry, while it executed a frontal attack directly into a Chinese-fortified zone. The first week of operations cost Adachi's regiment 466 casualties, including 128 killed. Consider these losses in light of the First Cavalry's Ia Drang casualties—234 killed, 240 wounded in four days of close combat.

In Shanghai in autumn of 1937, however, unit losses of between 10 and 15 percent were considered trifling. The Forty-fourth suffered 3100 casualties among 3500 effectives as the original unit ceased to exist. Unfortunately for the Japanese, the Forty-fourth's losses were typical. The Eleventh Division suffered a total of 2293 killed and 6084 wounded, or 65 percent casualties.

Officer losses were so heavy that they began stripping off their insignia of rank, making it more difficult for Chinese snipers to target them. Infantrymen found themselves either fighting through rubble-filled streets or throwing themselves head-on at concrete pillboxes, whose machine-gun teams skillfully covered all likely creek and canal crossing points with interlocking fire. Here Adachi showed beyond a doubt that he would share the hardships of his men. He accepted without complaint the field conditions, and repeatedly exposed himself to enemy fire to lead, to rally, and to inspire his troops.

In late September Adachi's regiment had to clear a line through a dozen small walled villages perpendicular to a major highway. Each village amounted to a walled fortress bristling with machine guns and covered by mortar batteries with preregistered fires. The Twelfth managed to crack this fortified string of villages, but at the cost of two battalion commanders killed in action and a third wounded. Early in the fighting, Adachi learned that the commander of his First Battalion had been killed. He quickly arrived at the scene for both a personal reconnaissance and to bolster the morale of his troops.[20]

Chinese gunners, however, had spotted his movement, and in the ensuing barrage of mortar rounds Adachi was severely wounded by fragments that hit him in the face, neck, and thigh. Adachi's first combat command lasted less than a month, but for breaking through the defensive line he received mention in the dispatches and a commendation.

Despite the severity of his wounds, Adachi was back with the Twelfth Infantry that December. His right leg now had a bent appearance, and he was hobbled with a cane. In typical fashion, after a few days Adachi threw away the cane not wanting to seem handicapped. Instead he bore the excruciating pain that accompanied the numerous falls he took on a still weak leg. The enlisted men believed that they had the toughest colonel in the Imperial Army.

Adachi's courage and leadership at Shanghai earned him a promotion to major general in March 1938 and temporary attachment to the Kwantung Army. Perhaps his most poignant moment of this tour came when he visited the Twelfth Infantry, now stationed in Manchuria. The meeting of a commander and his surviving officers and men was an emotional moment that remains a cherished memory for the veterans more than fifty years later.

That November Adachi took command of the Twenty-sixth Infantry Brigade, Twenty-sixth Infantry Division under Japan's Mongolian Garrison Army, leading it against communist guerrillas, Kuomintang regulars on raiding parties, and ordinary bandits. The rugged mountainous terrain of North China made this a tough proposition. So too did incursions by small guerrilla bands who sabotaged Japanese LOCs by blowing up brigades, dynamiting railroad tracks, cutting telegraph wires, and sowing propaganda. It was, in short, classic counter-guerrilla warfare with all its attendant frustrations.

In August 1940 Adachi was promoted to lieutenant general and received command of the Thirty-seventh Infantry Division then scattered across Shansei Province. By early 1941, however, the Japanese high command consolidated its fragmented units. The new strategy relied on encirclement and isolation to defeat the forces fighting against them in Shansei. In tactics familiar to the Apache fighter General George Crook, Adachi found his division involved in an advance by converging columns designed to drive the guerrilla bands from their mountain bases and into the hands of other columns. Between March and October 1941, the Thirty-seventh Division fought four pacification campaigns.

These deliberate operations threw Adachi's command style into sharp relief. He was merciless on his staff, demanding perfection. Yet he showed patience and concern for his junior officers, especially infantry platoon and company commanders. He insisted on seeing off night patrols venturing into no man's land and ordered his battalion commanders do the same. During operations the austerity at his headquarters reminded one officer of the strictness of a Zen temple with Adachi as the head monk.[21] Adachi's reticence enhanced this impression. Never verbose, he preferred to lead by example rather than by slogans. Much like the intuitive Zen monk, he understood his officers and men on an emotional level.

His first operation as a divisional commander, however, ended in failure as Japanese pincers failed to close in time to trap the retreating Chinese Nationalist Fifteenth Army. A disappointed Adachi ordered a thorough review to determine how the Chinese escaped. He also called his newly promoted brigade commander to his office to rehash the action and discover why the brigade failed to achieve its preassigned objectives. This postmortem escalated into one of the memorable nights in the Thirty-seventh's history. From the street, enlisted men and junior officers could see into the room where Adachi and the unfortunate brigade commander were drinking sake. They watched tempers explode in heated argument punctuated by the brigade commander leaping to his feet to contradict real or imagined slights to his honor. Whatever was said worked in Adachi's next campaign, the Nakahara Operation of May 1941.

It involved six divisions and two mixed brigades, almost the entire strength of Japan's North China Area Army. Five Japanese columns closed from east to west on the mountainous stronghold of the Chinese Fifth Army Group, which boasted twenty-six divisions comprising 180,000 troops. The Thirty-seventh Division's mission was to sever the southernmost Chinese line of communication. Adachi attacked in three columns on the night of 7 May in the middle of a dust storm. After eight hours of fighting, his main column broke through the Chinese defenses and eventually sealed off the Fifth Army Group's line of retreat. With the Fifth Army Group contained, the Japanese wiped out individual Chinese troop concentrations at will. Chinese losses were enormous; 42,000 killed and 35,000 captured.[22] Japanese casualties amounted to about 3000 killed and wounded. Adachi's successes merited yet another commendation. Although no one could know it, this triumph would be the greatest of Adachi's career.

FIGURE 5. Glory days: Adachi in command of the Thirty-seventh Infantry Division on China front. Courtesy of Mainichi shimbunsha

Adachi led the Thirty-seventh Division in a series of pacification operations until November 1941 when he was appointed chief of staff, North China Area Army. A month later Japan's declaration of war on the United States, Great Britain, and the Netherlands opened new battlegrounds that eventually reached to such exotic places as New Guinea and Guadalcanal. The expanded war also opened new opportunities for high-level command, and Adachi was perfectly positioned to become an army-level commander. Besides having extensive combat and staff experience plus the right credentials at all levels, he was in the proper year group. Between November 1942, when Adachi received command of the newly formed Eighteenth Army, and October 1943, seven members of the Twenty-second Academy Class became army commanders.[23] Just as significant, no one from the Twenty-second class made the rank of full general, and from subsequent year groups only three officers made general, all of them posthumously.[24]

Adachi's promotion to army commander was bittersweet, because that very day, 6 November 1942, he also received word that his wife had died after a lengthy illness. He did not attend her funeral. With orders for New Guinea, he instead stuck to his schedule of briefings and preparations. Passing through Tokyo three days later en route to Rabaul, New Britain, he spent his only spare time visiting his eldest daughter already hospitalized for the consumption (tuberculosis) that would eventually kill her. Adachi's personal tragedies on the eve of leaving for a decisive battle remind me of Longstreet's tribulations before the battle at Gettysburg. As Michael Shaara described so eloquently, Longstreet's wife and two daughters had recently died, yet he still had to go forth to lead men into battle. In both cases we have vivid reminders of commanders as frail human beings torn by the same emotions that beset all of us in times of personal tragedy.

Incidentally, if you think that all Japanese officers were long-suffering as Adachi was, consider the elevation of Lieutenant General Yamashita Tomoyuki, the Tiger of Malaya, to command the Twenty-fifth Army the previous year. When Yamashita came to Tokyo in November 1941 to receive his command from the emperor, he demanded to stay at the best room at the well-apportioned officers' club in downtown Tokyo just across the moat from the imperial palace. Told that the room was unavailable, because it was reserved for a honeymooning couple, Yamashita sulked the rest of the time in Tokyo denouncing the crass commercialism that denied a commanding general headed for the front lines the best room in the house.²⁵ If nothing else, Yamashita had a sure sense of his own importance. Adachi conversely was unassuming, straightforward, and sincere; qualities much admired by the Japanese.

Adachi reported to Lieutenant General Imamura Hitoshi at Rabaul in late November 1942. Imamura commanded the newly organized Eighth Area Army, which had operational control of the Seventeenth Army on Guadalcanal and the Eighteenth Army on New Guinea. Heavy fighting was in progress in Papua New Guinea, as Australian and American troops closed in on the coastal Japanese stronghold at Buna in a brutal battle of attrition. Adachi implored Imamura to let him go to Buna immediately to direct the defense, because he could not bear to sit idly around headquarters while his boys were getting killed. Adachi was so persistent that Imamura had to take the unusual step of issuing an order that the Eighteenth Army commander's place should be at Rabaul.²⁶ This is the pattern of Adachi's fighting career—a single-minded determination to lead from the front—wonderful for a subaltern; inappropriate for a corps' commander.

In January 1943 Adachi flew from Rabaul to Lae, Northeast New Guinea, a major Japanese stronghold, air base, and port, where he met the survivors of Buna. For the first time in his career he saw Japanese soldiers in defeat, uniforms in tatters, some propping themselves upright on crudely fashioned bamboo crutches, others being carried by exhausted comrades. Shocked by the sight, Adachi discarded his inspection schedule and instead talked to each man, encouraging and praising them for their efforts and telling them they looked like soldiers.²⁷

He also went inland, crossing jungled terrain that ranged from swamp to mountains, to see his front-line soldiers. Despite a recurrence of amebic dysentery that he picked up in China, Adachi shrugged off a headquarters doctor's advice to get complete rest. Saying he'd be all right, Adachi marched off into the night wearing common workmen's rubber-soled socks (*tabi*) and carrying his sword (which today incidentally reposes at the Australian War Memorial in Canberra). At first sight of Adachi the troops were formal and snapped to attention, but his obvious concern for their welfare drew them out. Soon more and more troops were crowding around their general and taking unheard-of liberties, including shouting out, "Hey general, how are things."²⁸ Things were bad, and reinforcements were needed.

Decisions made in Tokyo and at Rabaul transformed New Guinea into one of the major battlegrounds of World War II and one of the great killing grounds of Japanese. Allied local air superiority made troop convoys to Lae risky. Everyone understood that the farther west in New Guinea reinforcements landed, the safer they were from Allied air attacks. Two divisions, the Twentieth and Forty-first, had already arrived at Wewak. While Wewak was a safe haven to receive reinforcements, it was too far from the front lines at Lae to bolster Adachi's crumbling positions. Terrain made rapid overland movement impossible, which meant reinforcements for Lae had to come by sea.

In March disaster overtook Adachi's reinforcement scheme. In the Battle of the Bismarck Sea Allied airmen sank eight Japanese troop transports, killing about 3000 soldiers and destroying all the Fifty-first Division's equipment and stores. Adachi and the Eighteenth Army's command group were aboard a destroyer escort, itself damaged by Allied bombs. He returned ignominiously to Rabaul.

This was the operational crisis facing the Eighteenth Army in eastern New Guinea. Adachi's combat formations were scattered over 400 miles of the north New Guinea coast. The Forty-first Division farthest west at Wewak was 200 miles distant from the Twentieth garrisoning Madang, which was in turn another 200 miles from the broken Fifty-first Division clinging to Lae. Tokyo ordered Adachi to buy time for the army to consolidate an in-depth defense in western New Guinea and the Philippines. These orders reduced the Eighteenth Army to holding little more than strong points in eastern New Guinea that in turn depended for support on lightly guarded rear logistics or air bases that stretched along the coast. As the pace of the Allied counteroffensive intensified, Adachi confronted a classic dilemma. If he garrisoned every possible landing site with small numbers of troops, he risked them being overwhelmed piecemeal. If he concentrated his forces, he risked them being bypassed.

So in June 1943 Adachi decided to fight the main battle at Salamaua, because loss of that base would render Lae untenable. His decision played into the Allied plan to fix the Japanese at Salamaua while executing an air-sea envelopment at Lae. Adachi's orders to hold onto Salamaua unintentionally accommodated his opponent's plan. Yet what alternatives did Adachi have open to him? Both Imperial Headquarters and Eighth Area Army Headquarters had ordered him to fight forward. His assumption that Salamaua's loss imperiled Lae was correct. Adachi also counted on the Fourth Air Army at Wewak to check an Allied landing at Lae. This trump card, however, disappeared after a surprise attack by Allied fighters and bombers caught large numbers of planes on the ground and crippled Japanese airpower in a single day. To escape MacArthur's airborne and seaborne envelopment, 8000 Japanese marched into the mountains to escape; 2000 never came out.

Adachi reacted to contain the invaders around Lae by strengthening his forces at Finschhafen, which controlled the strategic Dampier Straits between New Guinea and New Britain. But events were beyond his theater of operations. Japan was on the strategic defensive throughout the Pacific, and IGHQ responded by contracting its strategic defense perimeter. This "zone of national defense" behind which Japanese air and ground strength could reconstitute excluded the Eighteenth Army's area of operations. Adachi's new mission was to conduct a strategic delay by holding Finschhafen.

The ensuing struggle saw Australian troops gradually and at great cost grind down the Japanese defenders. Insistent on leading from the front, Adachi and his key staff officers went by *daihatsu* to the scene of the Twentieth Division's fight. Adachi personally controlled the operations and delegated his chief of staff, Lieutenant General Yoshiwara Kane, to control the Eighteenth Army's rear area logistics and administration.[29] Determined leadership alone could not stem the Allied advance. By mid-December the Twentieth Division had suffered more than 5700 casualties, or 45 percent total strength. It could no longer stem the remorseless Allied push, and Adachi ordered a retreat to the Sio area.

Outnumbered, outmaneuvered, and written off by higher headquarters, Adachi still had the mission of delaying the Allied advance. Japanese staff studies had concluded that MacArthur's dependence on land-based fighter aircraft to cover landing beaches limited the distance of his seaborne envelopments to between 240 and 300 miles, the operational radius of Allied fighter aircraft.[30]

This appreciation in February 1944 led Eighth Area Army Headquarters and IGHQ to expect MacArthur's next landing in Hansa Bay. By concentrating two divisions on either shoulder of the bay, Adachi aimed to hurt his enemies by ambushing the Allies.[31] In retrospect, Adachi can be faulted for his dispositions. Yet it was Tokyo that opined that MacArthur would land next at Hansa Bay. And how could Adachi know that Allied cryptanalysts were routinely reading his current radio messages that described the Eighteenth Army's present dispositions as well as his future plans and intentions?[32] Moreover Adachi again counted on the Fourth Air Army, now based in the illusory safety of far-off Hollandia, to augment his ground forces and disrupt any Allied amphibious operation. Instead the Fourth Air Army was again destroyed on the ground in three massive

Allied air raids commencing on 30 March. MacArthur now commanded the air and the sea.

Under these circumstances Adachi could do little except push his rear echelon slowly westward, while his forward echelon waited the expected Allied landing between Hansa Bay and Wewak. So Adachi's blood must have run cold on 22 April 1944, when Hollandia radioed an emergency signal: "0500 to 1000—received a naval gun attack and same time bombing and strafing attack. Situation at airfield runway—unusable, weather—rain unsuitable for flying."[33]

MacArthur's 600-mile leap along the north coast and simultaneous Allied landings at Aitape and Hollandia captured the Eighteenth Army's largest rear area bases. Overnight 60,000 Japanese found themselves isolated in eastern New Guinea. The initial reaction among junior officers and men was one of dismay, because their choices were either to die fighting against a superior enemy force or to die withering away in the jungle.[34] Adachi understood, however, that indecision meant death. Four days after MacArthur's landings, Adachi announced his decision to attack the Allied forces at Aitape. By 5 May his staff had promulgated the outline of operations for the "A" Operation. Adachi's order of the day encapsulated his philosophy. "We desire life. We desire honor. If we cannot have both, we should discard life and cling to honor."[35]

Predictably Adachi was found in the van of the lead battalion moving west toward Aitape. Chief of Staff Yoshiwara stayed behind, responsible for logistics and daily administrative planning. Adachi ordered rations cut two-thirds yet insisted that his army maintain a pace through the swamp and jungle of 8 kilometers per day (or more appropriately per night). Everyone would endure. One Japanese soldier recorded his depression when passing through the once mighty base at Wewak. "We saw the skeletons of our aircraft littering graveyard airfields; we saw the countless masts of our sunken ships sticking out of the water; we knew no ships would ever again come to this port."[36]

Gradually Adachi's determination and leadership restored morale. Despite a painful hernia, he was always up front with the combat troops, always encouraging the infantry and exhorting them to whip the Americans. Encouragement, however, was not synonymous with laxity. Strict military discipline was enforced. In short, the men had to feel that they were still soldiers and that they had a chance to survive MacArthur's latest trap. As they neared Aitape, morale improved, and in their assembly areas soldiers were full of fight. Adachi had convinced them that they could win.[37]

Since early May MacArthur's General Headquarters had received numerous forewarnings based on decrypted Japanese radio messages of the Eighteenth Army's intent to storm Aitape. Nonetheless Adachi managed not only to move his 60,000 troops 300 miles overland through terrible jungle and swamp terrain, but he also achieved operational surprise with his main attack on 10 July 1944. The reasons for American commanders at the operational and strategic levels being caught unaware need not detain us. Adachi's order of the day, promulgated five days before the attack, called for an all-out effort to annihilate the enemy. Eighteenth Army's success would contribute to the overall campaign in New Guinea and "display the true merit of the Imperial Army."[38] As usual on the night of the attack, Adachi was with the assault battalions.

The restrictive jungle terrain forced Adachi to resort to attack in echelon—taking heavy losses to achieve a breakthrough.[39] Tough Japanese infantrymen ripped through the thinly manned U.S. covering force and sparked a month-long battle of attrition. By early August, though, it was clear that Adachi's counterattack had failed and that his surviving units were in danger of envelopment. Adachi led the breakout acting as battalion and regimental commander in front-line units.[40] Once clear of the Americans, he collected his shattered forces, still determined to contribute to Japan's war effort.

His defeat at Aitape cost 10,000 Japanese lives. Now Adachi had to hold together a broken, isolated force, thousands of miles from home, and without any hope of relief. His impartiality and common sense became the glue of the defeated army. So too did his October 1944 Emergency Punishment Order that gave his officers the power of summary field execution.[41] He adopted roles as necessary in the worst days of September 1944 to January 1945. One day he worked out ration distribution. Next he could be found encouraging the sick and wounded; then he might preside over a cremation of the dead; and always he reported his situation and forced a shattered system to perform routine administrative tasks that kept its sense of identity intact.[42]

Again Adachi led by example. He shared the hardships and short rations, losing nearly 80 pounds and all his teeth. Disdaining a painful hernia, he insisted on making daily visits to his front-line outposts, no matter how far distant from headquarters.[43]

By March 1945 Adachi believed that the war had entered a final, decisive stage. With the Australians closing in, the Eighteenth Army had to abandon its notions of passive resistance and prepare for decisive battle. Adachi's orders were brutally simple—healthy soldiers will kill three enemies; sick soldiers will kill one; incapacitated soldiers will fight and die in place; under no circumstances will one allow himself to be taken prisoner.[44] But Australian pressure was unrelenting. By August 1945 the Australians were pressing close to Eighteenth Army headquarters. Adachi's order of the day called on Eighteenth Army to "do its duty and die with honor."[45] Preparations for a final suicidal attack were under way when Japan surrendered. In defeat Eighteenth Army could muster only 10,000 men of the nearly 140,000 Japanese soldiers sent to eastern New Guinea, giving emphasis to the then current army wisdom that, "Heaven is Java; hell is Burma; but no one returns alive from New Guinea."

Humiliation is the handmaiden of defeat. When Adachi got off the Australian transport aircraft that brought him to the site of the Eighteenth Army's formal surrender ceremony at Wom, he saw that he was at the far end of the airstrip. The Australian commander had ordered the airstrip lined for parade with the added stipulation that each Australian soldier on parade had to be at least 5'10" tall. Adachi had to walk this psychological gauntlet to reach the table where he gave up his sword and signed the surrender documents. Further mortification waited with Adachi's subsequent indictment for alleged war crimes.

A major charge against Adachi was the illegal use of Indian prisoners of war in the Eighteenth Army. More significant was the catalog of Japanese atrocities that stretched from murdering civilians at Buna Mission to bayoneting or beheading Allied prisoners of war to killing natives.[46] One must wonder why up to the very last moment the Japanese insisted on leaving these bloody trophies skewed to trees for their comrades to discover.[47] Did they expect to terrify the American GI or Australian digger? Was it innate Japanese cruelty? Was it incomprehension that anyone would willingly be taken prisoner? Was it barbarism? Whatever it was, the Japanese record of rapine, pillage, and murder across Southwest Asia remains a bitter legacy.

While Adachi personally was involved in no executions, his silence condoned the practices. But in his own estimation, his moral responsibility was to fellow warriors, his subordinates, and to the Americans and Australians who died in battle. Adachi testified in defense of and encouraged every one of his subordinates under indictment at Rabaul for war crimes. Adachi himself was sentenced to life imprisonment, though he clearly would have preferred the death penalty—not because he thought himself guilty, but because in death he could atone for causing his emperor and nation so much grief. In the early morning hours of 10 September 1947, his goal of encouraging and supporting his officers and

FIGURE 6. Adachi at Bay: Wom, New Guinea, August 1945. Courtesy of Australian War Memorial, AWM 042743

men through their war crimes' trials accomplished, Adachi used a paring knife to commit suicide.

Adachi's last will and testament accepted the terrible responsibility for defeat in New Guinea and the attendant suffering and death of his command. Heavy on Adachi's mind were the more than 100,000 lost officers and men. "I have demanded perseverance far exceeding the limit of endurance of my officers and men, who when exhausted succumbed to death like flowers falling in the winds. Only the gods know how I felt when I saw them dying, but at that time I made up my mind not to set foot on my country's soil again. I will remain as a clod of earth in the Southern seas with my 100,000 officers and men, even if a time should come when I would be able to return to my country in triumph."[48]

The Eighteenth Army's eulogy, and that for all defeated armies, was penned by its chief of staff, Lieutenant General Yoshiwara Kane: "Meritorious deeds on the New Guinea battleground brought no laurels of victory, only funeral wreaths. The dead received no eulogies and no one recorded their glory."[49] The same might be said for Adachi Hatazo.

CHAPTER EIGHT

A SIGNALS INTERCEPT SITE AT WAR

Imagine yourself in a tropical rain forest a few degrees south of the equator. You're sitting in a *kunai* grass hut. Your "desk" is crudely fashioned from branches bound together. Breezes provide the only ventilation, but this is the wet season, so daily downpours leave a temporary chill and a permanent mold. In this most primitive setting, however, stands a modern marvel, the Kingsley AR7 intercept radio tethering you by your headset. During your six- or eight-hour duty shift, you manually search radio frequencies in hopes of overhearing enemy radio signals. Your reward for intercepting a broadcast is the chance to listen to a static-filled, coded gibberish broadcast in a most difficult language. From a Japanese pilot's voice transmission, for instance, you might hear something utterly incomprehensible, such as "SE NO SU/ME U TE/MU KU NO/," and so forth. Or you might overhear a Japanese radio station broadcasting International Morse Code. Then you would listen to packets of numerals, such as "2345 5810 6372 1111," for hours on end. But besides listening you must copy these messages exactly on a prescribed form. Then an officer or sergeant collects your work and sends it hundreds of miles away for analysis. You may or may not ever know the importance of your effort. You might even ask yourself how in the world you got into such an operation and what possible value such repetitive, seemingly mind-dulling work could possess.

To leave the jungle and return to the duller world of history, you ended up at a signals intercept site in New Guinea because of training, operational requirements, and chance. Fortune is difficult to assess, so I discuss the more mundane features—training, deployment, and operation of a specific intercept site at war, namely Number Fifty-five Australian Wireless Section.

Australia entered the war against Japan with a small, but expanding, signals intelligence (sigint) capability. In December 1939 the chief Australian general staff recommended the formation of an independent cryptographic organization, and the following month a small cipher section was established in Sydney. A few months later, in July 1940 the director of naval intelligence gave Paymaster Commander Eric Nave permission to establish an independent Royal Australian Navy (RAN) cryptologic agency. Nave had previously worked against Japanese naval codes at listening posts in Singapore and Hong Kong while attached to the Royal Navy's Far East Combined Bureau (FECB).[1] Back in Australia in early 1940, he quickly recruited all the Japanese linguists in uniform he could find. By September 1940, operating from an annex behind the blue stone walls of Victoria Barracks in Melbourne, Nave's small group was listening in on Japanese navy radio broadcast from the Mandates. Meanwhile the army cast its net wider, snaring university classicists, such as professors of Greek and French or mathematicians, for work as codebreakers. Nave gathered more Japanese linguists for an expanded mission—tracking Japanese ships moving in Asian waters. Then in mid-1941, under Nave's urging, the professors joined the servicemen now code cracking at the Monterey Building in Melbourne. With technical assistance from the British, they eventually progressed to solving Japanese J-19 consular and diplomatic traffic dispatched from the Japanese consulate generals in Sydney and Melbourne.[2] Around the same time in July 1941 the Australian Government Defense Committee authorized the Royal Australian Air Force (RAAF) to train personnel to intercept Japanese naval and military radio traffic.[3] The initial RAAF group underwent eight weeks of intensive training before being declared operational on 3 September 1941 and dispatched to Darwin. After a meandering eleven-day journey by train and army truck, the group set up an intercept site on the top floor of the Camera Obscura building at Darwin's RAAF airfield. From there they intercepted Japanese naval radio traffic from bases at Truk, Saipan, and the Palaus, as well as Tokyo and sent their intercepts to Nave's naval cryptology section in Melbourne for analysis.⁴ On 7 December 1941 one field intercept site and Nave's small center were the sum of Australia's sigint capability directed against Japan.

By April 1942 the Japanese thrust into the Bismarcks, Solomons, and New Guinea, which, coupled with their conquests in Malaya, the Netherlands East Indies, and the Philippines, left Australia exposed to Japanese air and naval attacks and possible invasion. During these dire circumstances, the Allies created Central Bureau, an independent cryptanalytic agency. In theory, because there wasn't much else in early 1942, Central Bureau had two complementary sections—a widespread intercept network and a centralized cryptanalytic organization. The creation and accomplishments of one link in the intercept network are the subjects of this chapter.

The Australian Special Wireless Group (ASWG) became responsible for the recruitment and training of intercept operators, signals officers, linesmen, and administrative personnel, as well as the provision of field sites.⁵ ASWG was organized around and consisted of about seventy officers and men of the Number Four Australian Special Wireless Section, just returned from service in the Middle East, plus local augmentees, including twelve British intercept operators who had escaped from Singapore. They trained and operated at Bonegilla, about 170 miles northeast of Melbourne. Their raw material came from scores of teenage recruits or volunteers throughout eastern Australia. Because of security considerations, prospective intercept operators were required to volunteer before being told the details of what they were volunteering for. One "volunteer," for instance, was pulled from his RAAF Morse Code class and taken to his commanding officer. The youngster was told that he had been specifically selected for a very dangerous mission, about which the commander knew nothing except it would probably be behind enemy lines. If the recruit wanted to know more, he would have to volunteer! Being young, adventurous, and concerned about appearing "chicken," the eighteen-year-old volunteered, unknowingly, as an intercept operator.⁶

Basic training lasted three months with no days off. All intercept operators had to learn International Morse Code and become proficient enough to copy at least twenty-five words per minute. The Japanese army and navy used International Morse Code to transmit their most secret administrative messages as four- or five-digit enciphered groups. These numbers concealed operational orders and weather reports, battle results, and so forth. After learning International Morse Code, the prospective intercept operator next had to master *kana* Morse, the Japanese version of Morse Code. This skill was needed to copy those Japanese naval and army air-to-ground communications transmitted as *kana* codes, as well as Japanese sent in plain text. These might include tests of radio signal strengths, estimated times of aircraft departure or arrival, destinations, landing instructions, tactical weather reports, and so forth. Based on the Japanese phonetic alphabet, *kana* Morse required learning seventy-one symbols, as opposed to the twenty-six-letter alphabet of International Morse Code. It also demanded proficiency, because expert Japanese naval operators were capable of transmitting at speeds of forty to fifty words per minute, although twenty to twenty-five words per minute was the norm. Moreover operators had to learn to transcribe Japanese *kana* symbols accurately. In the final stages of training, instructors evaluated students on their ability to copy actual Japanese naval message traffic. Twenty-four-hour-a-day shifts were set up, and trainees who had passed their proficiency tests competed to record the highest tally of intercepted Japanese messages. After all this training, at least another two months of regularly intercepting *kana* Morse was necessary to maintain the speed and proficiency to keep pace with Japanese radio operators. Alas life was not all intercept techniques. Drill and discipline occupied the days and most of the nights.

The cold mud and icy winds of south Australia's winter made the inevitable physical training even more grueling. A two and one-half mile morning march roused everyone's enthusiasm about the rest of the day. Inspections to ensure the recruits' conformity with the army way of doing business, lack of hot water, harassment from officers and camp NCOs about wear and tear of the uniform, mandatory parades, and the various petty details that armies seem to throw their limited imaginations into were constant sources of complaints in the barracks, easily recognizable by anyone who went through basic training. Certainly unfamiliar to most recruits undergoing basic training was the arrival at Bonegilla of members of the Australian Women's Army Service who had been recruited for intercept work. The young women wore dresses and skirts, drab military uniforms and shoes not having yet arrived. To chill prospective Romeos, a heavily armed guard promptly surrounded the women's barracks.[7]

While the putative intercept operators learned their trade, Central Bureau was simultaneously training the "Y" intelligence analysts that it would provide to and direct at field intercept sites.[8] Future cryptanalysts and intelligence specialists were studying their trade in the arcane classroom of Eric Nave at "Cranleigh." This gabled, ivy-clad mansion near Melbourne was the original home of Central Bureau. Appropriately enough in such an aristocratic setting, Nave taught what amounted to university seminars to small groups of carefully selected officers and enlisted men.⁹ The intellectual topic for this special classroom, however, was the solution of Japanese naval air codes. Meanwhile Central Bureau also trained and provided the cooks, drivers, and intelligence clerks for intercept sites. By August 1942 these disparate parts of Fifty-five Wireless Section were gathered at Bonegilla waiting orders to move north.

An Australian wireless section's table of organization divided the section into two parts. The signals group had two officers (a captain and lieutenant, respectively) and eighty-nine enlisted or other ranks of whom fifty-three were intercept operators. The "Y" or intelligence group also had two company grade officers, two noncommissioned officers, and eighteen enlisted ranks. At least that was what the book said. For its first four months of field operations, Fifty-five Wireless's "Y" intelligence group found itself operating with a third of its assigned enlisted strength.¹⁰ These young men, most of whom were just nineteen or twenty years old, were expected to supply immediate tactical radio intelligence to field commanders based on their analysis or decoding of Japanese army, army air force, or naval land-based air force radio traffic. The "Y" section in turn depended on the newly minted teenage intercept operators to copy Japanese radio traffic quickly and accurately. Together they would supply Central Bureau the raw materials that they obtained by copying enciphered Japanese military messages.¹¹

Fifty-five Wireless was the second Australian Army intercept site to deploy to the field, Number Fifty-one having displaced in June 1942 to Darwin, then under constant enemy air attack. In July a D/F detachment from Fifty-five Wireless was dispatched to Wanigela about 150 miles due east of Port Moresby on the north New Guinea coast. The ASWG commander's send-off was a model of understatement. "You are going into enemy territory. Never let your equipment be captured. If attacked, retreat and go in another way. Best of luck."¹²

The D/F unit reached its destination and, working out of a grass hut while relying on a gasoline-powered generator to run its equipment, tracked the Japanese advance across the Owen Stanleys toward Port Moresby. When the IJA retreated westward in late December, the D/F unit was withdrawn from Wanigela by ship. The detachment eventually reestablished its listening post at Kerema, nearly 150 miles east-northeast of Moresby on the south coast.

As the focus of the air and ground shifted war toward Port Moresby, Fifty-five Wireless was ordered there. The section moved to a separate

FIGURE 7. D/F operator in grass shack, New Guinea, October 1942. From Geoffrey Ballard, *On ULTRA Active Service*; used by permission

block of the Bonegilla camp to develop unit cohesion independent of the rest of the ASWG. Cross-country training coupled with intensive intercept training marked their last month in Australia. On 1 September Fifty-five Wireless departed Bonegilla. At Brisbane the section boarded a 3000-ton Dutch merchantman, which deposited the men at Port Moresby several days later. That first night, camping in the open, they witnessed an enemy air raid by three Japanese bombers. The war was now very immediate.

Fifty-five Wireless's arrival coincided with the Japanese land advance over the Owen Stanley range. Ignoring heavy losses and overcoming appalling terrain, the tough Japanese infantrymen pushed into and through the mountains. By 16 September the Japanese were perched on the second from last ridge blocking the route to Moresby. They could plainly see searchlight beams from Port Moresby poking the skies for Japanese naval warplanes raiding air bases and harbor installations there. Under the enemy's eyes, Fifty-five Wireless was setting up shop at Fairfax Harbor. Placed away from the main flow of traffic on the base, the unit occupied a ready-made intercept room with louvered walls for ventilation from the harbor breezes. The men pitched tents across a *kunai* grass plain beyond the building.[13] Life would never get any better.

The Allied intercept system in the Southwest Pacific Area in late 1942 was rudimentary and its relationship to operational commands vague. In a sense, this gave Fifty-five Wireless the freedom to accomplish its assigned mission. Yet viewed by base commanders, who had no idea what Fifty-five Wireless was supposed to be doing, the strange unit did as it pleased. Fifty-five Wireless was supposed to monitor Japanese army radio activity along the Kokoda Track controlled from Rabaul, New Britain.[14] Only two Japanese army radio stations, however, were audible from Fairfax Harbor. From these circuits, radio operators' chat, and occasional plain text transmissions, Central Bureau formed a rough estimate of the size of the Japanese forces advancing across the Owen Stanleys on Port Moresby.[15] General Douglas MacArthur, the SWPA commander, disregarded these estimates and insisted the Australian rabble was withdrawing in the face of numerically inferior Japanese forces.

In September Fifty-five Wireless began recording all radio frequencies being used by the enemy, reconstructing Japanese radio networks, locating by D/F the transmitting stations, and identifying Japanese unit call signs and radio frequencies.[16] The section forwarded a daily report and its collected intercepts to Central Bureau headquarters for further analysis. Such raw data were of little tactical value, but they became the essential building blocks for the future exploitation of Japanese military communications.

By late September the enemy drive on Moresby had spent itself. The direct threat was now the Japanese air forces. As a consequence, Fifty-five Wireless found itself devoting more and more intercept sets, operators, and intelligence analysts to monitoring naval air-ground traffic as well as Japanese tactical weather broadcasts. The seemingly innocuous weather reports were actually an intelligence bonanza, because broadcasts of atmospheric conditions over Allied-held areas always preceded planned Japanese air raids by several hours. Conversely, climatological reports intercepted from Japanese-held areas were especially useful in preparing Allied air attacks against enemy targets.[17]

These successes against air-ground systems and weather reporting codes, however, were wasted unless the intercepted messages were made available to field commanders in time for action. Sending raw data, for example, radio broadcasts from Japanese warplanes back to Central Bureau for evaluation and in turn having Central Bureau pass it back to field headquarters, took so long given the existing technology that the resulting intelligence became worthless. To overcome the problem, Central Bureau sent trained cryptanalysts forward to the intercept sites to evaluate intercepted naval air-ground messages and, whenever possible, decipher them on the spot.[18]

Fifty-five Wireless notified the Port Moresby fighter sector commander of impending Japanese air attacks as follows. Most air attacks occurred in the early morning hours or late in the afternoon, so Australian intercept operators worked special watches to cover those most dangerous periods. A direct phone line connected them to a D/F site 2 miles distant, which furnished the intercept operator with bearings taken on the approaching enemy planes. Decodes of Japanese pilots' radio messages combined with D/F reports enabled intelligence clerks to plot incoming raids in the intercept room. The site commander in turn either phoned or teletyped the unfolding intelligence to the air intelligence officer. This effort comprised the bulk of the section's work in October 1942.[19]

The commander of Fifty-five Wireless was Lieutenant John Vasey, a veteran of the Middle East, Greece, and Crete campaigns. He also happened to be nephew of the commander of the Seventh Australian Division, Major General George A. Vasey. Unfolding events would put the young lieutenant in need of powerful friends. Headquarters wanted Japanese field radio traffic, but precious little could be overheard from Fairfax Harbor. After four days of proposals, Vasey received approval to send a detachment about 40 miles northeast of Port Moresby to search medium and high frequencies for Japanese radio broadcasts.[20] The small party, commanded by a corporal, moved two intercept sets to a ridge overlooking an abandoned rubber plantation. A nearby waterfall provided a natural shower as did the daily rain shower. The towering Owen Stanleys rose ridge on ridge to the west. From their high ground, the detachment did intercept a large volume of messages, adding between 25 and 50 percent of the total messages intercepted daily by Fifty-five Wireless.[21] Many were transmitted in easily solved field codes or in plain text. Both were of immediate tactical value. The detachment remained on station until December when the rainy season forced it to shut down and return to the main section.²²

In mid-October Japanese navy bombers and flying boats launched a series of nighttime harassment raids against Moresby. Intercepted Japanese communications proved not only the most reliable tip-off of impending raids but also in most cases the sole indication of incoming enemy bombers. Technology usually made it possible for the field intercept station to provide a far longer warning time than a radar site. Depending on several factors, such as signal strength, weather conditions, atmospherics, and so forth, intercept operators might overhear an enemy aircraft broadcast at ranges of approximately 400 miles, which translated into as much as three hours' early warning. Radar at Port Moresby, by way of contrast, offered about twenty minutes' worth of warning. And it was not until 29 December that the Allies had comprehensive radar coverage for New Guinea.²³ In such circumstances, Fifty-five Wireless providing fighter sector command between one and two hours' early warning of Japanese raids on 19, 20, 22, and 25 October was an intelligence bonanza.²⁴ Japanese bombs fell harmlessly into the night, while Allied antiaircraft fire exploded just as harmlessly in the dark skies. Without radar coverage or sophisticated night fighters, it was difficult for fighter command's pilots to intercept much less engage the bulky Japanese flying boats. Following a week's respite three land-based bombers from the 751st Naval Air Group sortied against Moresby. Fifty-five Section again gave accurate bearings and warnings three hours before the enemy planes struck Port Moresby.²⁵ Once again results were inconclusive for both sides. Still Fifty-five Wireless was demonstrating the potential advantage that timely and accurate signals intelligence conferred on its holder. The question was, who controlled the intercept site. On 8 November the intelligence and signals' brass met at headquarters, New Guinea Force, to sort out that basic yet previously unconsidered issue.

The participants included SWPA's chief signal officer, Brigadier General Spencer Akin, and its intelligence chief, Brigadier General Charles A. Willoughby. Also present were two Australian brigadiers, two colonels, two majors, and a lowly Lieutenant Vasey. They decided the signals officer, New Guinea Force would have operational control over the section. They also agreed that the section would set aside watches expressly for air warning purposes.²⁶ In light of these high-level decisions, the happenings during the rest of the month may most charitably be described as puzzling.

Local commanders, usually not cleared for or knowledgeable about signals intelligence, did not necessarily accord intercept work either high priority or a fair share of resources. Thus the RAAF wing commander informed the section that he was taking over their intercept site for his personal headquarters. Within four days Brigadier General Akin, an Australian brigadier and air group commander, paid the surprised wing commander a hurried and unscheduled personal visit. Fifty-five Wireless, would stay where it was after all.[27]

A few days later there was another crisis. Because D/F equipment was scarce, Fifty-five Wireless was sharing the RAAF's fixed navigational aid installations to track incoming enemy aircraft. Fighter sector headquarters insisted, with some justification, that its navigational aid stations existed exclusively to guide Allied pilots safely to and from base. RAAF 10 Signals Unit sided with the pilots, ordering all available D/F equipment to be used only to guide and to track Allied fighter aircraft. The taking of D/F bearings on Japanese aircraft was relegated to lowest priority.[28] Without bearings Fifty-five Wireless could not plot the progress of incoming enemy air raids or provide timely warnings of imminent attacks. So Japanese air raids of 24 and 27 November against Port Moresby as well as Buna went unmolested. In both instances Fifty-five Wireless warned the fighter sector that Japanese bombers were airborne but, without bearings, could not provide vital headings or estimated times of attack.[29] After the second raid the RAAF D/F unit received orders to give the section all bearings it requested. This change enabled Fifty-five Wireless to give one hour's advance warning of a night raid carried out by three naval land-based bombers on Port Moresby on 29–30 November.[30] Another major conference at Advance Headquarters, Port Moresby, became necessary to resolve this latest competition for scarce resources. In a Solomon-like compromise, henceforth D/F facilities would be available to Fifty-five Wireless provided their use did not interfere with requests by friendly aircraft for bearings.[31]

Besides administrative squabbles, the handful of enlisted men of Fifty-five Wireless's "Y" intelligence group were gradually being overwhelmed by the growing volume of intercepted Japanese message traffic,[32] because the Japanese Eighteenth Army was about to enter the Buna fighting. Fifty-five Wireless first discovered references to an Eighteenth Army linked by radio with the Japanese garrison at Buna and a Second Shipping Group Headquarters broadcasting from Shortland Island. Both the Eighteenth Army and the shipping group were newly organized formations;

the Eighteenth Army being activated on 16 November, and the Second Shipping Group arrived in the Shortlands in November to augment the First Shipping Group's efforts to reinforce and resupply Japanese units fighting on Guadalcanal.[33] If radio transmissions among these units were to be believed, the Japanese focus was shifting to New Guinea.

Indeed, under the auspices of the Eighteenth Army, the Second Shipping Group was preparing its and First and Second Shipping Engineer Regiments to transport the Twenty-first Independent Mixed Brigade to Buna.[34] Unable to read the contents of the numerous messages crackling back and forth to coordinate this major deployment, Fifty-five Wireless nevertheless deduced, based on analysis of the Japanese radio message traffic, that the Eighteenth Army was reinforcing Buna. Analysts at Central Bureau Headquarters, however, rejected the intercept site's warnings, casting doubt on the very existence of an Eighteenth Army.[35]

Yet the appearance of several new Japanese military radio transmitters in New Guinea and the doubling of the daily volume of intercepted messages broadcast by shipping units and major headquarters by Fifty-five Wireless over the next two weeks were clear signs that the Japanese were intent on pushing reinforcements into Buna and Guadalcanal.[36]

Fifty-five Wireless, for instance, detected radio exchanges between Seventeenth Army Headquarters at Rabaul and shipping units on Guadalcanal in early December. By 4 December intelligence analysts at the intercept site deduced that these otherwise unreadable messages portended further reinforcement of Guadalcanal.[37] These radiograms were coordinating a resupply effort to Guadalcanal by ten Japanese destroyers set for three days hence. Again on 6 December Fifty-five Wireless overheard messages transmitted by the Eighteenth Army presaging its unsuccessful attempt to resupply Buna two days later. American B-17 heavy bombers struck the approaching convoy and forced it to turn back to Rabaul.[38]

The section accumulated still more evidence about the Eighteenth Army when it listened to a Japanese radio operator at Buna address the headquarters for a third time.[39] Five days later Central Bureau acknowledged Fifty-five Wireless's original warning by confirming that Eighteenth Army Headquarters was operating at Rabaul.[40] While the section was having success, the quickening pace was overwhelming the understrength intelligence group and was burdensome on the intercept operators as well.

Tight security, the lack of creature comforts at field stations, especially the forward-most detachments, loneliness, and alternating stress and boredom were problems facing Fifty-five Wireless. The strain on intercept

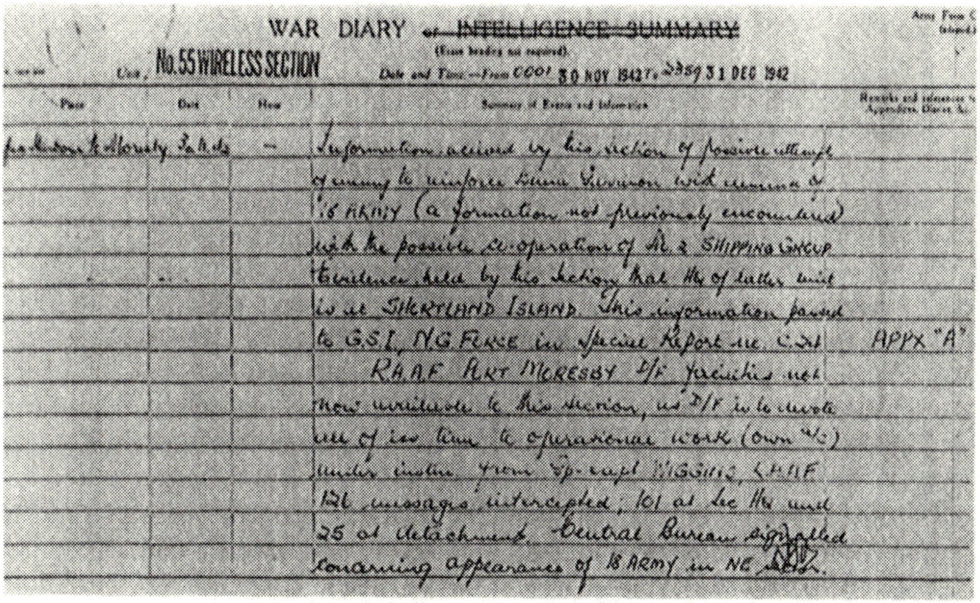

WAR DIARY ~~or INTELLIGENCE SUMMARY~~

Unit, No. 55 WIRELESS SECTION

Date and Time—From 0001 30 NOV 1942 To 2359 31 DEC 1942

Place	Date	Hour	Summary of Events and Information	Remarks and references to Appendices
Port Moresby	1 Dec	–	Information received by this section of possible attempt of enemy to reinforce Buna Division with elements of 18 ARMY (a formation not previously encountered) with the possible co-operation of the 2 SHIPPING GROUP. Evidence held by this section that HQ of latter unit is at SHORTLAND ISLAND. This information passed to GSI, NG FORCE in special Report No. C.21	APPX "A"
			RAAF PORT MORESBY D/F facilities not now available to this section, as D/F is to devote all of its time to operational work (own a/c) under instns from Gp. Capt HIGGINS, RAAF	
			126 messages intercepted; 101 at this HQ and 25 at detachment. Central Bureau signalled concerning appearance of 18 ARMY in NE ...	

FIGURE 8. Number Fifty-five Wireless Section log entry for 1 December 1942 identifying the Japanese Eighteenth Army. Courtesy of Australian War Memorial, AWM 52, File 7/39/21

operators from listening for four or five consecutive hours to very faint enemy signals with other signals superimposed over them (Armed Forces Radio being the chief villain) and a lot of crackling static interference remains the standard job description of the trade. The repetitious intercept work also took its toll. One intercept operator suffered a nervous breakdown and resorted to making up his own messages. This odd traffic was noted, but it took a month to discover him, because the externals of the message, the addresses, telegram numbers (*den dai*), preambles, and times—in other words the forms of the fabricated messages—were proper. It was the text that was offbeat and caused a few cryptanalysts to question the content of the messages. Other distractions occurred as well. It was not just a matter of tuning in and copying messages. Radio frequencies wandered, requiring the operator to keep a steady left hand on the tuner to hold a constant signal. Mosquitoes feasted on the exposed hand, leaving it swollen and raw. Frequent thunderstorms broke into messages seemingly at the most critical times and with ear-shattering consequences. Having headset earphones constantly clamped on the operator's head in the moist, tropical New Guinea climate produced painfully mildewed ear canals. Besides hard work, ingenuity, patience, and teamwork, it took character and determination to build an intercept network from scratch. And, of course, the enemy never rested.

Japanese air activity increased to keep pace with the enemy's ground reinforcements pouring into New Guinea. Central Bureau ordered Fifty-five Wireless to monitor Rabaul's naval control transmitter to glean information about the flow of aerial reinforcements moving into the theater.[41] Identifying aircraft and air base call signs, the section reconstructed the naval air arm's order of battle. By now the section was tracking the Eighteenth Army, providing early warning of Japanese air raids, monitoring Japanese naval air-ground traffic, and overhearing army air-ground messages as the newly organized Sixth Army Air Division moved into the Bismarcks. Lieutenant Vasey, meanwhile, was proselytizing the work of intercepts and D/F in warning of air raids to Four Fighter Sector. To underscore Vasey's work, the section then provided advance warnings of impending Japanese air attacks on 15, 16, and 17 December.[42]

Besides Japanese aircrew messages, Fifty-five Wireless Section was also intercepting more and more radio traffic sent by army or navy shipping units, because the Japanese were frantically attempting to resupply their isolated Buna garrison by any and all means. On 14 and 15 December, intercepted enemy messages revealed that two submarine units were now hauling cargo. Just four days later, two submarines, concealed by darkness, did manage to unload 20 tons of supplies at Buna.[43] A few days later communications between the major Japanese transshipment base in the Palaus pinpointed the First Shipping Transport Group there. Australian intercept operators were indeed overhearing the broadcasts sent by the First Shipping Transport Group's advanced detachment in the Palaus.

Overextended and fighting on two fronts, the Japanese were throwing more of their slender resources into a losing effort. More men and supplies meant more shipping units and radio messages. A new radio frequency being used on the Rabaul radio network displayed the characteristics of a headquarters or even a major new command, which turned out to be the Fourth Shipping Transport Unit organized to control shipping operations on Japan's now congested South Pacific front lines.[44]

Not all deductions formulated from radio traffic analysis were correct, however. Call signs were misread or assigned to nonexistent and far distant units. Geographical designations were confused, placing ships hundreds of miles from their actual locations. And sometimes deductions backfired, as was the case of radio traffic between unidentified shipping units at Buna and Rabaul increasing markedly on 26 December. Australian intelligence analysts supposed this latest upsurge of shipping-connected messages augured another major reinforcement convoy destined for Buna. The Fifth Shipping Engineer Regiment at Rabaul and its Second Company (reinforced) at Bakumbari, an anchorage about 7 miles north of the Buna garrison headquarters, were fixing the details for a shipment of troops. Rather than reinforcements, however, this latest upsurge in radio messages was about withdrawing survivors of Buna to safer locales. On 26 December the Eighteenth Army had ordered the Twenty-first IMB to relieve Buna, but two days later rescinded that directive by ordering Buna evacuated.[45] As December drew to a close Fifty-five Wireless's deductions were back on track as it identified the newly formed Eighth Area Army at Rabaul.[46]

January 1943 brought a new location and still more responsibilities. Fifty-five Wireless's operations were temporarily disrupted when the unit displaced from its comfortable accommodations in Fairfax Harbor to a newly prepared intercept site several miles north of Port Moresby, on a hill between two busy airfields, "7 Mile Strip" and "Ward's Drome." The section moved, because a detachment from Number One RAAF Wireless Unit arrived at Port Moresby to relieve Fifty-five Wireless of its air raid warning role. While One Wireless Unit was proficient against frequencies used by Japanese naval air-ground controllers, Fifty-five Wireless continued to intercept army air-ground communications until August 1943.[47] By early January 1943, for example, Fifty-five Wireless had confirmed that the Japanese Eleventh Army Fighter Squadron was flying from bases at Rabaul. This unit had arrived at Rabaul on 18 December, and fifteen of its aircraft raided Buna in the early morning hours of December 26.[48]

Together with the move, the section received reinforcements, bringing it to authorized strength for the first time in the campaign. As the newcomers marched out of the town, a banner stretched between two trees proclaimed, "Through these portals passes the best mosquito bait in the world." The new intercept site was a large, screened-in, thatched hut commodious enough to house the twelve intercept sets and intelligence function. The men lived in tents erected on platforms cut out of the side of the hill. A used kerosene can served as a pull string shower. Washing clothes was done by boiling them in water-filled kerosene drums. One nameless soul managed to set the entire hillside on fire when his fire got out of hand. Playing cards and chess served as entertainment as did grainy motion pictures. USO shows also toured the air bases, including Bob Hope's.[49]

With a full complement of personnel, a decent site location on high ground, understandings confirmed with the local air force commanders, as well as established reporting procedure to and from Central Bureau, plus invaluable operational experience, Fifty-five Wireless Section was a seasoned intercept site. It had evolved from passing tactical early warning of Japanese air raids to monitoring Japanese attempts to reinforce a series of bases in the Bismarcks and New Guinea. What started as giving local air raid alarms and intercepting battalion-level tactical ground communications now extended to eavesdropping on radio networks throughout the Japanese empire.

By February 1943 Fifty-five Wireless had reconstructed the Japanese army's radio network in the Southwest Pacific. Intercept operators tracked army transport ships and identified army shipping units, all harbingers of reinforcements. The section also uncovered a series of high-priority messages being transmitted to Guadalcanal connecting the Eighth Area Army and a shipping group, likely the Third Shipping Engineer Regiment.[50] This radio activity presaged the third stage of the Japanese evacuation of that island. D/F techniques isolated Japanese weather reporting stations at Lae and Wewak among other places.[51] Meanwhile a new embarkation unit, likely the First, also at Rabaul was passing messages back and forth with Wewak. This radio activity unmasked Wewak as an important port and base in Japanese plans.[52] Indeed the Twentieth Division had occupied Wewak between 17 and 23 January.[53] Within three weeks Fifty-five Wireless pronounced the Twentieth Division at Wewak, although believing incorrectly it had moved there in the second week of February. Analysts also identified a Japanese army message relayed by Rabaul to Wewak as having originated from Keijo, Korea, the recruiting district for both the Twentieth and Forty-first Divisions, suggesting the two divisions were deploying to New Guinea.[54]

By 9 February the site was eavesdropping on a Pacific-wide naval radio web woven around the Forty-first Division by shipping and embarkation units at Ujina in Japan, Singapore, Manila, Sourabaya in the Netherlands East Indies, Cebu, Philippines, and Rabaul.[55] On 12 February a three-stage convoy carrying the Forty-first Division departed from Tsingtao, North China, headed for Wewak. To support the huge operation, three shipping units, the Fifth Shipping Engineer Regiment and elements of the First and Second Embarkation Units, were constantly sending and receiving messages from Wewak. The Eighth Area Army was coordinating the shipment, so it too was in radio contact with Wewak. Moreover because of Japanese communications procedures, Rabaul was relaying messages to Wewak that had originated in the Palaus. Because part of the Forty-first Division was known to be in the Palaus, these references, taken together, betrayed the division's likely destination as Wewak.[56]

The Fifth Shipping Engineer Regiment was responsible for carrying and disembarking the men of the Twentieth and Forty-first Divisions. Stevedores and barge operators from the regiment's Second Company had redeployed to Wewak; from its First to Lae; and from its Third to Tuluvu, New Britain. One embarkation unit on New Britain was positioned near the Dampier Straits. All of them were transmitting and receiving information about the Forty-first Division's impending arrival at Wewak. Heavy radio traffic peaked along the Rabaul-Wewak-Madang radio network between 19 and 22 February, coinciding with the arrival of the Forty-first Division at Wewak and its disembarkation, which commenced on 20 February.[57] Five days later Australian cryptanalysts at Fifty-five Wireless confirmed that the Forty-first Division was at Wewak by deciphering its unit code name, KAWA, in the address routing of an otherwise routinely intercepted message.[58]

Still more Japanese reinforcements seemed destined for New Guinea. Analysts had previously identified a special call sign being used by a Lae radio station to pass hourly weather reports to Rabaul.[59] From mid-February the transmitter became increasingly active. At the same time the previous pattern of increased shipping-related radio messages now involved Hong Kong, Singapore, Manila, Cebu, and Davao, as well as Rabaul, Palau, and Wewak. Further reinforcements were bound for New Guinea.[60] The Rabaul-Wewak-Madang radio circuits again were extremely active, evidently preparing for them.[61]

Meanwhile radio centers at Rabaul, the Palaus, and Tokyo had been passing messages about shipping. Three shipping units at Rabaul, the First and Second Embarkation Units and the Eighth Shipping Engineer Regiment, were involved in the exchanges pointing to the imminent movement of another large convoy.[62] The Eighth Shipping Engineer Regiment was actually responsible for transporting the Fifty-first Division from Rabaul to Lae. The weather station at Lae increased the number of its daily weather reports to Rabaul, while the Second Shipping Group had withdrawn from Shortland Island to Rabaul, meaning the Japanese had switched their shipping priorities from Guadalcanal to the New Guinea front. At least six shipping units plus Headquarters Eighth Area Army and the Eighteenth Army at Rabaul were exchanging radio messages.

Besides the Second Shipping Group, these included boat companies of the Fifth and Eighth Shipping Engineer Regiments plus embarkation units. Furthermore, in an attempt to confuse would-be eavesdroppers, the Japanese had also switched call signs or resorted to alternative ones.[63] Marked increases in weather reporting, some being transmitted on an hourly basis, were overheard between Lae and Rabaul.[64] Taken together, traffic analysis conducted at Fifty-five Wireless and forwarded to Central Bureau by 1 March 1943 pointed to the following:

The Japanese were planning to ship reinforcements to New Guinea.
It was a major effort, evidenced by Pacific-wide coordination of army shipping units and bases.
The pattern of radio traffic was similar to that preceding the shipment of the Twentieth and Forty-first divisions from Rabaul to New Guinea.
To preserve secrecy, the Japanese had recently switched call signs, suggesting the reinforcement operation was imminent.
Extraordinary increases in weather broadcasts from Lae suggested that port as the most likely destination for the reinforcements.

On the night of 28 February 1943, the Eighth Area Army dispatched the Fifty-first Division from Rabaul for Lae. Because of advance warnings from intercept sites, including Fifty-five Wireless and U.S. Navy codebreakers, Australian and American flyers sank all eight Japanese troop transports plus four enemy destroyers in the decisive air-sea battle known to history as the Battle of the Bismarck Sea. I am not implying Fifty-five Wireless's role was decisive, but I am saying that Fifty-five Wireless made an important contribution to the overall intelligence estimate. Its intercepts and traffic analysis reinforced aerial photography showing Rabaul Harbor jammed with shipping and complemented decrypted Japanese naval messages announcing the convoy's destination as Lae.[65] Fifty-five Wireless, in short, produced intelligence that mattered. Moreover the unit's achievements had broader consequences than immediate tactical advantage. By demonstrating the practicality and enormous intelligence value of the field intercept site, Fifty-five Wireless ensured that the system was supported, funded, and accepted. By mid-December 1942 word of their achievements reached Australian Prime Minister John Curtin, who, based on Fifty-five Wireless's and other intercept sites' successes, approved the immediate formation of two additional units at Darwin and Moresby.[66] What better tribute could one pay to an intercept site at war?[67]

CHAPTER NINE

LEYTE: UNANSWERED QUESTIONS

Three U.S. Navy task forces converged on the central Philippines in mid-October 1944. Their objective was Leyte, a natural gateway to the rest of the islands. More than 150 warships of Task Force 77 protected the 518 ocean-going vessels included in Task Forces 78 and 79. These two task forces carried four U.S. Army divisions, the 160,000 troops set to invade Leyte. Meanwhile Admiral William F. "Bull" Halsey's Third Fleet, organized around four powerful carrier task groups, was steaming north and east of Leyte, striking Japanese targets on Luzon. Then his fast carriers returned to Leyte to soften up the beaches.

Just after midnight on 20 October the invasion convoys entered Leyte Gulf and approached the invasion beaches. Continual flashes of naval guns created an artificial sunrise in the otherwise somber gray skies. After several hours of bombardment, the four divisions landed simultaneously on Leyte's northeastern shore. By nightfall they had seized a lodgment at a cost of 247 army casualties, and more than 100,000 tons of supplies had been put ashore. The Japanese had fled into the rugged interior of the island.[1]

General Douglas MacArthur, commander in chief, Southwest Pacific Area, was jubilant. The general visited Red Beach just three hours after the first infantrymen had landed. He had made good on his promise to return to the Philippines. MacArthur had received personal congratulations from the president of the United States and the prime minister of Great

Britain. Now his thoughts focused on the next prize, the main Philippine island of Luzon. After all, the combined might of American air, ground, and naval forces was irresistible. The Japanese would grudgingly concede Leyte to conserve their men, ships, and planes for the decisive battle on Luzon, where they could fight the Americans on more favorable terms.

This preconception, shared by MacArthur and Halsey,[2] contributed to two unending questions about the Leyte operation—one on water, the other on land. First, why did Admiral Halsey steam north in pursuit of Japanese carriers, leaving the door open to Leyte Gulf and thereby exposing the vulnerable transports to Japanese surface attack?[3] Second, why didn't the Americans rapidly seize the high ground overlooking Carigara Bay when it was lightly defended?[4] A review of pertinent ULTRA documents, that is, signals intelligence available at the time, might provide the answers.

Signals intelligence, loosely defined, is knowledge obtained by monitoring, intercepting, analyzing, or deciphering enemy radio communications. During World War II the Allies gathered vast amounts of intelligence from analyzing Japanese military and naval radio networks. They were also able to decipher various Japanese government, naval, and military codes. This type of intelligence carried a code name, either MAGIC for foreign ministry decryptions or ULTRA for military ones. The former were read consistently throughout the war; the latter were not. Availability of intelligence forms one part of my story. How commanders interpret available data forms the other.

Neither Halsey nor MacArthur enjoyed a clear intelligence estimate of the likely Japanese reaction to an invasion of Leyte. Neither commander had the personality of, say, U.S. Civil War General George McClellan, who not only believed whatever dubious intelligence his "sources" reported to him but also insisted further intelligence had to be amassed before taking any action. Both Halsey and MacArthur used ULTRA when it was relevant to their plans, but neither of these aggressive officers allowed intelligence to dictate plans. A brief review of why Leyte was suddenly selected as the place for the return to the Philippines makes clear that neither Halsey nor MacArthur ever depended exclusively on ULTRA. Indeed had they been guided solely by signals intelligence, the great task force would never have been in Leyte Gulf that October morning.

In June 1944, General George C. Marshall, U.S. Army chief of staff, had already cautioned MacArthur that both ULTRA and MAGIC had revealed extensive Japanese preparations to defend the Philippines against the anticipated Allied counterattack.[5] The buildup continued throughout the summer and into the fall. For instance, two entire army air force divisions were overheard in radio communications as they deployed from faraway Manchuria to Luzon in July. Other fighter regiments from faraway Burma and nearby Formosa were also flying to the islands. By mid-August the newly formed Thirty-fifth Army was identified in the southern Philippines. Because a Japanese army headquarters controlled at least two divisions, the discovery portended more reinforcements there.[6] A few days later Allied cryptanalysts identified a newly organized Fourteenth Area Army in Manila. ULTRA also made known convoys carrying thousands of tough Japanese infantrymen who were Philippine bound. A large percentage of fifty-two major convoys that ULTRA detected in July and August were headed for Manila.[7] Clearly the Japanese were working overtime to reorganize and strengthen their Philippine defenses.

In late July, for instance, the war department estimated that 176,000 Japanese troops were defending the archipelago. In early September the number reached 200,000, in early October 225,000, and signals intelligence warned of more reinforcements on the way. ULTRA also tracked Japanese navy messages of early October, which mentioned unusually large numbers of navy planes moving from Japan to the Philippines.[8]

ULTRA then contradicted Admiral Halsey's mid-September optimism. After his carrier air strikes against Mindanao and Leyte drew such feeble Japanese reaction, an excited Halsey announced the central Philippines were just a "hollow shell with weak defenses and skimpy facilities." He proposed that Mindanao be bypassed in favor of Leyte, which might even be undefended.[9] Actually ULTRA revealed that the Japanese were strengthening, not abandoning, the region.[10] ULTRA also disclosed that the Japanese had intentionally conserved their airpower from battle during Halsey's raids by withdrawing it from the southern islands to bases on distant Luzon.[11] This signals intelligence was known to Halsey, MacArthur, and the JCS. What each saw was a chance to seize Leyte before the Japanese completed their entire scheme to reinforce the islands. It was also evident that Marshall and Nimitz relied on the estimates of their subordinates, MacArthur and Halsey, when making command decisions. So Lieutenant General Richard Sutherland replied to General Marshall's cable on 15 September 1944, affirming a direct assault on Leyte, with both officers fully aware of the strengthened, not weakened, condition of Japanese defenses on the island.

As preparations for the Leyte invasion went forward, ULTRA did offer some comforting news to the harried GHQ planners. American submarines, coached by ULTRA disclosures about Japanese convoy schedules, routes, and destinations, exacted a fearful toll in ships, men, and equipment. In some cases ULTRA also disclosed the fate of the Japanese victims. Five thousand Japanese troops of the Twenty-sixth Division were crammed aboard four troop transports sunk on July 31.[12] In early September ULTRA unveiled convoy losses to the Eighth Infantry and Second Armored Division. Radioed distress calls from stricken Japanese ships on the night of 2 October to rescue 2300 men off southern Formosa were overheard by Allied intercept operators as far away as Hawaii and Australia.[13] Allied submarines, warplanes, and mines sunk dozens more Japanese ships.[14]

ULTRA and other sources of intelligence—prisoner of war interrogations, Filipino guerrilla reports, captured documents—gave MacArthur an accurate picture of Japanese ground forces on Leyte, as well as the tactical dispositions of the enemy's Sixteenth Division. He knew only one division—the Sixteenth—defended Leyte while two protected Mindanao. As the invasion date neared, MacArthur was further reassured by Japanese ignorance of his intentions. ULTRA reported, for instance, the commander of the Southwest Area Fleet's opinion about an expected American landing on Mindanao sometime between 6 and 10 October.[15]

In sum, signals intelligence confirmed the still weak Japanese ground defenses on Leyte. Deciphered messages from Japanese convoys steaming toward the Philippines enabled American submarines to attack the heavily laden ships and cause alarming losses. So whatever ULTRA's role in the strategic decision to invade Leyte, it is certain that ULTRA was available and accurate at the time. This all changed following MacArthur's landings on Leyte. ULTRA's unavailability left the Americans unprepared.

Perhaps American optimism was a natural afterglow of Admiral Halsey's recent rampage against Luzon, the Ryukyus, and Formosa. A series of great air battles cost the Japanese 500 aircraft. That was bad enough, but the inexperienced Japanese pilots wildly inflated their battle claims. IGHQ announced the sinking of eleven American carriers and two battleships.[16] The Japanese themselves continued to believe and to act on the estimates. More than a month after the battle, the German naval attaché in Tokyo forwarded to Berlin a Japanese account of the battle claiming the destruction of 60 percent of the U.S. fleet and more than 1100 U.S. aircraft eliminated.[17] Furthermore, ULTRA tipped off the Allies that the Japanese really believed their claims.[18] "Continued emphasis on above figures [of exaggerated U.S. naval losses] suggest that the Japs themselves believe that a major portion of the US fleet is inoperative."[19] While MacArthur did not know his opponent's intentions, he surely did know the Japanese were making decisions based on wildly incorrect battle assessments and wishful thinking. MacArthur likely smiled or, given his recent sour taste of U.S. politics, maybe grimaced as he read an 18 October message sent by the vice chief of the Japanese general staff, which reassured Japanese military attachés that the Americans were attacking the Philippines to cover up earlier losses off Formosa and to influence the coming American presidential election.[20]

Japanese fantasies aside, the first few days at Leyte had gone well for the Americans. The staggering casualties inflicted on Japan's Sixteenth Infantry Division eliminated its ability to fight as an organized unit. The Japanese fleet had not contested the Leyte landings, so Halsey used the respite to rotate elements of his command on quick trips back to Ulithi in the Carolines to replenish stores and refresh spirits.[21]

Given the American Navy's previous success in breaking Japanese naval ciphers and the momentous role of its codebreakers in the naval battles of Coral Sea and Midway, one is surprised to learn that on the early evening of 21 October "the U.S. Navy was not sure where the bulk of the Imperial Japanese Navy was, nor what it was up to."[22] By this time the IJN's massive assault on Leyte was already under way. How could the Japanese move four separate fleets over thousands of miles of ocean stretching from southern Japan to Singapore without notice? Of greater interest, how could the enemy coordinate the arrival of these four fleets at the proper place to give battle? The second question is easier to answer than the first.

Japan's admirals had been planning for such an eventuality since June 1944. In late July, Imperial Headquarters in Tokyo issued its comprehensive "Plan for the Conduct of Future Operations," dubbed, rather optimistically, Shō, or "Victory." The Shō plan had four variations, and Shō 1 covered the expected attack on the Philippines.[23] By October the Japanese had already war-gamed their response to an invasion of the Philippines. Their scenario involved three likely landing points—Lamon Bay in the north, Leyte in the middle, and Davao Gulf in the south. Operational plans were hammered out at conferences. With so much coordination already having been effected, extensive radio messages for planning purposes were unnecessary. Everyone involved in Shō 1 knew their assigned roles,[24] nor was there any need to transmit by radio long operational orders. Those brief messages the Japanese navy did broadcast were probably enciphered in the flag officer code used to send operational orders to major warship and air units. The Allies solved very little of this particular cipher during the course of the war. In other words, the

Japanese fleets and headquarters relied on first-rate radio discipline and secure communications to escape detection. They were not completely successful, however.

Allied eavesdroppers did overhear Japanese navy messages regarding activating the "S" or Shō Operation, and Allied intelligence correctly identified Shō as the enemy plan to defend the Philippines.[25] Both the U.S. Seventh Fleet and MacArthur's General Headquarters, however, thought the Shō Operation involved night attacks by Japanese PT boats against Allied landing craft.[26] Later decryptions about the Japanese positioning small craft within striking distance of MacArthur's intended landing beaches near Tacloban seemed to "confirm" such assessments.[27] ULTRA was not able to interpret Japanese capabilities, let alone foretell enemy intentions. Just two days before the momentous battle of Leyte Gulf, for instance, MacArthur's headquarters still associated Shō with raids by small craft, because no major enemy naval units were believed in the area.[28] As far as the Americans knew, the IJN might be on the high seas, yet the exact whereabouts of its fleets was uncertain.

Intercepted, but not deciphered, Japanese naval messages implied that the First Mobile Fleet had issued operational orders to surface task forces, air fleets, and other units. Another indecipherable message was judged to be a sortie communication plan.[29] As late as 23 October naval intelligence reported that the Japanese striking force, commanded by Vice Admiral Ozawa Jisaburō, was likely at sea, location unknown, but probably heading from Japan for the Philippines. Ozawa's fleet was bait. He was to lure Halsey's carriers away from the Tacloban beachhead thereby uncovering the defenses for the First Diversionary Attack Force. Ironically a faulty radio transmitter thwarted Ozawa's efforts to advertise his location by broadcasting one radio message after another. With nothing to overhear, intercept stations remained unaware of Ozawa's southward thrust.[30]

Nonetheless, there were a few clues of Japanese maneuvers being transmitted on the airwaves. A decrypted message from a Japanese fleet oiler steaming to Coron Bay in the Pescadores provided the sole hint from signals intelligence that the First Diversionary Attack Force, under Vice Admiral Nishimura Shōji, was out of anchorage.[31] It still took an attack by U.S. Navy submarines against these warships to pinpoint their precise location.[32] The visual sightings confirmed that Nishimura's battle fleet had sortied from Singapore but not his destination. Where was he headed? ULTRA pointed to Coron Bay already sheltering seven fleet oilers waiting to refuel the warships.[33] Once fueled, the ships were ready for combat. There were more oilers at one anchorage than needed to refuel Nishimura's warships. The extra oilers likely awaited Admiral Kurita Takeo's Second Diversionary Attack Force. But the Americans thought Kurita's ships were in Manila, at least temporarily. According to naval intelligence, "A better picture of the Japanese fleet's location and intentions was obtainable from sub and aircraft sightings than from R[adio]. I[ntelligence]."[34]

Everyone knew the IJN's objective had to be the Allied anchorage off Tacloban. However, no one knew which route the Japanese would take to get there. ULTRA remained silent about such matters. With only piecemeal and ambiguous intelligence available, General Headquarters speculated that Vice Admiral Kurita and Admiral Nishimura might join forces west of the Philippines. From there they would be in a position to sortie through the central Philippines against the Leyte landing forces. The SWPA G-2, Major General Charles A. Willoughby, doubted the Japanese would make such a risky approach without air cover. Besides, he reasoned, the Allies would quickly detect any enemy fleet movement and quash it with their overwhelming air and naval might.[35]

The Japanese, Willoughby believed, would concentrate their forces and strike Leyte from the northeast via the Luzon Strait. Why? Because a southern thrust to the Celebes Sea was exposed to Allied airpower, one through the Visaya or Mindanao seas fraught with navigational hazards and restricted room to maneuver.[36] From the Japanese viewpoint, the northern Luzon route had two drawbacks. Besides exposing the fleet to American carrier aircraft, the circuitous route sacrificed the advantage of surprise.[37] Nishimura swept through the Celebes Sea into the Mindanao Sea and was nearly annihilated.

While Nishimura's force was being pounded, Halsey's airmen were punishing Kurita's central force. To Halsey, however, Japan's carriers were the major threat and remained his major concern. His mission was to protect the landing area, but surely that meant defending it against carrier air strikes, not merely surface ships. Without ULTRA forewarnings, he had to wait until American search planes located Ozawa's carriers. Searchers finally spotted the carriers in the late afternoon of 24 October. Still unaware of the overall Japanese plan, at dawn the next day Halsey steamed north to attack the carriers. His departure left the backdoor to Leyte Gulf wide open to Kurita.[38]

Kurita, maneuvering through shoal-filled waters of the central Philippines, found himself in trouble. Around 2 P.M. on 24 October he dispatched a signal to Headquarters Combined Fleet and the naval general

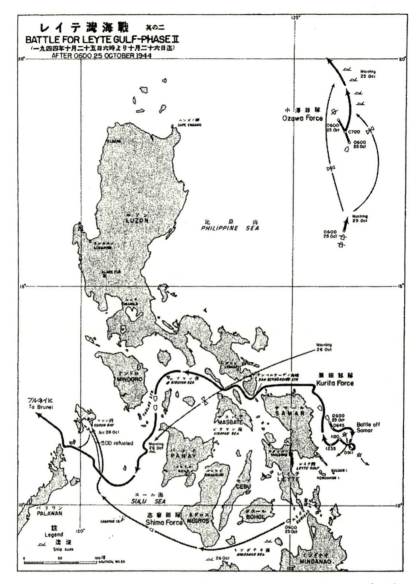

MAP 4. Battle for Leyte Gulf, Phase II. Source: U.S. Army Center of Military History

staff, stating his fleet had been under air attack for seven hours and was turning back. Pandemonium erupted among the naval staff. What was Kurita doing? Whatever could he be thinking? Combined Fleet was about to take the extraordinary step of ordering Kurita to resume the attack when his next radio message arrived: "Trusting in divine providence, the entire force is attacking: 1830 Kurita."³⁹ Halsey's departure may not have been exactly due to divine providence, but it gave the Japanese admiral the chance of a lifetime. Indeed Kurita's lunge nearly reached the landing beaches at Leyte. He then turned back.

There is no satisfactory explanation for Kurita's abrupt withdrawal. After the war, the admiral gave three rationalizations. First, intercepted enemy messages in plain language, he said, indicated the American fleet was deploying for battle. These messages were actually desperate appeals for help from the outnumbered and outgunned American ships standing in Kurita's path. Japanese intercept operators at the major intercept station in Owada, Japan, confirmed the communications were indeed calls for help.⁴⁰

Second, Kurita was unclear about the enemy situation in Leyte Gulf. Aerial reconnaissance had not located the American ships, tactical communications to Kurita's warships arrived too late to influence the fighting, and IGHQ never dispatched an updated intelligence estimate to him.⁴¹ This left Kurita in the dark about exactly what if any shipping awaited him in Leyte Gulf.

Third, he was, with good reason wary of enemy carriers, perhaps even obsessed with them. Kurita's conduct had been criticized after Midway for abandoning the cruiser *Mogami* to American planes and again for withdrawing too quickly following the 13 October 1942 bombardment of Guadalcanal. Now at Leyte he worried about reports of enemy carriers bearing to his north. The admiral left out a fourth reason.

The gossip traders in the corridors of IGHQ whispered that Kurita lacked aggressiveness or, less politely, "needed his butt kicked" (*shiri o tatakubekida*).⁴² Having suffered through seven hours of air strikes the day before, concerned about imaginary task forces bearing down on him, and with no one to order him otherwise, Kurita opted to pull back just when success was at hand. So he withdrew leaving an unending controversy in his wake.

Japanese losses in the battle of Leyte Gulf were four carriers, three battleships, six heavy and four light cruisers, eleven destroyers, and one submarine. They also lost about 500 planes, and about 10,500 sailors or airmen were killed. It was not a cheap victory. American losses were one light and two escort carriers, two destroyers, one destroyer escort, and more than 200 aircraft. About 2800 Americans perished in the fighting, and another 1000 were wounded. Yet by any standard the battle was an overwhelming American victory, except the Japanese used a different yardstick to measure success and had been doing so for some time.

During mid-October, Japanese and American pilots fought a series of air and naval battles ranging from Luzon to Okinawa to Formosa. Inexperienced and overexcited Japanese pilots reported that they inflicted enormous losses on the U.S. fleet. After the Battle of Leyte Gulf, their even greener replacements again claimed outrageous battle casualties. Raw untried pilots, pumped up on the adrenaline of combat, often forced to attack in night or in bad weather, understandably exaggerated their accomplishments. Yet in both instances, Tokyo uncritically accepted the pilots' versions of Leyte Gulf, which ranged as high as fifteen U.S. carriers and five cruisers sunk or damaged.[43] Classified foreign ministry cables informed all Japanese diplomatic posts overseas about the sinking of seven or eight American carriers, eight cruisers, and fourteen other vessels. They described eight more carriers, three battleships, four cruisers, and thirty-five other ships as damaged. Japanese losses were two cruisers and a destroyer, with a submarine sunk and a battleship damaged.[44] These fanciful figures could not be dismissed as crude propaganda promulgated to conceal the extent of Japanese losses. These misguided appreciations actually were guiding the Japanese decision to convert Leyte into the decisive battleground of the Pacific War.

Japan's determination to fight the decisive land battle of the Philippines on Leyte was contentious. Strategic considerations dictated defending the main island of Luzon, where the Americans would have to fight on extended lines of communication. That was the thinking of General Yamashita Tomoyuki, the newly appointed commander of the Fourteenth Area Army. IGHQ and the Southern Army disagreed. If the Americans took Leyte, they would convert the island into a great air base and anchorage, making any defense of Luzon untenable. Besides Leyte could be held, especially after the great Japanese naval victory in the Philippines. Southern Army ordered Yamashita to reinforce the island. Error drove the Japanese war machine's reinforcements to Leyte. Relying on the Japanese to do what was expected of them drove MacArthur's lackadaisical response to his unwelcome visitors.

After the successful landings near Tacloban, General Headquarters regarded Leyte as secure, subject to a little mopping up of Japanese stragglers. Any Japanese stand on the island was inconceivable. The staff college solution called for Yamashita to conserve his forces for a determined defense of Luzon. The Americans' first two weeks on Leyte seemed to bear out such classroom strategy. General Walter Krueger's Sixth Army units moved quickly inland. XXIV Corps ran into stiff resistance when it hit the mountainous central spine of Leyte. To the north X Corps, advancing along the coast, reached Carigara Bay twelve days after landing. The Japanese had no choice except to withdraw—Leyte's airfields were lost; 30,000 Japanese troops were slain; its surface fleets were sunk; hundreds of warplanes were destroyed; and surviving Japanese troops were surrounded. The SWPA press communiqé for 3 November announced, "the end of the LEYTE-SAMAR campaign is in sight."[45] Captivated by wishful thinking, it was easy to overlook or misinterpret clues pointing to other less palatable interpretations of Japanese intentions.

During the communications commotion created by the naval battles around Leyte, for instance, a U.S. Navy intercept operator picked up a brief, crackling Japanese radio message mentioning special transports unloading at Ormoc, a port on Leyte's west coast.[46] Were the transports carrying reinforcements or evacuating survivors of a wrecked division? Conventional military wisdom interpreted the report as describing a Japanese withdrawal. As Willoughby melodramatically put it, "The hopeless tactical situation meant that the curtain is about to fall on the Leyte operation."[47] The Japanese had no air cover, no surface fleet, and no reason to waste reinforcements on Leyte. As for Krueger, he had earlier asked for another division. MacArthur refused—better to withhold the fresh division for the Luzon landings. While MacArthur was looking beyond Leyte, Krueger was looking at the thickly forested ridges. Why didn't Krueger seize the high ground?

Perhaps the explanation to this second controversy over Leyte is a simple one. Krueger felt no urgency to take the heights. After all, if the campaign was over, and if Krueger was short of officers and men as well as on the wrong end of an overextended supply line, it was better to consolidate his gains. Why fight die-hard Japanese on their terms in the hills? Instead Krueger could rest his troops, conserve supplies, and save wear and tear on equipment as he readied for the Luzon operation. Taking territory for its own sake or slugging it out with the Japanese were not the Sixth Army's preferred way of war. GIs had bypassed and isolated the Japanese from the Admiralties to Morotai. Why should Leyte prove much different? Besides as far as Krueger, MacArthur, or anyone else in General Headquarters knew from available intelligence, no enemy reinforcements were en route to Leyte.

The invasion of Leyte coincided with one of several lengthy periods during the war when Allied cryptanalysts could not decipher the main Japanese army code system. On 8 April 1944, the Imperial Army cryptologists introduced a major change to the army code. They retained the current army codebook, *Rikugun angōsho* No. 4 (Army codebook, fourth edition), but switched to different encryption books.[48] Around the same time, they introduced a much more difficult encipherment system. Allied cryptanalysts were on the verge of reconstructing the new encryption books, when on 1 August 1944 the Japanese started enciphering message discriminants.[49] Allied cryptanalysts had yet another puzzle to solve. Taken together these security measures stymied Allied codebreakers' attempts to solve the army code until mid-November.[50]

Beyond these security measures, the Japanese army also relied on regional codes to further confuse would-be codebreakers. Units in New Guinea, for instance, used one system to encipher messages; those in the Philippines another; those in Manchuria yet another. In other words, solving the codes of the Japanese Eighteenth Army in New Guinea did not guarantee the solution to codes of units such as the First Division stationed in the Philippines or Manchuria.[51] Besides each Japanese division had its own unique codebook, meaning that in the summer of 1944 almost 100 division codebook systems were being used to conceal the contents of radio communications. This complex, complicated, and cumbersome system shielded the First Division's deployment to Leyte.

Denied the most reliable source of intelligence about Japanese army intentions during the most critical phase of the Leyte ground campaign, U.S. commanders relied on intelligence from other enemy code systems—naval, military, and diplomatic—which continued to be read with regularity. But without access to the secrets of the army code, any decisions had to be made on the basis of incomplete intelligence. Such circumstances are commonplace in warfare. Officers are trained and educated to make decisions in the "fog of war." Professional military education aims to reduce options and exclude alternatives, thus revealing the most likely course of action for a commander. At Leyte there were no options for the Japanese except to evacuate Leyte or die there. Given the circumstances, any professional officer would have withdrawn. With the campaign seemingly over, there was little reason to push GIs into the lush green hills. Let the Japanese starve and then occupy the high ground later. Similar to its counterpart at Leyte Gulf, however, by this stage of the war the Japanese army followed no conventional military wisdom. While the Americans congratulated themselves on another successful operation, the bullheaded Japanese reinforcement of Leyte had just begun.

On the day MacArthur's public relations' flacks proclaimed the end of the campaign was in sight, the Imperial Army's First Infantry Division already had landed, marched north, and was fortifying the heights overlooking Carigara Bay. Its unannounced appearance in the rugged, conical-shaped hills overlooking Carigara Bay became MacArthur's second nasty surprise at Leyte. An entire enemy division had moved from its home station in remote northern Manchuria to Ormoc Bay in complete secrecy. That in itself was a major operational success. By getting their "firstest with the mostest," the First Division forced Krueger to fight the rest of the long, grinding campaign of attrition on Japanese terms.

The division's 13,000 officers and men bore a distinguished unit lineage dating to the Russo-Japanese War (1904–5).[52] With the exception of a few veterans who fought at Khalkin Gol (Nomonhan) in 1939, the division lacked combat experience. Nevertheless it was still considered an elite formation. In the summer of 1944, IGHQ tabbed the First Division as the strategic reserve for the Shō Operation. In late July, Tokyo ordered the division to move from northern Manchuria to Shanghai in central China. For Allied intercept operators, other Japanese radio networks had priority over faraway Manchurian stations. Besides, those encrypted messages they did intercept could not be solved.

Moving by train the division headed for Shanghai on 20 August. Now internal division orders were either hand carried to their destination or passed by telephone. Messages transmitted in such fashion could not be detected by Allied radio intercept units. Eleven days after departing Manchuria, the First Division closed in on Shanghai. It surely coordinated its arrival and requirements via radio, likely in unreadable regional code systems. Its ranks spent the next month around Shanghai as did soldiers in every army—waiting for something to happen.

Something happened in late September. A staff officer arrived in Shanghai from IGHQ with orders in hand for the division. The First Division was destined for Luzon and the Fourteenth Area Army. Separate radio messages from Tokyo confirmed the First Division as part of the Fourteenth Area Army. On 22 September and again on 3 October, Allied intercept operators copied messages from Tokyo to all divisions and armies stationed in the Philippines. The contents were unreadable, but each address heading carried two more addressees than there were units known to be in the Philippines. An unidentified code name used in the messages hinted a new division might have been added to the Japanese order of battle in the Philippines.[53] These vague and tantalizing references told nothing about the division or its origins or its destination in the islands. The army code system was keeping its secrets. It was, however, only one of many Japanese code systems, some of which were most porous.

The Imperial Army had its own maritime transport network, which it coordinated with its own Army Water Transport code system. Radio messages flashed back and forth assembling ships to transport the troops; alerting port directors of impending arrivals; directing stevedore and anchorage units to debarking areas; passing convoy arrival and departure times; and coordinating a host of other administrative matters involved in moving 13,000 men and their equipment thousands of miles by sea. Reading Water Transport Code messages enabled the Allies to anticipate Japanese convoys, to attack them with warplanes or more likely submarines, and to choke off reinforcements. U.S. Army cryptanalysts had broken the Japanese army's Water Transport Code in April 1943, and since then sinkings of Japanese transports, oil tankers, and merchantmen increased dramatically.[54] The Twenty-sixth Division's fate, described earlier, was an example of the ruthlessly efficient union of signals intelligence and submarine warfare.

The First Division left Shanghai on 12 October bound for San Fernando in northern Luzon. U.S. carrier aircraft marauding through the East China Sea soon forced the ships to seek shelter alongside several small islands off Shanghai. Then the convoy turned back to Shanghai where the men heard about the great Japanese victory in the Taiwan air battles. With the American fleet destroyed, many soldiers assumed their next stop would be Japan. On the morning of 18 October, however, they cast off again for Luzon. The convoy crossed the same dangerous waters of the Luzon Straits that cost the Twenty-sixth Division so dearly. Their voyage was uneventful in large measure because the Allies knew so little about it.

On 9 October several partially decrypted messages from the Takao (Formosa) Guard District and Army Water Transport District mentioned convoys TAMA 28, 29, and 29A. TAMA was the code name of the First Division, but in the Japanese scheme of convoy identification could mean convoy sailing from Takao, Formosa, to Manila, Philippines. The messages themselves were inconclusive. The most readable one, and most likely involving the First Division, was "TAMA 28 Convoy—San Fernando (3 ̲ type planes to escort)."[55]

Troops were unloading the First Division's cargo and equipment at San Fernando on 25 October when the orders arrived to report immediately to Manila. No hint of the convoy appeared during this leg of its voyage, as operations orders to the First Division at San Fernando were likely transmitted in the unsolved Fourteenth Area Army code. Radio coordination between water transport units at San Fernando and Manila was not intercepted. The convoy closed at Manila on 30 October, but no one disembarked. General Yamashita came to review the troops onboard their transports and send them on to Ormoc. Fourteenth Area Army staff officers hand carried the division's written orders to the ships. In short, there were no radio broadcasts for Allied eavesdroppers to overhear. Besides, Manila was a busy port, and the TAMA convoys were not the only ones headed there.

General Headquarters was aware from signals intelligence of the desperate Japanese attempts to reinforce the Philippines, meaning Luzon not Leyte. Intelligence analysts and commanders probably had too much data to digest given all the other action taking place simultaneously. During the week after the Leyte landings, the following major Japanese convoys were detected:

A high-speed convoy, cargo unknown, left Japan for Manila on 20 October.
MOMA 06, an eleven-ship convoy, was assembling at Moji, Japan, for departure to Manila.
SIMA 03 departed Singapore bound for Manila on 22 October.
HI 79 was bound for Manila with oil.[56]

Convoys were steaming to and from Manila daily. Then there were fleet movements. In other words, thousands of Japanese radio signals cluttered the airwaves. Surely analysis of enemy fleet dispositions, the landing itself, and the subsequent Battle of Leyte Gulf all overshadowed the incomplete convoy intelligence. In that larger context, a single convoy was not that much news, especially when so many were bound for the Philippines.

Japanese radio traffic did suggest army reinforcements were moving to the Philippines via Formosa. U.S. submarine sightings of Japanese merchantmen and transports at Manila and Aparri in northern Luzon on 24 and 25 October also presaged arriving reinforcements.[57] ULTRA and the visual sightings could not be reconciled, leaving the units involved and the scope of activity a mystery. And besides, everyone thought Luzon would be the scene of the climatic battle. A reasonable conjecture was that Japanese reinforcements from China and Formosa were en route to Luzon.[58]

When faced with ambiguity, Willoughby endorsed it. His appreciation for 28 October included reasons the Japanese were reinforcing Leyte, complemented by arguments why they were withdrawing from the island. The Japanese were landing reinforcements on Leyte, he concluded, to bolster a rearguard action while simultaneously withdrawing service troops from the island.[59] In a separate appreciation dated the same day,

Willoughby asserted that heavy enemy losses and American advances made Japanese choices either a last stand or evacuation.[60] By 1 November he insisted that no sizable Japanese merchant vessels would again ever venture into the central Philippines.[61] By this time the First Division's large convoy, including four attack cargo ships, was nearing Ormoc (a talkative Japanese pilot said so).

Japanese airmen flying convoy cover were required to report enemy submarine sightings and to update convoy positions at preselected times during runs to and from Ormoc. Australian Number Six Wireless Unit at Tacloban intercepted the pilots' broadcasts and promptly alerted U.S. air and naval units about the location and destination of impending convoys. Throughout the Leyte campaign, twenty-four Japanese ships were sunk on the Ormoc run. American aircrews credited the intelligence provided by Australian eavesdroppers as instrumental in the destruction of seventeen of them.[62]

Yet here again the First Division slipped through the Allied intelligence net. On 1 November a Japanese pilot mentioned a Number Four convoy in an otherwise broken and static-filled report to his home base. Nothing else was known about this convoy or the three that presumably preceded it. Number Four convoy was the fourth, and largest, echelon of the First Division's transport to Leyte. By the time American pilots sighted four large transports, three destroyers, and two destroyer escorts headed for Ormoc late on the afternoon of 1 November it was too late.[63] Even after the First Division's arrival at Ormoc, ULTRA could not confirm its presence on the island for another five full days. Appropriately enough, the telltale clue appeared in a routine administrative cable.

A mundane message dealing with the commissioning of officer candidates suggested the possibility of another Japanese division in the Philippines. The message contents were not important but the list of fifty-one addressees on this 1 November cable was very important. All the addressed units were of division or higher echelon. One unidentified unit was the same one addressed at Shanghai in September and early October. This relationship suggested the mystery unit probably moved to the Philippines via Shanghai. If true, then the unit had to be a division, because army headquarters units were not transferred from one area to another.[64] A few days later the deciphered weekly intelligence circular from the vice chief of staff in Tokyo to Japanese military attachés in Europe confirmed the First Division was fighting on Leyte.[65] By this time, however, captured documents, POWs, and dog tags stripped from Japanese corpses had already revealed the First Division's presence on

Leyte. As SWPA sadly admitted, "No information has previously been available from ULTRA sources on the move of the 1st Division to Leyte."[66] The comment echoes that made about the naval actions of Leyte.

Indeed there are several parallels between the sea and ground controversies. Both controversies involve questionable decisions. Halsey decided to go north leaving Leyte Gulf lightly defended. If Kurita had a bit more courage, this might have led to a naval disaster. Krueger opted not to seize the high ground, allowing the Japanese First Division to occupy it. This prolonged the ground campaign on Leyte and delayed the return to Luzon. In each case ULTRA or other forms of signals intelligence were unavailable to the respective commanders, and the naval or ground commander made decisions on the basis of his assessment of the operation. Halsey determined Kurita had turned back and went north to destroy enemy carriers. He viewed the carriers as the major Japanese threat, never believing a surface fleet could get close to the Leyte beachhead. Similarly MacArthur and Willoughby viewed Luzon, not Leyte, as the enemy's center of gravity. Leyte was a warm-up for the decisive battle farther north. With higher headquarters insisting the Leyte show was over, Krueger saw no urgency about the high ground. In short, when peering into the fog of war, the naval and ground commanders applied the doctrines of a lifetime of professional experience. The navy went after warships; the army looked ahead to a decisive battle on Luzon. In neither case was ULTRA, or associated forms of signals intelligence, of much help. Resorting to the ULTRA documents would not settle Leyte's controversies.

The simplistic approach is to attribute Japanese successes (or near successes) by blaming an Allied "intelligence failure" of one sort or another for the lapse. The notion of a failure, however, sets an impossibly high standard for ULTRA. It assumes a symmetric relationship between codemaker and codebreaker when the context is actually asymmetric and usually in the codemaker's favor. It also reduces the human element in decision making by presuming that had Halsey or MacArthur had access to relevant ULTRA intelligence he would have done things differently. The justification for invading Leyte demonstrates the lack of wisdom of such a view. Neither Halsey nor MacArthur ever enjoyed uninterrupted access to the Japanese army or navy ciphers during the Pacific War.

This condition was especially true for MacArthur. At most he had access to the Japanese army code for twelve of his forty-five months at war. MacArthur never made a strategic decision solely on the basis of signals intelligence. In addition, he did not depend on ULTRA. He knew its limitations far too well. The same held true for Nimitz and Halsey. They understood that aggressiveness today might prevent greater bloodletting tomorrow. When assessing the generals and admirals in the Pacific War under ULTRA's harsh glare, it is useful to bear in mind the interplay of ULTRA and that great central processing unit, the human brain. Otherwise we risk underestimating several of the greatest commanders on land and sea in American history.

CHAPTER TEN

JAPANESE PREPARATIONS FOR THE DEFENSE OF THE HOMELAND

Imperial General Headquarters in Tokyo began planning for homeland defense in early 1944 following American air attacks against the eastern Carolines and Truk. In May Tokyo mobilized the General Defense Command and its subordinate district armies, Eastern, Western and Central. Beginning in July each district headquarters worked on improving coastal defenses and fortifications. Top priority went to building air bases, although fortifications in key areas and road improvements did receive some attention. Construction proceeded sporadically until 1945 when Tokyo accelerated plans for homeland defense. I will discuss the resulting Japanese preparations for the defense of the home islands in terms of manpower, resources, and doctrine.

Japanese manpower was already stretched thinly across Asian and Pacific battlegrounds, and 1944 left a quarter of a million Japanese dead in places such as New Guinea (50,000), Leyte (75,000), Burma (60,000), and the Marianas (64,000). By January 1945 Japan had only eight divisions available to defend the entire homeland (excluding Hokkaido).[1] Reinforcements could come from two sources: established divisions stationed in Manchuria or newly mobilized ones.

On 11 January 1945 Army Chief of Staff General Umezu Yoshijirō ordered all directorates in the war ministry to establish their immediate priorities for homeland defense. Nine days later the emperor approved, and the army promulgated, the overall concept for the defense of Japan.

General policy for homeland defense envisioned a decisive battle fought on Japanese soil. To buy time for defensive preparations in the home islands, Japanese forces in outlying garrisons would fight protracted operations against invading American or Allied forces. The outposts would be sacrificed, but they would inflict as many casualties as possible on the attackers, weakening them before the climactic battle on Japan's sacred shores. The Japanese high command expected this great clash to occur on the southernmost main island of Kyushu and the Tokyo plain around autumn of 1945.

By mid-February the army ordered a three-stage levee en masse. Plans emerged to mobilize sixteen new divisions by the end of May, eight more during June and July, and sixteen more during August, or forty new divisions totaling more than half a million men. Four other first-line divisions would be transferred from Manchuria to bolster the newly mobilized units.

Mobilized divisions were of three types and numbered accordingly. The 100-series divisions, for example, the 146th, 154th, and 156th, were coastal defense units mobilized in February 1945. This designation meant the troops would fight and die near the Allied beachhead. From hasty field fortifications, such as earthen bunkers with log revetments to permanent, ferroconcrete pillboxes, these soldiers would hold the ground near the beaches until killed or relieved by counterattacking Japanese forces. With nowhere to go, the 100-series divisions needed little mobility or firepower—they had few trucks or carts and no heavy artillery and only a handful of howitzers and field cannons. In short they were human breakwaters to the invader's tide. Sooner or later they would be washed away.

The 200-series units, including the 206th, 212th, and 216th divisions, were called to active service in April. After receiving just four to six weeks of basic training, they were declared operational. These divisions would counterattack and destroy the Allied beachhead. Armed with heavy artillery, mortars, and automatic weapons, they also had a generous supply of combat engineers for demolition work, mine clearing, and road and bridge repair.

The 300-series units, for instance, the 303d, 312th, and 351st divisions, were also intended for coastal defense. After mobilization and following minimal training, they would deploy to their operational areas in midsummer. The mobilization timetable for the three 300-series divisions slated for Kyushu was advanced both because of fear of imminent invasion and to allow the deploying units more time to familiarize themselves with their operational areas. The trade-off was even less organic artillery than the already considerably weakened 100-series divisions. Indeed, the 300-series units substituted a heavy mortar section for artillery.

Japan's military leaders also expected to throw civilians into the fighting as necessary. The "National Resistance Program" called for all ablebodied Japanese, regardless of sex, to engage the enemy. In early June Japanese men between the ages of fifteen and sixty and women from sixteen to forty were mobilized under military control into the People's Volunteer Corps, which, if required, could become the People's Fighting Unit.[2] This mobilization gives us the photographs and images of Japanese women training with bamboo spears, of children drilling with wooden rifles, and of a nation teetering on the brink of collapse. But this is a Janus-faced image.

A few months ago, I contacted my professor in Tokyo, who was sixteen years old in 1945 and well remembered the People's Volunteer Corps—he was in it. His "equipment" consisted of a bamboo spear and a backpack filled with two large stones. He practiced huddling in a dank, stinking foxhole, waiting for the Americans. If the enemy approached, he would exchange his stones for a land mine. His mission was to destroy an enemy tank, and himself, with it. Reflecting back, the training, indeed the whole notion, was similar to something out of a demented cartoon. But, he emphasized, the military was serious. And if the Americans landed, he is certain he would have perished. My point is the nation was facing disaster, but the idea of surrender remained inconceivable.

Resources were also in short supply, as Allied submarines and aircraft systematically destroyed Japan's merchant marine fleet. By January 1945, 69 percent of Japan's merchantmen, including 59 percent of its oil tankers, had been sent to the bottom. (By March 1945, the figures were 74 and 75 percent, respectively). Without an overseas supply of raw materials, production figures plummeted.[3] Where would resources for the defense of the homeland come from? Furthermore, would the Japanese be able to move raw materials and finished goods to front-line units? Rail movements were falling off sharply, although the railroad network had not yet been singled out for sustained Allied aerial attacks.[4] From mid-July, however, air strikes, especially against railroad bridges, seriously hampered traffic, which forced the Japanese to resort to a shuttle system to bypass downed bridges, leaving railroads to operate only at night.[5] IGHQ deployed the Fourth Anti-Aircraft Artillery Division to Kyushu, but it could not simultaneously defend the manufacturing centers of the north and the bridges, rail lines, and supply dumps of the south. Actually the Japanese expected that air attacks would completely disrupt rail lines in Kyushu by October. To overcome this disadvantage, planners relied on stockpiling, dispersing supplies in underground caches throughout the forward areas, and devising a relay system to carry supplies for troops in southern Kyushu by wagon or truck.[6] Aerial mining of Japanese inland waters also posed an increasingly serious problem, more or less closing ports such as Niigata by June 1945.[7]

Nonetheless, the Japanese had some advantages. For example, they had prepositioned in Kyushu sufficient ammunition, fuel, and stores for two combat divisions. They had also started stockpiling. The Second General Army, headquartered in Hiroshima and in overall charge of the defense of western Japan, feared an imminent Allied landing and accordingly accelerated the movement of supplies to Kyushu. From late May through early June, hundreds of freight trains, pulling more than 3400 boxcars loaded with munitions and equipment, ran back and forth throughout Kyushu. Despite damaged rail and road lines, sporadic Allied air attacks, transportation bottlenecks, and an inadequate distribution network, by the end of June the Sixteenth Area Army, entrusted with the defense of Kyushu, reported delivery of about 80 percent of the promised materiel.[8] Indeed by the end of July, the Sixteenth Area Army estimated that it had completed 80 percent of its base construction and procured 70 percent of all its supplies, this despite increasing the number of combat divisions defending Kyushu from two in April to fourteen by the middle of July.[9]

The Japanese cleaned their homeland cupboards to supply Kyushu. Defensive preparations around the Tokyo plain, for instance, had to be neglected to reinforce southwestern Japan. Even so shortages persisted. The ammunition available to the five-plus infantry divisions and two tank brigades of the Fifty-seventh Army, protecting southeast Kyushu, was sufficient for only the requirements of three and one-half divisions in sustained operations. The Japanese idea, which may sound familiar, was to fight one and one-half battles; the line units would receive a full share of ammunition, while the maneuver and attack forces would get only a half share. Sufficient rations were available to sustain its approximately 300,000 men and 20,000 horses for four months, and there was enough fuel for its 2000 vehicles and 300 tanks for a month and a half. All these supplies were in the hands of the Fifty-seventh Army units in August 1945. The four divisions and two brigades under the Fortieth Army, defending southwest Kyushu, were somewhat worse off, having about 40 percent of their required ammunition, but just

30 percent of their rations. The Fortieth Army also lacked fuel to feed its mobile forces.[10]

In late May hastily mobilized formations, such as the 146th and 156th Infantry divisions, did suffer from poor training, from shortages of weapons, ammunition, and equipment, and from inadequate headquarters command and control arrangements.[11] Under a carpet of American bombs, munitions' production was unable to keep pace with the vast mobilization. Shortages were ubiquitous. Only 68 percent of the necessary rifles were produced; 9 percent of mortars; 54 percent of heavy artillery; and 14 percent of antitank guns.[12] But there were also first-class divisions from Manchuria, such as the Twenty-fifth and Fifty-seventh, present in Kyushu to bolster the resolve of the newer units.

In early 1945 Japan's counter-amphibious doctrine was in flux. Was it better to risk all to defeat an invader on the beaches or to fight a protracted battle of attrition inland? The Japanese had tried both tactics. Neither brought success. Unlike their string of defeats on isolated Pacific islands, however, the Japanese high command now believed they could mass sufficient air and naval forces to strike a great blow against the invaders. For the first time, the army would be able to throw its main strength into decisive battle, fighting on shortened lines of communications, and with the full support of the population.[13]

In mid-March 1945, IGHQ was favoring a protracted defense to contain the invaders. The revised doctrine in its field manual for fortifications exemplified the concept. Fortifications would buy time by covering the assembly areas needed to launch the great counterattack. In the case of secondary landings, troops in fortified areas would fight a protracted defense. Pinning down enemy troops would enable Japanese mobile units to destroy the main enemy beachhead and win the decisive battle.

The projected layout of beach defenses was ambitious, likely compensating for the underequipped 100 and 300 series divisions. Dummy positions scattered throughout all three defensive belts would draw fire, exposing the enemy to Japanese counterfire. Invaders would meet a thin screen of squad- and platoon-size positions studded with machine-gun nests along the beaches. Pushing through these defenses, they would next encounter a covering force—company-size formations dug in for all-around defense. After fighting through this zone, they would hit the main defensive line, about a mile or a mile and a half inland. Veteran troops in battalion strength would be manning the weapons here and were expected to defend to the death.[14] These were the tactics of Iwo

Jima and Okinawa—fight a protracted battle of attrition after conceding the Americans a lodgment ashore.

On 8 April 1945, Tokyo announced its counter-amphibious doctrine for homeland defense. Relying on "our nation's unique special attack [i.e., suicide] tactics," air, surface, and underwater special attack units would aim to destroy the American transport fleet and landing craft. "Special attacks" (a euphemism for suicidal air and sea assaults) were the key to success in homeland defense. After the invasion convoy came within 200 miles of Japan, all army and navy special attack air forces and midget submarines would strike en masse. When the hostile invasion convoy had arrived, midget submarines, human torpedoes, and crash boats would constantly attack the transport fleet. Artillerymen firing from caves, kamikaze flyers, and suicidal frogmen would strike landing craft shuttling to and from the beaches.[15] The army had 1000 suicide planes committed as the main striking force against an invasion of Kyushu. Another 1000 army kamikaze and 1100 conventional warplanes were available to support the main attacks. As for the navy, it offered another 1750 suicide, bomber, and torpedo planes for the main attack with 2200 kamikaze and 1100 conventional aircraft in reserve.[16] Based on the results of war games, the navy expected such tactics could destroy 30 to 50 percent of the invasion forces. More conservative ground commanders expected perhaps 15 to 20 percent, or the equivalent of knocking out three entire divisions at sea. After running this air and sea gauntlet, the surviving invaders would meet the IJA on its home ground. IGHQ's orders were simple. All ground forces would execute continuous and violent counterattacks against the enemy's landing points, thereby destroying the invaders in the coastal areas.[17]

But neither IGHQ nor the on-scene commanders had much confidence they could destroy an American landing with existing tactics. After all, whenever the Americans had established an organized beachhead perimeter, it was impossible to dislodge them. So the invaders had to be hit hardest while they were most vulnerable. The Japanese high command was analyzing just when that critical moment would occur.

Tokyo might be rethinking doctrine, but there was no change about what the high command expected from its troops.

> Those wounded in the fighting or the sick will not be evacuated to rear areas. It is necessary to press wholeheartedly for destruction of the enemy remembering the noblest thing one can do for a wounded comrade is to promptly destroy the enemy. Tending to comrades cannot be condoned.

During the fighting medical personnel should have the responsibility to advance to the front lines to treat the wounded.

Units are not permitted to withdraw in the midst of fighting. Scouts, messengers, and volunteer assault units are permitted to advance in the direction of the rear after successfully completing their missions.[18]

Around the beginning of May, the Second General Army predicted that the Americans would soon attack southern Kyushu trying to end the war against Japan as quickly as possible. It correctly saw the enemy's aim as seizing a forward operational base for air and naval forces from which a final decisive attack against the Tokyo plain would be launched. The invasion of Kyushu might come any time after the final days of June 1945. The sense of urgency dictated immediate countermeasures.

Thus far the defenders conceded the beaches to the invaders. The 156th Division, for example, deployed its squads of infantrymen and antitank weapons along the beaches near Miyazaki on Kyushu's east coast. Their mission was to obstruct the enemy landing. The main force deployed on high ground about two miles inland from the beaches. Raiding units would roam between the higher ground and the beaches sowing confusion and further hampering the enemy push inland. Heavy artillery and firing from fortified positions would punish the invaders along the beaches, while mortars firing from defilade would hit attackers advancing on the main line of defense. A secondary line of defense, about 3 miles behind the main positions, would screen the division's reserves, who would be thrown into the fighting if the enemy appeared to be breaking out of the beachhead.[19] The plans followed the book, but the book was about to change.

The war minister and the commander, Second General Army, both regarded existing doctrine as too passive. From the results of tabletop war games conducted in May, they concluded an invader was most vulnerable after the landing but before the consolidation of the lodgment. This was the moment to destroy him. On 6 June Imperial Headquarters issued a new field manual announcing the revised tactical doctrine for the defense of the homeland.[20]

"The decisive battle for the homeland will be the last desperate battle that all Japanese should fight to the bitter end. We have to abandon the conventional protracted way of fighting and its way of thinking to defend ourselves. We should be determined to destroy the enemy landing forces at the water's edge by conducting an all-out decisive battle there using suicide attacks against the enemy."[21] No longer would the Americans be allowed to secure a foothold on Japan's sacred soil. Japanese forces would continuously attack the enemy after the landing but before the Americans could establish an organized lodgment. Closing with and fighting the Americans at close range was the way to neutralize the enemy's otherwise overwhelming advantage in artillery and naval gunfire support. Fighting on the beach and coast would also deny the Americans quick access to nearby inland air bases.[22]

Armed with these combat instructions, Sixteenth Area Army ordered its units to complete all preparations for the decisive battle by the end of September. Wherever the bulk of the enemy landed would become the site of the decisive ground clash. If the main landings proved difficult to identify, the battle would occur at the initial landing site. Coastal divisions would fix the enemy in place for mobile divisions to destroy it in the key beachhead area. Mobile units would reach the beaches by marching 15 to 20 kilometers per night. Cloaked in darkness, they could deploy with less interference from American aircraft and artillery. Within ten days of the invasion, Japanese mobile forces would launch their all-out counterattack against the enemy beachhead.[23]

A 20 June message from the vice chief of staff, Lieutenant General Kawabe Torashirō, to First and Second General Armies plus Air General Army, restated the revised doctrine and tactics. This message was intercepted and decrypted by Allied codebreakers. The Japanese commander's own words in the decrypted version give us the flavor of those desperate days in the summer of 1945.

> The battle will be literally the decisive battle—a fight to the finish. It is fundamentally contradictory for Japanese forces disposed along the coast—whatever tactical difficulties may arise—to count on continuing the struggle by retreating.
>
> If a landing on Japan proper is attempted, "a full scale offensive will be launched with the intention of utterly destroying Allied forces at sea or on the beaches."
>
> Japanese air and sea forces must annihilate the Allied invading forces at sea. Ground forces must expose the enemy's weak points at the water's edge and overwhelm and annihilate the enemy at the coast.
>
> If the Allied forces cannot be prevented from establishing a bridgehead, the main aim of coastal forces is to "cover the deployment of mobile troops who will smash the enemy."[24]

Another message, in a similar vein, was also decrypted. It described antitank tactics for the invasion. These lines convey the impression of an enemy determined to go down fighting and not interested in surrender. "The number one target on the beaches during an invasion is enemy tanks. Japanese units will construct anti-tank defenses in depth from the water's edge inland. Engineers will demolish all coastal roads forcing tanks into rugged terrain where they will be more vulnerable to attack by small suicide units. Tokyo is ordering all officers and men, regardless of branch of service, to execute such suicide attacks."[25]

Whether the Japanese could have carried out their ambitious schemes remains a moot point. Japan's military leaders understood the precarious nature of resources and equipment, but were still deadly serious about fighting the invaders on the beaches. American plans for a 1 November assault date ironically coincided with the Japanese preference for an invasion during the fall of 1945. Otherwise high-ranking Japanese officers feared stockpiled supplies would be consumed and troops would run short of rations should the invasion be postponed until the following spring.[26]

So by early August 1945, Imperial Headquarters had deployed fourteen divisions, five independent mixed brigades, and three armored brigades to defend Kyushu. They were working feverishly to raise, arm, equip, and train even more new units. And we need to recall that these material deficiencies were somewhat balanced, because the Japanese were reinforcing and fortifying the very beaches where the Americans would land; because they would be fighting from prepared positions on familiar terrain; and because they would be defending their very homeland against foreign invaders. Throughout the Pacific War, the Japanese soldier had gained a fearsome reputation of fighting to the death, and there was no reason for the Allies to believe that he did not intend to live up to it, or rather perish to preserve his repute. Besides, no Japanese soldier would openly question his superiors, and in a silently terrifying sort of way, both soldiers and civilians seemed resigned to their fate. Indeed commanders assured junior officers that counterattacking the invaders would be a most splendid way to die. Because it may be hard to imagine fifty years later does not make it any less true.

CHAPTER ELEVEN

INTELLIGENCE FORECASTING FOR THE INVASION OF JAPAN
Previews of Hell

OLYMPIC was a fitting code name for the American invasion of the land of the gods. A massive amphibious assault by nine divisions (six stormed the Normandy beaches) would seize three widely separate landing areas on the southernmost Japanese main island of Kyushu. A tenth would assault offshore islands. More than 400,000 American troops were slated for the assault forces.[1] By the spring of 1945 preparations for the invasion were under way. Simultaneously the Japanese were struggling around the clock to turn Kyushu's beaches into massive killing grounds. The showdown was set for 1 November 1945.

Intelligence forecasts predicted the landings forces would encounter at most ten Japanese divisions throughout all of Kyushu. Planners confidently expected American attackers to outnumber Japanese defenders two or three to one in the southern half of the island. But from early spring to midsummer 1945 the forecast changed dramatically. Intelligence, obtained mainly from reading Japanese military and naval codes, uncovered a Japanese buildup on Kyushu of mind-boggling proportions. By August more than ten Japanese divisions defended southern Kyushu alone. Standard tactics would include widespread suicide attacks on the invasion fleet with everything from kamikazes to human torpedoes.

Countless decrypted messages from the high command in Tokyo underlined Japanese determination to fight to the death against the invaders. Japan's planned defense of Kyushu, unwittingly told to the Allies in their own words, forecast beachheads running red with American blood. Concern about estimated U.S. losses for the operation runs through American decision makers' thinking. As more and more Japanese troops crowded into Kyushu, there were even suggestions to switch the landing elsewhere in the Japanese home islands. Finally the intelligence forecasts caused serious consideration about the tactical use of atomic bombs to clear Japanese defenders from the landing beaches.

Yet it all began innocently enough. In early April the JCS instructed General Douglas MacArthur to plan and prepare for the invasion of Japan. The same directive named MacArthur commander in chief, U.S. Army Forces in the Pacific in addition to commander in chief, Southwest Pacific area. He controlled almost all American Army and Air Force units and resources in the Pacific. In late May the Joint Chiefs set the date for the invasion, code named OLYMPIC, for 1 November 1945.

On 25 April Major General Charles A. Willoughby, MacArthur's intelligence chief, submitted his initial estimate of the enemy defenses on Kyushu.[2] Information gleaned from reading Japanese military codes formed the basis of his forecast. Such intelligence was code named ULTRA. Throughout April ULTRA revealed Japanese anxiety about an imminent invasion of the home islands. Navy messages ordered mining of several Kyushu bays "as soon as possible" and told of the evacuation of civilians from coastal areas, clearly counter-invasion measures.[3] The vice chief of staff predicted an American invasion of Kyushu sometime after the middle of the year.[4] This apprehension accounted for the urgency of Army Chief of Staff General Umezu's directive to all army commands to discover the time, place, and scale of the Allied invasion of Japan. Overseas commands duly alerted subordinate units to gather intelligence on an Allied invasion of Japan.[5]

ULTRA also identified two combat divisions on Kyushu, the Fifty-seventh in the north and the Eighty-sixth in the south. The total number of troops on the island was estimated at about 230,000 and was expected to increase. Messages from army harbormasters at Pusan were reporting another 30,000 to 60,000 Japanese troops embarking from Korean ports and heading for Kyushu.[6] Because Willoughby expected at least six and at most ten combat divisions defending the island, these reinforcements were not cause for alarm. Besides, the Japanese would not know the exact landing beaches, so they would have to protect Kyushu's entire coastline. That meant dispersing their combat divisions equally between northern and southern Kyushu. The Americans would still enjoy overwhelming superiority on the beachheads.

Willoughby predicted three enemy combat divisions, maybe 100,000 troops, would be deployed in southern Kyushu by D-day. About 2000 or 2500 Japanese aircraft would be ready to strike an approaching fleet. Granting that half the airplanes might be obsolete or trainers, they were a serious threat, especially if used in kamikaze fashion. The remnants of the once formidable imperial battle fleet were not considered a significant danger.[7]

Throughout May ULTRA continued to report on the steady, but unspectacular, reinforcement of Kyushu. The Twenty-fifth Division had arrived as predicted from Manchuria and was settling into central Kyushu.[8] An amphibious brigade redeployed from the Kurile Islands to southernmost Kyushu.[9] And an unidentified but important headquarters began broadcasting messages from Takarabe to major army command posts throughout Japan.[10] By month's end there were three divisions definitely identified on Kyushu with another three to five either present or expected. The Japanese were making feverish efforts to reinforce Kyushu. Yet the numbers fell within Willoughby's tolerances—the forecasted eight to ten divisions.

The Takarabe headquarters' mystery was solved in June by unveiling the Fifty-seventh Army in south Kyushu. Shortly afterward the Fifty-sixth Army was identified in the north half of the island.[11] Two armies fit Willoughby's original model of Japanese forces on Kyushu, divided between the northern and southern commands. An estimated 280,000 Japanese soldiers were now in Kyushu.[12] Coded addresses on intercepted messages, though, hinted at another major, as yet unidentified, headquarters somewhere in southern Kyushu.[13] Radio messages broadcast from the same region betrayed the Seventy-seventh Division's move from northern Japan to Kyushu.[14] It became the fourth division definitely located on the island.

Decryptions of Japanese naval and air force messages conjured up still fresh and painful memories of massed suicide attacks off the Philippines and Okinawa. The commanding officer of the Twelfth Naval Flotilla based in Kyushu intended to use his 900 planes of all types as kamikazes against an Allied landing.[15] Naval air depots throughout Japan were converting more than 400 biplane trainers into kamikazes, and staging bases were being readied to repel any invasion.[16] Sasebo Naval Base workers on double shifts were building suicide boats, and the command was deploying *kaiten*, the naval version of a piloted torpedo, to bases on the south Kyushu coasts.[17] Suicide weapons en masse would greet any invaders. By mid-June decrypted messages told of Japanese concern about an Allied landing in southern Kyushu.[18] The Japanese high command did not know the invasion was still months away, but they knew the Allies were coming. They suspected the beaches of Kyushu were the most likely landing areas and were doing everything possible to convert these beachheads into graveyards for Americans troops.

Japanese army air force communications showed the enemy concentrating all his available aircraft at fields stretching from Shanghai through Korea to Honshu. From bases inside this arc, Japanese aircraft were well within range of Kyushu's beaches, especially for their one-way missions.[19] Army construction battalions were busy working on underground aircraft hangers and concealing dispersal airfields throughout Kyushu.[20] With 1400 suicide training planes in the homeland augmented by 4000 other aircraft of varying quality, the prospect loomed of a bitter and protracted air war over the home islands for the next several months. Allied air attacks would destroy hundreds of Japanese planes before the scheduled invasion. Even so MacArthur's latest intelligence estimates forecast serious damage to invasion shipping from enemy air attacks. ULTRA really was telling two stories. One was a straightforward rendition of Tokyo's hurried efforts to transform Kyushu into a mighty bastion. The other was even more frightening. Nowhere in the enemy's mindset could ULTRA detect pessimism or defeatism. Instead Japan's military leaders were determined to go down fighting and take as many Americans with them as possible.

Marshall's preview of invasion beaches laced with mines, barbed wire, pillboxes, and thousands of Japanese defenders stiffened by massive numbers of kamikazes troubled him. Before discussing OLYMPIC with President Truman and the other JCS on 18 June, he cabled MacArthur. What was MacArthur's estimate of American casualties for OLYMPIC? The response was prompt—105,500 battle casualties for the first ninety days of fighting plus 12,600 more nonbattle losses.[21] Such unacceptably high estimates shocked Marshall. How long could a democracy be keyed up to fight a foreign war, especially with large numbers of dead and wounded?[22] He told MacArthur of his concern and added, "[The] President is very much concerned as to the number of casualties we will receive in OLYMPIC operation." MacArthur now understood what Washington wanted. He reassured Marshall. The earlier estimate it turned out was "purely academic and routine," and he had not even seen it. This was disingenuous. Nothing left MacArthur's headquarters, let alone a message to the chief of staff, without review and approval. Personally, MacArthur continued, he doubted losses would be that high.

Besides, Soviet intervention "sufficiently ahead of our target date" would prevent Japanese troops on the Asian mainland from reinforcing the home islands. OLYMPIC was a solid plan. No change was needed.

Within minutes of reading MacArthur's cable, Marshall went to see the president and other joint chiefs. Afterward he cabled MacArthur. Your message, Marshall wrote, "arrived with 30 minutes to spare and had determining influence in obtaining formal presidential approval for OLYMPIC."[23] It was not mere flattery. During the momentous meeting, Marshall had quoted verbatim an entire section of MacArthur's estimate supporting an invasion.[24]

American casualties remained a concern, but the invasion was on. Within weeks casualties became an obsession because of the changing intelligence picture of Japanese defenses on Kyushu. The forecast turned ominous for two reasons. First, Japanese army and navy code books captured on Luzon and Okinawa enabled Allied cryptanalysts to read the enemy's most important codes.[25] Second, newly mobilized Japanese divisions were organizing on Kyushu. Every day their radio operators tapped out a steady flow of messages to coordinate redeployments, to issue orders, and to administer all the other things involved in preparing a new unit for operations. In other words the appearance in radio communications of the new divisions coincided with the Allies' newfound ability to decipher the Japanese army's most secret messages. The result was startling.

As far as Marshall knew when he met the president, all the Japanese reinforcements earmarked for Kyushu were already there. That meant a maximum of eight enemy divisions would defend Kyushu. ULTRA had alerted the chief of staff about additional divisions being raised in Japan. Still American air and naval attacks, he told Truman, made further reinforcement of Kyushu suicidal. The Japanese would lose so many men and so much equipment that the attempt was just not worth it. Throughout July ULTRA made mockery of Marshall's estimate.

The Japanese navy was busy converting 2000 biplane trainers, plus assorted fighters and floatplanes, into kamikazes. Pilots were practicing for night attacks. Biplanes might sound ridiculous, but American radar could not detect the flimsy wood and fabric machines. By striking in darkness, determined suicide pilots might gain an edge. As if to underline their deadliness, suicide biplanes sank one U.S. destroyer and damaged another in a moonlight attack in late July.[26] Staging bases on Kyushu were being assigned for kamikaze units. ULTRA located new, secret airfields being built, underground storage dumps being constructed, and aircraft

FIGURE 9. Listening to and recording the enemy at Vint Hill Farms VA. This unit also intercepted Japanese diplomatic messages transmitted by radio from Europe. Courtesy of U.S. Army Intelligence and Security Command

being camouflaged and dispersed.[27] Indeed there was so much military construction under way in Kyushu that there were not enough airfield construction battalions to go around.[28] Appeals for thousands more men to fill labor battalions were sent as far away as central China.[29]

One reason for the labor shortage was so many men had been mobilized to form new divisions. During 1945 Japanese strength in the homeland doubled from 980,000 on 1 January to 1,865,000 on 10 July.[30] Allied intercept operators listened to the reverberations of the mass mobilization in southern Japan. Early in July two more divisions, the 206th and the 212th, were identified in Kyushu.[31] A week later the 154th Division was positively located on the south-central coast. Within a few days ULTRA exposed two tank regiments and three independent mixed brigades there. An estimated 380,000 Japanese troops now garrisoned

Kyushu.³² Shortly afterward Allied eavesdroppers overheard the 156th Division broadcasting orders to its subordinate regiments.³³ During the final days of July, another division, the 146th, was pinpointed in southernmost Kyushu along with three tank brigades.³⁴ ULTRA now confirmed nine divisions already on the island. The estimate of Japanese troops now ballooned to 455,000.³⁵

But the most important ULTRA find was a newly organized Fortieth Army headquarters in southwestern Kyushu. No longer was the Japanese high command regarding northern and southern Kyushu as equally liable for invasion. Two army headquarters in the south meant the Japanese had decided the invaders would hit the southern beaches. That was where they were concentrating their divisions. The allies had counted on Japanese defenders being dispersed throughout Kyushu. That was no longer true. The Kyushu reinforcements were swarming into the very areas designated for the OLYMPIC landings. Estimates of Japanese troops swelled to 525,000.³⁶

What the high command expected from its soldiers was also chillingly explicit. In early July the general staff completely reversed Japanese defensive doctrine. ULTRA provided, in Tokyo's own words, a preview of Kyushu's defense. According to Imperial Headquarters' guidance, air and sea forces had to annihilate the invaders at sea. If the allies were bold enough to risk a landing on Japan proper, a full-scale offensive would be launched. Fighting at the water's edge was a dramatic reversal of defensive doctrine, a return to the abandoned doctrine of 1943–44. Ground forces would expose enemy weaknesses at the water's edge then destroy him on the coast. If the enemy managed to establish a lodgment, mobile troops would counterattack and smash it by repeated attacks. Coastal troops would cover the concentration of the mobile units into attack assembly areas. No matter what tactically important points the Allies took, divisions deployed along the coast could not retreat. Continual counterattacks were the order of the day, and Japanese soldiers could not depend on passive defensive tactics. From the high command to the lowest private soldier, everyone would act boldly, aggressively, and decisively.³⁷ Either Japanese soldiers would die in their pillboxes and foxholes dotting Kyushu's beaches, or they would die attacking the invaders. But they were expected to die defending their sacred homeland.

The number one target on the beaches during an invasion was enemy tanks. Armor was the backbone of Allied ground units, and without it they would falter. Japanese units would build anti-tank defenses in-depth from the water's edge inland. Engineers would demolish all coastal roads forcing tanks into rugged terrain where they would be vulnerable to attack by small suicide units. Tokyo ordered all officers and men, regardless of branch or service, to carry out such suicide attacks.[38]

Navy pilots too would join the fighting at the water's edge. For them success depended on crashing into allied attack transports and landing craft while they were still loaded with troops. The floatplane kamikaze pilots, previously identified by ULTRA, were known to be practicing shoreline attacks. Their one-way mission was to smash into landing craft headed for shore.[39] Of the 2700 navy suicide training planes, 775 were already deployed somewhere in Kyushu.[40] Naval authorities claimed air and sea kamikazes could sink 30 to 40 percent of the invading convoy—more if the invasion came after August, because there would be more ships and thus more targets. Army staff officers were more conservative, but still expected 10 or 20 percent losses.[41]

The Japanese high command made the purpose of these suicidal measures brutally explicit. ULTRA told of the Japanese military's intention to inflict severe losses on the Allies. In so doing they expected to prolong the war and thereby convince the Allies of the futility of further bloody fighting.[42] These stark military objectives paralleled efforts by elites at the imperial court and the foreign ministry to obtain a negotiated peace for Japan.

ULTRA even let the Allies peer over their enemies' shoulders as Japanese commanders war-gamed the defense of the homeland. These practice maneuvers correctly predicted an Allied landing in southern Kyushu. D-day was forecast for 20 August. By D plus 15 the tabletop maneuvers had ten U.S. divisions ashore in southern Kyushu, but heavy fighting on the beaches still contained the invaders' amphibious lodgment. In this scenario, two American airborne divisions had dropped behind Japanese lines, but mobile forces had quickly counterattacked to check them.[43] From these June map maneuvers, Tokyo concluded a third of the assault troops could be destroyed at sea and another 15 to 20 percent of the first assault wave killed by artillery or beach defenses.[44]

As ULTRA continued to uncover more and more Japanese divisions in southern Kyushu, the forecast for the invasion steadily worsened. Six more Japanese divisions appeared in Kyushu during June and July, and even more reinforcements were on the way. The odds were against the invaders, because the defenders would soon equal or outnumber the attackers on the beaches. This was, as Willoughby candidly put it, "hardly a recipe for success."[45] On 1 August, because of the accelerated buildup of Japanese reinforcements on the island of Kyushu, General

Headquarters ordered an immediate air campaign to destroy bridges, railroads, barges, ports, and anything moving on Kyushu's roads.[46] It came too late to stop, or even slow down, the movement of troops.

During the first week of August, ULTRA identified four new divisions in Kyushu. The 312th Division had deployed there from central Japan. Washington now credited 545,000 Japanese soldiers on Kyushu.[47] ULTRA confirmed two other divisions, the 216th and the 303d, four days later.[48] In between a 351st Division was mentioned in messages passed from Imperial Headquarters to the Sixteenth Area Army in charge of the overall defense of Kyushu.[49] By now ULTRA had divulged thirteen of the fourteen Japanese divisions defending Kyushu. Besides the infantry divisions, the Fourth Artillery Command appeared in southwestern Kyushu to complement the First Artillery Command located on the southeastern half of the island.[50] As artillery coordination centers, they controlled at least six medium artillery regiments as well as two heavy artillery battalions.[51] Rocket gun units assigned to infantry regiments in the newly organized infantry divisions increased their firepower, making them seem quite formidable.[52] Washington's estimate of Japanese troops on the island jumped to 560,000.

These numbers were far beyond the original estimates used to plan the invasion. More troubling than the sheer number of divisions was their steady attraction to southernmost Kyushu. It was as though the beaches selected for the OLYMPIC landings were magnets pulling the Japanese to them. Following electronic footprints left by routine radio transmissions from mobile headquarters, Allied intelligence experts tracked the 86th Division from central Kyushu to Ariake Bay, where XI Corps would land. The 146th and 206th divisions had moved to the beaches of the southwest coast where V Amphibious Corps would invade. As mobile reserves, the 77th Division would have to contend with rugged terrain but might move against either landing area. In any case, it sat perched on Kagoshima City, the V Amphibious Corps' objective. And the 212th was readying to move farther south into the I Corps landing zone.[53] This buildup, stacking enemy troops on the very landing beaches, the accompanying tactics, and the overall Japanese objective of inflicting as many Allied casualties as possible were Marshall's preview of hell. A professional soldier could easily visualize the bloody carnage along the beachheads. The assault troops needed every weapon America possessed to get them across the beaches and inland with the fewest possible losses. By now these weapons included the atomic bomb.

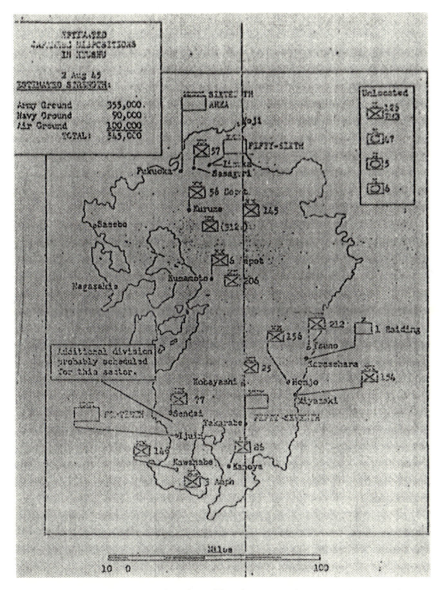

FIGURE 10. Japanese ground order of battle in Kyushu appearing in 2 August 1945 "'MAGIC' Summary, Far East Supplement." Courtesy of National Archives and Records Administration

Sometime earlier Marshall had asked Major General Leslie Groves, director of America's atomic bomb program, about using atomic bombs as tactical weapons. On 30 July Groves's written report of the bomb's tactical possibilities reached Marshall. The bomb blast alone could wipe out enemy resistance over an area 2000 feet in diameter, paralyze it seriously over a mile in diameter, and hinder it seriously over an area of 5 miles in diameter. The blast effect would kill soldiers in slit trenches within 800 feet of the explosion, but troops sheltering in deep caves a mile or so from ground zero would survive to fight. Eleven or twelve bombs might be ready by the invasion date.[54] In the meantime the bomb would be used as a strategic weapon against Japan's cities. Many thought the evidence of its awesome destructiveness would be enough to force Japan's surrender.

The first atomic bomb exploded on Hiroshima but without the results Marshall expected; it did not shock Japan's leaders into surrender. Codebreakers read dispassionate eyewitness Japanese military assessments from Hiroshima downplaying the enormous destruction. One vivid ULTRA description of 100,000 casualties actually seems to have affected Truman more than Japan's warlords. While they looked for countermeasures for atomic bombs, he secretly ordered no more bombs to be used without his express approval.[55] Marshall saw Hiroshima against a larger backdrop of strategic bombing. According to a deciphered message, an earlier air raid had killed 100,000 Japanese people in the capital of Tokyo in a single night, but seemingly had no effect whatsoever on Japanese determination to fight on. Even worse destruction to Hiroshima yielded no surrender. Japan seemed determined to fight. An invasion was still likely.[56] Indeed ULTRA had located three more Japanese divisions on Kyushu the day the Hiroshima bomb was dropped. The Sixteenth Area Army now had 600,000 troops on Kyushu and expected even more.

The quality of the divisions defending Kyushu varied enormously. There were first-class outfits, such as the Twenty-fifth and Fifty-seventh Divisions. Many of the newer ones though were desperately short of equipment, even uniforms. Training often consisted of slogans, because weapons were lacking. Certainly soldiers in line units knew little about higher headquarters' grand operational plans. One young lieutenant had the vague notion that three days after the enemy landing his company would be thrown against the beachhead. It would be, their division commander assured them, a most splendid death.[57] A conscript in another newly raised formation saw a vicious cycle of corruption undermining discipline, as soldiers openly traded gasoline for food on the black market. When the division commander arrived to inspect his brand new unit, his staff car, a luxury in itself, was crammed full of fresh meat, poultry, and vegetables. A recalled veteran of the China front wondered aloud if the general had come to inspect the officers' wives.[58] Other recruits, many previously graded 4-F, resorted to black humor, referring to themselves as victim units.[59] But it was one thing to be sullen and insubordinate, quite another to be openly defeatist. Except for the war minister, no Japanese soldier had any inkling about Japan's efforts to end the war. Besides, for a front-line soldier or sailor to surrender was a court-martial offense punishable by death. So the Kyushu reinforcements were a mixed bag, some just rag-tag units. Yet they were already digging in along the very beaches where the Americans would land. The invasion would be costly. The enemy would be fighting in prepared positions, for their homes, and for their families. They had nothing to gain by surrender, and everything to lose by defeat. And bitter experience from Guadalcanal to Okinawa made clear that they could be expected to fight to the death.

Seen or, more accurately, listened to from afar, the deficiencies of the new divisions were not that apparent. A special War Department analysis of the new Japanese divisions reached Marshall around 6 August. From 1937 to 1943, the Japanese army mobilized an average of eight divisions per year. In 1944 thirty were formed. But in the first seven months of 1945, at least forty-two were activated, twenty-three in Japan itself. And Japan had the potential manpower to create even more divisions, as many as sixty-five infantry and five armored by the time of the invasion. Equipment, especially artillery, was deficient, but the Japanese use of rocket units made up for their lack of artillery. According to decrypted messages, a single twenty-four-round volley from a rocket gun produced the equivalent in weight to 120 155-mm U.S. projectiles.[60] A bored naval watch officer in Hawaii noted in his log with malicious delight that all the "experts" on the Japanese army were quietly burning their estimates on enemy ground strength for late 1945 or early 1946.[61] To Marshall it was no laughing matter. The Japanese army was still expanding and would continue to right up to the invasion.

On 7 August, the day after the Hiroshima bombing, Marshall sent an "Eyes Only" message to MacArthur. He said he was frankly worried by intelligence reports about the large enemy buildup both of divisions and of air forces in Kyushu and southern Honshu. Marshall also foresaw the likelihood of discussions in Washington about the reported Japanese reinforcements. Did it make sense to attack into the teeth of the Japanese defenses? Maybe it was better to shift OLYMPIC to less well fortified places like Tokyo, Sendai, and Ōminato? What did MacArthur think? Imagine Marshall sending such a cable to Eisenhower asking him to consider switching the Normandy invasion to Norway just three months before D-day! MacArthur's reply, received two days later, dismissed reports of reinforcements as "greatly exaggerated." Besides there was no reason to change OLYMPIC in the slightest. Overwhelming logistical difficulties, exacerbated by his air campaign, would isolate and weaken Japanese forces on Kyushu before the invasion.[62]

MacArthur's determination to lead the greatest amphibious operation in history blinded him to ULTRA's disclosure of the growing risks of invasion. Indeed throughout the war, MacArthur had paid scant attention to intelligence forecasts urging caution or delay. He once remarked that there were only three great intelligence officers in the history of warfare "and mine is not one of them."[63] So far, talent, generalship, and good luck had allowed him to treat intelligence in such a cavalier fashion.

After Hiroshima (6 August), the Soviet declaration of war against Japan (8 August), and Nagasaki (9 August), the Japanese still offered only a conditional surrender (10 August). A rapid series of shock actions—each one thought capable by itself of forcing immediate capitulation—had failed to produce Japan's unconditional surrender. Grave doubts had replaced the certainties of a week before. Atomic bombs had not forced the Japanese to surrender, nor had the Soviet entry into the war. Thirteen divisions, not the anticipated ten, now protected Kyushu, and more were thought en route to the island fortress. Expected counter-amphibious doctrine was completely reversed, calling for all-out bloodletting on the beaches. The Imperial Army was mobilizing new divisions at a record pace. What other surprises could the Japanese have waiting for the Americans?

As far as Marshall, or anyone else knew, it would still take an invasion to subdue Japan. Impressions of blood-soaked Omaha Beach enabled him to picture the hell awaiting GIs on Kyushu's shores. MacArthur told him that to postpone or change the invasion was unacceptable. ULTRA told him the Japanese defenders were still massing on the proposed landing beaches. Groves told him the bomb could be used as a tactical weapon. Marshall needed some way to reverse the preview of hell on Japan's beaches. If the bombs could not shock the Japanese government into surrender, and judging from ULTRA reports and Japanese public braggadocio, they could not, then the bombs could be used to soften up invasion beaches before the American landings.

On 10 August Marshall instructed Groves that the third atomic bomb, which would be ready by the sixteenth, would not be dropped without the express authority of the president.[64] Truman was appalled at the thought of "wiping out" another "100,000 people." According to a confidant, he did not want to drop another atomic bomb on a Japanese city.[65] The next day Marshall told Groves not to ship more fissionable material to the Pacific. Then the head of army intelligence told Marshall not to expect atomic bombs to have a decisive effect in the next thirty days.[66] Believing further atomic attacks against Japanese cities would not force capitulation—and the days passed without any sign of Japan's unconditional surrender—Marshall reconsidered using the bomb as a tactical weapon. On the thirteenth, Lieutenant General John E. Hull, the assistant chief of staff for operations and plans, phoned Groves's aide, Colonel L. E. Seeman. Hull told Seeman about Marshall's idea for using atomic bombs in direct support of operations.[67]

Seeman said seven bombs might be available by the OLYMPIC invasion date. Then they talked about tactical bombs to support the landing forces. Seeman confirmed what Groves had earlier told Marshall. With U.S. soldiers and marines on ships about 6 miles offshore, atomic bombs would clear beaches by blast effect. A few days later the invaders would land. If the Japanese decided to continue the war, Hull, echoing the army G-2's estimate, doubted another atomic attack against a city would convince them to surrender.[68] In other words, Marshall now regarded the tactical use of atomic bombs to support the Kyushu invasion as a realistic alternative to the continued pounding of Japanese cities.[69]

Japan's seeming unwillingness to surrender unconditionally did shape Marshall's thinking. But the driving force behind his emerging plan to use atomic bombs on Japan's beaches was the intelligence sneak preview of thousands and thousands of Japanese infantrymen awaiting American GIs and marines on the landing beaches. ULTRA made Marshall well aware of the tough Japanese infantrymen waiting patiently for the invasion in their concrete pillboxes, camouflaged earth and log revetments, tunnels, caves, and rifle pits behind obstacle-strewn beaches and shorelines sowed with mines. Only their emperor or death could move them. Marshall's ULTRA-derived forecast gives special meaning to his later comment: "We had to visualize very heavy casualties unless we had enough atomic bombs at the time to supplement the troop action, if the bomb proved satisfactory for that purpose."[70] Japan's surrender made such decisions unnecessary. But what if the militarists had insisted on a fight to the bitter end?

An atomic attack on such a scale along Kyushu's shores would have rendered Hiroshima and Nagasaki mere footnotes to history. The atomic hell on the beaches though would have seared both ways. Thousands of Japanese troops, not to mention numerous Japanese civilians, would have immediately died on or near the beaches. But for those who survived the blast, including the American GIs and marines who would land on the radioactive beaches, a personal agony of radiation poisoning might just be beginning. Because no one yet understood the full implications of radioactive fallout, an atomic hell on the beaches would have been followed by a lingering one for veterans of both sides for decades. OLYMPIC would not have invaded the land of the gods but the world of the dead.

CHAPTER TWELVE

CHASING A DECISIVE VICTORY
*Emperor Hirohito and Japan's War
with the West (1941-1945)*

Between 18 March and 8 April 1946, Emperor Hirohito narrated his version of his tumultuous reign to a tiny circle of five court intimates. The five took notes of the imperial account as told to them in five sessions held on four separate days. One of them, Terasaki Hidenari, then an imperial household official after a varied foreign ministry career, based on his notes prepared an abbreviated version of the meetings. He placed his version, dated 1 June 1946, with his diary where it would remain unread for more than forty years.¹

Terasaki himself was a fascinating figure. He belonged to the staff of the Japanese Embassy in Washington DC in the months before Pearl Harbor. With his American wife, Gwen, whom he married in 1931; his fluent English; and his Ivy League connections—he was a Brown graduate—Terasaki seemed perfectly suited to present Japan's cause to the American government. Alas, he was too perfect because, in the words of Gerhard Krebs, Terasaki was "Japan's master spy in the Western Hemisphere." His duties included overseeing Japanese espionage activities in North and South America, paying spies, agents, and informants, as well as clandestinely collecting intelligence for Japan. Because the American authorities were decrypting Japanese diplomatic ciphers, they were well aware of Terasaki's double game.² They feared expelling or later prosecuting Terasaki for espionage might alert the Japanese foreign ministry to its porous cipher system. So Terasaki, his wife, and their young daughter, Mariko, were repatriated to Japan in 1942 where he spent the war working for the foreign ministry.

Given his background, it seems all the more remarkable that during the American occupation of Japan, General Headquarters allowed, indeed encouraged, Terasaki to serve as the emperor's liaison with General Douglas MacArthur, Supreme Commander for the Allied Powers (SCAP). Yet the reason was simple. Occupation authorities confronted Terasaki with his earlier espionage and pressured him into becoming an American controlled intelligence source reporting on the activities of Japanese political and military factions late in the war.[3] As an imperial counselor Terasaki was indeed a high-level American informant, and it was in his capacity as counselor that he participated in transcribing the emperor's monologue. Suffering from chronic hypertension coupled with overwork, Terasaki died at age fifty in 1951.

Gwen Terasaki published her memoirs, titled *Bridge to the Sun*, in 1957. The well received book became the basis for a movie of the same name starring James Shibata and Carol Baker. In 1958 Gwen received Hidenari's papers from his younger brother, but being unable to read Japanese, stored the materials with other of her late husband's effects. Years later Mariko's son took an interest in his grandfather and had the papers evaluated. Shortly afterward in 1988 Mariko decided to turn her father's notes over to *Bungei shunjū*, a major general-interest monthly magazine with a circulation of about 750,000. The emperor's monologue originally appeared in published form in the December 1990 issue of *Bungei shunjū* magazine, creating an immediate sensation in Japan. The publishing company reissued the document along with Terasaki's diary in book form in 1991. It became a best-seller going through four printings and selling 140,000 copies in just three months.[4] At long last Hirohito was speaking his mind about the war waged in his name.

As for so much about the late emperor, though, a great portion of his monologue remains unclear. Why, for instance, did he decide to leave such an account? One imperial counselor wrote that the account was to be the emperor's record of issues (*mondai*) related to the war crimes trials.[5] But by the time the monologue was transcribed, Hirohito already knew that he would not be indicted as a war criminal.

In September 1945 Washington had told MacArthur to take no action against the emperor as a war criminal pending further instructions.[6] That guidance came from the JCS in late November when they instructed MacArthur to investigate whether sufficient evidence existed to indict the emperor.[7] On 25 January 1946 the general responded in a lengthy communiqué that such a decision was beyond his level. Thus he warned Washington that if Hirohito were tried SCAP might need around 1 million American troops stationed indefinitely in Japan to maintain order.[8] MacArthur was well aware of the enormous public pressure in the United States for ever more rapid demobilization and reasoned correctly that the specter of an enormous occupation force would tip the balance against trying Hirohito. To be safe, the general also suborned the chief Allied prosecutor, telling him the emperor was not only off limits as a defendant, but also as a witness.[9] A few weeks later, on 13 February, Major General Courtney Whitney, one of MacArthur's senior staff officers then in charge while drafting Japan's new constitution, told high-ranking Japanese officials that the emperor would not be tried as a war criminal despite pressure to do so.[10]

Nonetheless, the International Military Tribunal for the Far East—the Tokyo Trial—was scheduled to convene on 3 May 1946, and the monologue may have been prepared in anticipation of the emperor's defense.[11] Conversely it may have been prepared as a friend of the court brief to assist the prosecution.[12] It could also have been prepared in anticipation of Hirohito's imminent abdication, because in late February Prince Mikasa suggested Hirohito was considering such a move, and on 20 March Terasaki sounded out a senior SCAP member about MacArthur's feelings on Hirohito's possible resignation.[13] Or it may simply have been prepared by a man who wanted his own views on the historical record. Whatever the reason, the appearance of the emperor's monologue has given us a point of departure, described to us in Hirohito's own words, to assess his wartime conduct.

Hirohito has been variously described as a pacifist, a reactionary, a constitutional monarch, a warmonger, a nationalist, and a victim of machinations by others. Before the monologue appeared, speculation substituted for evidence resulting in such widely contradictory interpretations of the emperor's role in Japan's war with the West (1941–45). The imperial version of events confirms previous conjecture and highlights shared assumptions that influenced key decisions.[14] Based on Hirohito's own words, my contention is that historical precedent combined with shared national values shaped Hirohito and his military and naval advisers' response to wartime events.

In Japan during the 1930s and 1940s, the experience of the Russo-Japanese War (1904–5) was the touchstone when history was used for the business of state. The war validated the bedrock principles of military discipline—nationalism, patriotism, and service to the emperor. Victory in that earlier conflict also ultimately shifted the basic assumptions of Japanese about themselves. Heretofore Japan looked to the West not only for material but also for ideological guidance. Such dependency acknowledged Japan's inferior status vis à vis the Western powers. After 1905 Japanese searched for national sources to explain their military and economic progress. Building on, adapting, and creating ideology, the government carefully cultivated the sense of national identity provided by Japan's triumph over the West. The new universally recognized and unquestioningly accepted models elevated the imperial house, according to one scholar, "as central not only to the nation but also to the fabric of society itself."[15]

These core values plus the accretion of myths, beliefs, faith, and customs binding the members of society together were embedded in the nation's culture. None was more powerful than *kokutai*, the notion of Imperial Japan as a unique nation by virtue of its sacred emperor. *Kokutai* remains difficult to define precisely in a few words, because the concept meant different things to different groups in Japan. Two examples: for Hirohito it meant the responsibility to his imperial ancestors to preserve the unbroken imperial line; for his imperial army it meant the preservation of the imperial system (*tennō-sei*), which became the repository for the values and virtues of the imperial army.[16]

Another inheritance from the Russo-Japanese War, especially relevant in military thought, was the concept of a decisive victory. Japan's overwhelming naval triumph in the Battle of the Japan Sea (1905) became the model for the definitive engagement—a single great battle deciding the war against a major European power in Japan's favor. As with *kokutai*, a definition of decisive battle is elusive, because its meaning evolved between 1941 and 1945 from victory, to negotiated truce, to bloody stalemate.

Japan's war with the West linked the concepts of *kokutai* and decisive victory. None of Japan's foreign wars and adventures since 1905 had been fought with the fate of the nation at stake. Even the great losses from Japan's undeclared war in China did not threaten Japan's national survival. A war with a third- or fourth-rate power, such as China, was one thing; war against two first-class Western powers was quite another. Hirohito's nightmare was that a confrontation erupting in one of China's international treaty zones, such as Tientsin or Peiping, might bring about a clash of arms with the Anglo-American powers.[17] Losing a war against major Caucasian powers would imperil national survival and *kokutai*. To preclude such a catastrophe, Japan required a decisive victory, either to win or to end the conflict. Japan's generals and admirals were responsible for planning and executing the master stroke. The most senior among them were accountable for keeping the emperor informed of military developments designed to achieve that goal.

The war and navy ministers personally advised the emperor on administrative matters of military import. The chiefs of the army and navy general staffs counseled him on operational ones. In all cases these generals and admirals relied on middle grade officers—colonels, majors, and captains—to prepare position papers or responses to imperial questions. Because the liaison conferences with the emperor involved operational affairs, midlevel staff officers in the army or navy general staffs drafted papers, staffed them to war, navy, and foreign ministries for comments and revisions, then revised them as required following liaison conference discussions—a classic example of the traditional Japanese practice of *ringisei* (lit. circular letter system).[18] If the emperor asked questions, as he did frequently, the generals returned to the majors and captains for answers. As for operational orders or directives, the responsible chief of staff had an imperial audience and submitted the appropriate documents to the throne for imperial sanction. If the emperor made further inquiries, his military aide-de-camp or the answerable aide-de-camp would relay the question to the proper office. In the case of operational orders, the respective staff responsible for the order would be asked for a response.[19]

The chief aide-de-camp attended meetings of senior leaders, but withdrew from the imperial chamber after scheduled matters were formally reported to the throne. This allowed the emperor to ask direct questions and chat informally with the service chiefs and was a major source of his detailed information about military and naval affairs. The chief aide-de-camp was not necessarily informed of these conversations unless other questions arose from them. In such cases, Hirohito's aide-de-camp would task the appropriate general staff office to provide answers to the aide for direct reply to emperor.[20]

The briefings Hirohito received were presented as information and not for decision making. Nevertheless they offered the emperor a fairly detailed grasp of military operations from the Japanese perspective. To believe that Hirohito was briefed "usually in the most general terms"[21] about military policies is incorrect. It slights the emperor's influence, as opposed to actual power, and oversimplifies his interaction with his military chieftains during these meetings. There was plenty of give and take at these imperial audiences as opposed to the highly ritualized Imperial Conferences.

By the time of Prince Konoe Fumimaro's short-lived third cabinet (18 July–18 October 1941), the army and navy leaders who would direct Japan's war against the West were already onboard. General Tōjō Hideki, the incumbent war minister, would succeed Konoe as prime minister. As prime minister, Tōjō retained his war minister portfolio, because he was still on active duty and served concurrently in both offices. He later added munitions minister and chief of the army general staff duties to his posts. General Sugiyama Hajime served as chief of the army general staff until replaced by Tōjō in February 1944. Sugiyama then became war minister, serving to April 1945. As for the Imperial Navy, Konoe's navy minister was Oikawa Koshiro, whom Tōjō replaced with Shimada Shigetarō in October 1941. Shimada served as navy minister until July 1944. Admiral Nagano Osami was chief of the naval general staff to February 1944 when Shimada replaced him and served concurrent appointments.

It is Hirohito the Shōwa emperor personally who tells us from his own lips his perspective on the tumultuous events between 1926 and 1945. Hirohito was forty-one years old in 1941, sixteen years younger than his youngest military adviser. He had ascended the throne in December 1925, but having served as regent for his mentally incapacitated father since 1921, he had, in effect, been emperor for twenty years. The tumultuous span witnessed Japanese aggression abroad, political terrorism at home, and the rise of Japan's military to a predominant role in affairs of state.

By all accounts, Hirohito was extremely intelligent and gifted with a remarkable memory. His scientific bent was well known, and he also took a keen interest in military affairs, perhaps a hangover from his childhood indoctrination in such matters. Hirohito made clear in the opening lines of his monologue his commitment to Japanese nationalism. The root causes of Japan's war with the West, according to the emperor, were the failure to insert a racial equality clause in the Versailles Treaty ending World War I and the California anti-Japanese exclusion acts.[22] Japan's aggressive expansion into Asia goes unquestioned, because the Great Japanese Empire (*Dai Nippon Teikoku*) was a given.

The emperor seemed full of nervous energy, wanting answers, action, or results immediately. When they were not forthcoming, Hirohito flashed a temper or resorted to sarcasm. He was often irritable, especially as the war turned against Japan and, for a Japanese, exceptionally frank. Hirohito tended, if we take his own words for it, to blame those around him for what went wrong. His later lament, for instance, about the causes for Japan's defeat included the pointed remark about the absence of men of the caliber of the military and political leaders of the Russo-Japanese War.[23] His monologue is peppered with caustic comments aimed at almost all his advisers. The man seems to have genuinely liked very few people.

This may be because of his introverted personality. Possessed of a conservative, even passive, character, Hirohito's innate caution pushed him to rely on advisers, mainly courtiers, rather than his instincts. But timidity was the institutionalized role of Japanese emperors. Even Hirohito's illustrious grandfather Meiji did not lead, but endured during his wars.[24] Nonetheless Hirohito developed an abiding respect and affection for his imperial forces that lasted throughout the war. In his official capacity as supreme commander he often appeared in public in uniform, riding his white horse. By reviewing troops, attending ceremonies, and seeing off departing servicemen, he not only symbolized the legitimacy of Japan's war but also lent imperial sanction to the conflict.[25] He fulfilled this role to the end. Between 2 January and 19 June 1945, for example, Hirohito, resplendent in his full dress army uniform, medals, and sword, presided at eight palace ceremonies where he bestowed 103 regimental colors—for the 103 new regiments mobilized for homeland defense. On 10 August 1945, he remarked how unbearable it was for his brave and loyal army to be disbanded and punished for war crimes.[26]

An orderly, bookish, and bright person, Hirohito possessed an excellent memory. He relied on these traits to keep close track of military operations. Between September 1941 and December 1944, he listened to 145 presentations on army operations. From October through December 1944 alone, navy leaders briefed him more than 100 times.[27] And he often became nervous or impatient when officers blathered on instead of directly answering his penetrating questions. Outwardly the bemedaled symbol of Japanese militarism, inwardly Hirohito was an introverted, even timid, person, who constantly sought reassurances, because his commanders could not guarantee him victory over the West.

During the course of Japan's war with the West, the emperor's main military advisers shuffled in, out, and around between 1941 and 1945. As they did, the style, tone, and content of advice to the throne also changed. Nagano, Shimada, Sugiyama, and Tōjō had the longest tenure with Hirohito during the war. How did they interact with the throne? What sort of advice did they provide to Hirohito?

Fifty-eight-year-old Nagano was so notorious for sleeping through conferences that young staff officers derided him as "the dozing admiral." He would sometimes fall asleep during meetings with a burning cigarette

FIGURE 11. Hirohito, on his favorite horse, Shirayuki (White Snow), reviews his troops in May 1941. Courtesy of USAMHI, Japan Miscellaneous Collection

dangling from his lower lip. The pressures of wartime and perhaps those of a fourth, and much younger wife, reinforced Nagano's proclivity to nod off during conferences. More damaging was his inability to formulate a strategic vision for the Imperial Navy or for Hirohito. Full of fight but not sure where to fight, he was called a hawk without a strategy.[28]

Navy Minister Oikawa was also fifty-eight years old. He is best remembered for questioning the foreign minister's sanity during a liaison conference. A mild, scholarly man, Oikawa liked to please everyone, a feat made especially difficult as naval factions grappled with the implications of war with the West. Still Oikawa usually accomplished his goals through ambiguity.[29] As navy minister he presided over the navy's acquiescence to the Tri-Partite Pact, because he lacked the courage to maintain opposition to the alliance.[30] Neither did Oikawa openly state his opposition to war with the United States, providing instead an "enigmatic reluctance to say whether Japan was ready for war or not."[31] Instead of clarity, Oikawa promoted obfuscation during the critical months from July to October 1941.

When Tōjō came to power he replaced Oikawa in the navy ministry with Admiral Shimada Shigetarō. The fifty-eight-year-old admiral was frankly miscast as navy minister. He lacked the skills of a military bureaucrat, being inept at political infighting or court politics. As did many Japanese navy officers, Shimada understood the risks of war with America but viewed the conflict as inevitable.[32] By late 1941, he believed that it was impossible to oppose war, because a breakdown of domestic law and order would result. Instead of devoting all his time to thinking through the momentous issues of war and peace, between 17 October 1941 and the end of that fateful year he visited various Shinto shrines at least twenty-eight times, perhaps praying for divine inspiration.[33]

Shimada was an intelligent if colorless personality, sometimes lacking common sense. Told by veterans, for instance, of the need to avoid a repetition of the losses at Attu or Tarawa, Shimada remarked that the loss of one or two islands was no reason for alarm.[34] His demeanor changed in neither victory nor defeat. The same was true of his daily routine. After rising, he prayed at the Meiji Shrine, then had breakfast. He arrived at the navy ministry every morning at 0805 sharp and left at 1730 every evening. Shimada disliked drinking, so nights out were rare, and he had little time for politicians, bureaucrats, or anyone else. More important he held the office position of prime minister, and thus Tōjō, almost in awe. His allegiance, not to say subservience, earned him ridicule as "Tōjō's adjutant" and much worse. During his tenure as navy minister and as chief of the naval general staff any advice he passed to the emperor came from Tōjō's brain.[35]

As for army chief of staff Sugiyama, he was always discreet and discriminating, a methodical, diligent personality from childhood. Lacking imagination and anxious to please, he fell victim to his own self-fulfilling prophecy. Twenty years older than Hirohito, at age sixty-one he still referred to himself as "the emperor's whipping boy" and believed it his job to accept imperial rebukes.[36] When the emperor vented his imperial anger and frustration, Sugiyama would shrug his shoulders and hang his head. His physical appearance exacerbated his body language. Sugiyama was a powerfully built man in top-notch physical shape, but his left eyelid drooped, his eyes were narrow, and he looked like an old country bumpkin. His countenance reminded many of someone lost in a fog, and junior officers derided him as "the out-of-touch field marshal." More senior officers referred to him as the "bathroom door," because his opinions swung whichever way he was last pushed. Yet Sugiyama was ever conscious of his role and duty to the emperor and the nation. "I think," he wrote, "I personally have to bear responsibility to His Imperial Majesty and to the people simultaneously. My burden is a greater one than the prime minister's."[37] Unlike Nagano, Sugiyama did not sleep through Imperial Conferences; he literally sweated through them often complaining about the cold, clammy perspiration running down his back in the presence of the emperor. His procrastination and prevarication misled Hirohito, sometimes intentionally. Sugiyama, true to form, eventually swung whichever way the emperor pushed. But similar to a swinging door, he never made progress. He just returned to his original position. His was a frustrating personality to deal with.

Prime Minister Tōjō, aged fifty-seven, was the best of this lot, which alone may account for Hirohito's favorable comments about his prime minister who led Japan to war with the West. But Tōjō did have undeniable talent. He was well organized and single-minded. Wine, women, and song bored him. So apparently did his family. Only once in fourteen years, for example, did he take his children to the movies.[38] Instead Tōjō cherished his regulations and respected the throne and the emperor. He treated Hirohito with respect and as an adult. As he put it, "In so far as I am able, in the process of studying serious issues, I bear in mind reporting these to the throne. Consequently, because His Imperial Majesty fully understands developments, when I present a draft for decision, it receives imperial approval without wasting time. Providing interim reports allows the true expression of direct imperial rule."[39] Tōjō's description accords with accounts of his close associates that the prime minister would appear several times at court to gauge the emperor's mood before cautiously presenting his report.[40] It was mutual admiration between two meticulous petty bureaucrats more concerned about forms than about people.

The same Tōjō who would get teary eyed talking to wounded soldiers kept his military policemen busy rummaging through garbage to keep up on what people were thinking. On his morning constitutional, Tōjō himself poked through people's trash ostensibly because of his concern about the smallest details of citizens' lives.[41] Still the reaction to his heavy-handed use of the military police was one reason Hirohito gave for Tōjō's downfall.[42] Tōjō gathered greater power during the war, but at heart he remained a competent military bureaucrat and was no strategic genius.

Marquis Kido Kōichi, lord keeper of the privy seal, was a superb bureaucrat. More important he had the emperor's confidence. Closer in age, fifty-two, to Hirohito, he was more in tune with the younger man's thinking than were the older generals and admirals. Kido was brought into the palace, one scholar asserts, "to preserve the transcendence of the imperial institution."[43] His mission was to preserve *kokutai* and the imperial line. As the emperor's confidant, Kido interpreted the imperial will, negotiated it in politics and decision making, and recorded it for posterity. Kido was extremely intelligent, a skilled negotiator, devoted to the emperor, and a workaholic. It was said Kido made every office he held more important than it would have been in the hands of other men. And that was the rub. He was the best mind advising the emperor, yet Japan was in a ruinous war with the West, because he was allegedly too willing to appease the generals if it meant keeping the emperor above the political fray. To some Kido was too smart for his own good; to others a man of expediency, not morality; and to still others a hardheaded practical man, very pragmatic, who carefully planned every aspect of life.[44] All these assessments contain fragments of truth. Working behind palace walls, Kido was extremely well connected with anyone who mattered in wartime Japan.

These personalities were Japan's key decision makers in the summer of 1941 when relations with the United States went from poor to dangerous. Since early 1941, the Japanese ambassador to Washington DC had been negotiating with his counterparts in the U.S. State Department to resolve differences. On 24 July, however, Japanese troops occupied southern French Indochina. Hirohito had told Tōjō that such a move would provoke American reaction and cause the Japanese people to suffer. Tōjō ignored the advice, which later proved correct. The American president reacted by freezing Japanese assets and funds and embargoing oil shipments to Japan. Because the Imperial Navy would run out of oil in eighteen months, Japan had to make decisions on war or peace quickly. The general staffs accelerated preparations for war with the West. Kido described the emperor at this time in a "state of dread" over U.S.-Japan relations.[45] There was good reason. Only a few days before, Sugiyama had told Hirohito he thought the army would be all right for one year in a war with the West. Hirohito's comeback encapsulated the emperor's wartime thinking: the need for decisive victory to ensure Japan's survival. "If you say that, are you thinking of winning in one year?" Sugiyama's reply was also a wartime staple; he evaded answering the emperor's question directly.[46] The chase for the elusive decisive victory had begun.

On 31 July 1941, Hirohito and Admiral Nagano discussed policy regarding the United States. Although insofar as possible wishing to avoid conflict, Hirohito conjectured that if it came to war, he was confident about Japanese victory. He asked Nagano about the chances of winning a decisive naval victory over the Americans similar to Japan's smashing naval success against Imperial Russia at Tsushima in 1905. The admiral replied that Japan could win the war but that he could not promise a decisive victory as at Tsushima. When Hirohito expressed his concerns about the dangers and uncertainties of warfare, Nagano simply brushed his worries aside.[47] Instead of offering reassurance, Hirohito's naval chief of staff, being unclear about any strategy, offered his emperor vague platitudes. Small wonder that Hirohito fretted about the navy's readiness to wage war with the West.

The pattern repeated itself in early September. On the fifth of the month, Prime Minister Konoe Fumimaro, another master of procrastination, had informed the throne of the Fiftieth Liaison Conference's (held two days earlier) decision to pursue diplomatic negotiations with the United States while simultaneously preparing for war. If negotiations made no progress by the last ten days in October, Japan would go to war.[48] Surprised by the October timetable, Hirohito summoned both his chiefs of staff to the palace to question them about the decision.[49]

The ensuing meeting began around 1700 and went badly. The emperor demonstrated his grasp of minute military details of the impending operations, while he betrayed his nervousness and temper. Admonishing the chiefs to give priority to diplomacy over warfare, he questioned them about opening hostilities. Sugiyama blandly told Hirohito that things were on track for a five-month campaign to secure Malaya and the Philippines.[50] As war minister in 1937, hadn't Sugiyama, the emperor asked, told him the China Incident would be wrapped up in one month? Yes, but China was a big country replied a flustered and sweating Sugiyama. His voice rising in frustration, Hirohito sarcastically asked if the Pacific Ocean wasn't larger than China? Speechless and conscious of his burden, Sugiyama could only hang his head in embarrassment.[51]

More concerns flooded out of Hirohito. The planned amphibious operations worried him, more so because of the recent exercises held in Kyushu, where large numbers of transports were declared lost. He fretted about the suitability of the weather at the planned invasion beaches. Told over and over that ironclad guarantees were impossible, but everything was going according to plan, the agitated emperor's frustration rose along with his voice: "Is victory certain?" he shouted. Nagano responded, "I cannot say it is certain, but it is probable."[52] Again the emperor had sought reassurance about going to war, and again his respective chiefs of staff responded with evasive generalizations. Sugiyama left the meeting with the impression that the emperor was displaying "reasonable anxiety" about embarking on war with the West.[53] Rather than a confident generalissimo directing a master war plan, an apprehensive and nervous Hirohito was plainly worried about going to war with the West.

FIGURE 12. Meeting of the Supreme Council for the Direction of the War, September 1941. Courtesy of Mainichi shimbunsha.

Hirohito regarded Imperial Conferences as "funny things" (*okashinomono*), because everything had already been discussed and agreed on in cabinet or at liaison conferences. He tells us that only the lord keeper of the privy seal, in this case Kido, was in a position to oppose the proposed agenda. The highly structured nature of the Imperial Conferences denied the emperor any decision-making authority in such meetings.[54] Hirohito's explanation is accurate though disingenuous. The emperor's own questions directed to his ministers or military chieftains at the various advance meetings made it possible for him to influence the shape of the emerging consensus that would become the Imperial Conference agenda. Still to exercise authority during a conference was beyond the imperial pale. Just before the 6 September Imperial Conference, for example, Hirohito approached Kido about the advisability of speaking out at the meeting. Kido dissuaded the emperor from doing so.[55]

At the fateful conference, Nagano reiterated his belief in the high probability of victory, even in a protracted war, and warned of the dangers of an illusory, short-term settlement. Sugiyama argued that time was running out for Japan and restated that the last ten days of October was the time to complete preparations for war with the West.[56] As for Navy Minister Oikawa's presentation, Hirohito dismissed it as pure sophistry, and later described this particular conference "a really troublesome meeting,"[57] one reason being because the chiefs of staff merely restated the same opinions Hirohito has berated them for the previous day, while Oikawa remained evasive. Moreover neither service chief could articulate a comprehensive strategy for war with the West. At one of the most pivotal moments in the history of modern Japan, Hirohito's military leaders contravened his attempt to shape a consensus by simply ignoring his previous questions. They were determined to go to war notwithstanding the emperor's realistic concerns about the implications of war with the West.

As hopes for a diplomatic solution with the United States dimmed, Konoe resigned his premiership. Before doing so, he recommended Prince Higashikuni, Hirohito's uncle, as his successor, a move supported by the army. Both Privy Seal Kido and Hirohito vetoed the notion, however. Installing a member of the royal family in a responsible post just before the outbreak of the Pacific War might cause the imperial house to be blamed for starting the war. Likewise, to avoid responsibility settling on the imperial line for war with the West, Hirohito had earlier agreed to replace the imperial princes who had served as chiefs of staff for the army and navy, respectively. He also refused to endorse bellicose proclamations and continually warned his wartime prime ministers that to do so was contrary to the traditions of the imperial house.[58] Hirohito betrayed his naiveté expecting that such cosmetic actions would disassociate the throne from a war being waged in its name. Still these decisions about the imperial family demonstrated his keen awareness of his responsibility to his imperial ancestors not to endanger the unbroken succession and preservation of the imperial line (*bansei ikki*), which, after all underpinned *kokutai*.[59]

Tōjō Hideki, the incumbent war minister, now became concurrently the new prime minister, in large measure because Hirohito and others thought only Tōjō could control the army. Although Tōjō personally believed a diplomatic settlement was still possible, some prominent Japanese viewed his appointment as a harbinger of imminent conflict[60] or even as a decision for war.[61] In a sense, they were correct.

From 11 to 20 September, a small group of naval officers had convened at the Naval War College in Tokyo for tabletop maneuvers designed to validate war plans against the West. On 16 and 17 September, in a separate building located near the war college, an even more select group had war-gamed the Pearl Harbor attack.[62] Hirohito's second brother, Prince Takamatsu Nobuhito, a navy lieutenant commander, had attended some sessions of the war game scenarios, but seems not to have participated in the closed-door Pearl Harbor meetings. As for Hirohito, the general staff briefed him on 20 October about the army's prospects for the first stage of operations in war against Britain and America. He did not, however, learn about the navy's Pearl Harbor operation until later.[63]

Not coincidentally, between 11 September and 30 October fourteen liaison conferences grappled with the issue of war or peace. IGHQ planners were counting down for war with the West. On 29 October, the service chiefs of staff approved joint campaign plans for war, anticipating hostilities would commence around the beginning of December. This timetable meant the choices were peace at any price or war with a deadline of 30 November.[64] Meeting at 0730 on 1 November, Sugiyama told Tōjō the army general staff wanted to curtail diplomatic negotiations immediately in favor of a decision for war. Besides the complicated logistics of deploying thousands of troops to the southern front to meet Japan's timetable for war, Sugiyama argued, recalling the soldiers if a diplomatic agreement was reached would adversely affect their morale. That might be so said Tōjō, but it would be unacceptable to the emperor who favored continuing diplomatic overtures as long as possible.[65] Immediately after their discussion, both officers marched into the Sixty-sixth Liaison Conference with the basic issue of war or peace still not close to agreement.

Because no consensus existed, the conference turned into a marathon session lasting seventeen hours. Concessions to the United States were not seriously considered, yet the prospect of war with the United States was troubling.[66] If Japan did not go to war and three years later the American fleet attacked, would the navy have a chance of winning? Nagano was unsure. Will the Americans attack Japan in three years? That too, according to Nagano, was unclear. It was a fifty-fifty proposition. The foreign minister interjected that war was unnecessary. Nothing can be taken for granted, said Nagano, because in three years the southern defenses would be stronger as would the enemy fleets. Then when could Japan go to war and win? "Now!" shouted Nagano, "The chance won't come again." One suspects his interlocutor wished Nagano would have gone back to sleep. The dilemma was plain to army vice chief of staff Tsukada Ko. No one was willing to say, "Don't worry, even if it is a prolonged war. I will take responsibility." With the status quo unacceptable, war became inevitable.[67]

Following the lengthy conference, Tōjō reported the results to the emperor, who accepted the decision for war while hoping for a diplomatic breakthrough in the meantime.[68] The next day, 2 November, Nagano,

Sugiyama, and Tōjō met with the emperor. Among other things, Hirohito asked the trio their thoughts on the justification for war, projected initial losses, and air defense measures for Japan's major cities.

On Monday, 3 November, a national holiday in honor of the Emperor Meiji, Nagano and Shimada spent the morning with Admiral Yamamoto Isoroku, who was visiting Tokyo, going over the latest details of the Pearl Harbor attack, the plan having been explained to them much earlier.[69] That afternoon, Sugiyama and Nagano were again at the palace answering the emperor's latest concerns about the projected southern operations. Hirohito questioned Sugiyama about Hong Kong's place in the overall Malaya operation and then turned to Nagano to ask the navy's target date for operations. Nagano replied 8 December. Because Hirohito was still unaware of the Pearl Harbor plan, he naturally assumed operations would commence on Monday, 8 December, Tokyo time. Wasn't that a Monday, the emperor asked? Yes, replied Nagano, but the timing was good, because the defenders would be tired the day after a holiday. By not mentioning 8 December in Tokyo was 7 December in the Hawaiian Islands, Nagano deliberately kept the emperor in the dark. The navy's briefings, after all, had intentionally omitted any mention of the Hawaii attack for security reasons![70] Hirohito informed Kido of these discussions on the eve of the 5 November Imperial Conference.

That conference determined Japan would go to war with the West in early December, although diplomatic efforts to break the impasse with the United States would continue.[71] Thirty minutes after the Imperial Conference adjourned, Sugiyama and Nagano met with Hirohito in the ornate Phoenix Room to explain the operational plans of their respective services. Sugiyama described the army's general plan of campaign already well known to the emperor. Hirohito then heard for the first time from Nagano the details of the Hawaii operation. Combined Fleet, organized around six aircraft carriers, would launch a surprise air attack against the enemy's main fleet concentration catching it at anchor in Pearl Harbor. Capitalizing on surprise to catch the enemy warships at anchor, Nagano told his emperor, the pilots would likely sink two or three battleships and carriers. By 1700 hours the emperor had sanctioned the operational plans, including the Hawaii operation.[72]

Hirohito wanted further information about the results of the Pearl Harbor war games conducted during September. The chief aide-de-camp arranged for map maneuvers to be played before the emperor at the palace from 1300 to 1600 on Saturday, 15 November. Even though the observers for these paper exercises would be limited to the emperor, his war and navy ministers, and Hirohito's aide-de-camp, the navy excluded the Hawaii operation from the exercises, ostensibly to preserve secrecy although from whom is not clear. The compulsive secretiveness was all the more bizarre, because on the previous Saturday, 8 November, the chief aide-de-camp had brought to the emperor detailed written staff responses to his inquiries about the navy's planned attack on Hawaii.[73] On 19 November 1941, he formally applied his imperial seal to the operational plans as requested by the naval general staff and Headquarters, Combined Fleet.[74]

But the ever cautious Hirohito was already having second thoughts. Although the cabinet had opted for war, he asked Kido to get a second opinion by sounding out Japan's senior statesmen about the decision. Hirohito later asserted that their opinions against going to war were too abstruse to counter the facts and figures the cabinet members brought to bear.[75] To further the emperor's anxiety, on 30 November, Prince Takamatsu, who had attended some of the navy's war games, told him naval officers considered the chances of defeating the United States as fifty-fifty and at best sixty-forty. An Imperial Conference was set for the next day, so Hirohito hurriedly summoned the chief of the naval general staff and navy minister to the palace for reassurance.[76]

At the brief, twenty-five-minute meeting held during the deepening twilight, Nagano assured the emperor that all the plans were in order and at tomorrow's conference he would provide the throne with the exact details. If imperial sanction was given, the attacks would proceed as planned. Then Hirohito asked a seemingly odd, but actually critical, question: What did his navy intend to do if Germany quit the war in Europe? Shimada never hesitated. Germany was unreliable and, even if Japan washed its hands of the German allies, it would not affect operations.[77] This was a breathtaking opinion. After all German military success against Great Britain underpinned Japan's war plans. Hirohito was well aware of this strategic tenet and later criticized his military advisers of exaggerating German strength, thereby leaving Japan depending on a German victory.[78] Although Shimada hastened to add that the navy's morale was high and its crews confident about the Pearl Harbor attack,[79] what was Hirohito to make of this opinion?

The next day's Imperial Conference approved going to war with the West on 8 December 1941, Tokyo time. Given his evident concern and constant worry, why didn't Hirohito just say no? One reason was that a veto in the face of unanimity (the famous Japanese consensus) was beyond a narrow circle of Imperial Household Ministry "handlers," notably Privy Seal Kido's interpretation of the emperor's constitutional role. Hirohito later explained that, "As a constitutional monarch, I had to recognize the unanimity of opinion between the government and the supreme command."[80] The emperor had to remain above the fray or place the imperial line at risk. A more immediate and practical concern was his fear that giving in to American demands because of the oil embargo might provoke a domestic coup d'état.[81] In the 1930s Hirohito had witnessed at least five major coup attempts, culminating in the great mutiny of February 1936. From 1921 through 1944, one authoritative source lists sixty-four incidents of right-wing violence, including foiled attempts to assassinate prime ministers, senior statesmen, Diet members, newspaper editors, scholars, generals, admirals, right and left wingers, and to attack the British and American embassies. Would-be assassins succeeded in wounding the president of the Seiyukai political party (1939) and, as late as August 1941, a minister of state.[82] Besides this undercurrent of rightist terror and violence, there had been an assassination attempt on Hirohito's life (the Toranomon Incident in 1923), and rumors abounded about replacing Hirohito with his oldest brother Prince Chichibu. The pattern of "government by assassination"[83] magnified Hirohito's ever-present concern that the next coup might be aimed directly against him. He rationalized that a foreign war fought by a united Japan was preferable to a nation divided by a craven peace. And domestic upheaval aimed against the throne would shake the very foundation of *kokutai*.

Although the emperor did not actively campaign for war with the West, neither did he take positive steps to avoid such an eventuality. As did many other Japanese he allowed himself to be swept along in the current of events. Hirohito acknowledged chances of victory were fifty-fifty, implicitly recognizing that Japan could not expect to defeat the United States. He later blamed defeat on the Tripartite Pact, rationalizing that without an entangling German alliance, Japan, with conquered strategic territories already in hand, could have created the window for a negotiated settlement.[84] Such equivocation was typical of Hirohito. As a monarch he surely owed more to his nation and his people than to wage war on a faulty premise or passively resign himself to the inevitable. Others have argued Hirohito may have wanted to avoid war with the West, but not at the cost of the Japanese empire.[85] But I suspect Hirohito was less concerned about war with the West than with the reluctance of his military advisers to guarantee him a victory in such a conflict, because no one knew what implications defeat would have for the imperial house.

Once Japan's war erupted into its Pacific phase, Hirohito monitored the progress of campaigns from a map room constructed in the palace.[86] He kept abreast of the fighting through daily situation reports as well as the numerous special operational briefings given by senior military and naval officials. The information Hirohito received was more or less accurate and candid about Japanese losses. He knew the details of the Midway disaster well before the army department of IGHQ, for example.[87] But the same briefers exaggerated Japanese successes. In other words, because IGHQ's analysis and verification was uncritical, not to say fictitious, the emperor found himself misled by the exaggerated battle claims.[88] This is why he believed the war was one of a punishing conflict with both sides suffering severe losses. So long as this was the case, Japan had a chance to force a decisive battle that would force the Americans to the conference table.

In the heady days following Pearl Harbor, Hirohito, as most other Japanese, was caught up in the drama of a panorama of sweeping victories. But at heart he remained cautious and conservative. Encouraging his military chieftains to exploit the early triumphs, he also told Tōjō on 12 February 1942 not to miss any opportunity to end the fighting. The emperor's stated reasons to seek a settlement exemplify his basic anxiety. On the one hand, he was concerned for human peace, but on the other fretted about the declining quality of Japan's forces in a prolonged war.[89] Hirohito wanted to end the war on Japanese terms. As this goal receded into defeat after defeat, he longed for a great victory to open the way for a negotiated settlement. Each new setback was another roadblock in his path. Hirohito's frustration was almost palpable as he searched for any way to inflict a stinging defeat on the Americans. Rather than "war mindedness"[90] one detects increasing desperation, as Hirohito grasps for the talisman of a decisive victory to end, not to expand, the war.

Japan's unbroken string of defeats began at the Coral Sea in May 1942. From information supplied by the chief aide-de-camp, Kido had informed Hirohito of that reverse on 8 May.[91] While the naval engagement in the Coral Sea might be considered a tactical draw, the momentous defeat at Midway was quite another matter. On Saturday, 6 June, the emperor's naval aide-de-camp, Vice Admiral Samejima Tomoshige, somberly gave Kido details of the disaster at Midway. Two days later, with Nagano present, Hirohito listened to the sobering account with perfect composure. Although Kido marveled at the imperial equanimity, Hirohito was truly shaken. Drawing on Admiral Tōgō Heihachirō's example from the Russo-Japanese as his model, he told Nagano to ensure the setback affected neither the navy's morale nor future operations.[92]

The Midway debacle was followed by a defeat in New Guinea, which coincided with the heavy fighting on air, land, and sea for the possession of Guadalcanal, a place where Admiral Nagano had dismissed the American landings in August 1942 as of no consequence.[93] By Hirohito's own account, the Japanese setback in New Guinea convinced him that the war was lost.

"From the time when our line along the Owen Stanley Mountain range in New Guinea was broken through (September 1943 [?]) I lost hope of victory. I thought that by thrashing the enemy somewhere we would be able to gain a negotiated peace. But we had a treaty with Germany against concluding a separate peace; and we could not violate an international agreement. So I was more or less thinking wouldn't it be good if Germany was quickly defeated."[94]

Preoccupied by the fighting simultaneously occurring on and near Guadalcanal, Imperial Headquarters ordered Japanese units to withdraw from the Owen Stanleys. The retreat began on 25 September 1942 with Australian troops in pursuit. By early November, the Australians had retaken Kokoda and seized Oivi thereby driving the Japanese from the mountains. This defeat ended the overland threat to Port Moresby and the Japanese menace to Australia.[95] Because Hirohito kept close track of military operations, it is unlikely he would have confused the pivotal Owen Stanley campaign with operations farther west along the New Guinea coastline a year later. Furthermore, by September 1942, Hirohito knew of the naval defeats at Coral Sea and Midway as well as the battle of attrition being waged for Guadalcanal. The emperor seems to have regarded the September 1942 repulse in the Owen Stanleys as a critical turning point in Japan's war with the West.

Hirohito then spent the next three years waiting in vain for a military or naval victory that would lead to a negotiated settlement of the war. Unwilling to break the alliance with Nazi Germany, hoping for a separate peace settlement, and underestimating American determination to fight Japan to the finish, Hirohito clung to the illusion that one great military victory would extract Japan from its war with the West. The chimera of the decisive battle, be it on land or sea, became not only the emperor's mantra but also that of the court, the bureaucracy, and ultimately of the die-hard military itself.

By November the emperor was cautioning his naval advisers to study the naval lessons of the Russo-Japanese War to avoid repetition of such disasters off Guadalcanal.[96] Colonel Ogata Ken'ichi, the emperor's military aide, recalled him asking penetrating questions about military history and wartime leadership, relying on examples from the Russo-Japanese War to drive home his points. "It's easy," Hirohito remarked, "to start a war but it's difficult to end one."[97] Hirohito was just understanding how difficult it was. Even his divine ancestors did not seem able to help him.

In December 1942, the emperor made a pilgrimage to the Grand Shrine at Ise where he prayed more for a quick return to peace than for victory.[98] The emperor had previously encouraged top advisers to seek an early settlement to the war. But perhaps the crisis on Guadalcanal shaped Hirohito's December invocation to his divine forbears. Guadalcanal was certainly on his mind, because he had requested immediate updates on the fighting there. The naval aide who carried the latest dispatches from Tokyo heard Hirohito hinting for the first time about ending the war.[99] Beyond that, the episode illustrates the importance Hirohito attached to keeping informed about the progress of military operations.

By late December, the services were hemming and hawing over requesting imperial approval for the decision to withdraw from Guadalcanal. On the twenty-eighth, the emperor told his aide-de-camp that neither Sugiyama nor Nagano seemed to have any confidence about the Guadalcanal situation. Hirohito wanted to know by 30 December whether or not Japanese forces should withdraw from Guadalcanal. Furthermore, Hirohito thought the larger question of how to force the enemy to surrender should be pursued at IGHQ and was at their disposal for an Imperial Conference on the matter at any time.[100] His remarks galvanized the service chiefs, who hurriedly organized an Imperial Conference to receive imperial sanction not to attack but to retreat. Just three days later Sugiyama and Nagano approached the throne to explain the plan to abandon Guadalcanal. Acknowledging their earlier mistakes on the Pacific front, the chiefs promised the army and navy would work more closely together to blunt the Allied counteroffensive in the Solomons and New Guinea.[101] Hirohito enjoined both officers to ensure that the services did cooperate to achieve objectives.[102] The imperial goal was to win a victory that would in turn force the Americans to the conference table.

This is why Hirohito closely interrogated Sugiyama about the loss of Buna, Papua New Guinea (January 1943), and the subsequent disastrous Battle of the Bismarck Sea (March 1943). For his part, Sugiyama assured Hirohito that airfield and road building projects were already under way to bolster Japan's defenses in eastern New Guinea.[103]

Japan's next defeat came at Attu in the Aleutian Islands (May 1943). Sugiyama listened uncomfortably as an impatient as well as frustrated Hirohito lamented the lack of cooperation between the army and navy, a matter he had emphasized to his service chiefs six months earlier. The absence of joint effort became another of Hirohito's recurrent themes and among the causes he later gave for Japan's defeat.[104] A few days later he learned that thick fog had prevented the navy from interfering with the Allied landings at Attu. Had no one, he asked Sugiyama, ever thought about fog in that part of the world? Why, the emperor continued impatiently, couldn't Japanese forces strike the Americans somewhere? Another chance for decisive battle had vanished into the fog.

Sugiyama's impressions of this audience encapsulate Hirohito's frustrations. The emperor was dissatisfied over the navy's reluctance to seek a decisive battle; he was worried about the lack of joint service cooperation; he was troubled about the direction the war was taking; and he was determined that Japan strike a heavy blow somewhere against American forces.[105] These became the themes of the final years of Hirohito's war. Hirohito's frustration and impatience were evident as was his increasing sense of helplessness about successive battlefield reverses. The emperor certainly had no strategic plan, but neither did his military experts. Instead both were grasping for the one great triumph that would reverse the unfavorable tide of battle and lead to a negotiated end to the war.

During the spring of 1943, Japan gained some breathing room as the United States reconstituted and reorganized its forces for the Central Pacific and Southwest Pacific advances set for later that year. Air battles inaugurated the Allied siege of the great Japanese naval base at Rabaul, New Britain; fighting continued in New Guinea's Markham Valley; and Allied preparations to recapture the northern Solomon Islands were under way. Yet the major Allied offensives were still months away. By June Hirohito thought things were going pretty well and stressed the need to hold fast in New Guinea. Sugiyama concurred and assured him that preparations were already under way to retake the initiative there.[106] The following month Hirohito spoke of his pride in the front-line troops, enjoining the staff to do everything to get them the wherewithal needed for the campaigns. But the optimism of early summer changed to pessimism by August.

Nowhere were things going well, declared Hirohito, who then recited his now familiar refrain about striking a blow the Americans somewhere. His aim was twofold, to hurt the enemy and to exploit the effects a great

Japanese victory would exert on other nations.[107] In brief, a decisive battle might open the way to negotiate an advantageous peace settlement.

On 24 August during discussions with his service chiefs about the defense of Rabaul, Hirohito reiterated the need for the navy to engage the Americans decisively.[108] By September a decisive blow had fallen, but on the Japanese. The Allied landing at Finschhafen, Northeast New Guinea, on 22 September provoked the imperial wrath. What most incensed Hirohito was the navy's inability to sortie against the transports carrying the invasion forces.[109] Again and again he had pleaded for a decisive naval battle, and now another chance for such an engagement had been lost. This latest defeat led to the fourth Imperial Conference held since the start of the war. On 30 September Imperial Headquarters created an "invincible" defensive perimeter by designating Rabaul and most of eastern New Guinea as self-sufficient outposts. Henceforth the Allies would be attacking, the Japanese defending.

U.S. Marines fought their way ashore at Kwajalein in the western Marshalls on 31 January 1944. Three weeks later, on 19 February, they stormed Eniwetok. The Americans' Central Pacific offensive was smashing through the "invincible" defense perimeter and threatening the Mariana Islands from where their long-range bombers could reach Japan itself. Around this time an increasingly pessimistic Hirohito made his remark about the Owen Stanley setback to his courtiers. Yet he still hoped for the elusive battlefield victory that would save Japan from defeat. The combination of desperation and inflated battle claims convinced him it was still possible.

On 8 March 1944, twenty Japanese naval bombers flew from Truk in a night attack against Majuro Atoll, a newly seized American fleet anchorage in the western Marshall Islands. The raiders, gaining surprise, dropped their bombs, and all returned to base safely. Pilots reported sinking one warship instantly, torpedoing two heavy cruisers, setting fire to several buildings, and leaving the airfield in ruins. The Japanese airmen mistook Engebi Atoll for Majuro and sank or damaged no warships, because none were anchored there; they did no damage to the runway at Engebi, which was still under construction and became operational only on 10 March; they dropped two bombs that exploded harmlessly on Parry Island, a small boat repair and seaplane base 1 mile away from their intended target; and they made mast-height bombing runs on the auxiliary ships anchored in the harbor, but dropped no bombs on them.[110] Certainly flying 1500 miles round-trip in pitch darkness over water through enemy-dominated skies was an impressive navigational feat. But its military value was nil.

Nevertheless, based on hyperinflated Japanese battle claims, Hirohito, faced with the unending string of Japanese reverses, seized on this trivial episode. On 11 March he announced his complete satisfaction with the counterattack, and word of his majesty's approval was dispatched to the fleet. He hoped the navy would conduct these types of operations insofar as they were possible. About two weeks later, during an update on the military situation, he asked about retaking Majuro. That was being studied, replied the chief of naval operations, but attacking fortified bases was not easy. A few days later the emperor again asked if the navy could pull off something similar to the Majuro raid.[111] In the end the navy did nothing.

Hirohito was not the only one alarmed by the rapid American seizure of the Marshalls. On 21 February, Tōjō dismissed Sugiyama and Nagano, replacing them with himself and Shimada, respectively. Along with a further cabinet reshuffle, Tōjō's announced purpose was to "permit closer coordination of administration and command."[112] Tōjō was counting on his close personal relationship with Shimada to ensure unity of command between the services. Even Hirohito recognized that the very closeness between Shimada and Tōjō made Shimada extremely unpopular with his subordinates throughout the navy.[113] Informed navy circles mocked Shimada as a "mild spring breeze," enveloped in a haze and unable to see into the future.[114] Tōjō disdained remarks that such concentration of military and political affairs in one man's hands had led the Germans to disaster at Stalingrad. As he put it, "Chancellor Hitler was a corporal. I am a general."[115] His secretary argued that total war demanded such a concentration of power simply to get things done in the Japanese bureaucracy.[116] It did not much matter, because the reorganized cabinet could succeed only if Japan's army or navy could win a major victory. In July 1944 the services tried at Saipan in the Marianas. They failed.

Shimada had led the emperor to believe that the Marianas would be the scene of the long-awaited decisive fleet engagement. Instead of a victory rivaling Admiral Tōgō's at Tsushima, Hirohito soon learned that the "A" Operation had failed to drive the American fleet from the high seas. Japan had 3 first-line carriers sunk, another 3 badly damaged, and had 500 aircraft lost.[117] From the Japanese viewpoint, it was not a one-sided battle. They reported five enemy carriers had been sunk and more than 100 planes shot down.[118] Japanese pilots had not even managed to hit an American carrier much less sink one. Still his military briefings left

Hirohito with the impression that Japan may have lost the battle, but both sides had suffered heavy damage. Accepting responsibility for the defeat, Shimada resigned.

Tōjō too had to go. He had already sounded out Prince Higashikuni about resigning to take responsibility for the loss of the Marianas.[119] Higashikuni then told Konoe that Tōjō should stay on as prime minister to the very end thereby taking responsibility for the war and by implication shielding the throne from such criticism. Konoe cynically mused about the difficulties Tōjō might create by committing suicide, unless he had the good sense to leave a confessional-style last will and testament absolving everyone except himself of any responsibility for the war.[120] Such wishful thinking did not translate into policy. Hirohito, unaware of Higashikuni and Konoe's discussions, wanted to avoid the appearance that the throne or court circles were plotting to oust the general from power.[121] And Hirohito genuinely lamented Tōjō's loss, remarking later that he had been unable to communicate his high regard for Tōjō to the nation.[122]

By 24 June, Imperial Headquarters had written off any attempts to relieve Saipan and informed the emperor its loss was inevitable.[123] Nonetheless, because of the strategic importance of the island neither chief of staff bothered to inform the emperor of the decision. That is why on 25 June Hirohito convened the first ever meeting of his field marshals, Princes Fushimi and Kanin, plus Nagano and Sugiyama to seek their counsel on what to do next about Saipan. The collective wisdom regarded Saipan as too difficult to defend and allowed that resources would be put to better use by strengthening rear-area defenses.[124] Unknown to Hirohito, any discussion was merely rhetorical, because Imperial Headquarters had already abandoned the island garrison and nothing was going to change their minds.

Meanwhile Japan and Germany's deteriorating military situations were forcing other influential Japanese to face the inescapable fact that defeat was almost certain. The preservation of *kokutai* now became a paramount consideration in any war termination scheme. While the Marshalls were crumbling in early 1944, Hosokawa Morisada, Konoe's son-in-law, recorded his concern about the fate of the imperial house and imperial line. On the basis of foreign newspaper accounts, Hosokawa surmised that the Americans seemed to regard the Japanese as savages, and he therefore feared they might eliminate the imperial system.[125] Konoe agreed that American public opinion might hold the emperor responsible for the war at least judging from the prejudiced remarks about the imperial household appearing in foreign reports, and Foreign Minister Shigemitsu Mamoru too believed defeat would mean the extinction of the imperial house.[126] As early as April 1944 the chief of IGHQ's War Guidance Section told recalled Lieutenant General Sakai Koji of the general staff that Tōjō himself was very pessimistic, wanting only to preserve the imperial house while accepting any other provisions of surrender.[127] Indeed shortly after the Allied landings in Normandy, France, Tōjō told his vice chief of staff on 29 June 1944, "When Germany collapses, we must also have a plan to end the war. In the worst case, we must preserve our *kokutai*."[128] The very next day, Yonai Mitsumasa, who would soon become navy minister, told Rear Admiral Takagi Sōkichi, "I don't know the details, but the war is lost. We're really beaten."[129]

On 26 September, Konoe met with Japan's senior statesmen to discuss the future course of the war. Former premier Hiranuma Kiichirō told him forcefully that there was no hope for ending the war quickly. Diplomacy would only lead to unconditional surrender. Japan had to fight on waiting to take advantage of changes in the international situation.[130] Now the senior statesmen too were buying into the external force, the great victory, as a solution to end a losing war. They were encouraged by Prince Takamatsu, who was also looking for ways to end the war yet maintain *kokutai*.[131] Japan's war aims had clearly changed. Initially the empire would negotiate a settlement from a position of military superiority while occupying most of the Pacific and Southeast Asia. Now Japan would negotiate a truce to preserve *kokutai*. The only consistent ingredient was a decisive victory as the sine qua non for opening any parleys. As war aims changed so too did the personalities advising the emperor.

Prime Minister Koiso Kuniaki (July 1944–April 1945) proved a transitional figure bridging the gap between the end of the Tōjō regime and Suzuki Kantarō's premiership. In the new cabinet, Oikawa replaced Shimada as chief of the naval general staff, and Yonai Mitsumasa became navy minister. General Umezu Yoshijirō became army chief of staff, and Sugiyama reemerged as war minister. The Koiso cabinet presided over the strategy that sealed Japan's defeat, although it was left to Suzuki to end the war. For his part, Koiso seemed overwhelmed by the rush of events from Leyte through Okinawa.

At age sixty-four, Koiso had chased power since his involvement in the abortive March Incident of 1931. When he finally caught up with it, Japan was facing ruin. The emperor did not trust him, and the services ignored him. Hirohito also worried about Koiso's tendency to go overboard about religious mysticism. A contemporary described him as "not a particularly bright person," and the president of the privy council regarded Koiso's remarks as nothing more than vague platitudes "like those used to deceive small children."[132] Koiso was no one's favorite for premier. As governor general of Korea he had been away from Tokyo for two years and was genuinely surprised at the turn for the worse the war had taken. Unclear about what to do, he opted to declare Leyte the decisive battle of the war in expectation that a victory there would make the Americans negotiate peace.[133] Koiso tried, and failed repeatedly, to control the military to gain access to their information. One such attempt was the establishment in August 1944 of the Supreme Council for the Direction of the War. This inner cabinet composed of the premier, foreign minister, war and navy ministers, and chiefs of the army and navy general staffs never became the policy-making agent Koiso envisioned. By the time he resigned much of Tokyo was in ashes, burned by American B-29s.

General Umezu Yoshijirō was sixty-two years old when he replaced Tōjō as the army chief of staff. He had spent the past five years commanding the once mighty Kwantung Army in Manchuria. Japanese regarded Umezu as impersonal, an impenetrable mind, lacking the highly desirable attributes of *ninjō* (human feeling). His poker face earned him the nickname of "the ivory mask."[134] Umezu's influence depended on his supposedly rational decision-making ability, yet it was known that he was in favor of fighting to the death.[135] As vice war minister from 1936 to 1939, he kept a copy of the army register on his otherwise immaculate desk.[136] His marginalia scrawled next to the names of various officers made or broke careers. Umezu was exceedingly ambitious, but seldom willing to place his career in jeopardy by taking an unpopular stand.

According to Admiral Yamamoto Isoroku, his close personal friend Yonai Mitsumasu might "not be smart but he has guts." Yonai had pressed for the army to dispatch troops to Shanghai in 1937 and the occupation in Hainan Island in 1938, irrespective that such actions would further expand the China War. In 1940 he opposed the Tripartite Pact because of his fear that Germany would prematurely involve Japan in a war with Britain and America as well as his strong aversion to Hitler in particular and Germans in general. He also opposed war with Britain and America. He was a down-to-earth sort,[137] so taciturn that some deemed him ineffectual. His deceptively frank manner earned him nicknames, including "the lamp shining in daylight" or the "goldfish minister."[138] In truth he was more like a shark. When Koiso asked him which cabinet post he wanted, the sixty-four-year-old Yonai self-effacingly demurred he was only suited to be navy minister. That portfolio gave him access to the military data Koiso was denied. Yonai would consistently advocate a negotiated end to Japan's war. His motivation was simple; *kokutai* and the imperial house must be preserved.[139]

Koiso Kuniaki, previously governor general of Korea, knew little of Japan's steady defeats, but was now prime minister. Calling in "a man from a colony" to head the new cabinet was later regarded as a mistake, especially because Koiso lacked knowledge of the domestic situation.[140] Within days of Koiso becoming prime minister, Imperial Headquarters announced its plans for decisive victory. The Shō operations, 1–4, were scenarios to defeat the next American thrust against Japanese-held territory. Having nothing better to offer, Koiso wholeheartedly bought into the strategy.

By early October 1944, it seemed apparent that the Philippines would be the Americans' next target. Once again wildly inflated battle claims misled Hirohito into thinking the series of air and sea battles stretching from Taiwan to Okinawa had ended in a great Japanese triumph. On 16 October Oikawa presented the emperor a detailed account of the air and naval engagement, concluding that sixteen U.S. carriers had been sunk or damaged as well as scores of other American warships sunk.[141] Actual U.S. losses were two cruisers heavily damaged and about ninety aircraft destroyed. To inflict this punishment cost the Japanese 500 warplanes. On the basis of this fanciful briefing, the emperor issued an Imperial Rescript commemorating the great victory.[142] Hirohito's military advisers had again left him with the vivid impression that the Americans had suffered heavy losses in the recent fighting. With a weakened enemy pushing toward the Philippines, the timing seemed perfect for the decisive battle. Armed with the same faulty estimates, the army and navy opted to fight the Shō Operation at Leyte, Philippines, where American forces landed on 20 October 1944. Besides smashing the enemy with a devastating blow, the Japanese army expected to capture General Douglas MacArthur when they retook Leyte. The War Guidance Section, Imperial Army Headquarters, expected MacArthur "to run up the white flag" sometime before 2 November. A victory communiqué had even been prepared.[143]

On 20 October Prime Minister Koiso announced Japan's latest naval victories to a huge rally at Hibiya Park in downtown Tokyo. His strategic policy, enunciated a few weeks later at a meeting of the Supreme Council for the Direction of the War, was simple: score one great victory then negotiate a settlement of the conflict.[144] Imperial Headquarters though was still withholding full details of the Leyte fighting from Koiso. As a consequence, in a national radio address broadcast on 8 November the premier described Leyte as momentous a struggle as Tennōzan (lit. imperial mountain)[145] thereby endowing the battle with enormous symbolic and emotional value. Appeals to samurai spirits of centuries past were of no help on Leyte. By late December Imperial Headquarters wrote it off by switching the "decisive" battle farther north to Luzon, the main island of the Philippine archipelago. Koiso learned of the military's action just before departing for an imperial audience. When the emperor questioned his prime minister about the decision, the badly flustered and humiliated Koiso stammered that he just found out about it himself. Hirohito added to his consternation by wondering aloud about the effect the abrupt change to Luzon might have on home front morale and productivity. Koiso after all had publicly proclaimed Leyte to be the climatic battle of the Pacific War.[146] An infuriated Koiso berated the army staff for making him look foolish and complained to others that his position was very difficult, because the army's and navy's policies were not clear to him. Oikawa disingenuously observed that he had taken it for granted that the navy minister had been passing on information to the premier. Yonai, who was supposed to be the co–prime minister, told Koiso he ought to admit his unfamiliarity with operations and ask for help.[147]

And what did Hirohito think about the decisive battle of Leyte? Between 25 and 28 October Oikawa provided him with daily updates on the Leyte fighting. As usual Oikawa's uncritical briefings exaggerated enemy losses, creating the impression for the emperor that Leyte was a battle of attrition where both sides had suffered more or less equal losses.[148] It was crucial to fight on Leyte and not give in to defeatism.

Here is what Hirohito said about Leyte in 1946. "It wasn't just that the army and navy did not have a unified concept of operations. Even within the army opinions differed between the general staff, the Southern Army commander, and Yamashita. Yamashita would have defended the Philippines [Luzon] and probably this would have been best. Contrary to the opinion of the army and navy general staffs, I supported a decisive battle at Leyte thinking that if we could strike a blow and force the Americans to withdraw, couldn't we then find room for a compromise settlement? However my opinion was not transmitted to the high command so the army, navy, and Yamashita went their separate ways. Yamashita poured in troops in despair and the navy recklessly launched the fleet. This irrational style of warfare ended in defeat."[149] His analysis remained consistent with his earlier remarks to Sugiyama. Deeply worried about the inexorable American advance, Hirohito again complained that no one in the high command had listened to him. There was no joint effort at Leyte, and still another chance to strike the enemy hard to gain a decisive victory was lost. Leyte then became still another vain attempt to win a great victory that would force the Americans to the conference table.

Instead it became grist for the Japanese man in the street. At 1920 on New Year's Day 1945, the prime minister announced in his national radio broadcast that Luzon was now Tennōzan. With justifiable gallows humor, Tokyoites quipped, "Koiso even seems to move mountains."[150] The magical mountain though kept moving from Luzon to Iwo Jima and then to Okinawa. Navy Chief of Staff Oikawa remained confident of victory in a decisive battle at Okinawa.[151] As chief of the naval general staff, Oikawa witnessed the worst naval defeats in Japan's history—Philippine Sea, Leyte Gulf, and Okinawa. Still wanting to please, he gave Hirohito equivocal answers about major questions of strategy. Others were already anticipating the consequences of military defeat.

In late January 1945 Konoe, Navy Minister Yonai, and former prime minister and retired admiral Ōkada Keisuke, as well as Prince Takamatsu met with the chief abbot of the Ninnaji temple in Kyoto to discuss the possibilities of Hirohito abdicating the throne.[152] The plan was to install Hirohito as the temple's abbot, thereby shielding the emperor from any postwar controversy yet still having him available for consultations on matters of state. Konoe had earlier discussed with Higashikuni the possibility of an imperial abdication. His idea, broached after the fall of Saipan, was for the Crown Prince, then age eleven, to succeed Hirohito. Prince Takamatsu would be appointed as regent to facilitate negotiations to end the war.[153] Konoe believed he could broker a settlement by forming his fourth cabinet and using Great Britain as an intermediary for negotiations with America.[154] Meanwhile Hirohito, who by this time was receiving briefings about the military situation every evening from Sugiyama and Oikawa, polled Japan's senior statesmen about continuing the war.

The emperor had to move circumspectly to avoid provoking the army. Under the pretext of welcoming the elder statesmen at the palace to pay their new year respects, Hirohito met individually with each man, confidentially seeking his advice. Not a single one, he thought, had a firm opinion on war termination. Instead the group was split between optimists and pessimists. When Konoe's turn came on 14 February, the prince told Hirohito that the war should be ended at once. "I told him," said Hirohito, "that since the army and navy were eager to fight the decisive battle on Okinawa, it would not be suitable to end the war at this time."[155]

Actually Umezu and the navy advised the emperor that if the enemy could be lured into battle off Taiwan, Japan could defeat the Americans and then have recourse to a diplomatic settlement.[156] That afternoon, during a briefing on the latest developments on the fighting fronts, Hirohito remarked to his aide-de-camp, Lieutenant Colonel Nakamura Tadahisa, "If we persist in this war, I'm absolutely convinced of victory, but until then I worry whether or not the people will be able to endure."[157] The emperor was still looking for his decisive victory.

Army chief of staff Umezu played on fears that the Americans were intent on liquidating the imperial house to convince Hirohito a decisive battle in the spring of 1945 would lead to a negotiated end to the war on terms acceptable to Japan.[158] The emperor did not need much convincing, because he still hoped a Japanese military victory would lead to a negotiated end to the conflict. At the very least it's fair to say that well into 1945 Hirohito held out hope a military victory would enable Japan's diplomats to negotiate a settlement to the war.[159]

He was not alone in this assessment. Marquis Kido Kōichi, lord keeper of the privy seal, and his chief secretary Marquis Matsudaira Yasumasa, for instance, agreed in mid-March that if the army could win one battle, the emperor could openly support ending the war.[160] Similar sentiments were voiced at the palace on the eve of the Okinawa campaign.[161] Umezu was quite willing to risk everything for the decisive battle on Okinawa while acknowledging complete Japanese success would inflict at most 50 percent casualties on the enemy.[162] One did not have to win the final battle; just inflicting heavy losses on the enemy might compel a negotiated peace. In the early spring of 1945 the Japanese leaders, both military and civilian, were again plainly deluding themselves that a single military success would somehow lead to the negotiating table. By now the decisive victory meant mauling the Allies so badly that the bloodletting might deter them from their next advance and lead to a negotiated settlement.

Because Hirohito was counting heavily on the elusive decisive battle, he kept close track of the Okinawa fighting. On 3 April, two days after the American landings on the island, Hirohito told Umezu that defeat would cause the people to lose confidence in the army and navy. Couldn't the Thirty-second Army on Okinawa attack the Americans somewhere? If they didn't have enough troops, how about staging a counter landing?[163] Imperial Headquarters radioed his imperial majesty's wishes to the Okinawa garrison the following day.

Hirohito's desires hardly mattered, because higher headquarters in Taiwan and in Tokyo were already pressuring the Thirty-second Army to attack. At Thirty-second Army Headquarters serious planning and internal squabbling over a counterattack already had begun on 3 April, that is, before receipt of the message bearing the emperor's wishes from Tokyo. The attack, set for 6 April, was canceled on the night of 4 April because of reports that the Americans were readying another amphibious assault.[164] Hirohito's recollections of the Okinawa struggle exemplify the tenacity of the "great victory" syndrome even as Japan was eyeball to eyeball with disaster. His postwar assessment restates the now familiar apologies.

"I think the cause of defeat at Okinawa was the lack of coordination between army and navy operations. I was concerned because Okinawa should really have been defended by three divisions. At first Umezu thought two were sufficient, but afterwards the lack of the military strength began to be felt and we needed to send another division of reinforcements. The situation did not permit transporting it."

Original plans called for three divisions to protect Okinawa. In December 1944, however, the Ninth Division departed the island, eventually redeploying to Taiwan where Imperial Headquarters and Umezu anticipated the decisive battle would occur. The Eighty-fourth Division was supposed to replace the Ninth on Okinawa, but the general in charge of the First Bureau (Operations) canceled its deployment insisting that the Eighty-fourth was needed for defense of Japan's four main islands.[165] In other words, a bureau chief had overruled the emperor.

Hirohito continued:

"So called special attacks were conducted but the weather was bad, ammunition lacking, and the planes were not good. Even if the weather were good, I wondered wasn't it pointless?

"You really cannot hide your sympathy for the special attack [kamikaze] pilots. It was an unreasonable step which was unavoidably tragic.

"The navy lost nearly all its warships at Leyte, so [at Okinawa] it sent out its highly valued *Yamato*. Because there was no coordination between *Yamato* and our aircraft, the operation ended in defeat."

During one of Oikawa's briefings on the general air offensive, that is, the kamikaze attacks, Hirohito had asked the admiral if the navy was just using air units against the Allied fleet at Okinawa. Oikawa answered that the navy would use combined air and surface units but intentionally withheld the vital information that Japan's super battleship the *Yamato* was setting out on its own one-way mission to Okinawa. The naval general staff was very rightly concerned that Hirohito might ask them to justify their foolhardy plan.[166]

Then the emperor continued:

"Although the army prolonged the decisive battle, the navy joined the decisive battle in desperation. Operations were not coordinated. It was a completely stupid, stupid battle. . . . I thought if we were defeated in this last decisive battle, unconditional surrender would be inevitable. After Okinawa there could be no expectation of a decisive naval battle. The one ray of hope I thought was to strike a blow against the Americans and British at Yunnan together with Burma operations. I spoke to Umezu about it, but he was opposed saying the logistics could not be sustained. When I spoke to Prince Kaya, Commandant of the Army War College, about it, he said something probably could be done as a temporary measure and he would try to research it. However it came to nothing in the end."[167]

After the loss of Okinawa, Hirohito rationally knew that only surrender remained. Yet almost in the same breath he could intellectualize that the chance for an elusive decisive battle still existed. With his empire crashing down around him, he could not rid himself of the irrational notion that a single battlefield victory would somehow allow Japan to negotiate its way out of a losing war. Rather than evidence of the fighting generalissimo, Hirohito's constant whining for a military victory demonstrates his comprehension that Japan had no bargaining chips to raise the ante for an unconditional surrender to levels the Americans would find unacceptable. Even considering that a peripheral theater of operations, such as Burma, could have the slightest possible effect on the doomsday scenario Japan was scripting for itself only revealed imperial desperation.

Okinawa's loss brought different faces before the emperor as Oikawa and Sugiyama departed in favor of Admiral Toyoda Soemu and General Anami Korechika. The newcomers did not bring unanimity with them, however. After Okinawa everyone agreed the war had to end, but no one agreed on how to end it. A split opened between Yonai and the Anami-Umezu-Toyoda trio. Yonai, allied with Kido and the new foreign minister, Tōgō Shigenori, would end the war immediately provided *kokutai* remained intact. The Anami-dominated threesome would end the war *after* scoring a decisive battlefield victory, which would serve as the lever for a negotiated settlement that would preserve *kokutai*. Because of the split, Hirohito was receiving conflicting advice at a time when enemy attacks on the homeland itself made it plain for all to see that Japan had lost the war. This institutional schizophrenia manifested itself in Japan's war termination schemes. Kido, Yonai, Tōgō, and Hirohito were involved in a clandestine effort to enlist Soviet meditation to end the war. Anami, Umezu, Toyoda, and Hirohito were involved in implementing a massive reinforcement of Kyushu in expectation of fighting the decisive battle of the homeland on that island. Both efforts proceeded apace, independent of each other, although both had the same goal—a negotiated end to the war. Paradoxically the linchpin for the military defensive and the diplomatic offensive was the Soviet Union. The army needed the Soviets to remain neutral to carry out its decisive battle of the homeland scenario, and those who favored ending the war immediately recognized that only the USSR had the great power stature and military strength to influence America.

This is why the service chiefs and ministers went along with the x-item, a plan endorsed after a three-day supersecret meeting of the prime minister and foreign, war, and navy ministers as well as both chiefs of staff held in mid-May 1945. According to the agreement, Japan would open a diplomatic effort with the Soviet Union to prevent the USSR from entering the war; to ensure continued Soviet neutrality; and to secure Soviet mediation to end the war. Only these top six Japanese leaders knew of the initiative. The emperor was not informed.[168]

One of the knowledgeable six, Suzuki Kantarō, the new prime minister, was a retired navy admiral having served as chief of the naval general staff in the late 1920s. From 1929 to 1936 he was the grand chamberlain to Hirohito. Gravely wounded in the 26 February 1936 incident, Suzuki withdrew from the public stage, although he continued to provide advice privately. In April 1945 he reluctantly reemerged as premier, seventy-eight years old, half deaf and given to drowsiness. Hirohito liked Suzuki and got along with him well, but Suzuki's bellicose public pronouncements certainly did not help the cause of peace or consensus. Suzuki's biographer says this was all "haragei" (saying one thing but meaning something entirely different) on the elderly premier's part. Yet as an eminent historian has observed, such an explanation fits any case and covers every seeming contradiction.[169] More probably Suzuki, a retired admiral, like Anami, Umezu, and Toyoda, was looking for one victory to serve as the basis of a negotiated end to the war.[170] His bellicosity in June and July 1945 was real. Suzuki was not yet ready to lead a peace faction to surrender.

Suzuki's innermost thoughts will never be known. Kido told Suzuki he alone could "save the nation" without explaining precisely what Suzuki had to do to end the war.[171] Nevertheless, Suzuki then told his putative foreign minister he expected the war to drag on for another few years, nearly convincing Tōgō to flee back to rural Karuizawa.[172] One explanation is that Suzuki simply did not know the real situation facing Japan.[173] Another is that among the conditions the army imposed on him for its support were continuation of the war and preparation for the decisive battle of the homeland. Yet these hardly explain Suzuki's bizarre maiden speech to the Eighty-seventh Extraordinary Session of the Diet. Delivered the day after the depressing 8 June Imperial Conference, Suzuki, nevertheless, proclaimed Japanese willingness to fight to the very end.[174]

When Prime Minister Suzuki Kantarō had served as grand chamberlain, Anami has served as military aide-de-camp to the emperor. Both men liked and respected one another. Suzuki wanted the general as his war minister, because he believed Anami could control the army, something Hirohito had worried Sugiyama would be incapable of during any effort to end the war.[175] Imperial concern over military discipline and a legitimate wariness about a military uprising of some sort colored Hirohito's calculations during 1945. To control the army, Suzuki had to buy the whole package. Yet he bought it enthusiastically. On 26 April Suzuki gathered the army and navy leaders at his official residence to urge them to cooperate for the sake of the war effort. Victory at Okinawa, he told them, would enhance diplomatic efforts.[176] Similar to the rest of the Japan's leadership in the spring of 1945, Suzuki was looking for one decisive military victory to become the springboard to a negotiated settlement to hostilities. In mid-June he may have changed his mind, becoming less certain of the efficacy of a decisive battle of the homeland.[177] Even in that respect, his attitude matched Kido and Hirohito's.

Admiral Toyoda as well as Generals Anami and Umezu all hailed from the same village in southern Japan's Ōita Prefecture. Toyoda was considered a moderate, and he certainly displayed more integrity as chief of the naval general staff than did Oikawa. Born in 1885 to an impoverished samurai family, Toyoda had the reputation as a stubborn hardheaded sort. Unwilling to compromise for the sake of appearance, he was regarded by the Japanese as outspoken. In 1941 Toyoda had opposed war against the West and criticized Oikawa for not speaking out against it. Unlike the other members of Suzuki's inner cabinet, Toyoda had no previous working relationship with the emperor. Toyoda was, according to one critic, a capable admiral, "but ultimately jumping over more senior admirals to become chief of staff exposed his shortcomings."[178] Toyoda announced he intended to be Yonai's accomplice in ending the war and did turn from operations to war termination in the navy ministry building. He supported dispatching a special emissary to the Soviet Union, but insisted that *kokutai* must be preserved.[179] Although he agreed in principle with Yonai, he ended up siding with Anami. His overriding concern for *kokutai* then left the appearance that he was under Anami's spell to the very end.

General Anami Korechika was the most influential and powerful man in Japan in mid-1945. Younger army officers believed they could count on Anami's support, and they deeply trusted him. Anami was a sharp contrast to Sugiyama. A trim, assertive front-line commander, Anami's receding hairline and pencil mustache gave him an avuncular look, and indeed many junior officers regarded him more as a friendly uncle than an imposing presence. And Anami was cut from different cloth than the older Sugiyama. At fifty-eight, he was eight years younger than his predecessor, and brought the vigor and initiative Sugiyama lacked to the ministry. While both officers respected the emperor, Anami did not approach Hirohito with the trepidation of Sugiyama. Instead to the very end Anami saw opportunities to wean the younger man from the unhealthy influence of the liberals and pacifists who surrounded him. Hirohito was uncomfortable with Anami, despite his earlier service as the emperor's aide in the late 1920s and early 1930s. Some believed him too strong willed to be close to the emperor.[180]

At age fifty-eight archery, kendo (Japanese fencing), and judo kept Anami in excellent shape. His strong suit was sincerity, a trait much admired by Japanese and one that excuses a multitude of sins. The war had touched Anami personally in 1943 when his second son was killed in action in central China. Thereafter he always kept the boy's picture on his desk. He was less interested in desktop plans of well-groomed staff officers than in the commanders and soldiers dying in the mud and jungle. Anami held deep convictions, none stronger than his philosophy of warfare. He viewed warfare as a brutal affair inflicting pain and suffering for both sides. Once committed to battle, however, Anami would fight to the finish regardless of the cost.[181] Warfare, Anami insisted, came down to a clash of wills, and the human spirit or esprit in combat, or *seishin*, outweighed any material factors and could turn the tide of battle. According to Anami, the decisive battle would preserve *kokutai*. The army, he was convinced, could fight such a battle, but it required firm leadership to keep morale from plummeting. His personality and attitude earned him trust and confidence throughout the army.[182] Although Umezu was senior to Anami, his stature nowhere rivaled Anami's. Umezu did have his admirers, but only Anami could command the respect of the entire army. For these reasons he deferred to Anami who was several years his junior.

Anami's counterpart in the navy ministry was also working to preserve *kokutai*. Since 1944 Yonai was linked to a cabal that liked to convey its view of events to the emperor. Former Prime Minister and now senior statesman Prince Konoe's son-in-law, Hosokawa Morisada, served as the conduit carrying political, military, and economic intelligence between Konoe and Prince Takamatsu. Others involved were Rear Admiral Takagi Sōkichi, a polished navy bureaucrat highly skilled in political matters, and Lieutenant General Sakai Koji of the general staff. Yonai received regular reports not only from Takamatsu, but also from Takagi. In a nutshell the group aimed to preserve the imperial institution in the face of Axis defeat.[183]

When Hirohito and the peace faction or any other Japanese who mattered talked about ending the war, they meant by a negotiated settlement, not a capitulation and certainly not an unconditional surrender. As might be expected, the army insisted on conditions for any settlement. These included provisions to allow the Japanese to try alleged war criminals, to disarm their own forces, to avoid foreign occupation, and to guarantee *kokutai*. Hirohito supported these demands, dropping his heretofore adamant opposition to disarmament of Japanese forces and punishment of war criminals in early May 1945, after the loss of Okinawa.[184] Not coincidentally, around this same time he surprised Kido by expressing his feelings about using the imperial influence to end the war.[185] Defeat, not compassion, drove Hirohito.

By mid-1945 Kido also wanted to end the war thereby preserving *kokutai*. As bright as he was, Kido too was counting on the military inflicting a major defeat on the Allies. Once that happened, he believed the emperor could go public and offer a magnanimous settlement to end the conflict. Otherwise he risked involving Hirohito directly in affairs of state, something Kido wanted to avoid if at all possible. Kido was no more out of touch than other Japanese who wanted to end the war and believed it was still possible to do so on Japan's terms to protect *kokutai*.

Shortly thereafter safeguarding *kokutai* took on a terrifyingly literal meaning. A firebomb attack on Tokyo created a conflagration that spread to the imperial palace. Thirty-three firefighters died trying to stop the flames from reaching the imperial sanctuary where the sacred jewel and a replica of the sacred mirror were housed. Together with the imperial sword, these three treasures symbolized the unbroken imperial line. Had the fire consumed the sanctuary, the loss of the sacred objects would have been an incalculable shock to the Japanese people.

"I probably should have brought the imperial mirror from Ise [whose shrine was also partially destroyed by fire bombings]," said Hirohito, "and the imperial sword from Atsuta shrine here so I could take care of them myself. But in deciding to move them I must act cautiously and take into account the effect it would have on the people's morale. Still, if worst comes to worst, I feel I have no choice but to guard the sacred objects and share with them whatever fate has in store."[186]

For the same reasons of protecting the imperial regalia he rejected the army's plans to displace Imperial Headquarters along with the throne to an alternate command post and palace being secretly constructed deep in the mountains at Matsushiro. Work on the alternate headquarters commenced in the fall of 1944, and in March 1945 secret army orders expanded the project's scope to include construction of a provisional palace. In May, Umezu informed Hirohito that an alternate command post was being built without telling him about the displaced palace scheme. Was Umezu afraid to tell the emperor because the chief of staff thought Hirohito would flatly refuse to move? Or did Umezu hold back because it showed, perhaps even more than the alternate command post, that Japan had reached the end of the road? Unaware of the alternate palace scheme, Hirohito said he intended to remain with his subjects in Tokyo. Umezu did not raise the issue again.[187]

By early June, however, the army had specific plans to relocate the imperial family from Tokyo to Matsushiro. A specially converted armored train had been secured for the purpose, and soldiers were preparing an office building in downtown Tokyo to house the royal family during the relocation. Kido heard from the emperor's military aide-de-camp of the army's scenario, sent an imperial household ministry official to check it out, and reported his findings in mid-July to Hirohito. "I'm not going," was Hirohito's brusque response. The issue arose again on the final day of July, and Hirohito rejected any move, being determined to share the fate of the imperial treasures.[188]

The episode had graver overtones. As John Hall has noted, in Japanese history possession of the emperor is the name of the game.[189] If the army succeeded in isolating Hirohito in the mountain redoubt, its leaders could carry on the war to suicidal extremes to preserve *kokutai* in his name. Besides Hirohito was surely aware of the current gossip about Prince Takamatsu assuming the throne or becoming regent. For any number of good reasons then the emperor did not want to move to distant Matsushirō, because he understood full well such a displacement would fatally weaken the throne's prestige and influence in addition to endangering the sacred treasures.

Hirohito survived as emperor by emphasizing his imperial prerogatives. He reacted quickly to any infringement because of the potential threat it posed to the imperial line. In early May 1945, for instance, Umezu requested imperial sanction to add the Seventeenth Area Army stationed in northern Korea to the order of battle of the Kwantung Army in neighboring Manchuria. In operational terms, the realignment made sense, because it streamlined command and control especially in the event of a Soviet invasion. Hirohito rejected the request, because Korea was part of the Japanese homeland, and it was unprecedented to place a homeland headquarters under the command of an overseas one. Yamada Akira insists this imperial veto demonstrates that Hirohito was determined to the very end to permit no infringements on his "supreme command authority" (*tōsui taiken*).[190] On closer examination, though, "supreme command authority," as with much about Hirohito, is more appearance than substance.

The order of battle change was one of four provisions in Umezu's draft memorial presented to the throne. It was also the only one of the four Hirohito returned for revision. Furthermore, just three weeks later, Imperial Order Number 1338, sanctioned by the emperor, simply redeployed the maneuver units of the Seventeenth Area Army to the Kwantung Army leaving the headquarters itself in Korea denuded of troops.[191] The army, as usual, got what it wanted while adhering to outward appearances, which count for so much in Japan. Rather than a display of imperial authority, the episode demonstrated two features of the early reign of the Shōwa emperor. First, there were examples of partial revisions of general staff plans and orders (as with the order described above) before the emperor sanctioned them. There was not, however, a single instance of the emperor's outright veto of an entire draft proposal. Second, there were numerous examples of the general staff ignoring or circumventing the emperor's requests.[192]

Although by now harboring grave doubts about the possibility of a decisive battle, Hirohito sanctioned the massive buildup in Kyushu as Japan's generals insisted on fighting the evasive decisive battle on Japan's main islands, the key, they argued, to open the door to a negotiated settlement. By May 1945, the reality was three years of uninterrupted military setbacks; the unconditional surrender of Japan's major ally, Nazi Germany; Japan's major cities in ashes; a threat of imminent invasion;

and, as Hirohito was about to learn, an army and navy ill equipped to repel an attacker much less force a decisive engagement.

In early June several distressing confidential evaluations of the fighting potential of the armed forces reached the emperor. Hirohito's mood matched the rain-filled and overcast skies that persisted through the week. On 8 June, despite an exceptionally bleak evaluation of Japan's war potential, the Imperial Conference opted to fight the war to the bitter end. Following tradition, the emperor said nothing during the conference, but after leaving the proceedings met with Kido and told him that he was waiting for him to speak out.[193] The privy seal promptly began his efforts to overturn the 8 June decision.

The next day chief of staff Umezu returned form his inspection trip to the continent. Besides conceding most of Manchuria to a potential Soviet invasion, according to Umezu just eight American Army divisions could defeat all the Japanese forces then in China. Hirohito had never before heard such pessimism voiced by Umezu. Stunned, he asked his chief of staff, "So we cannot even defend the homeland?"[194] Coming as it did on the heels of the bleak 8 June Imperial Conference, Umezu's frank report struck Matsudaira as offering "timely help" in reinforcing the emperor's desire to terminate the war.[195]

A few days later on 12 June Admiral Hasegawa Kiyoshi returned from a three-month inspection tour of front-line naval units ordered by Yonai. Hasegawa brought Hirohito exactly what Yonai knew he would—more bad news. Naval preparations for operations in China and the homeland were hopelessly incomplete. The war had to be ended as quickly as possible. The shaken emperor could only reply, "That's what I figured. I understand your explanations." He later described Hasegawa's report as "devoid of any hope."[196] The following day Kido reported on the Matsushiro goings-on. Prince Higashikuni then told Hirohito about the shabby state of homeland coastal defenses manned by rag-tag formations.[197] Now, for the first time, Hirohito understood the chasm between the rhetoric of the decisive battle of the homeland and the Japanese military's capability to execute it.[198] Perhaps the disillusionment Hirohito experienced when he finally realized that the army and navy had consistently, throughout the war, reported victories when in fact they suffered defeats convinced him in August 1945 to throw his influence behind the "end-the-war" faction.

Kido continued to lay the foundation for a formal reversal of the 8 June decision. On the morning of the eighteenth, he met with Anami. The general remained convinced that fighting the invaders on Japan's beaches would lead to a negotiated peace. Why should the enemy invade, asked Kido, when Japan's cities were already in ashes from enemy air attacks? Civilian morale was flagging. If the cost of a decisive battle was the annihilation of Japan, wouldn't *kokutai* also be lost? Anami carried Kido's remarks to the late afternoon meeting of the Supreme Council for the Direction of the War, where the participants agreed to seek Soviet mediation to end the war. Two days afterward Hirohito told Foreign Minister Tōgō on 20 June about the hopeless state of national defenses and encouraged him to end the war as quickly as possible.[199] The ensuing Imperial Conference of 22 June determined the war should be ended through Soviet mediation.

Then why didn't the emperor end the war in June? Because he was a timid and conservative monarch who was unwilling to abandon either of the military or the diplomatic strategies then in motion to end the war even though they were working at cross-purposes. Besides how would the army react to attempts by the court to end the conflict? Could or would Anami control the military? Would hotheaded officers rebel, insisting Japan must fight to the death? These uncertainties and the specter of a military coup d'etat haunted Hirohito to the end.[200]

The emperor was willing to concede Allied demands, painful as they appeared, about disbanding Japan's military, trying Japanese war criminals, and occupying Japan. Yet as long as the two most powerful groups pursued independent courses to end the war, consensus was impossible. Anami and his two cohorts insisted that fighting the last great battle on Japan's beaches would convince the Americans of the wisdom of a negotiated peace while Kido, Yonai, and Tōgō placed their faith in the Soviet Union to conclude a settlement.[201] Where even Umezu and Toyoda saw ruin, Anami stubbornly still saw opportunity. Incomplete preparations of homeland defense were reasons to encourage greater effort, not to give up.[202] The war minister exuded confidence whether addressing the Imperial Diet or in private conversations. He believed the initial American landings could be repulsed.[203] And neither Umezu nor Toyoda was willing to deny Anami the chance to prove his point. Unless Hirohito acted, Anami had the connections, the respect, and the authority to continue the deadlock throughout July. Had these dichotomous initiatives to end the war played out behind a curtain of secrecy, perhaps the stalemate would have resolved itself within the confines of the Japanese leadership. Unknown to the Japanese leaders, the United States was closely following Japan's diplomatic and military efforts to secure a negotiated settlement to the conflict.

From decrypted Japanese foreign ministry cables flowing between Tokyo and Moscow, the Americans were well-informed of Japan's attempts to enlist the USSR as an intermediary on its behalf. Simultaneously, through deciphered Japanese military and naval messages, leaders in the United States were apprised of the staggering numbers of Japanese reinforcements filling in the very beaches of Kyushu projected for the American invasion of Japan that November. In other words, it seemed the duplicitous Japanese were up to their pre–Pearl Harbor trick of negotiating peace to buy time for a military perfecting plans to continue the war. In such circumstances, the United States seemingly had little to lose and much to gain by its atomic attacks against Japanese cities.

For Japan the mirage of a decisive battle had degenerated to such a state that winning was neither the motivation nor even the anticipated outcome. In the delusion gripping Japan in midsummer of 1945, victory was detached from winning or losing. Victory now meant only enduring. While the emperor alone cannot be said to have been more responsible than anyone else for delaying Japan's surrender,[204] the unrealistic and incompetent actions of Japan's military and civilian leaders prolonged the war. Furthermore, by consistently misleading Hirohito about the possibility of a decisive battle reversing Japan's fortunes, his military chieftains nullified his influence. In other words, because of the deceptive advice and exaggerated battle claims reported by his supreme command, which he was in no position to verify one way or another, the emperor went along with the army and navy's plans for a climactic battle that would reverse the course of the war with a single blow. In that context, he cannot be thought to be one in this circle of unrealistic and incompetent leaders.[205] That dubious distinction belonged to Japan's generals and admirals who led the nation into a defeat they were unwilling to accept.

At ten minutes to midnight, 9 August, following two atomic bombings and the Soviet declaration of war, an Imperial Conference convened in the underground bunker on the grounds of the imperial palace. Everyone present agreed that preservation of *kokutai* and the imperial house were paramount goals. Anami, Umezu, and Toyoda still opposed a foreign occupation of Japan and wanted disarmament and punishment of war criminals left in Japanese hands, arguing these conditions were still negotiable. Yonai and Suzuki, among others, insisted the time had come when there was no room for any negotiation, and Japan had to accept the Potsdam Declaration. From his recent briefings on the desperate state of Japan's defenses, Hirohito could see no way to continue the war, because Japan lacked the means to fight.[206] Anami thought otherwise.[207] Kido stressed the emperor's responsibility to his imperial ancestors to preserve the imperial line. Hirohito wondered if the decisive battle of the homeland meant that the entire Japanese race must perish? "If this comes to pass," he said, "we will be unable to pass on to our progeny the country called Japan that we received from our imperial ancestors."[208]

Speaking to his court intimates in 1946, the emperor offered this explanation.

> My first decision was in such circumstances the Japanese race will perish. I cannot protect my loyal subjects. Second, Marquis Kido and I had the same opinion about preserving *kokutai*. If the enemy landed near Ise Bay, the imperial shrines at Ise and Atsuta would be under enemy pressure. There was no time or margin to remove the imperial regalia [mirror, sword, and jewel] and no prospect of protecting them. If it were seized by the enemy, it would be difficult to preserve *kokutai*. Consequently at this time I determined even to sacrifice myself because I believed we had to make peace.[209]

Hirohito was restating his earlier instructions to Kido about preserving the imperial regalia. Reacting to the 24 July air attack on the grand shrine at Ise, the emperor told Kido he had given up on the decisive battle of the homeland. His attention now shifted to preserving *kokutai* and its manifestations, the imperial regalia. If the three sacred treasures fell into enemy hands the symbols of the 2600-year plus imperial line would be lost and with them the imperial house and *kokutai*.[210] On 21 August 1945, the army moved the sacred sword from Atsuka to the remote Gifu Prefecture to protect it from the Americans.[211] Hirohito's insistence to the end about preserving *kokutai* and its symbols, the imperial regalia, was neither selfish nor craven. It was instead a fundamental expression of core Japanese values in whose names people were still willing to endure a hopeless war. After all, if the emperor and the sacred regalia disappeared, would Japan's *kokutai* remain? Would it still be possible to have a unified people identifiable as Japanese? No one in Tokyo during that hot summer could answer that question with authority.[212] What is clear is that the army's understanding and acceptance of the Potsdam Declaration depended on preserving *kokutai* in its macro sense—the emperor system (*tennō-sei*), which legitimized the military's role in Japanese society. Hirohito looked at the microcosm—without the symbols of the throne the framework itself was irrelevant.[213]

By midsummer of 1945 basic values, the raison d'tre of the Japanese, were directly threatened by overwhelming Allied military might. Japan

FIGURE 13. Generalissimo and high priest: The bemedaled emperor visits the Yasukuni Shrine in Tokyo to pray for Japan's war dead. Courtesy of USAMHI, Japan Miscellaneous Collection

was losing the war, and no one knew precisely what defeat might mean in terms of *kokutai* or the preservation of the imperial house. From the Japanese viewpoint, the Allied policy of unconditional surrender threatened the very values used to define "Japanese" since the Russo-Japanese War. Thus the individual emperor is willing to offer himself to the victors to ensure the preservation of the Japanese people, the imperial institution, and *kokutai*. To preserve Japan, Hirohito finally did take the initiative to act with resolution. The agonizing stalemate was finally broken. Japan could move toward surrender. Secret peace maneuvers began on 10 August when the Japanese government informed the Allied powers of the emperor's decision.

The American reply to Japan's acceptance of the Potsdam Declaration came by short-wave radio early on 12 August. By this time, the war ministry was already in an uproar, as threats and recriminations filled the corridors. Anami was shifting troops about the capital causing staff officers to wonder if a coup d'etat was in progress under their very noses.[214] Each passing day only fueled further speculation that an armed coup was imminent.[215] Catching wind of these rumors, Metropolitan Police Headquarters posted special guards throughout the city and kept suspected officers under surveillance.[216] They were wise to do so, because the very thought of defeat provoked headstrong younger staff officers in Tokyo to mutiny. Led by Major Hatanaka Kenji, these diehards aimed to isolate the emperor by eliminating his key advisers. Once these evil counselors had been removed, the emperor would surely agree to continue the war. Hatanaka and his confederates spent the next two days enlisting support for their conspiracy.

Meanwhile, on the afternoon of 12 August, the imperial princes gathered in Tokyo to hear Hirohito's explanation of the 9–10 August Imperial Conference and his reasons for accepting the Potsdam Declaration.[217] During the three-hour meeting, Hirohito explained why he was seeking peace. He had, the emperor told his kinsmen, lost confidence in the military because of its record since the Leyte operation.[218] Prince Asaka, Hirohito's uncle and the most hawkish of the royal clan, then asked him, if we cannot preserve *kokutai*, will the war continue (*senso wo keizoku suru ka*). "Of course," was Hirohito's blunt answer.[219] This was the final wartime example of the emperor's willingness to rationalize the harsh reality of utter defeat. But Hirohito was always willing to take an ambiguous answer even, as things turned out, if it came from the United States. Fortunately for the emperor and his nation, his resolve was never tested. But it might well have been.

Although Hirohito had decided on surrender, the cabinet continued to wrangle over the meaning of the Allied reply, especially as it related to the emperor's future status. Neither could a meeting of the Supreme Council for the Direction of the War held on 13 August break the impasse. A deadlocked cabinet facing threats of open rebellion, continuing enemy air attacks, and even the specter of a third atomic bomb was paralyzed, incapable of action.

Early on the morning of 14 August American aircraft dropped leaflets throughout Japan containing the Japanese government's offer to accept the Potsdam Declaration and the Allied reply. Now the secret negotiations were revealed. Fearful that the leaflets falling into the hands of the military might ignite a coup, Hirohito scrambled to convene another Imperial Conference to make clear his unwavering determination to accept the American reply and end the war.[220] Just before the scheduled 1100 meeting, he met with his field marshals to get their opinions about ending the war. Field Marshal Hata Shunroku had flown from Hiroshima to Tokyo for the meeting, and it so happened that he had breakfast with Anami at the war ministry. Hata remarked that the atomic bomb was not that powerful a weapon, having been on the receiving end of one. Anami urged him to pass this information to the emperor, because it might affect Hirohito's final decision for war or peace.[221] Meeting in the Imperial Library, the field marshals did counsel Hirohito to continue the war and further assured him about the safety of the imperial house, whether they really believed it or not.[222] But Hirohito disagreed. The war had to end now.[223] The emperor then walked the short distance to the underground bomb shelter tunneled into the ground next to the library to open the Imperial Conference to approve acceptance of the Potsdam Declaration. But there still remained fanatical officers who believed Japan must fight to the bitter end.

Late on 14 August Hatanaka's conspirators assassinated the commander of the Guards Division and his brother-in-law, who happened to be present when the plotters burst into his office. After issuing a bogus order over the dead commander's seal, troops surrounded the palace and cut all communications from the household ministry building to the outside world. Then they began searching for the emperor's recording that announced Japan's acceptance of the Potsdam Declaration. In 1946 Hirohito recalled seeing squads of soldiers surrounding the Imperial Library and remarked it was a lucky thing that the heavy steel shutters on the windows were closed because of the danger from air raids thus making it impossible for the troops to see him.[224] Unable to find the recording, the soldiers' frustration mounted. General Anami, now planning his ritual suicide, offered the rebels no support. Eastern District Army Headquarters not only refused to support the mutineers but also actively turned against them. By morning the coup had quickly collapsed, and the ringleaders committed suicide. In July 1944 a coup attempt to end the fighting had failed in Germany. After that failure, the Allies continued their strategy as before until Germany surrendered. Had Hatanaka's coup succeeded, in all likelihood Allied strategy against Japan would have continued apace with devastating results for both sides.[225]

On the basis of the available evidence, Hirohito does not measure up as a fighting generalissimo. He consistently reacted to military operations; he did not initiate them. Viewed against the backdrop of Japan's military operations between December 1941 and August 1945, he comes across as a cautious procrastinator, willing to let events take their course. In the face of total defeat, he valued the imperial institution more than his people, his army, and his empire. Only the immediate danger to *kokutai* jolted him from his passive role and forced him to action. Perhaps more than fire raids, atomic bombs, the Soviet entry into the war against Japan, and the specter of invasion, it was the threat to his imperial ancestors, and therefore the survival of the imperial institution itself, that provided the steel otherwise missing from Hirohito's regal backbone.

NOTES

1. Tradition and Circumstances

This chapter benefited from the critical comments of Drs. Robert H. Berlin, W. Glenn Robertson, and Roger J. Spiller. The definitive work in any language on Khalkhin-Gol is Alvin D. Coox, *Nomonhan: Japan against Russia, 1939*, 2 vols. (Stanford: Stanford University Press, 1985).

1. Bōeichō, Bōei kenshūjō senshibu (Japan, National Institute for Defense Studies, Military History Department), ed., *Senshi sōsho*, vol. 73, *Kantōgun* (Official military history: Kwantung Army), pt. 2 (Tokyo: Asagumo shimbunsha, 1971), 2.
2. Lieutenant Colonel Kobayashi, IJA, "Tai sensha yōhō (senhō) no hensen susei" (An overview of the changing employment and tactics of antitank warfare), mimeographed, ca. 1940. Photocopy in possession of author.
3. Rikujō bakuryōbu dai 5 buchō (Japan Ground Staff College, Fifth Department [Training]), ed., *Nomonhan jiken no hōheisen* (Artillery engagements during the Nomonhan Incident), mimeographed, 1965, 56–57. Copy in possession of author.
4. The former figure is from S. N. Shishkin, *Khalkhin-Gol* (Moscow: Military Publishing House, 1954, reprint of 1945 ed.), 56, and the latter from Colonel (Res.) V. Yezhakov, "Slavnaya Pobeda Na Khalkhin-Gol," *Voyenno: Istoricheskiy Zhurnal* 8 (1979): 72.
5. The main documents used are

   Dai 1 bu, dai 3 ka, Rikugun gijutsu honbu (First Department, Third Section, Army Technical Headquarters), "Heiki kentōkai kiji (Nomonhan jiken)"

(Ordnance investigation conference report [Nomonhan Incident]), 13–14 September 1939, Secret;

Daihon'ei rikugunbu (Imperial General Headquarters, Army Department), "Sanbōchō kaidō sekijō ni okeru dai 5 kachō kōen yōshi" (Summary of the presentation by the AGS Fifth Section chief at the chiefs of staff conference), 10 October 1939, Secret;

Daihon'ei rikugunbu, Nomonhan jiken kenkyū iinkai dai 1 kenkyū iinkai (Imperial General Headquarters, First Research Subcommittee of the Subcommittee to Investigate the Nomonhan Incident), "'Nomonhan' jiken kenkyū hōkoku" (Nomonhan Incident research report), 10 January 1940, Top Secret;

Kantōgun heibi kenkyū chōsa iinchō (Chairman, Armaments Research Committee, Kwantung Army), "Kenkyū hōkoku—Nomonhan jiken"(Research report on the Nomonhan Incident), 27 November 1939, Secret;

Konuma Haruo, Lieutenant Colonel, IJA, "Nomonhan jiken yori kansatsu seru tai 'So' kindaisen no jissō" (The realities of modern warfare against the Soviet Union based on the Nomonhan Incident), February 1940, Secret;

Murakami Keisaku, Lieutenant General, IJA, "Nomonhan jiken ni kansuru kansatsu" (Considerations on the Nomonhan Incident), 16 October 1939, Secret;

Shimanuki Takeharu, Major, IJA, "Sakusen yoheijō yori mitaru 'Nomonhan' jiken no kyōkun" (Lessons of the Nomonhan Incident from the viewpoint of handling troops in operations), 30 September 1939, Secret; and

Colonel Terada Masao, IJA, "Nomonhan jiken ni kansuru shoken" (Opinions concerning the Nomonhan Incident), 13 October 1939, Secret.

6. Lieutenant Colonel Konuma had chaired the Second Subcommittee, which dealt with operations, tactics, staff procedures, and logistics.
7. Shimanuki, "Sakusen yoheijō."
8. Terada, "Nomonhan jiken ni kansuru shoken."
9. Gijutsu honbu, "Heiki kentōkai kiji."
10. Bōeichō, Bōei kenshūjō senshibu, *Senshi sōsho: Kantōgun,* vol. 2, Appendix 2: "Dai 2 sōgun shuyō butai hensei saiyo" (Overview of TO&E for major units of Second General Army). The Eleventh, Twenty-fifth, and Fifty-seventh divisions were transferred to the Japanese home islands in April and May 1945.
11. The 205th, 206th, 212th, and 216th infantry divisions had a similar role and the identical TO&E in Kyushu.
12. Shimanuki, "Sakusen yoheijō."
13. Murakami, "Nomonhan jiken ni kansuru kansatsu."
14. Bōeichō, Bōei kenshūjō senshibu, vol. 27, *Kantōgun,* pt. 1, 199. The respective statistics for the Type 89, 95, and 97 were

Type	Main Gun	Speed	Range
89-Medium	57 mm	25 kph	140 km
95-Light	37 mm	40 kph	250 km
98-Light	37 mm	50 kph	300 km

Source: Hara Tomio and Takeuchi Akira, eds., *Nihon no sensha* (Japanese armor) (Tokyo: Shuppan kyōdōsha, 1961), 26, 29, 37.

15. Hara and Takeuchi, *Nihon no sensha*, 24.
16. According to one version, 279 Type 97 improved models were built.
17. See, for example, the remarks in Shimanuki, "Sakusen yoheijō," and Murakami, "Nomonhan jiken ni kansuru kansatsu." The proposal for eighteen artillery batteries as opposed to the contemporary nine was Shimanuki's.
18. At Khalkhin-Gol the Japanese heavy artillery weapons with the greatest range were their Type 92 cannon, a 105 mm gun capable of firing 18,200 meters, and a Type 89 cannon, a 150 mm piece with an equivalent range. Both were flat trajectory weapons. The Soviets had a 122 mm cannon with a range of 20,800 meters and two types of long-range howitzers. The ML-20 was a 1937 design of a 152 mm howitzer with a maximum range of 17,300 meters. The 203 mm howitzer could fire a projectile 18,000 meters. The howitzer's ability to hit targets on rear slopes was significant.
19. U.S. forces identified each as a self-propelled gun. The Japanese referred to the Type 1 as a gun tank.
20. See Shimanuki, "Sakusen yoheijō"; and Terada, "Nomonhan jiken ni kansuru shoken."
21. Rikugun gijutsu honbu, "Heiki kentōkai kiji (Nomonhan jiken)"; Daihon'ei rikugunbu, "'Nomonhan' jiken kenkyū hōkoku"; and Terada, "Nomonhan jiken ni kansuru shoken."
22. Rikugun gijutsu honbu, "Heiki kentōkai kiji (Nomonhan jiken)."
23. Kantōgun heibi kenkyū chōsa iinchō, "Kenkyū hōkoku—Nomonhan jiken."
24. Rikushi kenkyū fukyūkai ([Japan, Ground Self Defense Force, Command & Staff College] Committee for the dissemination of the study of ground warfare), ed., *Marē sakusen* (The Malaya operation) (Tokyo: Hara shobō, 1971), 18–21, 271–73.
25. In 1941–42 the number of motor vehicles assigned to infantry divisions was as follows: Japanese (Fifth Infantry Division), 860; Italian (Western Desert), 381; British (Western Desert), 4000; German (Western Desert), 2600.
26. By the time Japanese forces reached the island of Singapore, concern about their ability to seize the island was growing at all levels of the Japanese command structure. Field guns were critically short of ammunition, and there was pressure on Lieutenant General Yamashita Tomoyuki,

commander of the Japanese land forces, to call off the attack. Instead Yamashita pressed forward, but after the war he said, "I felt that if we had to fight in the city we would be beaten." He described his strategy for Singapore as "a bluff, a bluff that worked." Cited in John Toland, *The Rising Sun* (New York: Random House, 1970), 275–76.
27. Terada, "Nomonhan jiken ni kansuru shoken."
28. Daihon'ei rikugunbu, "Sanbōchō kaidō sekijō ni okeru dai 5 kachō kōen yōshi."
29. Konuma, "Nomonhan jiken yori kansatsu seru tai 'So' kindaisen no jissō."
30. Kantōgun heibi kenkyū chōsa iinchō, "Kenkyū hōkoku—Nomonhan jiken."
31. Bōeichō, Bōei kenshūjō senshibu, *Senshi sōsho: Kantōgun*, 2:142.
32. Bōeichō, Bōei kenshūjō senshibu, *Senshi sōsho: Kantōgun*, 2:153.
33. Bōeichō, Bōei kenshūjō senshibu, *Senshi sōsho: Kantōgun*, 2:136.
34. Shimada Toshihiko, *Kantōgun* (The Kwantung Army) (Tokyo: Chūkō shinsho, 1965), 152.
35. Imai Sei'ichi et al., eds., *Taiheiyō sensō 3 Nitchū sensō*. Vol. 2. (The Pacific War 3: The Sino-Japanese War II) (Tokyo: Aoki shoten, 1971), 247.
36. Rikujō jieitai Fuji gakkō (Japan, Ground self-defense force, Fuji school), ed., *Sentō senshi: Bōei*, kōhen (Tactical military history: The defense [part 2]) (Tokyo: Fuji gakkō, 1973), Appendix 2: "Kyūgun hensei sōbi" (TO&ES of the former Imperial Army), 319–20. The Fourteenth and Twenty-ninth divisions were destroyed at the Palaus and Guam, respectively. The Thirty-sixth Division was mauled and bypassed at Sarmi, Netherlands New Guinea, and the Fifty-second Division ended the war garrisoning Truk.
37. Based on comments by Japanese participants during the U.S. Army Command and General Staff College, Combat Studies Institute—Japan Ground Self-defense Force Staff College Military History Faculty Historical Exchange, 22–24 July 1981 in Tokyo, Japan.
38. Cited in Bōeichō, Kenkyū shiryō [Research materials], *Soren gawa shiryō kara mita Nomonhan jiken Soren no kokkyō funsō taisho* (The Nomonhan Incident viewed from Soviet documents: The Soviets handling of border conflicts), Series Document 78 RO-8H, 1978, 191.
39. James B. Crowley, "Japanese Army Factionalism in the Early 1930's," *Journal of Asian Studies* 21 (May 1962): 313–14; and James B. Crowley, *Japan's Quest for Autonomy: National Security and Foreign Policy 1930–1938* (Princeton: Princeton University Press, 1966), 90.
40. Leonard A. Humphreys, *The Way of the Heavenly Sword: The Japanese Army in the 1920s* (Stanford: Stanford University Press, 1995), 106.
41. Barbara Tuchman, *Stilwell and the American Experience in China* (New York: Macmillan, 1970), 90.

2. The Development of Amphibious Warfare Doctrine

1. Hans G. von Lehmann, trans. by Michael C. Halbig, "Japanese Landings Operations in World War II," in Lieutenant Colonel Merrill L. Bartlett, USMC (Ret.) ed., *Assault from the Sea: Essays on the History of Amphibious Warfare* (Annapolis MD: Naval Institute, 1987), 195–201.
2. Suekuni Masao, "Senshi ni miru jōriku sakusen to sono urakata" (Another perspective on landing operations seen through military history), *Hatō* 3 (July 1977): 13–22.
3. Tajiri Masaji, *Jōriku sakusen senshi ruirei shū* (Selected historical examples of amphibious operations) (privately published, Imperial Naval War College, Navy Education Department, 1932), appendix 2.
4. Rikusen gakkai (Committee for the study of land warfare), ed., *Kindai sensōshi gaisetsu (shiryō hen)* (An overview of modern war history: Documents) (Tokyo: Rikusen gakkai senshi bukai, 1984), 121.
5. Tajiri, *Jōriku sakusen senshi ruirei shū*, 123
6. Tajiri, *Jōriku sakusen senshi ruirei shū*, 161.
7. Kobe Tatsu, "Nanpō sakusen ni ozuru rikusen no kyōiku kunren," Kenkyū shiryō, 85RO-3H ([Imperial Army] amphibious training and doctrine for southern operations) (Tokyo: mimeo., 1985), 5, 23, and 26.
8. Kobe, "Nanpō sakusen," 17.
9. Kobe, "Nanpō sakusen," 19.
10. Edward Behr, *Hirohito: Behind the Myth* (New York: Vintage, 1990), 236.
11. Kobe, "Nanpō sakusen," 19–20.
12. Rikusen gakkai, *Kindai sensōshi*, 121
13. Kobe, "Nanpō sakusen," 21.
14. Kobe, "Nanpō sakusen," 23.
15. Ōe Shinobu, *Shōwa no rekishi*, vol. 3, *Tennō no guntai* (The history of the Shōwa reign, vol. 3, The emperor's army) (Tokyo: Shogakkan, 1982), 252.
16. Hata Ikuhiko, *Nankyō jihen* (The Nanking Incident) (Tokyo: Chūō kōronsha, 1986), 93.
17. Fujiwara Akira, *Taiheiyō sensō shiron* (A historical interpretation of the Pacific war) (Tokyo: Aoki shoten, 1982), 44.
18. Kojima Noboru, *Nitchū sensō*, vol. 3, *1937–1945* (The Sino-Japanese war, vol. 3, 1937–1945) (Tokyo: Bungei shunjū, 1984), 143.
19. Bōeichō kenshūjo senshibu, vol. 86, *Shina jihen rikugun sakusen*, pt. 1, *Shōwa jusan nen ichi gatsu made* (Official military history, vol. 86, Army operations during the China incident: to January 1938) (Tokyo: Asagumo shimbunsha, 1975), 277, 401–3, and vol. 89, *Shina jihen rikugun sakusen*, pt. 2, *Shōwa juyon nen kyugatsu made* (Official military history, vol. 89, Army operations during the China incident: to September 1939) (Tokyo: Asagumo shimbunsha, 1976), 232, 238, 243–44, 339.

20. Fujiwara, *Taiheiyō sensō shiron*, 53–54.
21. Kobe, "Nanpō sakusen," appendix 9.
22. Allan R. Millett, *Semper Fidelis: The History of the United States Marine Corps* (New York: Macmillan, 1980), 320–21.
23. Fujiwara, *Taiheiyō sensō shiron*, 54.
24. Jeter A. Isely and Philip A. Crowl, *The U.S. Marines and Amphibious Warfare: Its Theory and Its Practice in the Pacific* (Princeton: Princeton University Press, 1951), 45.
25. William F. Atwater, "United States Army and Navy Development of Joint Landing Operations, 1898–1942" (Ph.D. diss., Duke University, 1986), 122, 134–35.
26. Von Lehmann, "Japanese Landings Operations," 195.

3. IJA *Strategy and the Pacific War*

1. Carl von Clausewitz, *On War*, ed. and trans. by Michael Howard and Peter Paret (Princeton: Princeton University Press, 1976), bk. 3, chap. 1, 177.
2. Fujiwara Akira, "The Role of the Japanese Army," in Dorothy Borg and Shumpei Okamoto, eds., *Pearl Harbor as History* (New York: Columbia University Press, 1971), 189–91.
3. Ōe Shinobu, *Nihon no sanbō honbu* (The Japanese General Staff) (Tokyo: Chūkō shinsho, 1985), 200.
4. Kobe, "Nanpō sakusen," 11–12.
5. Fujiwara, *Taiheiyō sensō shiron*, 53.
6. John Hunter Boyle, *China and Japan at War 1937–1945* (Stanford: Stanford University Press, 1972), 44–60; and Mark R. Peattie, *Ishiwara Kanji and Japan's Confrontation with the West* (Princeton: Princeton University Press, 1975), 267–308.
7. Hata Ikuhiko, "The Japanese-Soviet Confrontation, 1935–1939," trans. with an introduction by Alvin D. Coox, in *Deterrent Diplomacy: Japan, Germany, and the USSR 1935–1940*, ed. James William Morley, *Japan's Road to the Pacific War Series* (New York: Columbia University Press, 1976), 129–33.
8. Fujiwara, *Taiheiyō sensō shiron*, 53.
9. Coox, *Nomonhan: Japan against Russia*, 1034–49; and Shimada, *Kantōgun*, 153–58.
10. Fujiwara, *Taiheiyō sensō shiron*, 62–63.
11. Fujiwara, *Taiheiyō sensō shiron*, 64.
12. Fujiwara, *Taiheiyō sensō shiron*, 72, 75–76.
13. Ikuda Makoto, *Nihon rikugun shi* (A History of the Japanese Army) (Tokyo: Kyōikusha, 1980), 200.
14. Ōe, *Nihon no sanbō honbu*, 208–9.

15. Sanbō honbu sensō shidōhan (War guidance section, general staff), ed., "Daihon'ei kimitsu sensō nisshi" (IGHQ confidential war dairy), *Rekishi to jimbutsu* (September 1971), 354.
16. Ikuda, *Nihon rikugun shi*, 203.
17. Sanbō honbu sensō shidōhan, "Daihon'ei kimitsu sensō nisshi," 366.
18. Ikuda, *Nihon rikugun shi*, 204; Toyoda Jō, *Kaigun gunreibu* (The naval general staff), (Tokyo: Kodansha bunkō, 1993), 289-90.
19. Hayashi Saburō, *Taiheiyō sensō rikusen gaishi* (An overview of army operations in the Pacific war) (Tokyo: Iwanami shoten, 1951), trans. by Saburo Hayashi and Alvin D. Coox, *Kogun: The Japanese Army in the Pacific War* (Quantico VA: Marine Corps Association, 1959).

4. An Allied Interpretation of the Pacific War

1. Rikusen gakkai, *Kindai sensōshi*, 99; Fujiwara Akira, *Nihon gendaishi taikei: Gunjishi* (An outline of modern Japanese history: the history of military affairs) (Tokyo: Tōyō keizai shimpōsha, 1961), 186.
2. Christopher Thorne, *Allies of a Kind: The United States, Britain, and the War against Japan, 1941-1945* (New York: Oxford University Press, 1978), 56.
3. David Ignatius, "How Churchill's Agents Secretly Manipulated the U.S. before Pearl Harbor," *Washington Post*, 17 September 1989, Outlook Section, 1,1.
4. Louis Morton, *Strategy and Command: The First Two Years*, United States Army in World War II: The War in the Pacific (Washington DC: U.S. Government Printing Office, 1967), 81.
5. Allan R. Millett, "The United States Armed Forces in the Second World War," in *Military Effectiveness*, ed. Allan R. Millett and Williamson Murray, vol. 3, *The Second World War* (Boston: Unwin Hyman, 1988), 55.
6. Johanna Meskill, *Hitler and Japan: The Hollow Alliance* (New York: Atherton Press, 1966).
7. Hayashi Shigeru, *Nihon no rekishi* (The history of Japan), vol. 25, *Taiheiyō sensō* (The Pacific war) (Tokyo: Chūō kōronsha, 1967), 124-26.
8. Shimada, *Kantōgun*, 166, 171.
9. Morton, *Strategy and Command: The First Two Years*, 139.
10. Millett, "The United States Armed Forces," 55.
11. Thorne, *Allies of a Kind*, 266.
12. Akira Iriye, *Across the Pacific: An Inner History of American-East Asian Relations* (New York: Harcourt, Brace, and World, 1967), 232.
13. Throne, *Allies of a Kind*, 294.
14. Richard M. Leighton and Robert W. Coakley, *Global Logistics and Strategy 1940-1943*, United States Army in World War II: The War Department (Washington DC: U.S. Government Printing Office, 1955), 390-91.

15. Morton, *Strategy and Command: The First Two Years*, 441.
16. John Miller Jr. *Cartwheel: The Reduction of Rabaul*, U.S. Army in World War II: The War in the Pacific (Washington DC: U.S. Government Printing Office, 1959), 538-39.
17. Millett, "The United States Armed Forces," 57-58.
18. Morton, *Strategy and Command: The First Two Years*, 399.
19. Morton, *Strategy and Command: The First Two Years*, 460.
20. Morton, *Strategy and Command: The First Two Years*, 585-90.
21. Maruyama Shizuo, *Inpāru sakusen jūgunki* (A military correspondent on the Imphal operation) (Tokyo: Iwanami shinsho, 1984), 118-22.
22. Field Marshal Viscount Slim, *Defeat into Victory* (London: PAPERMAC, 1987).
23. Fujiwara, *Taiheiyō sensō shiron*, 175, 178.
24. Roy A. Appleman, James M. Burns, Russell A. Gugeler, John Stevens, *Okinawa: The Last Battle*, United States Army in World War II: The War in the Pacific (Washington DC: U.S. Government Printing Office, 1948), 473-74, 489-90. The figure for American casualties includes 12,250 killed or missing in action on Okinawa. Among the dead were 4907 U.S. Navy casualties. In addition, perhaps 100,000 Okinawan civilians were killed, trapped in the terrible artillery bombardments that marked this siege warfare.
25. U.S. Department of State, *Foreign Relations of the United States: Diplomatic Papers: The Conference of Berlin (the Postdam Conference), 1945*, vol. 1 (Washington DC: U.S. Government Printing Office, 1960), 905, 907-8.
26. Edward J. Drea, *MacArthur's* ULTRA: *Codebreaking and the War against Japan, 1942-1945* (Lawrence: University Press of Kansas, 1992), 202-25.

5. U.S. Army and IJA Doctrine during World War II

1. FM 100-5, *Tentative Field Service Regulations, Operations* (Washington DC: U.S. Government Printing Office, 1939), 29.
2. FM 100-5, *Tentative Field Service Regulations*, 31-33.
3. Kent Roberts Greenfield, *The Historian and the Army* (New Brunswick NJ: Rutgers University Press, 1954), 81.
4. FM 100-5, *Field Service Regulations, Operations* 5.
5. FM 100-5, *Field Service Regulations*, 235.
6. Ernest J. Fisher Jr., comp., "Weapons and Equipment Evolution and Its Influence upon Organization and Tactics in the American Army from 1775-1963," 64, Historical Manuscript Collection, U.S. Army Center of Military History, Washington DC. See also Jonathan M. House, "Towards Combined Arms Warfare: A Survey of Tactics, Doctrine, and Organization

in the Twentieth Century," Research Survey No. 2, Combat Studies Institute, Fort Leavenworth KS, mimeo., 69–78 for an excellent summation of major trends in the U.S. Army during the interwar period.
7. Fisher, "Weapons and Equipment Evolution," 4; Henry F. Pringle, "Weapons Win Wars," Historical Manuscript Collection, U.S. Army Center of Military History, Washington DC, 27.
8. Fisher, "Weapons and Equipment Evolution," 62–63 and 89. Also see John English, *A Perspective on Infantry* (Westport CT: Greenwood Press, 1981), 139. On infantry losses see U.S. Army Ground Forces, Plans Section, "Study of AGF Battle Casualties," 25 September 1946, 11.
9. Lieutenant Colonel H. E. Dager, USA, "Modern Infantry," C&GSS *Military Review* 20:76 (March 1940), 9–10.
10. War Department, Replacement Board, "Statements of Colonel Arthur S. Collins," *Replacement System World Wide World War II: Report of the Replacement Board*, Department of the Army, 1947, bk. 5, Annex 35 Historical Manuscript Collection, U.S. Army Center of Military History, Washington DC.
11. Katogawa Kotarō, *Sanjuhachi shiki hoheijū* (Type 38 infantry rifle) (Tokyo: Shirogane shobō, 1975), 137.
12. Kuwada Etsu and Maebara Tomio, eds., *Nihon no sensō zukai to dēta* (The wars of Japan: graphics and data) (Tokyo: Hara shobō, 1982), pt. 2, appen. 5, 6, 10.
13. Ikuda Makoto, *Nihon rikugunshi* (A history of the Japanese army) (Tokyo: Kyōikusho, 1980), 157.
14. Katogawa, *Sanjuhachi shiki hoheijū*, 242–44.
15. Rikugun daijin (War minister imperial Japanese army), *Sakusen yōmurei dai 2 bu* (Field service regulations, pt. 2 [1938]), ed., Nihon bungeisha (Tokyo: Nihon bungeisha, 1969 reprint of the 1938 FSR), 129–32.
16. Kobe Tatsu, "Nanpō sakusen ni ozuru rikugun no kyōiku kunren" (Army training and doctrine for southern area operations), Bōei kenshūjō, Kenkyū shiryō 85RO-3H mimeo., 1985, 179.
17. Kobe, "Nanpō sakusen," 22 and 182.
18. Kobe, "Nanpō sakusen," 79.
19. Kobe, "Nanpō sakusen," 110.
20. Kobe, "Nanpō sakusen," 89. The maneuvers were canceled as preparations accelerated in mid-1941 for war against the Western powers in Asia.
21. Christopher R. Gabel, *The U.S. Army GHQ Maneuvers of 1941* (Washington DC: U.S. Army Center of Military History, 1991).
22. Rikusenshi kenkyū fukyūkai, ed., *Ruson shima shinkō sakusen* (Offensive operations on Luzon Island) (Tokyo: Hara shobō, 1969), 57.
23. Allied Forces, Southwest Pacific Area, "Report of the Commanding General Buna Forces on the Buna Campaign, Dec. 1, 1942–Jan. 25, 1943,"

U.S. Army Center of Military History Historical Records Collection, Washington DC, 54.
24. "Report of the Commanding General Buna Forces," 54.
25. "Report of the Commanding General Buna Forces," 54.
26. "Report of the Commanding General Buna Forces," 66 and 76; statistics on artillery at Buna from Edward T. Lauer, *32d Infantry Division World War II* (Madison WI: Thirty-second Infantry Division History Commission, 1955?), 56.
27. "Report of the Commanding General Buna Forces," 73.
28. Harry Knight, Colonel, "Report Concerning Observations in the Southwest Pacific Theater during the Period October 16 to December 30 1942," Army Ground Forces Observer Report, Southwest Pacific Area, Historical Records Collection, U.S. Army Center of Military History, Washington, DC.
29. Daihon'ei rikugunbu (Imperial general headquarters, army department) "Tōbu 'Nyūginiya' homen tai Bei-A gun sentō no keiken ni motozuku jakkan no kyōjun" (Some lessons based on combat experience on the eastern New Guinea front against the American and Australian armies), *Senkunhō dai 7 go* (Lessons learned bulletin No. 7), 25 September 1943, 5.
30. "Comments and Off-the-Record Remarks to [BG Julian] Cunningham, CG 112th Cavalry RCT-COL [Philip] Hooper interview," 8 April 1947, in Robert Ross Smith Papers, U.S. Army Military History Institute, Carlisle Barracks PA.
31. Letter, MG C. P. Hall to LTG Walter Krueger, 16 July 1944, in Smith Papers.
32. Edward J. Drea, "Defending the Driniumor: U.S. Army Covering Force Operations in New Guinea, 1944," *Leavenworth Paper* No. 9 (Washington DC: U.S. Government Printing Office, 1984), 37.
33. Cited in Dager, "Modern Infantry," 7.
34. 32d Infantry Division, "Report After Action: Aitape Operation, 28 June–25 Aug 44," Annex 13, Intelligence Section, 4, microfilm, U.S. Army Military History Institute, Carlisle Barracks PA.
35. M. Hamlin Cannon, *Leyte: The Return to the Philippines*, United States Army in World War II: The War in the Pacific (Washington DC: Office of the Chief of Military History, 1954), 244–52. This section is based on General Krueger's personal critique of the Leyte operation.
36. Kobe, "Nanpō sakusen," 181.
37. Kobe, "Nanpō sakusen," 63.
38. Kobe, "Nanpō sakusen," 114–15.
39. Tsunoda Fusako, *Sekinin Rabauru shogun Imamura Hitoshi* (Imamura Hitoshi: The general responsible for Rabaul) (Tokyo: Shinchōsha, 1984), 261.
40. Inagaki Ri'ichi, "Nyūginiya furyoki" (A New Guinea POW's account)

Rekishi to jimbutsu: Zōkan Hiroku Taiheiyō sensō (September 1982), 230.
41. Bōeichō Bōeikenshūjō senshishitsu, ed., Senshi sōsho, vol. 84, Minami Taiheiyō rikugun sakusen, pt. 5, Aitape-Puriaka-Rabauru (Official military history, vol. 84, Army operations in the south Pacific, pt. 5, Aitape, Empress Augusta Bay, Rabaul) (Tokyo: Asagumo shimbunsha, 1975), 335.
42. Yutani Kohisa, "Kyūriku kaigun shōkō no sembatsu to kyōiku" (Education and personnel selection policies of officers of the Imperial Army and Navy), Bōei kenshūjō, Kenkyū shiryō 80RO-12H, mimeo., 1981, 71.
43. Ōe Shinobu, Shōwa no rekishi, vol. 3, Tennō no guntai (A history of the Shōwa period, vol. 3, The emperor's army) (Tokyo: Shogakkan, 1982), 94.
44. Yutani, "Kyūriku kaigun," 187.
45. Ōe Shinobu, Nichi-Rō sensō to nihon guntai (The Russo-Japanese War and the Japanese army) (Tokyo: Rifu shobō, 1987), 187–90.
46. Hori Eizō, "Yamashita Hirobumi taisho kujū nichikan no kunō" (General Yamashita Tomoyuki's ninety days of suffering), Rekishi to jimbutsu Taiheiyō sensō shiriizu Nihon rikukaigun no senreki (December 1986), 325.
47. Ienaga Saburō, The Pacific War 1931–1945 (New York: Pantheon, 1978), 46. On deficiencies in officer education also see Jōhō Yoshio, Rikugunsho gunmukyoku (The military affairs bureau, war ministry) (Tokyo: Fūyō shobō, 1979), 517–20.
48. Kobe, "Nanpō sakusen," 63.
49. "A Military History of the US Army Command and General Staff College, Fort Leavenworth, Kansas, 1881–1963," typescript, n.d., 27, Historical Manuscript Collection, U.S. Army Center of Military History, Washington DC, n.d.
50. Charles E. Kirkpatrick, An Unknown Future and a Doubtful Present: Writing the Victory Plan of 1941 (Washington DC: U.S. Army Center of Military History, 1990), 121.
51. Field Marshal Viscount William Slim, Defeat into Victory (New York: D. McKay, 1961), 538.

6. "Trained in the Hardest School"

The views and opinions expressed in this paper are those of the author and not those of the Department of the Army. An earlier version of this paper was presented at Washington and Lee University on 1 May 1986. I am indebted to Drs. Roger B. Jeans, Roger Spiller, and Carl Boyd for their comments and criticism of this essay.

The title quotation is from Thucydides, History of the Peloponnesian War, trans. Rex Warner (New York: Viking Penguin, 1985 ed.), bk. 1, 85. "There is no need to suppose that human beings differ very much one from another:

but it is true that the ones who come out on top are the ones who have been trained in the hardest school."

1. See Alvin D. Coox, "The Japanese Army Experience," in *New Dimensions in Military History*, ed. Russell F. Weigley (San Rafael CA: Presidio, 1975) for a succinct overview of the early years of the IJA. Ikuda Makoto, *Nihon rikugunshi* (A history of the Japanese army) (Tokyo: Kyōikusha, 1980), 20–44, offers a useful summary of the establishment of the IJA. Ōe Shinobu, *Nihon no sanbōhonbu* (The Japanese general staff) (Tokyo: Chūkō shinsho, 1985), chaps. 2 and 3, discusses the new army. Matsushita Yoshio, *Meiji no guntai* (The Meiji military) (Tokyo: Shibundō, 1958), an abbreviated version of his two-volume work, is still valuable.

2. Fujiwara Akira, *Nihon gendaishi taikei: Gunjishi* (An Overview of modern Japanese history: military history) (Tokyo: Tōyō keizai shinpōsha, 1961), 149, makes the estimate for the Meiji Era (1868–1912). By 1912 perhaps 70–80 percent of the officer corps were from samurai stock, but within fifteen years this figure had fallen to 50–60 percent. By the 1930s, previous lineage was not officially recorded. Fujiwara's seminal research revealed that, during the 1920s and 1930s, the proportion of serving officers who were sons of farm families declined, while that of sons of professional officers increased. See Fujiwara, 159. On this same point also refer to Nobutaka Ike, "War and Modernization," in *Political Development in Modern Japan*, ed. Robert E. Ward (Princeton: Princeton University Press, 1968), 189.

3. The Takebashi Incident of 23 August 1878 exploded when about 260 NCOs and men of a guards artillery battalion mutinied and murdered their officers. Dissatisfied because they had received no official recognition or reward for their service against the rebels in the Satsuma Rebellion, the men plotted to burn the imperial residence. One measure of the gravity with which the government viewed the revolt was the execution by firing squad of the ringleader and fifty-three other participants.

4. Roger F. Hackett, "The Meiji Leaders and Modernization: The Case of Yamagata Aritomo," in *Changing Japanese Attitudes toward Modernization*, ed. Marius B. Jansen (Princeton: Princeton University Press, 1965), 259, makes the point that the rescript "amplified and elevated" the "Admonition to Soldiers" previously circulated in 1878. The latter appealed "to all military personnel to adopt loyalty, bravery and obedience as guiding ideals." Also see Coox, "Japanese Army Experience," 133.

5. Sample Japanese casualty figures are Attu, 2350 killed, 350 prisoners, as cited in Stetson Conn, Rose C. Engelman, Byron Fairchild, *Guarding the United States and Its Outposts*, United States Army in World War II: The Western Hemisphere (Washington DC: U.S. Government Printing Office, 1964), 295; Tarawa, 4000 to 5000 killed, 146 prisoners, as cited in Captain James R. Stockman, *The Battle for Tarawa*, Historical Section,

Division of Public Information, Headquarters, U.S. Marine Corps, 1947, appen. C; Iwo Jima, 19,900 killed, 1033 prisoners, as cited in Kuda Etsu and Maebara Toru, *Nihon no sensō zukai to dēta* (The wars of Japan: graphics and data) (Tokyo: Hara shobō, 1982), 60. The revised 1941 Field Service Code enjoined soldiers, "Do not be taken prisoner alive." Cited in Ienaga Saburō, *The Pacific War*, trans. Frank Baldwin (New York: Pantheon, 1978), p. 49. John Dower, *War without Mercy: Race and Power in the Pacific War* (New York: Pantheon, 1986), notes that the reluctance of the American soldier to take Japanese prisoners exacerbated Japanese determination to fight to the end. Lee Kennett, *GI: The American Soldier in World War II* (New York: Scribner, 1987), also notes the fundamental difference in the GIs' attitude toward killing a Japanese instead of a German that was first identified in Samuel Stouffer et al., eds., *The American Soldier*, vol. 2 (Princeton: Princeton University Press, 1949), 34, and 158–65, for the GIs' more vindictive attitude toward the Japanese than the German enemy.

6. Postcards of the specific examples cited and an explanation of their provenance may be found in Mainichi shimbunsha, ed., *Ichiokunin no Shōwashi, 2, Ni-ni roku jiken to Nitchū sensō* (The history of one hundred million people in the Shōwa era [1926–]), vol. 2 (The February 26 [1936] Incident and the Sino-Japanese War) (Tokyo: Mainichi shimbunsha, 1975), 94–97.

7. Ōe Shinobu, *Shōwashi no rekishi*, vol. 3, *Tennō no guntai* (A History of the Shōwa reign, vol. 3, the Emperor's army) (Tokyo: Shogakkan, 1982), 63–64. Also see Fujiwara, *Gunjishi*, 144–45.

8. Actual conscription figures appear in Rikusen gakkai senshibu (Military History Department [National Institute for Defense Studies], committee for the study of land warfare), ed., *Kindai sensōshi gaisetsu (shiryō hen)* (Overview of modern war history: documents) (Tokyo: Rikusen gakkai, 1984), 32–35. In 1938 all 153,000 "A" and 17,000 of the more than 470,000 "B" qualified males were conscripted, a total of 170,000 draftees from a pool of 742,422 men examined that year.

9. Ōe, *Tennō*, 64.

10. Ōe, *Tennō*, 63–64.

11. Ōe, *Tennō*, 55–57. Ienaga, *The Pacific War*, 214–15, also offers examples of draft evasion in Japan. On the army's idealization of the Japanese peasantry see, for example, Ike, "War and Modernization," 200–201; Carol Gluck, *Japan's Modern Myths: Ideology in the Late Meiji Period* (Princeton: Princeton University Press, 1985), 181 and 273, offers a probing analysis of the place of the farming village in army thinking.

12. Iizuka Kōji, ed., *Nihon no guntai* (The Japanese army) (Tokyo: Hyōronsha, 1968 reprint), 95. This 1950 effort of five Japanese scholars to analyze and assess the ideological or "spiritual" indoctrination of the

Japanese people for war was a pathbreaking one. All five had served in the armed forces and spoke from personal experience. An impressionistic account, it is, despite a less rigorous methodology, comparable to Stouffer's analysis of the American soldier.

13. Mikiso Hane, *Peasants, Rebels, and Outcasts: The Underside of Modern Japan* (New York: Pantheon, 1982), 59–60.
14. The Imperial Guards Division was an exception, inducting its recruits on 1 December and separating them from active duty on 1 June.
15. "Guntai naimurei" (Handbook of Squad Regulations, 1934 ed.), 1–4, and 15, in Nihon Bungeisha, ed., *Sakusen yōmurei* (Field Service Regulations, 1938) (Tokyo: Nihon bungeisha, 1969 reprint of the 1938 FSR). The injunction to NCOs appeared in "Papers Related to the Reasons for Revision of the Handbook of Squad Regulations," as cited in Ōe, *Tennō*, 83.
16. Ōe, *Tennō*, 85.
17. I am paraphrasing the concept best expressed by Thomas C. Smith, *The Agrarian Origins of Modern Japan* (Stanford: Stanford University Press, 1959), 205. Smith argues that during the Meiji Restoration Japanese leaders used tradition to "mobilize and hold support" of the nation for change.
18. Hane, *Peasants, Rebels, and Outcasts*, 20.
19. On the pervasiveness of the Imperial Rescript in the barracks, see Hillis Lory, *Japan's Military Masters* (New York: Viking, 1943), 53; Yamamoto Katsue, *Kizoku no bo monogatari* (A blockhead's tale) (Tokyo: Senshi kankōkai, 1985), 37, provides the example of reciting the principles before eating; Richard J. Smethurst, *A Social Basis for Prewar Japanese Militarism: The Army and the Rural Community* (Berkeley CA: University of California Press, 1974), 155, notes that the Imperial Military Reserve Association (*Zaigō gunjinkai*) required rural teenage Japanese males enrolled in the reservist-sponsored youth training centers to memorize the fourteen-page rescript. An English translation of the rescript is available in Lory, 239–45. The five principles were: (1) The soldier should consider loyalty his essential duty; (2) The soldier should be strict in observing propriety; (3) The soldier should esteem valor; (4) The soldier should highly value faithfulness and righteousness; and (5) The soldier should make simplicity his aim. Besides the principles themselves, recruits also had to memorize an accompanying explanation of these points.
20. Edwin O. Reischauer, *The Japanese* (Cambridge: Belknap, 1977), 162–66, provides an insightful narrative on hierarchical relations in Japan.
21. Hane, *Peasants, Rebels, and Outcasts*, 59–60; Ienaga, *The Pacific War*, 51–54; Iizuka, *Nihon no guntai*, 127. Also refer to Iizuka, chap. 1, "Bōryoku to ōnjo" (Violence and compassion), 35–62, for a roundtable discussion of the pervasive violence in the IJA barracks. Of all the postwar

Japanese antiwar or antimilitary literature, perhaps the most depressing descriptions of life in the barracks are found in Gomikawa Junpei, *Ningen no jōken* (The human condition), pts. 1–4 (Tokyo: San'ichi shobō, 1956–57), subsequently made into an eight and one-half hour equally morose movie and later a television series in the early 1970s.
22. "Guntai naimurei," 1.
23. Reischauer, *The Japanese*, 151–53.
24. Japanese postmortems on the spectacular suicide of author Mishima Yukio in 1970 provide a postwar case in point. See Robert Jay Lifton, Shuiichi Kato, and Michael Reich, *Six Lives Six Deaths: Portraits from Modern Japan* (New Haven: Yale University Press, 1979), 231–74, for an extended commentary on Mishima's public suicide. Ivan Morris, *The Nobility of Failure: Tragic Heroes in the History of Japan* (New York: Holt, Rinehart, and Winston, 1975), analyzes the phenomenon of death before dishonor across Japan's traditional and modern cultures.
25. Iizuka, *Nihon no guntai*, 36.
26. Iizuka, *Nihon no guntai*, 120–21. Additional examples are available in Ōe, *Tennō*, 86–90.
27. Rikusen gakkai, *Kindai sensōshi*, 62. In 1937 the army recorded 290 courts-martial convictions from among the 250,000 men stationed in Japan. The ratio per 1000 troops was lower in Manchuria, 54 convictions among 200,000 men, 270; and China, 177 convictions among 50,000 soldiers, 354.
28. Ōe, *Tennō*, 85.
29. Reischauer, *The Japanese*, 134–39, discusses the rationale for employing go-betweens to maintain group solidarity to achieve cooperativeness and reduce, if not eliminate, forcefulness and individual self-assertion.
30. Rikusen gakkai, *Kindai sensōshi*, 47.
31. Prices may be found in Irogawa Daikichi, *Aru Shōwashi* (One man's Shōwa history) (Tokyo: Chūō kōronsha, 1973), 13; and Asahi shimbunsha, ed., *Me de miru Shōwashi* (Shōwa history before your eyes), vol. 1 (Tokyo: Asahi shimbunsha, 1972), 54.
32. Cited in Ōe, *Tennō*, 57–58.
33. Suematsu Taihei, *Watakushi no Shōwashi* (My Shōwa history) (Tokyo: Misuzu shobō, 1963), 83–84.
34. Yamamoto, *Kizoku no bo monogatari*, 49.
35. Yamamoto, *Kizoku no bo monogatari*, 45. Yamamoto was assigned to a front-line unit in North China in 1941 during this period of his training.
36. Reischauer, *The Japanese*, 15, discusses Japanese fatalism.
37. Hane, *Peasants, Rebels, and Outcasts*, 32; also Ienaga, *The Pacific War*, 54, makes the same point.
38. Senjō shinri chōsa hōkoku (Report of the battlefield psychological investigation), "Senjō shinri chōsa ni motozuku shōken" (Observations based

on the investigation of battlefield psychology), Secret, 1939, National Institute for Defense Studies, Military History Archives, Tokyo, Japan.
39. Alvin D. Coox, *Nomonhan: Japan against Russia, 1939*, 2 vols. (Stanford: Stanford University Press, 1985), provides the most thorough English language account of this battle. Edward J. Drea, "Nomonhan: Japanese-Soviet Tactical Combat," *Leavenworth Paper* No. 2 (Washington DC: U.S. Government Printing Office, 1981), follows the progress of single Japanese infantry battalion through the fighting.
40. Senjō hōkoku, "Senjō shinri."
41. Field Marshal, the Viscount Slim, *Defeat into Victory* (New York: David McKay, 1961), 446–47. Slim compared the Japanese soldiers to ants. For both the context and criticism of Slim's remark see Louis Allen, *Burma, The Longest War 1941–45* (New York: St. Martin's, 1984), 609–12.
42. Senjō hōkoku, "Senjō shinri."
43. Ardant DuPicq, *Battle Studies: Ancient and Modern Battle*, trans. John N. Greely and Robert C. Cotton (Harrisburg: Military Service, 1946) and S. L. A. Marshall, *Men against Fire: The Problem of Battle Command in Future War* (Washington DC: Combat Forces, 1947).
44. John Masters, *The Road Past Mandalay* (New York: Harper, 1961), 155.

7. Adachi Hatazo: A Soldier of His Emperor

1. Hata Ikuhiko, *Shōwashi no gunjintachi* (Military men of the Shōwa era) (Tokyo: Bungei shunjū, 1982), 325. The others were Lieutenant General Kuribayashi Tadamichi, defender of Iwo Jima, and Lieutenant General Ushijima Mitsuru, defender of Okinawa.
2. Fujita Yutaka, "Adachi Hatazo: meian no senjō ni tatsu" (Adachi Hatazo: living on the bright and dark sides of the battlefield), *Rekishi to jimbutsu zōkan shogen Taiheiyō sensō* (September 1984), 169.
3. Tanaka Kengorō, "Adachi Hatazo," in *Nihongun no kenkyū: Shikkikan, jō*, eds. Imai Takeo and Terasaki Ryūji (Japanese army studies: the commanders), vol. 1 (Tokyo: Hara shobō, 1988), 62. Tanaka was a staff officer with the Eighteenth Army on New Guinea.
4. Komatsu Shigerō, *Ai no tōsotsu Adachi Hatazo* (Beloved commander—Adachi Hatazo) (Tokyo: Kōjinsha, 1989), 10.
5. In 1916 the ratio was 17.3 to 1 and even in 1920, a year of strong antimilitary sentiment, still 9 to 1. "Kyūrikukaigun shōkō no sembatsu to kyosei: Kyōiku jinji" (The selection and cultivation of officers of the former army and navy: personnel and education), (Bōei kenshūjō kenkyū shiryō 80RO-12H, 1980), mimeo., 46. Children of military officers paid reduced fees, and the army did give special consideration to offspring of military members. Nevertheless, more than family connections was necessary to gain entrance to one of the regional cadet academies. See

Theodore F. Cook, "The Japanese Officer Corps: The Making of a Military Elite, 1872–1945," (unpub. diss. Princeton University, 1987), 51–52, 72; and Ōe Shinobu, *Shōwa no rekishi, Tennō no guntai* (A history of the Shōwa emperor's reign: the emperor's army) (Tokyo: Shogakkan, 1982), 92.

6. Kojima Noboru, *Shikkikan*, jō (The commanders), vol. 1 (Tokyo: Bungei shunjū, 1974), 49.
7. Cook, "The Japanese Officer Corps," 99.
8. Japan's Military Academy opened in May 1875 and graduated eleven classes totaling 1285 students to the year 1889. In 1887, however, the Japanese army adopted the German military school model and renumbered graduating classes. Thus the first class educated under the new system graduated in 1890 and became the First Academy Class. Between 1890 and 1945 the academy graduated 50,018 students, but nearly half matriculated in the 1941–1945 period. See also Cook, "The Japanese Officer Corps," 40–41 and note 24.
9. Fujiwara Akira, *Nihon gendaishi taikei: Gunjishi* (An overview of modern Japanese history: the history of military affairs) (Tokyo: Tōyō keizai shinpōsha, 1965), 143; and Cook, "The Japanese Officer Corps," 362.
10. Komatsu, *Ai no tōsotsu Adachi Hatazo*, 11.
11. Komatsu, *Ai no tōsotsu Adachi Hatazo*, 16.
12. Fujita, "Adachi Hatazo," 172.
13. Based on the Thirty-fifth War College Class, whose 72 graduates were drawn from 5626 members of the Twenty-second through Twenty-ninth Military Academy classes. Equally impressive was Adachi's ability to pass the demanding examinations on his first try. Future general Yamashita Tomoyuki, the Tiger of Malaya, failed on his first try; future war ministers Itagaki Seishirō and Minami Jirō also failed on their initial tries; and Japan's last war minister, General Anami Korechika, needed three tries to pass the hellish entrance exam.
14. Ōe, *Tennō*, 95–96. See also "Rikugun jinji seidō gaisetsu" (An overview of the army's personnel system) kōhan (Bōei kenshūjō kenkyū shiryō 80RO-1H, 1981) mimeo., 187. On the deficiencies in Japanese officer education see Jōhō Yoshio, *Rikugunsho gunmukyoku* (The military affairs bureau, war ministry) (Tokyo: Fūyō shobō, 1979), 517–20. See also the critical comments of General Anami and Prince Higashikuni Naruhiko about War College instructors and instruction in Higashikuni Naruhiko, *Higashikuni nikki: Nihon gekidōki no hiroku* (The Higashikuni diary: a confidential account of Japan's time of upheaval) (Tokyo: Tokuma shoten, 1968), 164, 168, and 191.
15. Hori Eizō, "Yamashita Tomoyuki taishō kujūkan no kunō" (General Yamashita Tomoyuki's ninety days of suffering) *Rekishi to jimbutsu* (December 1986), 325.

16. Hata Ikuhiko, ed., *Nihon rikukaigun sōgō jiten* (Comprehensive dictionary of the Japanese army and navy) (Tokyo: Tokyo daigaku shuppankai, 1991), 542–43. Twenty-two were serving on active duty in September 1945; two committed suicide; one had died of natural causes in 1933; one was executed for war crimes; and eight were either killed in action or died of battle-related illness.
17. Domon Shupei, "Shō no rinri—Adachi chūshō jijin" (The ethical commander—Lieutenant General Adachi's suicide) *Will* 1 (1983): 57.
18. Japan acquired the eastern Chinese railroads as a result of the Russo-Japanese War. In 1906 an Imperial Rescript consolidated the former Chinese lines into the South Manchurian Railway Company as a joint government and private venture. Besides rail lines, the company managed coal mining, mines, and transportation and was the prime exploiter of the natural resources of Manchuria, which it developed into an economic enterprise zone. Joseph M. Goedertier, *A Dictionary of Japanese History* (New York & Tokyo: Walker/Weatherhill, 1968), 181. Moreover, the South Manchurian Railway Company was a vital cog in Imperial Army operational planning, because its defense and later its use to support forward operations against the Soviet Union was a centerpiece of mobilization, deployment, sustainment, and tactical considerations.
19. Fujiwara, *Nihon gendaishi taikei*, 175. The shake-up of the officer corps involved seven full generals forced into retirement, dozens more officers ranging in rank from lieutenant to lieutenant general seconded to the reserves, and transfers of three thousand officers.
20. Fujita Katsu, "Adachi butaichō no omoide" (Remembering our unit commander Adachi) in *Hohei dai juni rentai hyakujunensai kinenshi omideki*, ed. Ho juni henshuu iinkai (Recollections for essays in commemoration of the 110-year history of the Twelfth Infantry regiment) (privately published, 1985), 143. Fujita was a medical corps captain assigned to the Twelfth Infantry as its regimental surgeon. Miyoshi Kenzan, *Shanhai tekimae jōriku* (Amphibious assault at Shanghai) (Tokyo: Tōsho shuppansha, 1979), 122–23. I am indebted to Professor Aizawa Kiyoshi of the Military History Department, National Institute for Defense Studies, Tokyo, Japan, for sharing this information with me.
21. Domon, "Shō no rinri," 75; and Fujita, "Adachi butaichō no omide," 171.
22. Hata Ikuhiko letter, 15 December 1992; and Mainichi shimbunsha, eds., *Ichiokunin no Shōwashi, Nihon no sensō Nitchū sensō* 6(4) (December 1979): 82.
23. Hata letter.
24. Furukawa Toshiaki, "Rikugun taishō hyakusanjuyon' nin no keireki," (The careers of 134 army general officers) *Rekishi to jimbutsu* (September 1982), 342–43. The three were generals Suzuki Sosaku (Twenty-fourth

Class) of Leyte fame; Obata Eiyo (Twenty-third), killed in action on Guam; and Kuribayashi Tadamichi (Twenty-sixth) of Iwo Jima.
25. Kojima Noboru, *Shisetsu Yamashita Tomoyuki* (Yamashita Tomoyuki—a historical view) (Tokyo: Bungei shunjū,1979), 152.
26. Tsunoda Fusako, *Sekinin Rabauru no shōgun Imamura Hitoshi* (The general responsible for Rabaul: Imamura Hitoshi) (Tokyo: Shinchōsha, 1984), 101; and Domon, "Shō no rinri," 58. See also Ugaki, *Fading Victory*, 283–84 and 292. Diary entries for 24 November 1942 and 4 December 1942, respectively.
27. Domon, "Shō no rinri," 58–59.
28. Kojima, *Shikkikan*, 160.
29. Lieutenant General Yoshiwara Kane, "Southern Cross, An Account of the Eastern new Guinea Campaign," 141 (trans. Miss Doris Heath for Australian War History Section), copy in U.S. Army Center of Military History Files, Washington DC. Yoshiwara was Adachi's chief of staff.
30. Bōeichō, Bōeikenshūjō, *Senshi sōsho*, vol. 40, *Minami Taiheiyō rikugun sakusen: Munda Saramao*, pt. 3 (Official military history, vol. 40, Army operations in the south Pacific: Munda and Salamaua, bk. 3) (Tokyo: Asagumo shimbunsha, 1970), 520.
31. Bōeichō, *Senshi sōsho*, vol. 40, 458. See also GHQ, SWPA, G-2, "Situation Report 5 March 1944," RG 457, National Archives and Records Administration, SRH-203, pt. 2, GHQ, SWPA, MIS, "Special Intelligence Bulletin," 618.
32. GHQ, Far East Command, MIS, GS, "Operations of the Military Intelligence Section, GHQ, SWPA/FEC/SCAP," vol. 3, Intelligence Series (pt. 1), 1950 Documentary Appendices, appen. 1, table 4, plate 1.
33. "Special Intelligence Bulletin," 25 April 1944, 802. This bulletin lists decrypted Japanese radio messages reporting the Hollandia landing three days earlier.
34. Yamamoto Katsue, *Kizoku no bo monogatari* (A blockhead's tale) (Tokyo: Senshikankōkai, 1985), 157. Yamamoto served with a mountain artillery unit on New Guinea until captured at Aitape.
35. Fujita, "Adachi butaichō no omide," 127.
36. Yamamoto, *Kizoku no bo monogatari*, 160–61.
37. Yamamoto, *Kizoku no bo monogatari*, 174–75 and 178.
38. Adachi's order of the day is cited in part in Supreme Commander Allied Powers, *Reports of General MacArthur: Japanese Operations in the Southwest Pacific Area*, vol. 2, pt. 1 (Washington DC: U.S. Government Printing Office, 1966), 299.
39. Adachi is criticized by some Japanese historians for replaying his rigid tactics of the China front. See Fujita, "Adachi butaichō no omide," 176.
40. Yoshiwara, "Southern Cross," 151.
41. W. M. Anderson, major general, "Form for Assembly and Proceedings

of a Military Court," 4 March 1947 and appended documents contain the charges and specifications brought against Adachi. I am indebted to Lieutenant General (Ret.) John M. Coates, Australian Army, for providing me with photocopies of these documents.
42. Kojima, *Shikkikan*, 162.
43. Kojima, *Shikkikan*, 161.
44. Domon, "Shō no rinri," 60; and Yoshiwara, "Southern Cross," 172–73 citing Mō (Eighteenth Army) operations order 18 March 1945.
45. Yoshiwara, "Southern Cross," 191, Mō (Eighteenth Army) operations order number 371, 25 July 1945.
46. Komatsu, *Ai no tōsotsu Adachi Hatazo*, 201; and Coates material (see note 41). See, for example, Majima Mitsuru, *Jigoku no senjō: Nyūginiaya senki* (Hell's battleground: a New Guinea war diary) (Tokyo: Kōjinsha, 1989), 89, who states that higher headquarters at Lae had notified line units to kill captured American pilots after interrogating them.
47. If the Japanese intent was to frighten Allied ground troops, it backfired. "The frequent evidence of Japanese atrocities had a remarkable effect on the morale of the troops. It developed a feeling a disgust which caused men to enter battle with a greater determination to eliminate the enemy whatever the cost." Gavin Long, *The Final Campaigns* (Canberra: Australian War Memorial, 1963), 342.
48. Long, *The Final Campaigns*, 387.
49. Yoshiwara, "Southern Cross," 28.

8. *A Signals Intercept Site at War*

1. David Jenkins, "Our War of Words," *The Sydney Morning Herald*, 19 September 1992, 37. I am indebted to Dr. David Horner for sharing this article with me.
2. Wayne Gobert, Lieutenant Commander, RANC, "The Evolution of Service Strategic Intelligence 1901–1941," *Australian Defence Force Journal* 92 (January/February 1992): 61–62. See also David Jenkins, *Battle Surface! Japan's Submarine War against Australia 1942-44* (Sydney: Random House Australia, 1992), 42–46. I am indebted to Jozef H. Straczek, senior naval historian and archives officer, Department of Defence (navy), Canberra for providing me these materials.
3. Jack Bleakley, *The Eavesdroppers* (Canberra: Australian Government, 1991), 7. Bleakley served as a radio intercept operator in Australian signals intelligence during World War II
4. Bleakley, *The Eavesdroppers*, 10.
5. "Central Bureau Technical Records, Part J—Field Sections," 4, Australian Archives (Victoria): Central Bureau, CRS B5436/1, Technical Records 1945-1946, Item No. IT J, 28. Hereafter cited as CBTR, JCBTR, J.

6. Bleakley, *The Eavesdroppers*, 26.
7. Geoffrey Ballard, *On ULTRA Active Service: The Story of Australia's Signals Intelligence Operations during World War II* (Richmond, Victoria, Australia: Spectrum, 1991), 150–53. Ballard served in Australian signals intelligence during World War II. Also see Bleakley, *The Eavesdroppers*, 8–10, 32–33, 49.
8. CBTR, J, 32. "Y" or intelligence specialists actually were in separate units designated Australian Special Intelligence personnel sections and attached to respective wireless sections for analysis and decoding purposes.
9. Ballard, *On ULTRA Active Service*, 164.
10. CBTR, J, pt. 2, para. 2.
11. CBTR, J, pt. 1, para. 1–4; Bleakley, *The Eavesdroppers*, 83. Throughout the Pacific War, Australian government policy prohibited the sixty-five women of One Wireless Unit's Women's Australian Auxiliary Air Force (WAAF) from leaving Australia for posting at advanced field sites in New Guinea and the Philippines. War Cabinet Addendum No. 205/45, "Allied Central Bureau," 16 May 1945 and Cabinet War Minute, 28 May 1945. Australian Archives (Victoria); File MP 729/8/0, Item 41/431/18. This was unfortunate, because many of the women were excellent intercept operators as demonstrated by their outstanding service in Australia.
12. Ballard, *On ULTRA Active Service*, 201.
13. Ballard, *On ULTRA Active Service*, 202.
14. CBTR, J, 29.
15. "Central Bureau Technical Records, Part A—Organisation," 2, Australian Archives (Victoria): Central Bureau, CRS B5436/1, Technical Records 1945–1946, Item No. IT A., 5. Hereafter cited as CBTR, A.
16. CBTR, A, 5.
17. Edward J. Drea, "Were the Japanese Army Codes Secure?," *Cryptologia* 19(2) (April 1995): 133.
18. CBTR, A, 6.
19. CBTR, J, 29.
20. No. Fifty-five Australian Wireless Section, "War Diary," 7 October 1942, Australian War Memorial, Canberra: AWM 52, File 7/39/21. Hereafter cited as "War Diary" with date.
21. "War Diary," 7 October 1942. For a representative sample see "War Diary" entries for 11 October 1942 showing 48 messages intercepted at the main site and 16 at the detachment; 13 October, 99 and 26, respectively; 14 October, 118 and 55, respectively.
22. Ballard, *On ULTRA Active Service*, 203.
23. "B II, Australia and India Reports, Air Ground Traffic Beginning 31 October 1942," Australia Report No. 3, 31 December 1942, 2, Box 1045, RG 457, National Archives and Records Administration, College Park MD; and Ballard, *On ULTRA Active Service*, Appendix "Report of Air Raid on

Port Moresby, Early Morning of November 30th, 1942," "Report of Air Raid on Pt. Moresby between 1955/L and 2127L 14th December," and "Report of Air Raid on Pt. Moresby between 2040/L and 2300L on 15th December 1942." The Japanese used naval land-based bombers as well as flying boats for the raids. See Takano Nao, "Taiheiyō saizensen otei wa seisuku" (Flying boat attacks on the Pacific front line) *Rekishi to jimbutsu* (winter 1986): 51–52. Takano piloted a flying boat against Port Moresby. John F. Kreis, *Air Warfare and Air Base Defense 1914–1973* (Washington DC: Office of Air Force History, 1988), 242 discusses radar installations at Port Moresby.

24. "War Diary," 19, 20, 22, and 25 October 1942.
25. "War Diary," 1 November 1942.
26. "War Diary," 8 November 1942. Akin was also director, Central Bureau.
27. "War Diary," 14 and 18 November 1942.
28. "War Diary," 22 November 1942.
29. "War Diary," 23, 24, 25, and 27 November 1942.
30. "War Diary," 30 November 1942.
31. "War Diary," 22–25, 27, and 30 November and 7 December 1942.
32. "War Diary," 13 December 1942.
33. "War Diary," 30 November and 1 December 1942. The Eighteenth Army was provisionally announced by Japan's war minister on 9 November 1942 and activated seven days later. The Second Shipping Group controlled the First and Second Shipping Engineer Regiments. For information on the shipping units see Nakaoka Shigenari, "Sempaku kōhei to Gadarukanaru shima sakusen" (Shipping engineers and the Guadalcanal island operation) *Maru*: Bekkan 5 "Taiheiyō sensō shogen shiriizu—Saiaku no senjō" (Pacific war eyewitness series—the worst battleground) (March 1987), 133 and 138. Nakaoka served with the First Shipping Engineer Regiment at Guadalcanal.
34. Drea, *MacArthur's ULTRA*, 39 and 53. A Shipping Engineer Regiment consisted of a headquarters, three boat companies, and a service company. Each boat company was organized as a headquarters and four platoons. Each platoon had four to seven boats depending on its mission.
35. "War Diary," 4 December 1942.
36. "War Diary," 21 December 1942.
37. "War Diary," 4 December 1942.
38. "War Diary," 6 December 1942; and Drea, *MacArthur's ULTRA*, 54.
39. "War Diary," Appendix D, 14 December 1942. Cf. GHQ, SWPA, Military Intelligence Summary No. 268 x 15/16 December 1942, Special Intelligence—miscellaneous, RG 3, Box 27, Folder 6, SWPA MIS Daily Summaries Nos. 273x–283x, 21–31 December 1942, MacArthur Memorial Bureau of Archives, Norfolk VA. Hereafter cited by MIS number and date.

NOTES TO PAGES 120–125 • 239

40. "War Diary," 19 December 1942. Cf. MIS No. 274 x 21/22 December 1942.
41. "War Diary," 2 December 1942.
42. "War Diary," 11, 15, 16, 17 December 1942.
43. "War Diary," 14, 15 December 1942. Cf. MIS No. 268x 15/16 December 1942. Two submarines unloaded about twenty tons of supplies at Buna on 19 and 20 December. Ugaki Matome, *Fading Victory: The Diary of Admiral Matome Ugaki, 1941–1945*, trans. Masataka Chihaya, ed. Donald M. Goldstein and Catherine V. Dillon (Pittsburgh: University of Pittsburgh Press, 1991), 310. Diary entry for 22 December 1942.
44. "War Diary," Appendix F, 24 December 1942. Information about the Fourth Shipping Transport Unit may be found in Bōeichō Bōei kenshūjō senshibu, *Senshi sōsho*, vol. 28, *Minami Taiheiyō rikugun sakusen*: pt. 2, *Gadarukanaru-Buna sakusen* (Official history: Army operations in the south Pacific—operations at Guadalcanal and Buna), vol. 28. (Tokyo: Asagumo shimbunsha, 1968), 467.
45. "War Diary," Appendix H, 27 December 1942. For details on these shipping units see Shibata Masatoshi, "Shūtei kidō 'senpaku kōhei' ichidaiki" (The life of a shipping engineer in a mobile boat unit) *Maru* Bekkan 3: "Taiheiyō sensō shogen shiriizu—Jigoku no senjō" (Pacific war eyewitness series—Hell's battleground) (January 1987), 310. Shibata served as a junior officer with the Fifth Shipping Engineer Regiment. Regarding the withdrawal orders refer to Lida Mayo, *Bloody Buna* (Chicago: Playboy, 1979), 171. The assembly point at Bakumbari had already witnessed an evacuation of sick and wounded Japanese soldiers on 19 January.
46. "War Diary," Appendix J, 29 December 1942. Cf. MIS No. 281 x 28/29 December 1942. Eighth Area Army Headquarters was activated on 16 November 1942 and became operational at Rabaul ten days later. It controlled Seventeenth and Eighteenth Army operations on Guadalcanal and New Guinea, respectively.
47. CBTR, J, 23.
48. "War Diary," 15 January 1942.
49. Ballard, *On ULTRA Active Service*, 205.
50. "War Diary," 7 February 1943.
51. "War Diary," 5 February 1943.
52. "War Diary," 6 February 1943. The First Embarkation Unit had deployed to Rabaul with the Eighteenth Army, its controlling headquarters.
53. Drea, *MacArthur's ULTRA*, 66.
54. "War Diary," 16 February 1942.
55. "War Diary," 9 February 1943.
56. "Addenda to comment to w/T (IS) Activity Report (Period—14.2.1943)," "War Diary," 15 December 1943, 3. Cf. U.S. Navy CINPAC Intelligence

Bulletins, 3, 19, 22, and 26 February 1943 in U.S. Navy CINPAC Intelligence Bulletins, 1 June 1942–23 February 1943 and 24 February 1942–30 June 1943, SRMN-013, Parts I and II, RG 457, National Archives and Records Administration.

57. "War Diary," 22 and 23 February 1943; Shibata, "Shūtei kidō," 313–14.
58. "War Diary," 24 February 1942. The Japanese army used code names for its units. It then encoded the codenames on message routings. For example, the First Shipping Engineer Regiment's code name was AKATSUKI 6170. This was encoded as 4443 (AKATSUKI), 3463 (61), 0389 (70), or an address reading 4443 3463 0389. KAWA, the Forty-first Division's codename, was encoded as 2181.
59. "War Diary," 11 February 1943.
60. "War Diary," 21 February 1943.
61. "War Diary," 24 February 1943.
62. "War Diary"; Shibata, "Shūtei kidō," 313.
63. "War Diary," 25 February 1943.
64. "War Diary," 28 February 1943.
65. For example, compare CINPAC Intelligence Bulletins previously cited and HG Allied Air Forces, SWPA, "Intelligence Summary" 10 and 17 February 1943, RG 4, Box 17, Richard K. Sutherland Papers, MacArthur Memorial Bureau of Archives as well as SWPA, MIS, Daily Summaries, RG 3, MMBA, "Military Intelligence Summary," 22/23, 23/24, 24/25, and 27/28 February 1943 with Fifty-five Wireless Section's War Diary entries for February 1943.
66. Minister for Air (Arthur S. Drakeford) to prime minister and minister for defense, "Mobile Wireless Units," 16 December 1942, Australian Archives (Dickson, ACT); Series A5954/1, Item 245/16.
67. As for Fifty-five Wireless Section, in March 1943 a fifteen-man detachment was sent to an advanced intercept site to support Australian operations in the Markham Valley. The unit itself moved to Nadzab in October. In February 1944 the section redeployed to Finschhafen and was reorganized and redesignated as Fifty-three Australian Wireless Section. In July 1944 it deployed forward to Hollandia. In July 1945, owing to the virtual cessation of organized fighting on New Guinea, the section was inactivated.

9. Leyte: Unanswered Questions

1. M. Hamlin Cannon, *Leyte: The Return to the Philippines*, United States Army in World War II: The War in the Pacific (Washington DC: Office of the Chief of Military History, 1953), 41–42, 60–62, 84.
2. Ronald Spector, *Eagle against the Sun* (New York: Free Press, 1985), 426.

3. Thomas J. Cutler, *The Battle of Leyte Gulf 23–26 October 1944* (New York: HarperCollins, 1994), 207–9 and 288–97 for the enduring controversy.
4. See Spector, *Eagle against the Sun*, 513–15 for one viewpoint; and William M. Leary, "Walter Krueger: MacArthur's Fighting General," in *We Shall Return! MacArthur's Commanders and the Defeat of Japan*, ed. William M. Leary (Lexington KY: University Press of Kentucky, 1988), 74–76 for an opposing viewpoint.
5. CofS (Marshall) to CINCWSPA (MacArthur), 24 June 1944, in GHQ, FEC, MIS, Historical Division, "Historical Records Index Cards," mimeo., n.d., copy at U.S. Army Military History Institute, Carlisle Barracks, PA.
6. Military Intelligence Section, general staff, GHQ, SWPA, "Special Intelligence Bulletin," 14/15 August 1944, SRH-203, RG 457, U.S. National Archives and Records Administration, Washington DC.
7. Military Intelligence Section, "Special Intelligence Bulletin," 31 August/1 November.
8. Office of Assistant Chief of Staff, G-2, War Department, "MAGIC—Far East Summary," 4 October 1944, SRS-01-547, RG 457, U.S. National Archives and Records Administration, Washington DC.
9. On this issue see Spector, *Eagle against the Sun*, 419; John Winton, *Ultra in the Pacific* (Annapolis MD: Naval Institute, 1993), 179–80; Drea, *MacArthur's ULTRA*, 157–58; and Douglas MacArthur, *Reminiscences* (New York: McGraw Hill, 1964), 246–47.
10. Office of Assistant Chief of Staff, "MAGIC," 11 September; Military Intelligence Section, "Special Intelligence Bulletin," 11/12 September.
11. Military Intelligence Section, "Special Intelligence Bulletin," 9/10 September.
12. Office of Assistant Chief of Staff, "MAGIC," 31 July and 1 August.
13. Office of Assistant Chief of Staff, "MAGIC," 5 October.
14. Office of Assistant Chief of Staff, "MAGIC," 12 November.
15. Office of Assistant Chief of Staff, "MAGIC," 5 October.
16. Spector, *Eagle against the Sun*, 424–25.
17. On the Japanese estimates see Shigeru Fukudome, "The Air Battle off Taiwan," in *The Japanese Navy in World War II*, ed. David C. Evans (Annapolis MD: U.S. Naval Institute, 2d ed., 1986), 351–54. For American knowledge of Japanese estimates see Office of the Assistant Chief of Staff, "Magic," 25 October.
18. Office of the Assistant Chief of Staff, "Magic," 16 October 1944 and Military Intelligence Section, "Special Intelligence Bulletin," 17/18 October.
19. Military Intelligence Section, "Special Intelligence Bulletin," 25/26 October.
20. For MacArthur's political whirl see D. Clayton James, *The Years of*

MacArthur, vol. 2, *1941-45* (Boston: Houghton Mifflin, 1975), chap. 10, "Political Misadventure," 403-40.
21. Stanley L. Falk, *Decision at Leyte* (New York: Norton, 1966), 123 and 138.
22. Cutler, *The Battle of Leyte Gulf*, 89.
23. Falk, *Decision at Leyte*, 42. Vice Admiral Ugaki Matome, commander, First Battleship Division, received a briefing on Shō 1 operational orders onboard the heavy cruiser Atago on 21 October. Ugaki, *Fading Victory*, 485. Also see Cutler, *The Battle of Leyte Gulf*, 89.
24. On planning aspects see Tomiji Koyanagi, "The Battle of Leyte Gulf," in *The Japanese Navy in World War II*, ed. David C. Evans (Annapolis MD: U.S. Naval Institute, 2d ed., 1986), 358-61.
25. Joint Intelligence Center, Pacific Ocean Area, "Summary of ULTRA Traffic," October 16 and 17, 1944, SRMD-009, RG 457, U.S. National Archives and Records Administration, Washington, DC.
26. Military Intelligence Section, "Special Intelligence Bulletin," 17/18 October.
27. Military Intelligence Section, "Special Intelligence Bulletin," 18/19 October.
28. Military Intelligence Section, "Special Intelligence Bulletin," 22/23 October.
29. Joint Intelligence Center, "Summary of ULTRA," 20 October.
30. Joint Intelligence Center, "Summary of ULTRA," 23 October.
31. Military Intelligence Section, "Special Intelligence Bulletin," 20/21 October.
32. Joint Intelligence Center, "Summary of ULTRA," 23 October.
33. Joint Intelligence Center, "Summary of ULTRA," 19/23 October.
34. Joint Intelligence Center, "Summary of ULTRA," 23 October.
35. Military Intelligence Section, "Special Intelligence Bulletin," 17/18 October.
36. Military Intelligence Section, "Special Intelligence Bulletin," 19/20 October.
37. Toyoda Jō, *Kaigun gunreibu* (The naval general staff) (Tokyo: Kodansha bunkō, 1993 reprint of 1987 ed.), 401.
38. Spector, *Eagle against the Sun*, 431-33. For a concise, lucid analysis of the Leyte Gulf controversy see George W. Baer, *One Hundred Years of Sea Power: The U.S. Navy, 1890-1990* (Stanford: Stanford University Press, 1994), 257-61.
39. Toyoda, *Kaigun gunreibu*, 412-13.
40. Toyoda, *Kaigun gunreibu*, 423; Cutler, *The Battle of Leyte Gulf*, 262; Ugaki, *Fading Victory*, 494.
41. Toyoda, *Kaigun gunreibu*, 425-28; and Ugaki, *Fading Victory*, 492.

42. Toyoda, *Kaigun gunreibu*, 416; Cutler, *The Battle of Leyte Gulf*, 263; and Ugaki, *Fading Victory*, 497. Kurita survived the war and died in 1977. During those thirty-two postwar years, he repeatedly rejected offers to present his side of the story of Leyte Gulf, brushing aside requests by saying the defeated shouldn't talk.
43. Joint Intelligence Center, "Summary of ULTRA," 27 October.
44. Joint Intelligence Center, "Summary of ULTRA," 30 October.
45. GHQ, SWPA, Communique No. 940, 3 November 1944, in SIB, 2/3 November 1944, 1554.
46. Joint Intelligence Center, "Summary of ULTRA," 25 October.
47. Military Intelligence Section, "Special Intelligence Bulletin," 29/30 October.
48. Drea, *MacArthur's ULTRA*, 115; Kamaga Kazuo, Fujiwara Kuniki, and Yoshimura Akura, "Zandankai: Nihon rikugun ango wa naze yaburarenakattaka?" (Roundtable: Why couldn't the Japanese army codes be broken?) *Rekishi to jimbutsu* (December 1985), 155.
49. "History of the Signal Security Agency," vol. 3, "The Japanese Army Problems: Cryptanalysis, 1942–1945," SRH-362, 106, RG 457, U.S. National Archives and Records Administration, Washington DC.
50. "Selected Examples of Commendations and Related Correspondence Highlighting the Achievements of U.S. Signal Intelligence during World War II," SRH-059, 54, RG457, U.S. National Archives and Records Administration, Washington DC.
51. Which is the reason for Marshall's otherwise paradoxical message to MacArthur requesting that the Japanese Eighteenth Army, then isolated on New Guinea, be allowed to transmit coded radio messages. "For MacArthur from Marshall," 11 June 1944, Chief of Staff Record Files, CINC, USAF, PAC, RG 4, Box 14, MacArthur Memorial Bureau of Archives, Norfolk VA.
52. Unless otherwise noted, information regarding the First Division may be found in Ōka Shohei, *Reite senki*, jō (Leyte war record), vol. 1 (Tokyo: Chūkō bunkō, ed., 1974), 356–70.
53. Office of Assistant Chief of Staff, "MAGIC," 14 October.
54. Drea, *MacArthur's ULTRA*, 74–75.
55. Joint Intelligence Center, "Summary of ULTRA," 9 October.
56. Military Intelligence Section, "Special Intelligence Bulletin," 23/24 October.
57. Military Intelligence Section, "Special Intelligence Bulletin," 26/27 October.
58. Military Intelligence Section, "Special Intelligence Bulletin," 28/29 October and 31 October/1 November.

59. Military Intelligence Section, "Special Intelligence Bulletin," 27/28 October.
60. Military Intelligence Section, "Special Intelligence Bulletin," 29/30 October.
61. Military Intelligence Section, "Special Intelligence Bulletin," 31 October/1 November.
62. Jack Bleakley, *The Eavesdroppers* (Canberra: Australian Government, 1991), 186–87.
63. Military Intelligence Section, "Special Intelligence Bulletin," 2/3 November.
64. Office of Assistant Chief of Staff, "MAGIC," 4 October.
65. Office of Assistant Chief of Staff, "MAGIC," 6 October.
66. Military Intelligence Section, "Special Intelligence Bulletin," 7/8 November.

10. Japanese Preparations for Defense

1. *Reports of General MacArthur*, vol. 2, pt. 2, *Japanese Operations in the Southwest Pacific Area* (Washington DC: U.S. Government Printing Office, 1966), 583; and Matsumoto Keisuke, "Daitō A sensō ni okeru minami Kyushu kessen jumbi: kokudō Bōei no genten wo sagasu: Shibushiwan no mizugiwa gekimetsu sakusen," vol. 3, pt. 1 (Preparations for the decisive battle in southern Kyushu during the great East Asia war: Tracing the origin of defense of the homeland: Annihilation at the water's edge operations in Shibishi bay) *Rikusen kenkyū* (August 1988): 38.
2. *Reports of General MacArthur*, 612; and Kyoto daigaku bungakubu kokushi kenkyūshitsu, ed., *Nihon kindaishi jiten* (Dictionary of modern Japanese history) (Tokyo: Tōyō keizai shinpōsha, 1958), 188.
3. *Reports of General MacArthur*, 575–76.
4. *Reports of General MacArthur*, 668.
5. Ohta Kiyoshi, "Statement on Preparations for Transportation and Line of Communications in the Kyushu Area during the Summer of 1945," 15 December 1949, General Headquarters, Far East Command, Military Intelligence Section, general staff, allied translator and interpreter section, *Statements of Japanese Officials on World War II* (English Translations), vol. 3, 168–69. (Hereafter cited as *Statements*, vol., page.)
6. Hirano Tosaku, "Statement on the State of Operational Preparations (Line of Communications) in Kyushu," 10 November 1948, *Statements*, vol. 1, 431.
7. Bōeichō, Bōei kenshūjō senshishitsu, *Senshi sōsho*, vol. 57, *Hondō kessen jumbi*, pt. 2, *Kyushu no bōei* (Official military history, vol. 57, Preparations for the decisive battle of the homeland, bk. 2. The defense of Kyushu)

(Tokyo: Asagumo shimbunsha, 1972), 479–80. Hereafter cited as *Kyushu no Bōei*.
8. Bōeichō, *Kyushu no bōei*, 393. Also Hirano, "Statement on the State," 430.
9. Hirano, "Statement on the State," 431. The reinforcing units included four regular divisions and eight newly mobilized ones.
10. Bōeichō, *Kyushu no bōei*, 551.
11. *Reports of General MacArthur*, 623.
12. *Reports of General MacArthur*, 667.
13. *Reports of General MacArthur*, 688. Such a rationale also appears in "Kongo torubeki sensō shidō no konpon taikō ni kanshi gozenkaigi keika gaiyō" (Outline of the course of the imperial conference dealing with the fundamental policy for future wartime guidance) 8 June 1945, in Sanbō honbu shozō, ed., *Meiji hyakunenshi sōsho*, vol. 39, *Haisen no kiroku* (Meiji centennial history, vol. 39, Record of defeat) (Tokyo: Hara shobō, 1979), 259.
14. Kondō Chūjō, "Taiheiyō sensō ni okeru Nihon rikugun no taijōriku sakusen shisō" (The Japanese army's concept of counter amphibious operations during the Pacific war), Bōei kenshūjō kenkyū shiryō, *Kenkyū shiryō*, 92RO-4H, mimeo., 1992, 164–65.
15. Alvin Coox, *Japan: The Final Agony* (New York: Ballantine, 1970), 71.
16. *Reports of General MacArthur*, 642–45.
17. Cited in Matsumoto, "Daitō A sensō ni okeru minami Kyushu kessen jumbi," 41.
18. "Kokudō kessen kyōrei," (Guidance for the decisive battle of the homeland) 20 April 1945. Cited in Bōeichō, Bōei kenshūjō senshishitsu, *Senshi sōsho*, vol. 51, *Hondō kessen jumbi*, pt. 1, *Kantō no bōei* (Official military history, vol. 51, Preparations for the decisive battle of the homeland, pt. 1, The defense of the Kantō region) (Tokyo: Asagumo shimbunsha, 1971), 337.
19. Bōeichō, *Kyushu no bōei*, 317–18.
20. Kondo, "Taijōriku sakusen shisō," 182; and *Reports of General MacArthur*, 625. The new manual was "Kokudō kessen sempō hayawakari" (The key to homeland decisive battle tactics).
21. Matsumoto Keisuke, "Preparations of Decisive Battle in Southern Kyushu in Great East Asia War," U.S.–Japan Military History Exchange, 25 October 1987, 21.
22. Kondo, "Taijōriku sakusen shisō," 182.
23. Matsumoto, "Preparations of Decisive Battle," 26–28.
24. Cf. Office of ACofS, G-2, War Department, " 'MAGIC'—Far East Summary," 12 July 1945, SRS SERIES, RG 457, National Archives and Records Administration, Washington DC, and the Japanese original, Sanden 885 (General staff electrical message No. 885) "Hondō kessen komponshu

no tettei ni kansuru ken" (Matters to drive home about fundamental principles for the decisive battle of the homeland), 20 June 1945, cited in Bōeichō, *Kantō no bōei*, 501–2.
25. "'MAGIC'—Far East Summary," 26 July 1945.
26. *Reports of General MacArthur*, 619. On the state and the prospects of Japan's war economy, see "Kongo torubeki sensō shidō no konpon taikō ni kanshi gozenkaigi keika gaiyō," 8 June 1945, *Haisen no kiroku*, 261–62; "Kokuryoku no genjō" (The present state of national power), in *Kyushu no bōei*, 427–30. This document is summarized in Robert J. C. Butow, *Japan's Decision to Surrender* (Stanford: Stanford University Press, 1954), 94–95. Concern for an extended blockade and aerial bombing strategy to render Japan powerless before any invasion appears in Daihon'ei rikugunbu, "Shōwa 21 nen haru goro mokuto to suru jōsei handan" (Intelligence estimate for spring 1946), 1 July 1945, cited in Bōeichō, *Kyushu no bōei*, 432. Also see Hirano Tosaku, "The condition of and future outlook concerning army provisions in the Kyushu area in the summer of 1945," *Statements*, vol. 1, 438. Lieutenant General Arisue Seizo, "Considerations and Observations of the 'Brains' of Imperial Headquarters Regarding American Strategy against Japan around June of 1945," 10 May 1949, *Statements*, vol. 1, 63.

11. Intelligence Forecasting for the Invasion of Japan

1. General Headquarters, U.S. Army Forces, Pacific, "DOWNFALL" Strategic Plan, Annex 3d (1) (c) "Estimate of Troop Lift Requirements," 28 May 1945.
2. General Headquarters, U.S. Army Forces, Pacific, Military Intelligence Section, G-2, "G-2 Estimate of the Enemy Situation with Respect to an Operation against Southern Kyushu in November 1945," 25 April 1945, RG 4, USAFPAC, Intelligence, General, MacArthur Memorial Bureau of Archives, Norfolk VA. Hereafter cited as MMBA.
3. War Department, Military Intelligence Service, "'MAGIC' Summary, Far East Supplement," 9 April 1945, SRS series, RG 457, National Archives and Records Administration, Washington DC (NARA).
4. War Department, Military Intelligence Service, "'MAGIC'," 15 April.
5. General Headquarters, Southwest Pacific Area, Military Intelligence Section, "Special Intelligence Bulletin," April 27/28, 1945, SRH-203, RG 457, NARA.
6. War Department, Military Intelligence Service, "'MAGIC'," 13 April.
7. "G-2 Estimate," 25 April 1945.
8. War Department, Military Intelligence Service, "'MAGIC'," 25 May.
9. War Department, Military Intelligence Service, "'MAGIC'," 29 May.
10. War Department, Military Intelligence Service, "'MAGIC'," 16 May.

11. War Department, Military Intelligence Service, " 'MAGIC'," 1/7 June.
12. War Department, Military Intelligence Service, " 'MAGIC'," 7 June.
13. General Headquarters, "Special Intelligence Bulletin," 10/11 June.
14. General Headquarters, "Special Intelligence Bulletin," 13/14 June.
15. General Headquarters, "Special Intelligence Bulletin," 11/12 June and War Department, Military Intelligence Service, " 'MAGIC'," 11 June.
16. General Headquarters, "Special Intelligence Bulletin," 9/10, 14/15 June.
17. War Department, Military Intelligence Service, " 'MAGIC'," 17 June.
18. General Headquarters, "Special Intelligence Bulletin," 14/15 June.
19. General Headquarters, "Special Intelligence Bulletin," 15/16 June.
20. General Headquarters, "Special Intelligence Bulletin," 6/7, 8/9 June.
21. Marshall to MacArthur, War Department (WD) 1050, 16 June 1945 and MacArthur to Marshall, WD 1052, 17 June 1945, RG 4, USAFPAC, Folder 4 (WD 1001–1095) 29 April–2 August 1945. MMBA.
22. Forrest C. Pogue, *George C. Marshall: Statesman 1945–1959* (New York: Viking, 1987), 6.
23. Marshall to MacArthur, WD 1056, 19 June 1945; MacArthur to Marshall, WD 1057, 19 June 1945; Marshall to MacArthur, WD 1060, 19 June 1945, MMBA.
24. U.S. Department of State, *Foreign Relations of the United States: Diplomatic Papers: The Conference of Berlin (The Potsdam Conference), 1945*, vol. 1 (Washington DC: U.S. Government Printing Office, 1960), 906.
25. Memorandum, Lieutenant Colonel A. W. Sanford, general staff, to commander in chief, Australian Military Forces (Blamey), 30 June 1945, in SRH-219, 64, RG 457, NARA.
26. War Department, Military Intelligence Service, " 'MAGIC'," 3 August.
27. General Headquarters, "Special Intelligence Bulletin," 3/4 July.
28. General Headquarters, "Special Intelligence Bulletin," 10/11 July.
29. General Headquarters, "Special Intelligence Bulletin," 1/2 August.
30. General Headquarters, "Special Intelligence Bulletin," 15/16 July.
31. General Headquarters, "Special Intelligence Bulletin," 8/9 July and War Department, Military Intelligence Service, " 'MAGIC'," 13 July.
32. War Department, Military Intelligence Service, " 'MAGIC'," 20 July.
33. General Headquarters, "Special Intelligence Bulletin," 15/16, 23/24 July.
34. General Headquarters, "Special Intelligence Bulletin," 28/29, 25/26 July.
35. War Department, Military Intelligence Service, " 'MAGIC'," 21 July.
36. War Department, Military Intelligence Service, " 'MAGIC'," 30 July.
37. General Headquarters, "Special Intelligence Bulletin," 14/15 July and War Department, Military Intelligence Service, " 'MAGIC'," 12 July.
38. General Headquarters, "Special Intelligence Bulletin," 29/30 July.
39. General Headquarters, "Special Intelligence Bulletin," 15/16 July.
40. General Headquarters, "Special Intelligence Bulletin," 17/18 July.
41. Supreme Commander for the Allied Powers, *Reports of General*

MacArthur, vol. 2, *Japanese Operations in the South-West Pacific Area*, pt. 2, 652 and 654. Bōeichō, Bōei kenshūjō senshishitsu, *Senshi sōsho*, vol. 51, *Hondō kessen jumbi*, pt. 1, *Kyushu no bōei* (Official military history, vol. 51, Preparations for the decisive battle of the homeland: Defense of Kyushu, pt. 1) (Tokyo: Asagumo shimbunsha, 1972), 500.

42. War Department, Military Intelligence Service, "'MAGIC'," 29 June.
43. War Department, Military Intelligence Service, "'MAGIC'," 26 July and General Headquarters, "Special Intelligence Bulletin," 3/4 August.
44. David Westheimer, *Downfall: The Top-Secret Plan to Invade Japan* [originally published as *Lighter Than a Feather*] (New York: Bantam, 1972), 447. Senshi kenkyū gurupu, "Hondō kessen moshi okonawarereba" (What if the decisive battle of the homeland had occurred?) *Rekishi to jimbutsu* 1 (August 1977): 344.
45. General Headquarters, "Special Intelligence Bulletin," 29 July.
46. General Headquarters, U.S. Army Forces, Pacific, G-2 (Willoughby) to G-3 (Sutherland), "SUBJECT: Kyushu Reinforcement," 28 July 1945 and Sutherland to commanding general Far East Air Forces, "SUBJECT: Destruction of Enemy Lines of Communication and Enemy Forces in Kyushu," 1 August 1945, S. J. Chamberlain Papers, U.S. Army Military History Institute, Carlisle Barracks PA.
47. War Department, Military Intelligence Service, "'MAGIC'," 2 August.
48. War Department, Military Intelligence Service, "'MAGIC'," 7 August.
49. General Headquarters, "Special Intelligence Bulletin," 5/6 August.
50. General Headquarters, "Special Intelligence Bulletin," 4/5 August.
51. General Headquarters, "Special Intelligence Bulletin," 6/7 July.
52. General Headquarters, "Special Intelligence Bulletin," 5/6 August.
53. War Department, Military Intelligence Service, "'MAGIC'," 4 August and General Headquarters, "Special Intelligence Bulletin," 9/10 August.
54. Barton Bernstein, "Eclipsed by Hiroshima and Nagasaki: Early Thinking about Tactical Nuclear Weapons," *International Security* 15(4) (spring 1991): 161.
55. Bernstein, "Eclipsed by Hiroshima and Nagasaki," 164.
56. Larry I. Bland, ed., *George C. Marshall: Interviews and Reminiscences for Forrest C. Pogue* (Lexington VA: George C. Marshall Research Foundation, 1991), 423. The figure of 100,000 killed in the Tokyo bombing was known to the Allies via a decrypted message by early April. This ULTRA was likely the source for Marshall's figure. See Joint Intelligence Center Pacific Ocean Area, "Summary of ULTRA Traffic," 7 April 1945, SRMD-007, RG 457, NARA.
57. Senshi kenkyū gurupu, "Hondō kessen moshi okonawarereba," 341.
58. Hosokawa Morisada, *Hosokawa nikki,* ge (The Hosokawa diary), vol. 2 (Tokyo: Chūkō bunko, 1979), 378.
59. Westheimer, *Downfall: The Top-Secret Plan*, 437.

60. War Department, Military Intelligence Service, "'MAGIC'," 15 July.
61. "Summary of ULTRA Traffic," 7 August 1945.
62. Marshall to MacArthur, War 31897, 9 August 1945: MacArthur to Marshall, War 31897, 9 August 1945. Photocopies in author's possession.
63. Cited in Drea, MacArthur's ULTRA, 187. An evaluation of MacArthur's use of intelligence appears on pages 230–31.
64. Marc Gallicchio, "After Nagasaki: General Marshall's Plan for Tactical Nuclear Weapons in Japan," *Prologue* 23(4) (winter 1991): 397.
65. Cited in Bernstein, "Eclipsed by Hiroshima and Nagasaki," 164–65.
66. Major General Clayton Bissell to chief of staff, "Estimate of Japanese Situation for the Next 30 Days," 12 August 1945, WD, general and special staffs, OPD, File 2, Box 12, RG 165, NARA.
67. Gallicchio, "After Nagasaki," 400.
68. Gallicchio, "After Nagasaki," 401.
69. Gallicchio, "After Nagasaki," 402.
70. Cited in Bernstein, "Eclipsed by Hiroshima and Nagasaki," 151–52.

12. Chasing a Decisive Victory

1. Terasaki Hidenari and Mariko Terasaki Miller, eds., *Shōwa Tennō dokuhakuroku—Terasaki Hidenari goyōgakari nikki* (The Shōwa emperor's monologue: Court official Terasaki Hidenari's diary) (Tokyo: Bungei shunjū, 1991), 88. Hereafter cited as DHR. Besides Terasaki, those present were Marquis Yasumasa Matsudaira, wartime private secretary and aide to the lord keeper of the privy seal; Matsudaira Tsuneo, minister of the imperial household (until June 1945); Kinoshita Michio, vice grand chamberlain, and Inada Shuichi, chief cabinet secretary. See also Herbert P. Bix, "The Shōwa Emperor's 'Monologue' and the Problem of War Responsibility," *Journal of Japanese Studies* 18(2) (summer 1992): 298.
2. Gerhard Krebs, "The Spy Activities of Diplomat Terasaki Hidenari in the USA," mss. n.d. (apparently spring 1995).
3. Kinoshita Michio, *Sōkkin nisshi* (The diary of a close associate [of the emperor]) (Tokyo: Bungei shunjū, 1990), 393–94.
4. DHR, 390–93; and Bix, "Shōwa Emperor," 298.
5. Kinoshita, *Sōkkin nisshi*, 170, entry for 18 March 1946.
6. "Report by the State-War-Navy Coordinating Subcommittee for the Far East," SWNCC 57/3, 12 September 1945 in *Foreign Relations of the United States: Diplomatic Papers 1945*, vol. 6, *The British Commonwealth: The Far East* (Washington DC: U.S. Government Printing Office, 1969), 936.
7. Stephen S. Large, *Emperor Hirohito and Shōwa Japan: A Political Biography* (New York: Routledge, 1992), 139, citing Robert E. Ward, "Presurrendur Planning: Treatment of the Emperor and Constitutional Changes,"

Democratizing Japan: The Allied Occupation, eds. Robert E. Ward and Sakamoto Yoshikazu (Honolulu: University of Hawaii Press, 1987), 15.
8. General of the Army Douglas MacArthur to the chief of staff, U.S. Army (Eisenhower), 25 January 1946, in *Foreign Relations of the United States 1946*, vol. 8, *The Far East* (Washington DC: U.S. Government Printing Office, 1971), 395–97.
9. Arnold C. Brackman, *The Other Nuremberg: The Untold Story of the Tokyo War Crimes Trials* (New York: Quill-Morrow, 1987), 78.
10. Kojima Noboru, *Tennō to sensō sekinin* (The emperor and war responsibility) (Tokyo: Bungei bunkō, 1991), 98–99.
11. Large, *Emperor Hirohito*, 133.
12. Bix, "The Shōwa Emperor's 'Monologue,'" 299, 331–33. Bix argues a possible indictment was a motivating factor and makes his point more forcefully in "Emperor Hirohito's War," *History Today* 41 (December 1991): 326–32. But also see Itō Takashi, Kojima Noboru, Hata Ikuhiko, and Handō Kazutoshi, "'Dokuhakuroku' wo tettei kenkyū suru" (Thoroughly studying the 'Monologue') *Bungei shunjū* (January 1991): 129–31.
13. Yoshida Yutaka, *Shōwa tennō no shūsenshi* (Tokyo: Iwanami shoten, 1992), 89; and Kinoshita, *Sokkin nisshi*, 222, on Terasaki.
14. Itō Takashi et al., "'Dokuhakuroku' wo tettei kenkyū suru," 139. Bix, "The Shōwa Emperor's 'Monologue,'" 299. Copious, and well-edited, extracts from "The Shōwa Emperor's 'Monologue'" have appeared in English in Yasumasa Matsudaira, "The Japanese Emperor and the War," in Supreme Commander for the Allied Powers, *Reports of General MacArthur: Japanese Operations in the Southwest Pacific Area*, vol. 2, pt. 2 (Washington DC: U.S. Government Printing Office, 1966), appen., 763–71.
15. Leonard A. Humphreys, *The Way of the Heavenly Sword: The Japanese Army in the 1920s* (Stanford: Stanford University Press, 1995), 171. Carol Gluck, *Japan's Modern Myths: Ideology in the Late Meiji Period* (Princeton NJ: Princeton University Press, 1985), 93. The shift obviously did not occur overnight, but the new paradigm was firmly in place by the time of the Emperor Meiji's death in 1912. From an obscure figure in 1868, the emperor had emerged as a symbol of Japan and Japanese ability to claim a place in "the forefront of the civilized world." Indeed this transformation is regarded as a key achievement of the Meiji leaders. Mikiso Hane, *Modern Japan: A Historical Survey*, 2d ed. (Boulder CO: Westview, 1992), 184.
16. Humphreys, *The Way of the Heavenly Sword*, 80. See Large, *Emperor Hirohito*, 133, citing Itō Takashi, Hirohashi Todamitsu, and Katashima Norio, eds., *Tōjō naikaku sōridaijin kimitsu kiroku* (Confidential record of prime minister Tojo's cabinet) (Tokyo: Tokyo daigaku shuppankai,

1990), 526 on this point. Also see Kinoshita, *Sōkkin nisshi*, 1–2 and 229 on the responsibility for the imperial ancestors.
17. DHR, 35.
18. Nobutaka Ike, trans. and ed., *Japan's Decision for War: Records of the 1941 Policy Conferences* (Stanford: Stanford University Press, 1967), xvii explains the system. The notion of *ringisei* is explored in Janet E. Hunter, *The Emergence of Modern Japan: An Introductory History since 1853* (London: Longman Group, 1989), 304–5.
19. Yamada Akira, *Shōwa tennō no sensō shidō* (The Shōwa emperor's wartime leadership) (Tokyo: Shōwa shuppan, 1990), 12.
20. Robert J. C. Butow, *Japan's Decision to Surrender* (Stanford: Stanford University Press, 1954), 44n, 46.
21. Large, *Emperor Hirohito*, 80, citing Yale Candee Maxon, *Control of Japanese Foreign Policy: A Study in Civil-Military Rivalry 1930–1945* (Westport CT: Greenwood, 1975), 61–62.
22. DHR, 20. See also "Seidan haichōroku genkō" (Manuscript of the record of listening to the imperial dialogue); Kinoshita memo, vol. 1, 211, and Kinoshita memo, vol. 3, 215–16 in Kinoshita, *Sōkkin nisshi*.
23. DHR, 84.
24. Stewart Lone, "The Sino-Japanese War, 1894–95, and the Evolution of the Japanese Monarchy," *Japan and China: Miscellaneous Papers* Discussion Paper No. 1S/93/269, London School of Economics (September 1993), 12–14.
25. Ben-Ami Shillony, *Politics and Culture in Wartime Japan* (Oxford: Clarendon, 1981), 42.
26. Alvin Coox, *Japan: The Final Agony* (New York: Ballantine, 1970), 67, describes the regimental flag ceremonies. Kido Kōichi nikki kenkyūkai, *Kido Kōichi nikki gekan* (Kido Kōichi dairy, vol. 2) (Tokyo: Tokyo daigaku shuppankai, 1966), 1224, entry for 10 August 1945.
27. Yamada, *Shōwa tennō no sensō shidō*, 13–20, 24.
28. Kojima Noboru, *Sanbō, jō* (Staff officers, vol. 1) (Tokyo: Bunshun bunko, ed., 1975), 211–12, 215; Hata Ikuhiko, *Shōwashi no gunjintachi* (Military men of Shōwa history) (Tokyo: Bungei shunjū, 1982), 32 and 321; Hata Ikuhiko, "Shūsen to tenno to rikugun," (The end of the war and the emperor and the army) *Rekishi to jimbutsu* (August 1983): 23.
29. Hiroyuki Agawa, *The Reluctant Admiral: Yamamoto and the Imperial Navy*, trans. John Bester (Tokyo: Kodansha International, 1979), 187.
30. Robert J. C. Butow, *Tojo and the Coming of the War* (Stanford: Stanford University Press, 1961), 168.
31. Butow, *Tojo and the Coming of the War*, 268–69; and Large, *Emperor Hirohito*, 109.
32. "Shimada Shigetarō taishō kaisen nikki" (Admiral Shimada Shigetarō's diary at the opening of the war) *Bungei shunjū* (December 1976): 362–63.

33. Hata, *Shōwashi no gunjintachi*, 149.
34. Takagi Sōkichi, *Takagi kaigun shōsō oboegaki* (Rear Admiral Takagi's memorandum) (Tokyo: Mainichi shimbunsha, 1979), 20, entry for 7 March 1944.
35. Hata, *Shōwashi no gunjintachi*, 156–57.
36. Kojima, *Sanbō*, 215.
37. Kojima, *Sanbō*, 207–8, 214.
38. Kojima Noboru, *Shikkikan*, jō (Commanders, vol. 1) (Tokyo: Bunshun bunkō ed., 1974), 185–86, 190, 193
39. Cited in Yoshida, *Shōwa tennō no shūsenshi*, 17. Also see Butow, *Tōjō*, 294. Ito Takashi et al., eds., *Tōjō naikaku sōridaijin kimitsu kiroku*, 259? Despite the title, the document is the prime minister's daily appointments' calender with limited notations.
40. Irogawa Daikichi, *The Age of Hirohito: In Search of Modern Japan*, trans. Mikiso Hane and John K. Urda (New York: Free Press, 1995), 82–83.
41. Akamatsu Sadao, "Tōjō ron" (A discourse on Tōjō), Asahi shimbunsha, ed., *Kataritsugu Shōwashi gekidō no hanseki* (Shōwa history handed down from one generation to another—the violent half century) (Tokyo: Asahi shimbunsha, 1976), 16. Akamatsu, an army colonel, was Prime Minister Tōjō's confidential secretary.
42. DHR, 88.
43. David Anson Titus, *Palace and Politics in Prewar Japan* (New York: Columbia University Press, 1974), 330.
44. Edward Behr, *Hirohito: Behind the Myth* (New York: Vintage ed., 1990), 177–78; John Toland, *The Rising Sun: The Decline and Fall of the Japanese Empire 1936–1945* (New York: Random House, 1970), 79.
45. DHR, 59, on Hirohito's advice to Tōjō. See also Large, "Emperor Hirohito and Early Shōwa Japan," *Monumenta Nipponica* 46(3) (1991): 363. On the "state of dread," see Large, *Emperor Hirohito*, 106, citing Kido, *Kido Kōichi*, 2, 894, entry for 25 July 1941. Ōe Shinobu, *Gozen kaigi: Shōwa tennō jugokai no seidan* (The imperial conference: The Shōwa emperor's 15 sacred decisions) (Tokyo: Chūkō shinsho, 1991), 86 argues the emperor's chronology in DHR is incorrect and questions why Hirohito spoke to Tōjō, then war minister, as opposed to the foreign minister, because diplomatic negotiations with the French over the issue were under way. Ōe also observes that Hirohito approved the move into southern Indochina on 19 July. This leads him to conclude that it is almost impossible that the emperor acted to prevent this latest aggression.
46. Sanbō honbu, ed., *Sugiyama Memo*, jō (Field marshal Sugiyama Hajime's memoranda), vol. 1 (Tokyo: Hara shobō, 1967), 277, entry for 22 July 1941. Hereafter cited as *Sugiyama memo* 1.
47. On Hirohito's concern about victory see *Sugiyama Memo* 1, 81 and Kido,

Kido nikki, entry for 895–96, entry for 31 July 1941. *Sugiyama Memo 1,* 310, entry for 5 September 1941. The English-language translation of this meeting is available in Ike, *Japan's Decision,* 135.
48. Ike, *Japan's Decision,* 129.
49. DHR, 62. See Ōe, *Gozen kaigi,* 86–99, for a dissenting viewpoint.
50. *Sugiyama Memo 1,* 310, entry for 5 September 1941. Konoe was present at the meeting and recorded what Sugiyama left out.
51. My account is taken from Kojima Noboru, *Tennō dai 4 kan Shōwa 16 juroku nen zengo* (Tokyo: Bungei shunjū, 1974), 298. See also DHR, 63; Large, *Emperor Hirohito,* 108; and Butow, *Tōjō,* 254–55.
52. *Sugiyama memo 1,* 310; and Yamada, *Shōwa tennō no senso shidō,* 81.
53. Cited in *Sugiyama memo 1,* 311. Sugiyama used the term "nanpō sakusen" or southern operations, which was Japanese for the offensive into Western colonies of Southeast Asia. For contrary interpretations see Bix, "Monologue," 299 and his "Hiroshima in History and Memory," 233, as well as David Bergamini's, *Japan's Imperial Conspiracy* (New York: Pocket Book ed., 1972), 822–28; and Behr, *Hirohito: Behind the Myth,* 221–25.
54. DHR, 47.
55. Ike, *Kido Kōichi,* 134. Kido deflected Hirohito's initiative by suggesting that the president of the privy council ask the questions and his majesty conclude the meeting with a brief statement. Butow, *Tojo,* 254–255.
56. Ike, *Kido Kōichi,* 139–41.
57. DHR, 66.
58. DHR, 69.
59. "Full translation of 'From Memorandum of Hoshina Zenshiro, Former Chief of Naval Affairs Bureau of Navy Ministry,'" 27 December 1949, 4, in General Headquarters, Far East Command, Military Intelligence Division, *Statements of Japanese Officials on World War II* (English translations), vol. 1. Hereafter cited as *Statements.*
60. Irie Sukemasu, *Irie Sukemasu nikki,* vol. 2, *Shōwa 15 nen 1 gatsu—Shōwa 20 nen 8 gatsu* (Tokyo: Asahi bunkō ed., 1994), 111, entry for 17 October 1941.
61. Chihaya Masatake et al., eds., *Takamatsu no miya nikki* dai 3 kan (Prince Takamatsu's diary), vol. 3 (Tokyo: Chūō kōronsha, 1995), 307, entry for 17 October 1941.
62. Chihaya, *Takamatsu no miya nikki,* n 3, 294.
63. Yamada Akira, *Daigensui Shōwa tennō* (Generalissimo: The Shōwa emperor) (Tokyo: Shin Nihon shuppansha, 1994), 150–52 and 156–57. Large, *Emperor Hirohito,* 111, citing Gordon W. Prange, *At Dawn We Slept: The Untold Story of Pearl Harbor* (New York: McGraw-Hill, 1981), 309, states the emperor learned of the Pearl Harbor attack at the October briefing. This is incorrect.

64. Ike, *Japan's Decision*, 196.
65. "Juichigatsu tsuitachi Tōjō rikusō to Sugiyama sōchō to no kaidan yōshi," (Gist of the November First discussion between War Minister Tojo and Chief of Staff Sugiyama) in *Taiheiyō sensō e no michi*, eds. Inaba Masao et al. (The road to the Pacific war), *bekkan shiryōhen* (Collected documents) (Tokyo: Asahi shimbunsha, 1963), 548–49. Cf. Tanemura Suketaka, *Daihon'ei kimitsu nisshi* (Imperial headquarters confidential diary) (Tokyo: Fūyō shobō, 1979 rpt. of 1952 ed.), 127, entry for 1 November 1941
66. Ike, *Japan's Decision*, 199–200.
67. Ike, *Japan's Decision*, 201–2 for Nagano's remarks and 207 for Tsukada's.
68. Ike, *Japan's Decision*, 208.
69. Sanbō, *Sugiyama Memo*, ge (Field marshal Sugiyama Hajime's memoranda), vol. 2 (Tokyo: Hara shobō, 1967), 6. Hereafter cited as *Sugiyama memo 2*. See also "Shimada kaisen nikki," 364.
70. *Sugiyama Memo 1*, 387–88, minutes of 3 November imperial audience by both chiefs of staff. On Hirohito's ignorance of the Hawaii operation see Ōe Shinobu, *Gozen kaigi*, 213. Behr, *Hirohito: Behind the Myth*, errs in stating that on 2 November 1941 Hirohito asked his chiefs of staff about projected losses for the first stage of wartime operations; was reminded by Nagano that 8 December in Tokyo was actually 7 December in Hawaii so everyone there would be tired after the weekend holiday; and that surprise was all important. The actual chronology was as follows: (a) on 2 November Tōjō, Nagano, and Sugiyama briefed the emperor on the results of the Sixty-fifth and Sixty-sixth Liaison Conferences held on 30 October and 1 November. They also answered several of Hirohito's questions as Behr describes on the bottom of page 233 and the top of 234; (b) The comments ascribed to Nagano on page 234 of Behr were made the following day, 3 November, when Nagano and Sugiyama met with the emperor. Contrary to Behr, however, Nagano made no mention of Hawaii in this exchange, although picking a Sunday was an important factor in scheduling the attack. The rest of Behr's context is accurate. *Sugiyama memo 1*, 386–88; and (c) As for Nagano's remarks about the necessity of gaining surprise, these occurred at the 5 November Imperial Conference. See *Sugiyama memo 1*, 430, and Ike, *Kido Kōichi*, 224. Thus on 4 November Hirohito actually told Kido information from the two previous days of briefings. Kido, *Kido nikki*, 921, entry for 4 November 1941.
71. Ike, *Japan's Decision*, 221 and 237–38.
72. A version of Nagano's remarks is available as Sanbō sōchō—Gunreibu sōchō (Chief of staff, army and chief of naval general staff), "Heiki ni yoru sakusen keikaku osetsumei ni kansuru hen" (Matters related to

the explanation to the emperor of operational plans based on tabletop exercises), 8 November 1941. The full document may be found in Yamada, *Shōwa tennō no sensō shidō*, documentary appen. 3, 231–36.

73. Yamada, *Shōwa tennō sensō shidō*, 91 and Yamada, *Daigensui Shōwa tennō*, 156 assert the entire operational plans of the army and navy, including the Pearl Harbor attack, were presented to the emperor at the imperial tabletop maneuvers held 15 November, but this is clearly wrong. See Bōeichō, Bōei senshishitsu, *Senshi sōsho*, vol. 20, *Daihon'ei rikugunbu*, pt. 2 (Official history, vol. 20, Imperial General Headquarters, army department, pt. 2) (Tokyo: Asagumo shimbunsha, 1968), 634; and Gomikawa Junpei, *Gozen kaigi* (The imperial conferences) (Tokyo: Bungei shunjū, 1984), 360. According to Jō Ei'ichirō, *Jiji bukan Jō Ei'ichirō nikki* (Imperial aide-de-camp Captain Jō Ei'ichirō's diary) Nomura Minoru, ed. (Tokyo: Yamakawa shuppan, 1982), 109, entry for 8 November. The chief aide-de-camp reported to the throne about the war games on that date.

74. Yamada, *Shōwa tennō no sensō shidō*, 91.
75. DHR, 72–74.
76. DHR, 75. Kido, *Kido nikki*, 928, entry for 30 November 1941. Unfortunately the tenth volume of Takamatsu's unpublished diary ends with a 14 November 1941 entry, and the eleventh starts with 1 December 1941. Chihaya, *Takamatsu no miya nikki*, vol. 3, n. 4, 318.
77. DHR, n 76–77.
78. DHR, 54.
79. "Shimada kaisen nikki," 368.
80. DHR, 75–76.
81. DHR, 71 and 75. The emperor later stated that the lack of oil made it inevitable that the navy would have to go to war. See Kinoshita, *Sōkkin nisshi*, 74, entry for 11 December 1946.
82. Shakai mondai kenkyūkai, ed., *Uyoku—minzokuha jiten* (The right wing—the nationalist factions) (Tokyo: Kokusho kankōkai, 1976), 78–91. Major attempted coup d'états included the March and October incidents (1931), the Blood Pledge Corps and the May 15th incidents (1932), the Heaven Sent Soldiers and Saitama incidents (1933), the Military School Incident (1934), the 2-26 Incident (1936), and the 7-5 Incident (1940).
83. Hugh Byas, *Government by Assassination* (New York: Knopf, 1942), reflects a reporter's view of coups, killings, and plots in prewar Japan. For a differing interpretation see Bix, "Monologue," 350–51.
84. DHR, 54.
85. Large, *Emperor Hirohito*, 80.
86. Large, *Emperor Hirohito*, 115.
87. See Kido, *Kido nikki*, 967, entry for 8 June 1942. Also see Sanbō honbu sensō shidōhan, ed., "Daihon'ei kimitsu sensō nisshi" (Imperial general

headquarters' confidential war diary), *Rekishi to jimbutsu* (September 1971): 366–67.
88. Yamada, *Shōwa tennō sensō shidō*, 190–91.
89. Large, *Emperor Hirohito*, 116, quoting Kido, *Kido nikki*, 945.
90. The term is Bix's, "Hiroshima in History and Memory: A Symposium: Japan's Delayed Surrender: A Reinterpretation," *Diplomatic History* 19 (spring 1995): 203.
91. Kido, *Kido nikki*, 945, entry for 8 May 1942.
92. Kido, *Kido nikki*, 966–67, entry for 8 June 1942; and Yamada, *Shōwa tennō sensō shidō*, 110. During the Russo-Japanese War, two Japanese battleships, one third of the navy's capital ships, were lost to Russian mines. The losses were kept secret, and Tōgō went out of his way to appear confident in victory.
93. Hata, "Shūsen to tennō to rikugun," 23.
94. DHR, 102. From the version prepared for the MacArthur history series. "I recall one day after the war ended the Emperor, speaking to us, his entourage, reminisced: 'From the time when our line along the Stanley Mountain Range in New Guinea was penetrated, I was anxious for peace, but we had a treaty with Germany against concluding a separate peace; and we could not violate an international commitment. This was a dilemma that tormented me." Matsudaira Yasumasa, "Appendix—The Japanese Emperor and the War," *Reports of General MacArthur: Japanese Operations in the Southwest Pacific Area*, vol. 2, pt. 2, 763. The version from the 1991 edition of the monologue giving the date as September 1943 is questionable given existing documentary evidence. This dating first appeared in parentheses in the 1991 edition of the emperor's monologue. No date was inserted in the text of the original publication in December 1990, however. Moreover a contemporary document prepared by Kido's chief secretary in 1946 contains the identical statement about the Owen Stanley defeat without any date. See DHR, 102; "Shōwa tennō no dokuhakuroku hachijikan" (The Shōwa emperor's eight-hour monologue) *Bungei shunjū* (December 1990): 129; and Matsudaira, "Tennō heiki wa itsu goro shūsen wo gokesshin shite imashitaka" (Around when did his imperial majesty determine to end the war?), undated ms., but apparently written in December 1946; original in Charles A. Willoughby Papers, the Gettysburg College Library, Gettysburg PA, 1. On the provenance of the document see Yoshida, *Shōwa tennō no shūsenshi*, 156–57. A translated English language version of the document titled "The Japanese Emperor and the War" is also available at the above-mentioned archive. This version became the basis for the appendix, "The Japanese Emperor and the War," in *Reports of General MacArthur: Japanese Operations in the Southwest Pacific Area*, vol. 2, pt. 2.
95. Supreme Commander for the Allied Powers, *Reports of General*

MacArthur: *Japanese Operations in the Southwest Pacific Area*, vol. 2, pt. 1 (Washington DC: U.S. Government Printing Office, 1966), 164–70.
96. Yamada, *Shōwa tennō sensō shidō*, 120.
97. Morimatsu Toshio, "Shōwa tennō wo shinobi hōzuru—Ogata jijū bukan nikki kara" (Reminiscences of serving the Shōwa emperor—from aide-de-camp Ogata's dairy) in *Shōwa gunji hiwa*, chū, ed. Dōdai kurabu kōenkai (Secret tales of military affairs in the Shōwa era) (privately published, 1990), 3–4.
98. DHR, 83.
99. Morimatsu, "Shōwa tennō wo shinobi hōzuru—Ogata jijū bukan nikki kara," 4.
100. Yamada, *Shōwa tennō sensō shidō*, 121. For the larger context see Bōeichō Bōei kenshūjō senshibu, *Senshi sōsho*, vol. 66, *Daihon'ei rikugunbu*, pt. 6 (Official history, vol. 66, Imperial General Headquarters, army department, pt. 6) (Tokyo: Asagumo shimbunsha, 1973), 28.
101. Cited in Yamada, *Shōwa tennō sensō shidō*, 250–51.
102. *Sugiyama memo* 2, 18–19. Notes on imperial audiences, 31 December 1942.
103. *Sugiyama memo* 2, 19. Notes on imperial audiences, 9 January 1943, and 3 March 1943.
104. See DHR, 84 on lack of interservice cooperation. *Sugiyama memo* 2, 20–21. Notes on imperial audience, 6 and 8 June 1943.
105. *Sugiyama memo* 2, 21, 8 June 1943.
106. *Sugiyama memo* 2, 21–22. Notes on imperial audience, 9 June 1943.
107. *Sugiyama memo* 2, 22–25. Notes from 5 and 8 August 1943.
108. Yamada, *Shōwa tennō sensō shidō*, 154–55.
109. Yamada, *Shōwa tennō sensō shidō*, 160.
110. For the Japanese version see Yamada, *Shōwa tennō sensō shidō*, 173. For the American account refer to "War Diary, U.S.S. Chincoteague," 8 March 1944, U.S. Naval Historical Center, Washington DC. I am grateful to Cathy Lloyd of the Naval Historical Center for locating this document for me.
111. Yamada, *Shōwa tennō sensō shidō*, 173.
112. Shillony, *Politics and Culture in Wartime Japan*, 54.
113. DHR, 103.
114. Takagi Sōkichi, *Takagi kaigun shōsō oboegaki*, 20, entry for 7 March 1944.
115. Shillony, *Politics and Culture in Wartime Japan*, 54. The original account of the exchange between the two appears in *Sugiyama memo* 2, 28–29.
116. Akamatsu, "Tōjō ron," 45.
117. As related to Takagi by Prince Takamatsu on 20 June 1944. See Takagi, *Takagi kaigun shōsō oboegaki*, 61.

118. Tokyo, *Asahi shimbun*, 24 June 1944, 1.
119. Higashikuni Naruhikō, *Higashikuni nikki: Nihon gekidōki no hiroku* (Prince Higashikuni's diary—confidential record of Japan's turbulent time) (Tokyo: Tokuma shoten, 1968), 132–33, entries for 20 and 23 June 1944.
120. Hosokawa Morisada, *Hosokawa nikki,* jō (Hosokawa diary, vol. 1) (Tokyo: Chūō kōbunkō ed., 1991), 244–45, entry for 23 June 1944. Hereafter cited as *Hosokawa nikki* (jō). This is an expanded version of Hosokawa's two-volume *Jōhō tennō ni tassezu* (Reports that did not reach the emperor) originally published in 1953.
121. DHR, 95–96.
122. DHR, 88.
123. Sanbō honbu sensō shidōhan, ed., "Daihon'ei kimitsu sensō nisshi" (Imperial General Headquarters' confidential war diary), *Rekishi to jimbutsu* (October 1971): 309, entry for 24 June 1944.
124. Higashikuni, *Higashikuni nikki,* n 133.
125. Hosokawa, *Hosokawa nikki* jō, 121, entry for 7 February 1944.
126. Hosokawa, *Hosokawa nikki* jō, 131 and 144, entries for 18 February and 3 March 1944. Shigemitsu's remarks are cited in 158–59, entry for 16 March 1944.
127. Hosokawa, *Hosokawa nikki* jō, 183, entry for 13 April 1944.
128. Yamada, *Shōwa tennō sensō shidō*, 180.
129. Takagi, *Takagi kaigun shōsō oboegaki*, 75, entry for 30 June 1944.
130. Cited in Hosokawa Morisada, *Hosokawa nikki,* ge (Tokyo: Chūō kōbunkō ed., 1991), 308–9, entry for 30 September 1944. Hereafter cited as *Hosokawa nikki* (ge).
131. Takagi, *Takagi kaigun shōsō oboegaki*, 104–6, entry for 17 September 1944.
132. Hosokawa, *Hosokawa nikki* (ge), 284, entry for 22 July 1944; and Kojima Noboru, *Tennō*, dai go kan, *Teikoku no shūen* (The emperor, vol. 5, End of empire) (Tokyo: Bungei shunjū, 1974), 204. DHR, 97.
133. Itō Takashi, "Koiso chinjutsu wo megutte" (Concerning Koiso's statement) *Rekishi to jimbutsu* (December 1985): 390.
134. Toshikazu Kase, *Journey to the Missouri* (New York: Archon, 1969), 144.
135. Hosokawa, *Hosokawa nikki*, ge, 343, entry for 10 January 1945.
136. Ōe Shinobu, *Shōwa no rekishi*, vol. 3, *Tennō no guntai* (A history of the Shōwa emperor's reign, vol. 3, The emperor's army) (Tokyo: Shogakkan, 1982), 94.
137. Concerning Yonai's opinions on China and the Tripartite Pact refer to Steven E. Pelz, *Race to Pearl Harbor: The Failure of the Second London Naval Conference and the Onset of World War II* (Cambridge MA: Harvard University Press, 1974), 213–14; and Morimatsu Toshio, *Daihon'ei*

(Imperial General Headquarters) (Tokyo: Kyōikusha, 1980), 191. On Yonai's "guts" see Agawa, *The Reluctant Admiral*, 126 and 143–44.
138. David Bergamini, *Japan's Imperial Conspiracy*, 1176.
139. Takagi, *Takagi kaigun shōsō oboegaki*, 236, entry for 16 May 1945. See *Reports of General MacArthur: Japanese Operations in the Southwest Pacific Area*, vol. 2, pt. 2, 670, on Yonai's entitlement to firsthand military information.
140. Takagi, *Takagi kaigun shōsō oboegaki*, 119, entry for 17 January 1945.
141. Gunreibu sōchō, "Senkyō ni kanshi sōjō," Shōwa 19 nen 10 gatsu 16 nichi (Report to the throne on the war situation, 16 October 1944), cited in Yamada, *Shōwa tennō sensō shidō*, Documentary appen. 9, 263–69.
142. "Senkyō ni kanshi sōjō," 183–84.
143. Bōeichō, Bōei Kenshūjō senshishitsu, *Senshi sōsho*, vol. 41, *Shōgo rikugun sakusen: Reite kessen*, pt. 1 (Official history, vol. 41, Shō ground operations: the decisive battle of Leyte, pt. 1) (Tokyo: Asagumo shimbunsha, 1970), 316.
144. Kojima, *Teikoku no shūen*, 242.
145. Kojima, *Teikoku no shūen*, 241–44.
146. Kojima, *Teikoku no shūen*, 252; and DHR, 101.
147. Takagi, *Takagi kaigun shōsō oboegaki*, 126, entry for 25 January 1945.
148. Gunreibu sōchō, "Senkyō ni kanshi sōjō," 25–28 October 1944, cited in Yamada, *Shōwa tennō sensō shidō*, Documentary appen. 10–13, 269–82.
149. DHR, 100. Yamashita had favored concentrating his defense of the Philippines on Luzon, but was overruled by Southern Army and Imperial General Headquarters, who ordered him to reinforce Leyte.
150. Kojima, *Teikoku no shūen*, 257.
151. DHR, 101–2.
152. Yoshida, *Shōwa tennō no sensōshi*, 21; Hata, *Shōwa tennō itsutsu no ketsudan* (Five decisions of the Shōwa emperor) (Tokyo: Bungei shunjū ed., 1994), 101–3. Okada Keisuke had been prime minister during the February 1936 mutiny and was spared only because rebel officers murdered his brother-in-law by mistake. As retired admiral he had access to high-level navy deliberations and shared the navy's resentment of Tōjō. He also favored striking a blow against the Americans before negotiating.
153. Shillony, *Politics and Culture in Wartime Japan*, 61; and Hata, *Shōwa tennō itsutsu no ketsudan*, 103.
154. Higashikuni, *Higashikuni nikki*, 135, entry for 8 July 1944.
155. DHR, 102. See also Butow, *Japan's Decision*, 62n, 50.
156. Although Hirohito says "Okinawa" in his 1946 recollections, at the time the decisive battle was anticipated to occur off Taiwan, when confiding details of the meeting to Hosokawa, Konoe told them Taiwan, not Okinawa. See *Hosokawa nikki*, ge, 354, entry for 16 February 1945.

157. Kojima, *Teikoku no shūen*, 270.
158. Hosokawa, *Hosokawa nikki* jō, 354, entry for 16 February 1945.
159. Yamada, *Shōwa tennō sensō shidō*, 201.
160. Takagi, *Takagi kaigun shōsō oboegaki*, 176, entry for 16 March 1945.
161. Irie, *Irie Sukemasu nikki*, 346. See, for instance, his entry for 27 March 1945.
162. Hosokawa Morisada, *Hosokawa nikki* ge, 373, entry for 30 March 1945.
163. Yamada, *Shōwa tennō sensō shidō*, 197–98.
164. Thomas M. Huber, "Japan's Battle of Okinawa, April–June 1945," *Leavenworth Papers* No. 18 (Ft. Leavenworth KS: Combat Studies Institute, 1990), 30–31.
165. Saburo Hayashi in collaboration with Alvin D. Coox, *Kogun: The Japanese Army in the Pacific War* (Westport CT: Greenwood, 1978 rpt. of 1959 ed.), 140.
166. Hata, *Shōwa tennō itsutsu no ketsudan*, 62.
167. DHR, 113–14.
168. DHR, 116, 117n, and 120. Hatano Sumio, "Suzuki Kantarō no shūsen shidō" (Prime Minister Suzuki's leadership to end the war) in *Dai ni ji sekai taisen*, vol. 3, *Shūsen*, ed. Gunjishi gakkai (The second world war, vol. 3, War termination) (Tokyo: Kinshosha, 1995), 61. See also *Reports of General MacArthur: Japanese Operations in the Southwest Pacific Area*, vol. 2, pt. 2, 688 on the need for Soviet neutrality. On the X diplomatic strategy see Butow, *Japan's Decison*, 81–85.
169. Butow, *Japan's Decision*, 70–71.
170. Hata, *Shōwa tennō itsutsu no ketsudan*, 65.
171. Butow, *Japan's Decision*, 63.
172. Shillony, *Politics and Culture in Wartime Japan*, 161.
173. Hatano, "Suzuki Kantarō," 63.
174. Butow, *Japan's Decision*, 68–69.
175. Handō Kazutoshi, *Seidan: Tennō to Suzuki Kantarō* (The sacred decision; the emperor and Suzuki Kantarō) (Tokyo: Bungei shunjū, 1985), 225–26. Hosokawa, *Hosokawa nikki*, 365, entry for 4 March 1945.
176. Handō, *Seidan*, 251.
177. Hatano, "Suzuki Kantarō," 55n, 76.
178. Nomura Minoru, "Nihon kaigun no gankosha, Toyoda Soemu no ketsudan" (The Japanese navy's stubborn man—Toyoda Soemu's decisions) *Rekishi to jimbutsu* (August 1985), 178.
179. Nomura, "Nihon kaigun," 177–78.
180. Hata, *Shōwa tennō itsutsu no ketsudan*, 66; and Hosokawa, *Hosokawa nikki*, 297, entry for 26 August 1944.
181. Jerome Forrest, "The General Who Would Not Eat Grass," *Naval History* 9 (July/August 1995): 22.

182. Hata, *Shōwashi no gunjintachi*, 24–25; and Takeshita Masako, "Anami Korechika taishō" (General Anami Korechika), in Imai Takeo and Terasaki Ryuji, *Nihongun no kenkyū shikkikan*, jō (Studies of Japanese military commanders) (Tokyo: Hara shobō, 1980), 6–13.
183. On the aims of the peace group see Hosokawa Morisada, "Genrō jūshin no hataraki" (The workings of the genrō and senior statesmen), in *Kataritsugu Shōwashi, Gekidō no hanseki*, vol. 3 (Stories of Shōwa history handed down from one generation to another—the violent half century) (Tokyo: Asahi shimbunsha, 1976), 306–7.
184. Takagi, *Takagi kaigun shōsō oboegaki*, 228–29, entry for 13 May 1945. Kido told Takagi the emperor's change of heart occurred two or three days before 5 May. See also Hosokawa, *Hosokawa nikki*, ge 394, entry for 24 May 1945.
185. Hosokawa, *Hosokawa nikki* (ge), 394, entry for 24 May, 1945 reads, "Kido said, 'Recently His Imperial Majesty, probably as a result of my [Kido's] prodding, feels he would be able to use his imperial will to end the war.' " Takagi, *Takagi kaigun shōsō oboegaki*, 228, entry for 13 May 1945, recounts the emperor's "changed feelings" and records other information similar to Hosokawa's later entries. This suggests Kido and the emperor had the discussion in early May.
186. Toshiaki Kawahara, *Hirohito and His Times: A Japanese Perspective* (Tokyo and New York: Kodansha International, 1990), 121–23.
187. Hata Ikuhiko, *Shōwa tennō itsutsu no ketsudan*, 59; Handō, *Seidan*, 269–70. There were also earlier rumors that the army intended to move the emperor to Manchuria. Shillony, *Politics and Culture in Wartime Japan*, 61. Higashikuni had also heard about the Matsushiro redoubt. Higashikuni, *Higashikuni nikki*, 135–36, entry for 8 July 1944.
188. Kido, *Kido nikki*, 1221, entry for 31 July 1945; Hata Ikuhiko, "Shūsen to tennō to rikugun" (War termination, the emperor, and the army) *Rekishi to jimbutsu* (August 1983), 21 and 24. For an opposing view see Ōe Shinobu, *Gozen kaigi*, 237, who asserts the same evidence shows an intent to relocate the court to Matsushiro. Hirohito did say he occasionally thought of moving the court. See Hara Takeshi, " 'Maboroshi no Matsushiro Dai hon'ei' no zenyo" (The full story of the illusion of an imperial headquarters at Matsushiro) *Rekishi to jimbutsu* (December 1986): 313–14. In Hara's opinion, any move was probably impossible.
189. John Whitney Hall, "A Monarch for Modern Japan," in Robert E. Ward, ed., *Political Development in Modern Japan* (Princeton: Princeton University Press, 1968), 44.
190. Yamada, *Shōwa tennō sensō shidō*, 203. Yamada's *Daigensui Shōwa tenno*, 302 provides a revised version of this espisode, which is more consistent with the account in my narrative.
191. "Tairikumei 1338," 30 May 1945 (Imperial general headquarters army

department order number 1338) in General Headquarters, Far East Command, Military Intelligence Section, Historical Division, "Translation of Japanese Documents," vol. 4, 57. Bōeichō Bōei kenshūjō senshishitsu, *Senshi sōsho*, vol. 73, *Kantōgun*, pt. 2, *Kantōkuen shusenji tai Sosen* (Official military history, vol. 73, The Kwantung Army, pt. 2, The Kwantung special exercise and operations against the USSR at the end of the war) (Tokyo: Asagumo shimbunsha, 1974), 374 and 378.

192. Hata, *Shōwa tennō itsutsu no ketsudan*, 61.
193. Hata, *Shōwa tennō itsutsu no ketsudan*, 68; DHR, 47 on the ritualized nature of the conferences; and Butow, *Japan's Decision*, 94–95 on the bleak assessment presented at the conference.
194. DHR, 116–17. Handō, *Seidan*, 272.
195. Takagi, *Takagi kaigun shōsō oboegaki*, 288–89, entry for 14 June 1945.
196. DHR, 119; and Hasegawa Kiyoshi, "Statement Concerning Inspection Report Submitted to the Emperor in Regard to the Naval Strength Near the Termination of the War," 24 March 1950, 3, in *Statements*.
197. DHR, 119–20 n.
198. Hata, *Shōwa tennō itsutsu no ketsudan*, 59.
199. DHR, 119–20n. Hayashi Shigeru, *Nihon no rekishi*, vol. 25, *Taiheiyō sensō* (A history of Japan, vol. 25, The Pacific war) (Tokyo: Chūō kōronsha, 1967), 446. General Headquarters, Far East Command, Military Intelligence Section, General Staff, Allied Translator and Interpreter Section, "Full Translation of Questions and Answers Concerning Termination of the War, answered by former Lord Keeper of Privy Seal KIDO," in *Statements*, 8.
200. DHR, 133. As late as 14 August 1945, Hirohito still feared a military coup might erupt.
201. Kawabe Torashiro, "Statement Concerning TEN and KETSU Operations," 13 June 1949, 5 in General Headquarters, Far East Command, Military Intelligence Division, *Statements of Japanese Officials on World War II* (English Translations), vol 2. Hereafter cited as *Statements 2*. Miyazaki Shuichi, "A Composite of Replies to Questions Regarding the Cessation of Hostilities," 29 December 1949, 1 and 4 in *Statements 2*.
202. Kawabe, 2–3, and Miyazaki, 2–3 in *Statements 2*.
203. Hayashi Saburo, "Statement Regarding the Attitudes of War Minister Anami and Others toward Peace Just Prior to Surrender," 23 December 1949, 3 in *Statements*. Amano Masakazu, "Statement Concerning Ketsugo Operations Plan," 10 June 1950, 1, and "Reply by Amano Masakazu," 29 December 1949, 2 in *Statements*.
204. Bix, "Monologue," 354.
205. For an opposite view see Bix, "Hiroshima," 223 and 197.
206. DHR, 125; Kido, *Kido nikki*, 1223–24, entry for 10 August 1945: Butow, *Japan's Decision*, 175.

207. As late as 13 August Anami favored continuing the war and argued Japan would gain a more advantageous settlement after "giving the enemy a terrible beating in the decisive battle on the homeland." See "Full translation of questions and answers concerning termination of the war, answered by former Lord Keeper of the Privy Seal KIDO," 11 August 1950, 7–8 in *Statements* 2. The document gives the date as 18 August. This is clearly a typographical error for 13 August, Anami having killed himself on 13 August.

208. "Memorandum of Hoshina Zenshiro," 4. Hoshina was describing the 9 August imperial conference. The emperor's remarks are cited in Kojima, *Tennō*, vol. 5, 386. Cf. The Pacific War Research Society, compiler, *Japan's Longest Day* (Tokyo: Kodansha International, 1968), 34.

209. DHR, 125–27, 129. Hirohito was restating his 31 July 1945 discussion with Kido, *Kido nikki*, 1221. This is clearer in "Sengo sōkkin ni arishi goro haichō shita okotoba" (The [emperor's] words listened to while a postwar close associate) in Kinoshita, *Sōkkin nisshi*, 228.

210. Handō, *Seidan*, 320. Kido, *Kido nikki*, 1220, entry for 25 July 1945.

211. Kinoshita, *Sōkkin nisshi*, 400.

212. Hata, *Shōwa tennō itsutsu no ketsudan*, 106.

213. On this point see Hata Ikuhiko, "'Shōwa tennō dokuhakuroku' wo yomiwakuru" (Reading and understanding the Shōwa emperor's monologue) in Hata Ikuhiko, *Shōwashi no nazo wo ou*, ge (Pursing the mysteries of Shōwa history, vol. 2) (Tokyo: Bungei shunjū, 1993), 23.

214. "Rikugun no shūsen nikki, Gunmuka 'Kimitsu shūsen nisshi'" (The army diary for the end of the war; the military affairs section confidential diary at the end of the war) in *Haisen no kiroku*, ed. Sanbō honbu shozō (Records of defeat) (Tokyo: Hara shobō, 1979), 365, entry for 11 August 1945.

215. Sanbō honbu shozō, ed., "Rikugun no shūsen nikki," 367, entry for 12 August 1945.

216. Pacific War Research Society, *Japan's Longest Day*, 50.

217. Higashikuni, *Higashikuni nikki*, 200–201, entry for 12 August 1945, has a brief account of the meeting.

218. Pacific War Research Society, *Japan's Longest Day*, 49. "Rikugun no shūsen nikki," 367–68, entry for 12 August 1945. Earlier that day, Anami had visited Prince Mikasa to enlist his support to continue the war. The prince had brushed him off saying that since 1931 the army had acted contrary to the emperor's wishes. Sanbō honbu shozō, ed., "Rikugun no shūsen nikki," 368.

219. DHR, 129.. Also see Kinoshita, "Sengo sōkkin ni arishi goro haicho shita okotoba" (The [emperor's] words as listened to by a postwar close associate), 228.

220. Butow, *Japan's Decision*, 206, and *Reports of MacArthur*, vol. 2, pt. 2, 724, place the initiative in Kido's hands. DHR, 134, puts it in Hirohito's.
221. Pacific War Research Society, *Japan's Longest Day*, 76; and Sanbō honbu shozō, ed., "Rikugun no shūsen nikki," 370, entry for 14 August 1945.
222. DHR, 133. Hata, *Itsutsu*, 75.
223. DHR, 133.
224. DHR, 134.
225. Gerhard L. Weinberg, "Grand Strategy in the Pacific War," *Air Power History* (spring 1996): 13.

LIST OF PERSONALITIES AND TERMS

Personalities

Adachi Hatazo. Japanese army officer and commander, Eighteenth Army in eastern New Guinea.
Anami Korechika. Japanese army officer. Japan's last war minister.
Chiang Kai-shek. Chinese officer and politician. Leader of the Kuomintang Party and generalissimo of Chinese armies during World War II.
Chichibu Yasuhito. Japanese army officer, imperial prince, and Hirohito's oldest brother.
Clausewitz, Carl von. Nineteenth-century German officer and military philosopher.
Fushimi Hiroyasu. Japanese navy officer, imperial prince, and chief of naval general staff, 1932–41.
Halsey, William. U.S. Navy officer and commander, U.S. Third Fleet from June 1944.
Hasegawa Kiyoshi. Japanese navy officer and in 1945 a member of Supreme War Council.
Hata Shunroku. Japanese army officer and field marshal in 1945.
Hatanaka Kenji. Japanese army officer and leader of attempted coup d'tat in August 1945.
Higashikuni Naruhiko. Japanese army officer, imperial prince, and Hirohito's uncle.
Hirohito. Emperor of Japan, 1926–89. Known as the Shōwa Emperor.

Hosokawa Morisada. Scion of aristocratic family. Prince Konoe's son-in-law and confidential secretary.

Ishiwara Kanji. Japanese army officer and theoretician. Opposed enlarging the war with China in 1937 in favor of conserving resources for a showdown with the USSR.

Kanin Kotohito. Japanese army officer, imperial prince, and field marshal. Chief of staff of the Japanese army, 1931–40.

Kido Kōichi. Japanese aristocrat and lord keeper of the privy seal, 1940–45. Hirohito's closest adviser.

King, Ernest. U.S. Navy officer and chief of naval operations and commander in chief, U.S. Navy, 1942–45.

Koiso Kuniaki. Japanese army officer and later prime minister of Japan 1944–45.

Komatsubara Michitarō. Japanese army officer and commander, Twenty-third Infantry Division at Khalkhin Gol in 1939.

Konoe Fumimaro. Japanese aristocrat and politician. Three-time prime minister of Japan and an adviser to Hirohito.

Krueger, Walter. U.S. Army officer and commander of U.S. Sixth Army in New Guinea and the Philippines, 1943–45.

Kurita Takeo. Japanese navy officer and commander of diversionary force at Leyte in 1944.

MacArthur, Douglas. U.S. Army officer and commander, Southwest Pacific Area, 1942–45.

Mao Tse-tung. Chinese revolutionary leader and commander of Chinese Communist forces during World War II.

Marshall, George C. U.S. Army officer and army chief of staff during World War II.

Matsudaira Yasumasa. Japanese aristocrat and chief secretary to Kido Kōichi. Postwar adviser to Hirohito.

Meiji, Emperor. Japanese emperor from 1868 to 1912. Hirohito's grandfather.

Mutaguchi Renya. Japanese army officer and commander of the Fifteenth Army in Burma.

Nagano Osami. Japanese navy officer and chief of the naval general staff, 1941–44.

Nimitz, Chester. U.S. Navy officer and commander of U.S. Pacific Fleet during World War II.

Oikawa Koshirō. Japanese navy officer and navy minister, 1940–41.

Okada Keisuke. Japanese navy officer and prime minister. During World War II, an influential adviser to naval circles.

Ozawa Jisaburō. Japanese navy officer and commander of naval strike force at Leyte in 1944.

LIST OF PERSONALITIES AND TERMS • 267

Sakai Koji. Japanese army officer. Recalled to active duty in 1943 and assigned to general staff.
Shimada, Shigetarō. Japanese navy officer and navy minister, 1941–44.
Slim, William. British army officer and commander of XIV Army in Burma.
Stark, Harold. U.S. Navy officer and chief of naval operations, 1939–42.
Stillwell, Joseph. U.S. Army officer, chief of staff to Chiang Kai-shek, and commander of U.S. forces in China-Burma-India theater during World War II.
Suematsu Taihei. Japanese army junior officer and political activist. Imprisoned following the 26 February 1936 mutiny.
Sugiyama Hajime. Japanese army officer and chief of staff, 1940–44, and later war minister.
Suzuki Kantarō. Japanese navy officer and Japan's last wartime prime minister.
Takagi Sōkichi. Japanese navy officer and military bureaucrat.
Takamatsu Nobuhito. Japanese army officer, imperial prince, and Hirohito's second brother.
Terasaki Hidenari. Japanese foreign ministry official, prewar spy in United States, and postwar counselor to Emperor Hirohito.
Tōgō Heihachirō. Japanese navy officer who defeated the Russian Fleet at the Battle of the Sea of Japan in 1905. Later Hirohito's tutor.
Tōgō Shigenori. Japanese career diplomat and foreign minister in 1945.
Tōjō Hideki. Japanese army officer and prime minister, 1941–44. Concurrently served as war minister and later as chief of staff. Also served as home minister (October 1941–February 1942). He also became munitions minister in November 1943 and army chief of staff in February 1944.
Tsukada Osamu. Japanese army officer and vice chief of staff in 1941. Killed in plane crash in China in December 1942.
Umezu Yoshijirō. Japanese army officer and chief of staff in 1945.
Willoughby, Charles A. U.S. Army officer and General MacArthur's chief of staff for intelligence during World War II.
Wingate, Ord. British army officer and promoter of long-range penetration operations against Japanese forces in Burma. Killed in plane crash in 1944.
Yamashita Tomoyuki. Japanese army officer. Conqueror of Singapore in 1942. Later commander of the Fourteenth Area Army on Luzon.
Yonai Mitsumasu. Japanese navy officer and politician. Prime minister of Japan 1940. Recalled as navy minister, 1944–45.
Zhukov, Georgi. Soviet army officer and commander of Soviet forces at Khalkhin Gol. He achieved later fame during World War II at Moscow and Stalingrad.

Terms

"A" Operation. Japanese combined air and naval plan to force a decisive battle with U.S. fleet in the Pacific in 1944.

Bungei shunjū. Japanese general interest monthly magazine.

bushido. Lit. the way of the warrior. By the 1930s a much romanticized version of derived values of Japan's warrior, or samurai, class.

"C" Operation. A series of five amphibious assaults executed by Japanese forces in the vicinity of Canton, China, in early 1941.

Changkufeng. Hillock in Manchuria along the borders of northern Korea and southern Siberia. It provided the Japanese name for a border war fought with the Soviet Union during the summer of 1938.

daihatsu. Japanese landing craft. See also *kohatsu*.

Fuji Maneuvers. Annual grand field exercises and war games conducted by the Japanese army on its training ground at the base of Mt. Fuji.

FS Operation. Japanese plan in early 1942 to occupy Fiji (F) and Samoa (S), thus severing the Allied line of communication between America and Australia.

Ichigō Operation. Japanese campaign from late 1944 into spring 1945 to destroy American air bases in China and open a continental rail line of communication from Saigon, French Indochina, to Pusan, Korea.

Ichigaya. Section of downtown Tokyo where the Army Military Academy and later Imperial Headquarters were located.

Ichiki Detachment. Japanese infantry unit commanded by Colonel Ichiki Kiyonao, annihilated by U.S. Marines on Guadalcanal in August 1942.

Imperial Conference. Extra constitutional conferences on matters of grave national importance convened in the presence of the emperor between 1894 and 1945.

Imperial General Headquarters. Established in 1937, it was composed of the army and navy general staffs, respectively. Its purpose was to coordinate and direct the military phase of Japan's national war effort. IGHQ for short.

Imperial regalia. Collective name for the three sacred objects—mirror, jewel, and sword—that are the symbols of the legitimacy and authority of the emperor of Japan.

Imphal-Kohima. Towns 60 miles apart in Manipur Province, India, close to the Burmese border and the sites of two decisive battles between the British and Japanese in 1944.

Indian National Army. Organized in 1942 with Japanese support, consisted of Indian soldiers taken prisoner at Singapore in 1942.

International Military Tribunal for the Far East. Judicial body to conduct trials of war criminals after World War II. The Tokyo Tribunal opened in May 1946 and closed 417 days later.

Joint Chiefs of Staff. U.S. interservice body composed of American chiefs of staff of the army, navy, marine corps, and army air forces and responsible for operational strategy in the Pacific as well as coordinating operations elsewhere with Allies.

Khalkhin Gol. River on the Manchurian–Inner Mongolian border. Scene of a four-month long undeclared war between the Soviet Union and Japan in the summer of 1939. See also Nomonhan.

kohatsu. Japanese landing craft. Smaller version of *daihatsu.*

kokutai. The concept of Imperial Japan as unique among nations by virtue of its sacred emperor.

Kuomintang. Chinese political organization headed by Generalissimo Chiang Kai-shek during World War II.

Kwantung Army. Designation for the Japanese army forces occupying the northeastern Chinese provinces collectively known as Manchuria.

Liaison conferences. Established in 1937 as a coordinating mechanism, it was attended by the prime minister, war, navy, and foreign ministers, plus both chiefs of staff.

MAGIC. Codename to indicate intelligence derived from breaking Japanese Foreign Ministry ciphers. See also ULTRA.

Manchukuo. The name of the Japanese-sponsored regime in Manchuria from 1933 to 1945.

Marco Polo Bridge Incident. Outbreak of fighting between Japanese and Chinese troops near the Marco Polo Bridge on the night of 7 July 1937. The incident escalated into full-scale, but undeclared, warfare between the two nations.

Matsushirō. Village in Japan's mountainous Nagano Prefecture where Imperial Headquarters was constructing an alternate command post and palace in 1945.

Ninnaji temple. Japanese temple that until the beginning of the Meiji period in 1868, customarily chose its abbot from tonsured members of the imperial family

Nomonhan. Japanese name for the Battle of Khalkhin Gol.

OLYMPIC. Code name for the American invasion of Japanese island of Kyushu scheduled for 1 November 1945.

Ormoc. Port city on Leyte's west coast used by Japanese to land reinforcements on the island in 1944.

Owen Stanley range. Mountain range in eastern New Guinea dividing northern and southern halves of the island, figuring prominently in 1942 fighting.

Port Arthur. English name for Chinese city of Lushun, a railway terminus and ice-free port on Liaodung Peninsula.

Potsdam Declaration. Statement issued by U.S. President Harry Truman from Potsdam, Germany, on 26 July 1945, calling on Japan to surrender unconditionally or face utter destruction.

Satsuma Rebellion. Abortive uprising in 1877 of disaffected Japanese samurai against the Meiji regime.
Seiyūkai. One of leading Japanese political parties, 1900–40.
Shō Operations. Japanese plans of 1944 to fight a decisive battle against the Americans. Sho, or Victory, had four contingencies: Sho 1, action in the Philippine Islands; Sho 2, Formosa and the Ryukyus; Sho 3, the Japanese home islands, less the northernmost main island of Hokkaido; and Sho 4, Hokkaido.
Shōwa. The official name for the era of Emperor Hirohito's reign, 1926 to 1989, and Hirohito's posthumous name. Shōwa means Enlightened Peace.
Supreme Council for the Direction of the War. Established in August 1944 to replace and streamline the existing liaison conference, it became an inner war cabinet.
Takebashi Incident. Mutiny in 1878 of a Japanese artillery battalion stationed in Tokyo.
Tennōzan. Site of a decisive Japanese battle in 1582 when Hideyoshi defeated the rival forces, opening the way for the warlord's campaign for national hegemony.
Toranomon Incident. 1923 assassination attempt on Hirohito's life outside the gate of the same name.
Tripartite Pact. Military pact signed by Japan, Germany, and Italy in Berlin in September 1940.
ULTRA. Code name to designate intelligence derived from breaking main axis military message ciphers as opposed to diplomatic messages. See also MAGIC.
Yamato damashii. Lit. Japanese spirit, the belief in the unique qualities and national characteristics of the Japanese people.

BIBLIOGRAPHIC ESSAY

Archival research for several of these essays involved work in archival repositories in Australia, Japan, and the United States. The essay on Number Fifty-five Wireless Section capitalized on the section's war diary and daily log with appendices available at the Australian War Memorial, Canberra, ACT, Australia. Filed among other operational records, to my knowledge, Number Fifty-five's account is the sole declassified day-by-day account of the actual workings of a signals intercept site, and for that reason its documents are unique. Holdings at the Australian Archives, Dicksen, ACT, shed light on Australian government policy regarding signals intelligence. These documents are complemented by the partially declassified Allied Central Bureau Technical Reports and associated items available at the Australian Archives, Victoria, since the early 1990s. In 1996 the U.S. National Security Agency (NSA) turned over to the U.S. National Archives and Records Administration (NARA) more than 5000 individual files under the title "Historical Cryptographic Collection, Pre–World War I–World War II" in Record Group 457. These include a complete and unredacted set of Central Bureau's Technical Reports. These records are now available for researchers at the NARA College Park, Maryland, facility. Also housed at College Park is the remainder of Record Group 457, which contains NSA material released since 1977, much of which appears in essays throughout this collection.

The outstanding collections of public and private papers at the George C. Marshall Library and Archives, Lexington VA, the MacArthur Memorial Bureau of Archives, Norfolk VA, and the U.S. Army Military History Institute,

Carlisle Barracks PA, were also used to prepare these essays. In addition, I consulted the U.S. Army, Far East Command, Military History Section, *Interrogations of Japanese Officials on World War II*, 2 vols., and *Statements of Japanese Officials on World War II*, 4 vols., sets of which are available at the U.S. Army Center of Military History in Washington DC.

In Japan work at the Defense Agency's Military History Department and Military History Archives in Tokyo was always a pleasure, and I am indebted to a number of directors who over the years supported my research. The documents used in the opening piece about Nomonhan all are available at the Tokyo archives. Besides the materials in Japan, I also made use of the "Kyūrikukaigun monjō" (Records of the former Imperial Army and Navy) duplicates about 400,000 pages of the Japan Defense Agency archival documents on 163 reels of microfilm. This collection is available at the Library of Congress, well indexed in John Young's *Checklist of Microfilm Reproductions of Selected Archives of the Japanese Army, Navy, and Other Government Agencies, 1868–1945* (Washington DC: Georgetown University Press, 1959).

I have relied extensively on collections of documents published in Japanese. *Sugiyama memo* (The memoranda of General Sugiyama Hajime), 2 vols. (Tokyo: Hara shobō, 1967) documents Sugiyama's pivotal role in national strategy and policy making between 1940 and 1944. It includes minutes of deliberations at imperial conferences, imperial headquarters–cabinet liaison conferences, and the Supreme War Council. Its sequel, *Haisen no kiroku* (Record of defeat) (Tokyo: Hara shobō, 1979), carries the documentary trial forward from early 1944 until late 1945. Appended to *Haisen no kiroku* is the confidential diary of the Military Affairs Section, War Ministry, a hard-liner to continue the war in August 1945. For day-to-day appreciations I relied on "Kimitsu sensō nisshi" (Confidential war diary), the daily journal of the War Guidance Section. Although slanted in favor of the Imperial Army's view of the world, the dairy goes beyond mere operational considerations to relate the army's role in total war and its relation to the navy, the economy, and the national policy. The diary was published serially from September to November 1971 in the monthly *Rekishi to jimbutsu*. It was also the basis for the early postwar publication by Tanemura Suketaka, *Daihon'ei kimitsu nisshi* (Confidential Imperial Headquarters diary) (Tokyo: Daiyamondosha, 1952; reprinted by Fūyō shobō, 1985), which is Tanemura's private account of policy formulation by midlevel officers in the War Guidance Section based on the section's official journal.

Before turning to more recently published sources, a word is in order about the Japan, Bōeichō, Bōei kenshūjō, Senshi shitsu (War history office, National defense college, Defense agency) *Senshi sōsho* (Official military history) series. This 102-volume enterprise, published between 1965 and 1980 is somewhat uneven in quality, reflecting how the loss or destruction of unit and other official documents hampers the creation of an accurate official history. For example, despite their terrible defeat at Nomonhan in 1939, the Japanese units survived as entities and preserved their records. Volume 27 dealing with that campaign, *Kantōgun*, pt. 1: *Tai So senbi, Nomonhan jiken* (The Kwantung Army, pt. 1, Military preparations against the Soviet Union and the Nomonhan Incident) (Tokyo: Asagumo shimbunsha, 1969), is an excellent one. The same cannot be said for those treating the disintegration of the Eighteenth Army in the New Guinea wilds. There are five volumes on the ground campaigns in New Guinea, vol. 14, *Mainami Taiheiyō rikugun sakusen*, pt. 1: *Potō Morezubi—Gashima shoki sakusen* (Army operations in the south Pacific: Port Moresby and the opening stages of the Guadalcanal island operations), vol. 28, *Minami Taiheiyō rikugun sakusen*, pt. 2: *Gadarukanaru-Buna sakusen* (Guadalcanal and Buna operations), vol. 40, *Minami Taiheiyō rikugun sakusen*, pt. 3: *Munda-Saramoa* (Munda and Salamaua), vol. 58, *Minami Taiheiyō rikugun sakusen*, pt. 4: *Fuinshuhaben-Tsurubu-Tarokina* (Finschaffen, Cape Gloucester, Torokina), vol. 84, *Minami Taiheiyō rikugun sakusen*, pt. 5: *Aitape-Puriaka-Rabauru* (Aitape, Puriaka, Rabaul) (Tokyo: Asagumo shimbunsha, 1969–1975). The volumes suffer from lack of documentation and incompleteness, in part because of the loss of unit records. Information regarding Adachi Hatazo had to come from accounts by former officers and soldiers who served with him and, ironically enough, from his messages, which now survive only in English via ULTRA intercepts. Nonetheless, the official histories are an especially valuable source of information, especially about top-level decision making. They are written at operational and strategic level and contain information and published records unavailable elsewhere. Most volumes rely on extensive, multipage quotations from official documents or military records as the framework for the narrative. This is especially true of the ten-part *Daihon'ei rikugunbu* (Imperial general headquarters, army department) set of the 102-volume series. Personalities are deemphasized, a common failing in all official history programs. Analysis is sometimes sketchy, and service viewpoints pervade the volumes, hardly surprising when one recalls that they were written by former staff officers of the defunct army and navy. Having said all that, the series remains incomparable and an absolutely essential source for anyone writing about the Japanese side of the 1937–45 war in Asia and with the West.

At the tactical level one can turn to the Rikusenshi kenkyūkai (Association for the study of the history of land warfare) series of more than twenty volumes, each analyzing in professional detail various military campaigns ranging over battlegrounds from ancient China to Korea between 1950 and 1953. *Marē sakusen* (The Malaya operation) (Tokyo: Rikusenshi kenkyūkai, 1966) is an excellent operational and tactical account of Japanese operations in Malaya 1941–42. The two-volume set, *Inpharu sakusen* (The Imphal operation) (Rikusenshi kenkyūkai, 1969), covers Mutaguchi's ill conceived offensive, and *Ruson shima shinkō sakusen* (Offensive operations on Luzon island) (Rikusenshi kenkyūkai, 1969), adds the Japanese dimension to the defeat of MacArthur's forces in 1941–42. In general the studies of earlier Japanese campaigns, say to 1943, are more critical and rewarding because of better documentation. Later studies like Iwo Jima rely heavily on American sources to fill in gaps in the missing Japanese records. Still the series is first-rate and contains several splendidly written narratives.

As for general guides, Itō Takashi's *Nihon riku-kaigun no seidō, soshiki, jinji* (Command and control, organization, and personnel of Japan's former army and navy) (Tokyo: Tōyō daigaku shuppankai, 1971), and Hata Ikuhiko's *Nihon riku-kaigun sōgō jiten* (Composite dictionary of the Japanese army and navy) (Tokyo: Tokyo daigaku shuppankai, 1991), are indispensable reference works containing extensive bibliographic entries on thousands of Japan's generals and admirals as well as extensive information about the military institutions of modern Japan. In similar fashion, Kuwada Etsu and Maebara Toshio's *Nihon no sensō zukai to dēta* (The wars of Japan: maps and graphics) (Tokyo: Hara shobō, 1982) provides detailed operational maps and order of battle information with a brief narrative of the major wars of modern Japan, and Sunekuni Masao, ed., *Riku-kaigun nenpyō fuheigo, yōgo no kaisetsu* (Chronology of the army and navy with appended explanations of military terms and usage) (Tokyo: Asagumo shimbunsha, 1980) has an enormously useful chronology of military and naval affairs from the outbreak of the war with China in 1937 through the end of World War II. It is fittingly the final volume of the 102-volume senshi sōsho series. Readers interested in a fuller explanation of Japanese language materials for this period should consult Sadao Asada, ed., *Japan and the World, 1853–1952: A Bibliographic Guide to Japanese Scholarship in Foreign Relations* (New York: Columbia University Press, 1989), which, despite the title, also covers military historiography in Japan.

The most sensational primary materials to appear in Japan in recent times are surely those of Terasaki Hidenari and Mariko Terasaki Miller, eds., *Shōwa tennō dokuhakuroku—Terasaki Hidenari goyōgakai nikki* (The Shōwa emperor's monologue and court official Terasaki Hidenari's diary) (Tokyo: Bungei shunjū, 1991). The provenance of the volume has been explained in the text, but it is important to note that the emperor's monologue tends to be more confirmatory than revelatory in its pronouncements. It shows great internal consistency when compared to the standard source for court affairs during the Pacific War, Kido Kōichi's dairy in two volumes and related papers, Kido Kōichi nikki kenkyūkai, eds., *Kido Kōichi nikki*, 2 vols. (Tokyo: Tokyo daigaku shuppankai, 1966); and *Kido Kōichi kankei bunsho* (Tokyo: Tokyo daigaku shuppankai, 1980). Kido's meticulous daily, compilation of life close to the throne provides the historian with a rare glimpse of the inner workings of Hirohito's court and is a required source for the period. Several statements appearing in the *Dokuhakuroku* have previously appeared in similar form in Kido's extensive notes. His related papers consist of an explanation of his diary, his own memoirs, and attempts to prevent and then terminate the Pacific War plus other materials. The emperor's monologue also matches well with *Sōkkin nisshi* (The diary of a close associate [of the emperor]) (Tokyo: Bungei shunjū, 1990), an account of the immediate postwar court by imperial adviser Kinoshita Michio. Kinoshita's account is especially valuable for its additional revelations about circumstances of the emperor's soliloquy and occupation connections with the court. Terasaki Hidenari's diary for the immediate postwar years, appended to the *Dokuhakuroku*, illuminates Terasaki's role in the court during that uncertain time. The Hosokawa Morisada diaries, *Hosokawa nikki*, 2 vols. (Tokyo: Chūō bunko ed., 1991), reissued in expanded form in 1991, also complement the *Dokuhakuroku* as do accounts left by Admiral Takagi Sōkichi. Takagi's material, based on his work in naval policy making and his close personal connections with men such as Admiral Yonai, Hosokawa, and others, plus access to classified or otherwise sensitive navy material, makes his commentary especially helpful in comprehending the relationships between 1944 and 1945 Japanese military, political, diplomatic, and court history. Although Takagi's entire diary has yet to be published, his *Takagi kaigun shōsō oboegaki* (The memoranda of rear admiral Takagi Sōkichi) (Tokyo: Mainichi shimbunsha, 1979) records events and meetings from December 1943 to September 1945 and is especially helpful in understanding the Japanese navy's attempts to end the war. *Takagi Sōkichi nikki* (Takagi Sōkichi diary) (Tokyo: Mainichi shimbunsha, 1985) covers two distinct periods, the formation of the Tri Partite Pact in 1940 and efforts to undermine the Tōjō cabinet in 1944. Also quite useful is the emperor's uncle Prince Higashikuni's diary *Higashikuni nikki: Nihon gekidōki no kiroku* (Prince Higashikuni's diary—confidential record of Japan's turbulent time) (Tokyo: Tokuma shoten 1968), whose selective entries cover the period from January 1941 to October 1945. More diaries continue to appear, most notably to date the thus far disappointing recollections of Prince Takamatsu as edited by Chihaya Masatake, et al., *Takamatsu no miya nikki* (Prince Takamatsu diary) (Tokyo: Chūō kōronsha, 1995–). It is likely more primary evidence about Hirohito's wartime role will emerge in the future.

Itō Takashi, ed., *Tōjō naikaku sōridaijin kimitsu kiroku* (Confidential record of prime minister's Tōjō's cabinet) (Tokyo: Tokyo daigaku shuppankai, 1990) is a somewhat misleading title, because much of the publication is merely a list of Tōjō's daily appointments as prime minister. The substantive material is devoted to Tōjō's discussions with the German envoy to Tokyo or the Indian nationalist Chandra Bose or the Greater East Asia Conference held in Tokyo in 1943. Amid this miscellany one finds insightful comments and descriptions of Tōjō's workings with Hirohito. The translation of Irogawa Daikichi's work into English as *The Age of Hirohito: In Search of Modern Japan* (New York: Free Press, 1995) is disappointing, because it fails to capture the highly nuanced and culturally sensitive narrative of the Japanese original. The recently reissued *Politics and Culture in Wartime Japan* (Oxford: Clarendon Press, 1981) by Ben-Ami Shillony is a well-written account of the Japanese home front during the war, containing informative sections on the emperor's role during the conflict.

The Shōwa emperor was controversial in life and remains so in death. For examples of Hirohito interpreted as a pacifist see Yasumasa Matsudaira, "The Japanese Emperor and the War," in Supreme Commander for the Allied Powers, *Reports of General MacArthur: Japanese Operations in the Southwest Pacific Area*, vol. 2, pt. 2 (Washington DC: U.S. Government Printing Office, 1966), appen., 763–71; and Colonel Bonner Fellers, USA, Retired, "Hirohito's Struggle to Surrender," *Foreign Service*, July 1947, 90–95; as a reactionary, Inoue Kiyoshi's *Tennō no sensō sekinin* (The emperor's war responsibility) (Tokyo: Gendai hyōronsha, 1975); as a constitutional monarch, Matsudaira, "Japanese Emperor," and Robert J. C. Butow, *Japan's Decision to Surrender* (Stanford: Stanford University Press, 1954), and by the same author *Tojo and the Coming of the War* (Stanford: Stanford University Press, 1961); as a warmonger, David Bergamini, *Japan's Imperial Conspiracy* (New York: Pocket Book ed., 1972), Yamada Akira, *Shōwa tennō no sensō shidō* (The Shōwa emperor's wartime leadership) (Tokyo: Shōwa shuppan, 1990), Edward Behr's *Hirohito: Behind the Myth* (New York: Vintage ed., 1990), and Herbert P. Bix, "Emperor Hirohito's War," *History Today* 41 (December 1991); as a nationalist, Stephen S. Large, *Emperor Hirohito and Showa Japan: A Political Biography* (New York: Routledge, 1992); and as manipulated, Yale Candee Maxon, *Control of Japanese Foreign Policy: A Study in Civil-Military Rivalry 1930–1945* (Westport CT: Greenwood, rpt., 1975), and Charles D. Sheldon, "Scapegoat or Instigator of Japanese Aggression? Inoue Kiyoshi's Case against the Emperor," *Modern Asian Studies* 12:1 (1978). David A. Titus *Palace and Politics in Prewar Japan* is a superior analysis of the workings of the imperial court based on the Kido diaries. Stephen S. Large, "Emperor Hirohito and Early Showa Japan," *Monumenta Nipponica* 46:3 (1991), offers a useful critique of four recently available Japanese language primary sources on the Shōwa emperor, including Hirohito's monologue. Nagai Nagomu, "Shōwa tenno wa tosuiken no unyo wo ayamattaka—Ōe Shinobu *Chō saku rin ansatsu* wo hyosuru" (Was he mistaken in the Shōwa emperor's application of command authority?—Comments on Ōe Shinobu's The assassination of Chang tso lin) *Ritsumeikan daigaku shigaku* 11 (November 1990), offers a withering critique of Professor Ōe's misunderstanding and anachronistic interpretation of the emperor's authority in operational military matters that is useful for comprehending Hirohito's role vis-à-vis his military chieftains throughout the early period of his reign.

Kojima Noboru's five-volume *Tennō* (The emperor) (Tokyo: Bungei shunjū, 1974) is clearly based on extensive primary source material but lacks documentation. Hata Ikuhiko's *Tennō no itsutsu no ketsudan* (Five decisions of the Shōwa emperor) (Tokyo: Bungei shunjū ed., 1994) examines five major decisions of Hirohito's prewar and wartime reign in balanced fashion. The paperback edition includes an additional chapter evaluating the *Dokuhakuroku* and reactions its publication provoked. It is valuable to compare Hata's analysis of the Shōwa emperor with the interpretation found in Ōe Shinobu's *Gozen kaigi: Shōwa tennō jugokai no seidan* (The imperial conference—the Shōwa emperor's 15 imperial decisions) (Tokyo: Chuko shinsho, 1991). Whereas Hata sees the emperor as influencing decisions but frustrated by the decision-making system and his sometimes less than helpful military and political advisers, Ōe, comparing sources and accounts such as the *Sugiyama memo* and Tanemura diary and other primary and secondary sources with the *Dokuhakuroku* version of events, insists that Hirohito was much more of an activist whose reservations about going to war had less to do with preserving peace than with a lack of confidence in ultimate military victory.

Already, however, the new revelations have sparked renewed interest in the early Shōwa period in Japan and in the United States. The death of the Shōwa Emperor in 1989 may also have marked the end of the imperial taboo, which shielded the imperial house, and Hirohito in particular, from serious criticism. By 1989 Yamada Akira's *Shōwa tennō sensō shidō* (The Shōwa emperor's wartime leadership) was frankly a polemic indictment of the emperor's wartime conduct based on Yamada's extensive, if selective, work in the Japanese defense archives. The great contribution was to publish the several key documents he located in the Defense Agency archives as appendices to his book. He has since revised the work as *Dai gensui tennō* (The generalissimo emperor) (Tokyo: Shin Nihon shuppansha, 1994) in light of publication of the *Dokuhakuroku* and criticisms leveled at *Shōwa tennō sensō shidō*. Though less strident, *Dai gensui tennō* still remains highly selective in its choice of material. Herbert Bix has drawn on Yamada and others for his reinterpretation of "Japan's Delayed Surrender." Bix claims, based on Yoshida Yutaka's arguments in *Shōwa tennō no shusenshi* (History of the Shōwa emperor's at war's end) (Tokyo: Iwanami shoten, 1992), that the Japanese succeeded in writing the emperor out of the war by striking agreements with the postwar occupation authorities. Yoshida's insightful account of how history was written after 1945 may indeed be accurate, but whether how it was written is indicative of what actually happened is debatable. In any case, by asserting the Japanese would confess to anything to save the emperor and the imperial institution, Bix and Yoshida force us to take a second look at Robert J. C. Butow's interpretation of Hirohito in his masterful *Japan's Decision to Surrender*.

Yamada is in the tradition of Inoue Kiyoshi, who since the mid-1970s has been denouncing Hirohito for imaginary war crimes. Inoue simply fabricates evidence or insists on mighty leaps of faith to demonstrate his extremely shaky, if politically popular in leftist circles, opinions. Sheldon's already mentioned "Scapegoat or Instigator of Japanese Aggression? Inoue Kiyoshi's Case against the Emperor," presents an insightful critical analysis of the flaws and shortcomings of Inoue's thesis and methodology. Inoue shares that stage with Ienaga Saburō, whose *Taiheiyō sensō* has been translated into English under the title *The Pacific War 1931–1945* (New York: Pantheon, 1978). Opinion and sincerity count for more than historical scholarship in both cases. Both might be likened to David Bergamini's royal plot-drenched narrative, *Japan's Imperial Conspiracy*. Edwin Behr follows on Bergamini's trail mixing and matching evidence to suit his needs. A more reasoned view of Hirohito is available in Stephen Large's political biography of the late emperor.

There is a wealth of excellent secondary material available on the Pacific War. One must begin with the U.S. Army's official history of World War II, the series The United States Army in World War II. Several volumes in The War in the Pacific subseries are especially relevant: two volumes by Robert Ross Smith, *The Approach to the Philippines* (Washington DC: U.S. Government Printing Office, 1953) and *Triumph in the Philippines* (Washington DC: U.S. Government Printing Office, 1963); Samuel Milner's *Victory in Papua* (Washington DC: U.S. Government Printing Office, 1957); John Miller Jr., *Cartwheel: The Reduction of Rabaul* (Washington DC: U.S. Government Printing Office, 1959); Louis Morton's *The Fall of the Philippines* (Washington DC: U.S. Government Printing Office, 1953), and *Strategy and Command: The First Two Years* (Washington DC: U.S. Government Printing Office, 1967). Robert Coakley and Richard Leighton's *Global Logistics and Strategy 1940–1943* (Washington DC: U.S. Government Printing Office, 1955), a volume in the subseries The War Department, is also essential for an understanding of Pacific operations. Companion volumes in the U.S. Air Force, Navy, and Marine Corps' accounts of their war against Japan complement the army version by filling in the south and central Pacific Ocean operations as well as the air campaign against the Japanese empire. Ronald Spector's *Eagle against the Sun* (New York: Free Press, 1985) is the best one-volume overview of the conflict. John Dower's *War without Mercy: Race and Power in the Pacific War* (New York: Pantheon, 1986) demonstrates the racial aspect of the fighting in the Pacific but seems close to monocausal in its analysis of the ferocity of the war. His *Japan in Peace and War* (New York: New Press, 1993) contains several excellent essays about Japanese culture, society, and the home front at war. Akira Iriye's *Across the Pacific:*

An Inner History of American-East Asian Relations (New York: Harcourt, Brace, and World, 1967) and *Power and Culture: The Japanese-American War, 1941–1945* (Cambridge: Harvard University Press, 1981) have enjoyed great influence as multiarchival, broad treatments of international relations focusing on the effect of the translation of ideas, ideologies, and cultures into foreign policy. Iriye approaches his topic as a diplomatic historian, not a military one, and too often accepts Japanese wartime rhetoric at face value. As for military history accounts of the war, *The Reports of MacArthur*, 3 vols. in 4 pts., although embarrassingly biased to make Douglas MacArthur appear omniscient, still offers information, documentation, and graphics unavailable elsewhere. The two volumes in the series of Japanese operations against MacArthur remain unsurpassed in English. A more balanced view is available in William Leary's *We Shall Return: MacArthur's Commanders and the Defeat of Japan, 1942–1945* (Lexington: University of Kentucky Press, 1988), which offers compelling portraits of the officers who implemented MacArthur's commands. Louis Allen's masterwork *Burma: The Longest War 1941–45* (New York: St. Martin's, 1984) should be required reading both in staff colleges and academic halls. Field Marshal Viscount William Slim's *Defeat into Victory* (New York: David McKay, 1961) is perhaps the best memoir of a senior commander in any theater during World War II. Making strategic, operational, and tactical points, Slim also conveys the sense of place and emotion that so often disappear from more antiseptic accounts by generals and admirals of their exploits. A special issue of *War and Society* 11:1 (May 1993) analyzes the events of 1942 in the southwest Pacific and Asia through Japanese, American, and Australian perspectives. MHQ 7:3 (spring 1995) similarly devotes an entire issue to the final stage in the Allied war against Japan drawing on American, British, Australian, and Japanese scholarship. For naval affairs from the Japanese perspective, David Evans's fine editing of *The Japanese Navy in World War II* (Annapolis MD: Naval Institute, 2d ed., 1986) is first-rate as is Paul Dull's *A Battle History of the Imperial Japanese Navy (1941–1945)* (Annapolis MD: Naval Institute, 1978). Read in conjunction with Admiral Ugaki Matome's extensive diary published as *Fading Victory: The Diary of Admiral Matome Ugaki 1941–1945* (Pittsburgh: University of Pittsburgh Press, 1991), one gets a sense of the inner workings of the Imperial Navy. Meirion and Susie Harries's *Soldiers of the Sun: The Rise and Fall of the Imperial Japanese Army* (New York: Random House, 1992) is an uneven study marred by numerous factual errors about World War II operations and suffers from incomplete citations and a lack of documentation, which makes it impossible to determine the degree of Japanese language sources they used.

Carol Gluck's *Japan's Modern Myths: Ideology in the Late Meiji Period* (Princeton: Princeton University Press, 1985) may seem an odd transition into the Japanese army, but her deft analysis and insightful commentary illuminates the culture and intellectual underpinnings of Japan's prewar military. Iizuka Koji's now dated *Tennō no guntai* (The emperor's army) (Tokyo: Hyōronsha, 1968 reprint) still offers an impressionistic version of the Imperial Army that remains valid and underscores the values Gluck identifies. Fujiwara Akira's seminal *Nihon gendaishi taikei: Gunjishi* (Systematic contemporary Japanese history: Military history) (Tokyo: Tōyō keizai shimpōsha, 1961) has been reissued as a two-volume set (Tokyo: Nihon hyōronsha, 1987) but adds little to the 1961 original. Ōe Shinobu's volume in the *Shōwa no rekishi* series (History of the Shōwa reign), vol. 3, *Tennō no guntai* (The emperor's army) (Tokyo: Shogakkan, 1982) is a thematic work containing extensive data on the organization and institutions of the Imperial Army and Navy. His *Nihon no sanbō honbu* (The Japanese general staff) (Tokyo: Chūkō shinsho, 1985) is less useful for the Japanese general staff per se, because he digresses into essays about European staffs and the nature of a staff. Individual Japanese commanders receive good treatment in Hata Ikuhiko's *Shōwashi no gunjintachi*, (Military men of the Shōwa era) (Tokyo: Bungei shunjū, 1982); Imai Takeo and Terasaki Ryuji, eds., *Nihongun no kenkyū: Shikkikan, jo* (Research about the Japanese military: the commanders, vol. 1) (Tokyo: Hara shobō, 1980) and Kojima Noboru's *Shikkikan* (The commanders) and *Sanbō* (The staff officers) (Tokyo: Bunshun bunko, ed., 1974). Mark Peattie's *Ishiwara Kanji and Japan's Confrontation with the West* (Princeton: Princeton University Press, 1975) makes excellent use of Ishiwara to develop the intellectual and strategic vision of Japanese staff officers in the 1930s. But, as Alvin Coox pointed out years ago, where have all the great Japanese commanders gone? There are far too few good studies of Japan's generals and admirals. Arthur Swinson's *Four Samurai: A Quartet of Japanese Army Commanders in the Second World War* (London: Hutchinson of London, 1968) is unsurpassed for encapsulating the careers and leadership as well as breathing life into the selected Japanese general officers, such as Yamashita Tomoyuki and Mutaguchi Renya. Works such as Kojima's *Yamashita Tomoyuki* (Tokyo: Bunshun bunko, 1979) are helpful, and John Bester's *The Reluctant Admiral: Yamamoto and the Imperial Navy* (New York: Kodansha International, 1982), a translation of Agawa Hiroyuki's best-seller, is first-rate biography. *Kuroi hata* (Dark waves) (Tokyo: Shinchosha, 1974), Agawa's novel chronicling the fate of several Japanese junior naval officers caught in the war, is one of the finer pieces of World War II fiction in any language.

But much additional work needs to be done on the Japanese commanders of the twentieth century. Individual memoirs range from the elegant prose of an idealistic and committed former junior officer, Suematsu Taihei *Watakushi no Shōwashi* (My Shōwa history) (Tokyo: Misuzu shobō, 1963), to more prosaic accounts of former enlisted men, such as Yamamoto Katsue, *Kizoku no bo monogatari* (A blockhead's tale) (Tokyo: Senshi kankōkai, 1985) or Majima Mitsuru *Jigoku no senjō: Nyūginia senki* (Hell's battleground: New Guinea war record) (Tokyo: Kojinsha, 1988). Another good source of reliable first-person accounts was the journal *Rekishi to jimbutsu*'s special issues on wartime Japan, usually appearing each August and December. Unfortunately the series ceased publishing these special numbers in the 1990s. There is no shortage of veterans' memoirs in Japan, though similar to those written in the United States, quality varies enormously. Among interpretative works, in the mid-1980s Fujiwara Akira's *Taiheiyō sensō shiron* (A historical interpretation of the Pacific war) (Tokyo: Aoki shoten, 1982) incorporates recent scholarship, a Marxist interpretation, and extensive experience to produce thought-provoking reinterpretations of Japan's war.

Thomas Cutler, *The Battle of Leyte Gulf 23–26 October 1944* (New York: Harper Collins, 1994) covers the naval aspects of Leyte Gulf in fascinating style, and Stanley Falk's book *Decision at Leyte* (New York: Norton, 1966), remains unsurpassed in English for an overview of the entire operation. The best work on Leyte in any language though belongs to Ōka Shohei. Using the official U.S. and Japanese histories, various unit and first-person accounts, and his own experience as a POW talking to hundreds of Leyte veterans, Ōka crafted an outstanding campaign narrative, *Reite senki* (Leyte war record) (Tokyo: Chūō kōron, 1972), that covers air, ground, and naval aspects of the prolonged fighting.

The most interesting work being done on ULTRA's role in the Pacific is happening in Australia. Former Central Bureau veterans Geoffrey Ballard, *On ULTRA Active Service: The Story of Australia's Signal Intelligence Operations during World War II* (Richmond, Victoria: Spectrum, 1990) and Jack Bleakley, *The Eavesdroppers*, (Canberra: Australian Government, 1991) offer vivid firsthand accounts of the use of ULTRA in the war against Japan. The latter half of Ballard's book is full of information and revelations about the inner workings of Central Bureau. Bleakley's book is special, because it is the only one to date written by a traffic analysis expert. A former intercept operator, Bleakley describes the efforts of Australian wireless units in the war against Japan. David Jenkins, *Battle Surface: Japan's Submarine War against Australia 1942–44* (Sydney: Random House Australia, 1992), a well illustrated coffee-table edition about Japan's submarine war against Australia is surprisingly full of ULTRA material as well as firsthand Australian and Japanese accounts of that campaign. My own *MacArthur's ULTRA: Codebreaking and the War against Japan, 1942–1945* (Lawrence: University Press of Kansas, 1992) is also available for those interested in the subject.

Any discussion of American writings about the Japanese military must begin with Alvin Coox. From *Kogun: The Japanese Army in the Pacific War* (Quantico VA: Marine Corps Association, 1959) to his majesterial two-volume history of *Nomonhan* (Stanford: Stanford University Press, 1985) and beyond, he has set the standards for scholarship for others to emulate.

Frequent references to Coox's other books and essays reflective of nearly fifty years of study and scholarship are found throughout my notes. Particular mention must be made of the series *Japan's Road to the Pacific War* (New York: Columbia University Press, 1976–94) edited by James Morley. Superb translations of selected essays in the pathbreaking Nihon kokusai seiji gakkai, eds., *Taiheiyō sensō e no michi* (The road to the Pacific war) seven volumes plus documentary appendix (Tokyo: Asahi shimbunsha, 1962–1963) series originally published in Japan in 1961 and recently reissued with full citations, allow the English-language reader to glimpse the sophisticated Japanese scholarship underpinning these works. Volumes from the series used in these essays are: *Deterrent Diplomacy: Japan, Germany, and the USSR 1935–1940; The Fateful Choice: Japan's Advance into Southeast Asia, 1939–1941; The China Quagmire: Japan's Expansion on the Asian Continent 1933–1941;* and *The Final Confrontation: Japan's Negotiations with the United States, 1941.* John Boyle's *China and Japan at War: The Politics of Collaboration* (Stanford: Stanford University Press, 1972) gives rare insights into the nature of the continental war that erupted in 1937 as well as the complexity of collaboration in the conflict, subjects still little known or understood by Western military historians. *Japan's Quest for Autonomy: National Security and Foreign Policy, 1930–1938* (Princeton: Princeton University Press, 1966), James Crowley's seminal reevaluation of Japanese policy making in the troubled decade, though dated, has no peer in the English language, and Nobutaka Ike's splendid translations in *Japan's Decision for War: Records of the 1941 Policy Conferences* (Stanford: Stanford University Press, 1967) make available the documentary sources that help to explain Japanese strategic decisions in 1941. Leonard Humphreys's long-awaited *The Way of the Heavenly Sword: The Japanese Army in the 1920s* (Stanford: Stanford University Press, 1995) is an excellent account of the development of Japanese army factionalism in the 1920s and its pernicious influences. Humphreys's detailed account also adds much to our understanding of the army as an institution.

The emotional firestorm ignited by the Smithsonian Institution's Air and Space Museum's proposed concept to display the Enola Gay, the B-29, which dropped the atomic bomb on Hiroshima, demonstrated anew the depth and incompatibility of opponents and proponents of the use of the atomic weapons. The historical literature on the subject in the United States is vast. Two recent essays stake out the differing interpretations of the event. Murray Sayle's "Letter from Hiroshima: Did The Bomb End the War?" *The New Yorker*, 31 July 1995, questions the use of the weapon and its historical consequences. A rebuttal by Donald Kagan, "Why America Dropped the Bomb," *Commentary* (September 1995) concludes the decision to use the bomb was the least repugnant choice available to American leaders. Samuel J. Walker's "The Decision to Use the Bomb: A Historiographical

Update," *Diplomatic History* 12 (winter 1990) and an updated version, "History, Collective Memory, and the Decision to Use the Bomb," *Diplomatic History* 19 (spring 1995) are helpful bibliographic introductions to the scope of the dispute and the volume of published material about the still controversial decision. The former director of the Air and Space Museum, Martin Harwit's *An Exhibit Denied: Lobbying the History of Enola Gay* (New York: Copernicus, 1996) contends a conservative cabal did in his ambitious and controversial exhibit thereby denying the American public access to its thought-provoking themes. Conversely Robert P. Newman's *Truman and the Hiroshima Cult* (East Lansing: Michigan State University Press, 1995) argues forcefully that belief, not scholarship, rules those who deny the necessity of the bomb. Although no end is in sight, nor indeed ever to be seen, over this controversy, those interested in the Japanese perspective should read Ian Buruma's fascinating comparison of collective memory in the former Axis powers. His *Wages of Guilt: Memories of War in Germany and Japan* (New York: Farrar Straus Giroux, 1994) is an impressionistic account of how the Japanese regard Hiroshima, culled from interviews with numerous Japanese from all strata of society, the Japanese media, and Buruma's own perceptive insights into Japanese culture.

Understanding that I wrote these essays over the course of fifteen years, I certainly profited from recent American scholarship that has not appeared otherwise in the sources. Richard Frank's *Guadalcanal: The Definitive Account of the Landmark Battle* (New York: Random House, 1990) lives up to its billing by the author's skillful integration of Japanese and American source material. Edward Miller's *War Plan Orange: The U.S. Strategy to Defeat Japan, 1897–1945* (Annapolis MD: Naval Institute, 1991) narrates the evolution of strategic thought in American naval circles. The essays in Saki Dockrill, ed., *From Pearl Harbor to Hiroshima: The Second World War in Asia and the Pacific, 1941–45* (London: Macmillan, 1994) present refreshing British, American, Japanese, Chinese, and German historians' views of the Asian war. Her own contribution, which reconsiders the use of the atomic bomb, is well worth reading. Theodore and Haruko Cook's *Japan at War: An Oral History* (New York: New Press, 1992) chronicles first-person accounts by ordinary Japanese ranging from convicted war criminals to schoolgirls and places a human face on the all too often faceless Japanese. Ray Skates's *The Invasion of Japan* (Columbia SC: University of South Carolina Press, 1994) and Norman Polmar and Tom Allen's *Codename Downfall: The Secret Plan to Invade Japan and Why Truman Dropped the Bomb* (New York: Simon & Schuster, 1995) synthesize existing military historiography while adding new evidence and different perspectives that rekindle the ongoing controversy about the decision to use the atomic bomb on Japanese cities. Finally Gerhard Weinberg's massive study *A World at Arms: A Global History of World War II* (Cambridge: Cambridge University Press, 1994) places the war in the East in its proper global perspective. There is, however, no single-volume treatment of Japan's war against Asia in English or for that matter Japanese. Hattori Takushiro's now dated *Dai Tō A sensō zenshi* (Complete history of the greater East Asia war), 8 vols. (Tokyo: Masu shobō, 1953–56) reprinted in one volume by Hara shobō in 1965, is still useful if self-serving. A former general staff officer, Hattori headed the Japanese history section involved in researching and writing the Japanese volumes of the *Reports of MacArthur*. His subsequent account is best considered a semi-official history. For differing reasons Japanese treat the Pacific War as distinct from their continental war, and American scholars focus on the Pacific War, usually ignoring events in China unless they somehow affected Americans operations or interests. Southeast Asia campaigns are also given little attention by American military historians, that area being left to the British and Japanese to study. If anything is certain, it is that we can expect more high-quality historical studies of the momentous events in Asia and the Pacific that occurred between 1937 and 1945.

INDEX

Adachi Hatazo, x, xiv, 91; description of, 92–93, 94, 95, 96–97, 103; education of, 95–96; endures pain, 93, 99, 103; and enlisted ranks, 95, 97, 99, 103; family life of, 91–92, 96–97, 102; as junior officer, 94–95; last will of, 109; leadership of, 98–100, 103, 106–7; and New Guinea campaign, 102–9; suicide of, 109; surrender of, 108; as war criminal, 108–9
aircraft, Japanese: losses of, 39; production of, 39, 53
Aitape, North-East New Guinea, 54–55; campaign, 106–7. *See also* Adachi Hatazo: and New Guinea campaign; Driniumor River
Akin, Spencer, 118, 119
Aleutian Islands, 34, 50; and MI operation, 36, 37. *See also* Attu
amphibious doctrine, Japan, x, xiii, 14; assessment of, 22, 25; exercises of, 17–18, 22; and landing tactics, 15–16; operations in China, 21–22; stages of development of, 14–17, 20–21; waning interest in, 18–19
amphibious doctrine, U.S., 24–25
Anami Korechika, 201, 209; and atomic bomb, 214; and decisive battle, 201, 203, 204, 208, 263 n.207; demands conditional negotiations, 210; and Hirohito, 204; and Kido Kōichi, 208–9; and *kokutai*, 201; and Japan's surrender, 213; personality of, 204; suicide of, 215; and U.S. invasion, 209, 210
anti-tank weapons, Japan, 5–7; lack of, at Khalkhin-Gol, 2, 3, 5, 6; tactics for, at Kyushu, 152–53, 160–61
armor, Japan: at Khalkhin-Gol, 2; models, 7–9, 218 n.14; recommended improvements to, 7–8; tactics for, 2
artillery, Japan, deficiencies in, 3, 8, 9, 218 n.9

286 • INDEX

Asaka, Yasuhiko, Prince, and *kokutai*, 213
atomic bomb, xiii, 58–59, 210, 214; availability of, for invasion of Japan, 167; downplayed by Japanese military, 214; tactical use considered, 155, 163–64, 166–67. See also Hiroshima, Japan
atrocities, 108, 236 n.47; at Nanking 43
Attu, 177, 190. See also Aleutian Islands
Australia, xi, xiv, 36, 46, 113, 115; Allied base in, 46–47; signals intelligence capability of, 111–12
Australian Number Six Wireless Unit, 142
Australian Special Wireless Group (ASWG), xix, 114, 115; mission of, 112
Axis alliance, 44–45; Allied strategy against, 45, 59; Hirohito on, 185, 188

B-29 (bomber): attacks Japanese cities; bases in China, 54; waning interest in China, 56
Bataan, Philippine Islands, 65, 69
Biak Island, Netherlands East Indies, 38, 52, 55
bicycle troops, 64
Bismarck Archipelago, 36, 112, 122; and Allied counteroffensive, 37; Japanese army assessment of, 35; and Japanese navy plans, 33–34. See also Rabaul, New Britain
Bismarck Sea, 50; battle of, 104, 125–26; Hirohito on, 189
Bolshevik Revolution (1917), effect of, on Japanese army, 28
Buna, Papua New Guinea, 123; Adachi Hatazo and, 103; campaign, 65–66, 103; Hirohito and, 189–90; Japanese troops at, 70, 119–20, 122, 123; Japanese defeat at, 38; signals intelligence and, 119–20, 122–23; and validation of U.S. Army doctrine, 65–66
Burma, 44, 53, 73; Allied operations on, 54, 57; Japanese invasion of, 48
bushido, 13, 90

Cairo Conference (1943), 48; decides on central Pacific drive, 51
Casablanca Conference (1942), 70–71
casualties, Japan, 145, 228 n.5; in China (1937–41), 30, 43; at Hiroshima, 164; at Okinawa, 58; at Tokyo, 164
Central Bureau, 112, 113, 114; Battle of Bismarck Sea, 126; and Fifty-five Wireless Section, 116, 120, 122, 124; problems, 117
Chiang Kai-shek, 43, 47; criticized over Henyang battle, 54; and communists, 54
Chichibu Yasuhito, Prince, 186
China: Allied air bases in, 51, 54, 59; Japanese operations in, 29–30, 31, 42–43, 54, 57, 98–100; war effort against Japan, 47
Chinese army units: Eighth Route Army, 20, 43
Churchill, Winston S., 44, 47, 48; attitude on British empire, 49
Clausewitz, Carl von: quoted, 26
codebreaking: Allied submarine offensive, 50; Australia and, 111–12; detects Japanese diplomatic and military initiatives, 209–10; and MacArthur's leapfrog operations, 54; in New Guinea campaign, 105. See also Fifty-five Wireless Section; intelligence, Allied; ULTRA
Combined Fleet, 133; and Kurita Takeo, 134–35
conscription, Japan, 75; characteristics of draftees, 78–79; draft resistance, 79; recruiting districts, 77, 78, 79–80; system, 77–79

INDEX • 287

convoys, Japan: at Bismarck Sea, 104, 125–26, detected in ULTRA, 141–42; at Leyte, 140, 142. *See also* ULTRA
"C" Operation, 22
Coral Sea Battle, 46, 131
counter-amphibious doctrine, Japan, xi, 70; in 1945, 149; revisions to, 151, 160, 166; and special attack tactics, 150, 154
coup d'etat: in 1945, 213–15; fear of, 186. *See also* February 26, 1936 Incident
Cunningham, Julian W., 67
Curtain, John, 126

daihatsu (barge), 21, 24, 105; description, 18
decisive battle, 173, 179; anticipated in Kyushu, 146, 151, 156, 199, 210; changing concepts of, 172, 210; concept for Kyushu, 148–49, 207; doctrine for, 146, 149–50; Hirohito and, 190–91, 199–200, 211; homeland defense, 145, 149–51, 160, 161; Koiso Kuniaki and, 196; at Leyte, 136, 195, 196–97; after loss of Okinawa, 201, 198–200; at Luzon, 143, 197; at Marianas, 192; relation to exaggerated battle claims, 187, 190, 210; relation to *kokutai*, 172, 186, 209; and Russo-Japanese War precedent, 172; and war termination, 187–89
direction finding (d/f) xix, 114, 116; role in air raid alerts, 122, 117. *See also* Fifty-five Wireless Section
doctrine, Japanese army, 64–65; artillery and, 63; emphasis on intangibles, 63; jungle warfare, 63–64, 65, 70; limitations, 74; Malaya operations, 65; reluctance to change, 69–70; special attack, 151–52. *See also* fight-to-the-death mentality; infantry, Japan: and intangibles; kamikaze

dokuhakuroku. *See* emperor's monologue
Doolittle, James, 37
Driniumor River, North-East New Guinea: campaign, 67–68. *See also* Aitape, North-East New Guinea

Eichelberger, Robert L., 65
Eighth Route Army (Chinese), 20, 43
emperor's monologue: provenance of, 169–70, 249 n.1; reasons for 170–71; value of, 171
Endo Saburō, 13
exaggerated battle claims: at Leyte, 130–31, 196–97; at Marianas, 192–93; at Marshalls, 191–92; effect on Japanese operations 130–31; effect on Hirohito, 187, 191, 210

Far East Combined Bureau (FECB), xix, 111
February 26, 1936 Incident, 86, 97, 259 n.152. *See also* coup d'etat
Field Service Regulations (FSR), xix; Japan, 1928, 13; Japan, 1938, 25, 63, 64; U.S. 1939 Tentative, 61; 1941, and operations, 61
Fifty-five Wireless Section, x, xiv, 111, 240 n.67; and air raid alerts, 117–18, 124; assessment of, 118–19, 126–27; and Bismarck Sea battle, 126; Central Bureau and, 116, 120; and field conditions, 120–24; mission of, 114, 122, 123; organization of, 114; at Port Moresby, 114–16
fight-to-the-death mentality, xi, xiv, 3, 71, 76, 90, 96; Adachi Hatazo and, 107–8; correlation to training, 89; and Kyushu, 160; reasons for, 76; Umezu Yoshijiro and, 195. *See also* kamikaze; special attack tactics; surrender policy, Japan
First Mobile Fleet, 55; at Leyte, 132

Formosa, 55–56, 130; in Japanese and U.S. planning, 55–56, 131
XIV Army (British), 57, 73
French Indochina, 31, 59; Hirohito and, 179, 252 n.45
FS Operation, 35
Fuji maneuvers (1941), 22, 65

general staff, Japan, 11, 17, 18, 19, 20, 28; assumes German victory, 34; decisive battle, 39; and emperor, 173; favors protracted war, 33–34; and French Indochina, 31; functions of, 27; at Guadalcanal, 38; at Leyte, 131; and Midway operation, 37; and navy's decisive battle, 36; redeploys against Soviet Union, 32, 34, 45; revised defense policy, 28–29; at Saipan, 39; and Soviet Union, 30; strategy of, 38; surprised by navy's plans, 27, 32; underestimates Allies 34, 47, 68. *See also* Imperial General Headquarters
German-Soviet War (1941), 31, 45
Germany-first strategy, 45, 46
Gilbert Islands, 38; U.S. assault on, 52. *See also* Tarawa, Gilbert Islands
Great Britain, 69, 127; attempt to isolate, 36, 45, 185; covert operations in U.S., 44; defeat presumed, 34–35, 45, 47; disagreements with U.S. on strategy, 50–51; Hirohito and, 201; as intermediary to end war with U.S., 198; and strain of two-front war, 51; strategy in southwest Asia, 48, 49
Groves, Leslie: tactical atomic bombs, 163–64, 166–67. *See also* OLYMPIC
Guadalcanal, 49, 69, 103; battle of, 37–38; Hirohito and, 189; Japanese reinforcements and, 120; withdrawal from, 124
Guam, 29; prewar Japanese plans for, 16, 28, 29; prewar U.S. plans for, 24
Guntai naimusho (Army handbook for Squad Administration), 81

Hall, Charles, P., 67
Halsey, William F., 37; advocates invasion of Philippines, 56, 129; decisions at Leyte, 128, 143; Leyte and, 55–56, 127–28, 131, 133; use of ULTRA, 143–44
Hansa Bay, North-East New Guinea, 105, 106
Hasegawa Kiyoshi: pessimistic report to Hirohito, 208
Hata Shunroku: opinion of atomic bomb, 214
Hatanaka Kenji, 213; leads coup d'etat, 214–15
Hawaii operation (1942), 36. *See also* MI operation; Midway
Higashikuni Naruhiko, Prince: imperial abdication, 198; pessimistic report to emperor, 208; Tōjō and, 193
Hirohito, Shōwa Emperor, x, xii, 41, 87; abdication considered, 171, 198; Anami Korechika and, 204; approves battle of homeland, 145, 202, 207; assessment of, 171, 215; and August 1945 coup d'etat, 214–15; believes war lost, 188, 201, 210, 256 n.94; and Chinese relations, 172, 180; as constitutional monarch, 186; decision of, to end war, 214; fear of coup d'etat, 186, 203, 209, 214; and French Indochina, 179, 252 n.45; and German relations, 185, 188; and Guadalcanal, 189; Higashikuni and, 182; and imperial conference, 173, 181; and imperial house, 182; influence versus authority of, 173, 181, 186, 192, 207; Kido Kōichi and, 208; Koiso Kuniaki

and, 194, 197; and *kokutai*, 172, 211, 213; and Konoe appeal to end war, 198; and liaison conference, 173; and Marianas, 192; and Matsushirō issue, 206, 208; and Midway, 187–88; and military, 173, 175, 179–184, 186–93, 197–203, 207–9, 211, 213; Nagano Osami and, 179; nationalism of, 174; and national morale, 197, 199, 206; and New Guinea, 188, 190; Oikawa Koshirō and, 181–82; and Okinawa, 199–201; and Pearl Harbor, 183–85, 254 n.70, 235 n.73; personality of, 174–75, 180; and Potsdam Declaration, 213; and Russo-Japanese War precedents, 175, 187–88, 189; Sugiyama Hajime and, 177–78, 179, 180, 184, 189–90; Tōjō Hideki and, 178, 179, 192, 193; and war criminal allegations, 170–71; and war termination, 59, 187, 188, 189, 198–99, 201–2, 205, 213; and war with West, 172, 179, 180, 183–86; and Western racism, 174; and Yunnan issue, 201. See also emperor's monologue

Hiroshima, Japan, 17, 148, 166, 167; atomic bomb, 68, 164

Hitler, Adolph, 43, 44, 45, 48, 51; Tōjō's comparison, 192

Hollandia, Netherlands New Guinea, 54–55; Allied operations, 105–6

homeland defense, Japan, x, xv, 58–59; beach defenses, 149–51; fight-to-the-death mentality, 160; Hirohito's evaluation of, 211; plans detected in ULTRA, 155; rationale for, 40; shortages, 148; suicide tactics, 161; tactics, 150–52. See also decisive battle: and homeland defense

Hong Kong, 21, 22, 44; "C" operation, 21, 22; disregarded by Great Britain, 24; as intercept site, 111; Japanese seizure of, 48

Hosokawa Morisada: and *kokutai*, 193–94; and war termination, 205

Ichigō operation, 11; objectives, 54

Ichiki Kiyoano, 69

imperial conference, 28; 6 September 1941, 181–82; 3 July 1941, 31; 5 November 1941, 184; 1 December 1941, 185; 30 September 1943, 191; 8 June 1945, 203, 208; 22 June 1945, 209; 9 August 1945, 210; Hirohito and, 181–82; nature of, 181

imperial defense policy (IDP), xix, 27; 1936 revision, 29; initial Japanese strategy, 46

Imperial General Headquarters (IGHQ) xix, 5, 10, 11, 12, 20, 22; abandons Saipan, 193; anticipates MacArthur attack, 105; and concept of decisive battle, 56, 57, 149–50; confidential war diary of, 35, 37; downplays Hiroshima destruction, 164; exaggerates battle claims, 130, 136, 187; expectations of troops, 150–51; functions of, 27–28; and homeland defense, 145; and Imphal operation, 53; Kurita Takeo and, 135; and Kyushu defense, 147, 153, 162, 207; and Matsushirō plan, 206; and New Guinea operations, 104; and Okinawa operations, 199–200; revises doctrine, 151; and Shō operations, 139; and zone of national defense, 105. See also general staff

imperial house: avoid war responsibility, 182; imperial regalia and, 205–6; possible extinction, 194, 199; preservation of, 194, 210, 211

Imperial Japanese Army (IJA), ix, x, xi, xii, xiii, xiv, xix; appeal of,

290 • INDEX

Imperial Japanese Army (IJA) (*cont.*) 79–80, 82, 88–89; assessment of Khalkhin-Gol, 5; code systems, 137–38; conditions for negotiated war termination, 205; doctrine, 64–65; emphasis on intangibles, 12–13, 63, 89–90; extension of Japanese family, 77–78, 81, 90; Hirohito and, 175; hypothetical opponents, 16, 19; initial war plans, 24, 27; jungle warfare, 63–64, 65; lack of expertise on U.S., 32, 64; legacy, 75; logistics, 3, 9–11, 39; Malaya operations, 65; motorization, 6, 9–10; prepares for southern operations, 64; prestige of, 92; self-image of, 77; special relationship with emperor, 82; and Soviet Union, 12, 19, 25, 27, 28–30, 31, 42, 64, 65, 71, 96, 97; underestimates Western powers, 32, 69; unquestioning obedience of, 153; wartime expansion of, 20. *See also* Imperial General Headquarters; infantry, Japan; Japanese army units; officer education, Japan

Imperial Japanese Navy (IJN), xix, 26, 28, 32, 41; anti-submarine warfare doctrine of, 50; and decisive fleet engagement, 33, 36, 39; Hirohito and, 190–91, 192; initial success of, 36; and oil embargo, 179; plans offensive operations, 33–34, 49. *See also* Kurita Takeo; Leyte Gulf; Midway; Pearl Harbor; Shō operation

imperial liaison conference, 28; 66th conference, 183; 5 November 1941, 33, 180; dynamics of, 173; preparations for, 173

imperial regalia: air raid and, 205; importance to Hirohito, 206–7, 211

Imperial Rescript to Soldiers and Sailors (1882), 76, 80, 230 n.19

Imperial War College, 24, 71, 74; curriculum of, 71–72, 95–96; mission, 96. *See also* officer education, Japan

Imphal, India, 11; battle of, 53, 54. *See also* Burma

India, 44; and British counteroffensive, 57; Japanese invasion of, 48, 53. *See also* Imphal, India

infantry, Japan, 69–70, 73, 80; assessment by opponents, 89, 90; compared to U.S. Army, 70–71; defeated at Buna, 70; Japanese emphasis on, 63; force structure of, 63; ignorance of U.S. tactics, 70; and intangibles, 12–13, 63, 69, 83, 89–90; Japanese overreliance on, 71; tactics, 73. *See also* training, Japan

infantry, U.S.: compared to Japanese, 70–71; deficiencies at Buna, 66–67; deficiencies at Driniumor, 67–68; deficiencies at Leyte, 68–69; force structure of, 62; infantry-artillery team and, 61–62; Japanese assessment of, 67; percent of total casualties, 63; tactics of, 61–63; training of, 62–63

Infantry Manual (1908), 63, 69. *See also* field service regulations

intelligence, Allied, xiv, xv; Aitape operation, 107; and Australia base, 111–12; detects Japanese duplicity Kyushu, 210; and Hollandia operation, 105–6; and invasion of Japan, 58; at Leyte, 128–30, 137–38; and MacArthur leapfrog operations, 54; Philippines and, 56, 130; supports U.S. submarine offensive, 50. *See also* Fifty-five Wireless Section; signals intelligence; ULTRA

International Military Tribunal for the Far East, 171
interservice rivalry, 27-28, 33, 49; Hirohito and, 189, 190, 197, 200-201
invasion of Japan. *See* decisive battle, homeland defense, OLYMPIC
Ishiwara Kanji, 29
Iwo Jima, 39, 56, 57, 70

Japanese army units:
  armies:
    Fifteenth, 11; and Imphal, 53
    Seventeenth, 37, 103, 120
    Eighteenth, xiv, 103, 121, 123; and Bismarck Sea battle, 104, 125-26; and New Guinea operations, 104-9; in ULTRA, 119-20
    Thirty-second, 199; dispute over strategy, 199-200
    Thirty-fifth, 39; at Leyte, 129
    Fortieth: defends Kyushu, 148-49; and shortages, 148-49; significance of, 160
    Fifty-seventh, 148, 156
  area armies:
    Eighth, 37, 103; and Bismarck Sea battle, 125-26; and New Guinea operations, 104-5, 123, 124; in ULTRA, 124-25
    Fourteenth, 39, 136, 139, 140
    Sixteenth, 148, 152, 162, 164
  general armies:
    Second, 148; expects Kyushu invasion, 151; homeland defense role, 148; revises tactical doctrine, 151
    Southern, 40, 136
  infantry divisions:
    Guards, 10, 22; Adachi Hatazo and, 94, 96; mutiny by, 73; recruitment of, 94
    First, 14, 15, 68; at Leyte, 138-41; mutiny of, 97
    Second, 14, 86
    Third, 15, 16, 21; and amphibious exercises, 17
    Fifth, 7, 10, 18, 29, 64; and amphibious exercises, 17, 19; and China operations, 19-20
    Eighth, 39, 68; detected in ULTRA, 130
    Ninth, 18; redeployment of, 200
    Eleventh, 6, 9, 10, 29, 218 n.10; and amphibious training, 17, 19; casualties of, 20, 22, 98; and China operations, 20-21, 98-99
    Twelfth, 20, 22; amphibious training, 17-19; and China operations, 20-21, 98-99
    Sixteenth, 21, 64, 65, 68; at Leyte, 130-31
    Eighteenth, 10, 17, 20, 21, 22
    Twentieth, 80, 124, 125; and New Guinea operations, 104-5
    Twenty-third: at Khalkhin-Gol, 2, 3, 11, 12-13; reactions to combat, 89
    Twenty-fifth, 6, 9, 218 n.10; on Kyushu, 149, 156, 164
    Twenty-sixth, 68, 99, 130
    Thirty-seventh, 99-100
    Forty-first, 104, 124, 125
    Fifty-first, 126
    Fifty-fifth, 22, 65
    Fifty-seventh, 6, 9, 10, 218 n.10; identified in ULTRA, 155; on Kyushu, 149, 164
    Seventy-seventh, 7, 156, 162
    Eighty-fourth, 200
    Eighty-Sixth, 155
    146th, 146, 160, 162
    154th, 146, 159
    156th, 146, 151, 160
    206th, 146, 159, 162, 218 n.11
    212th, 146, 159, 162, 218 n.11
    216th, 146, 162, 218 n.11
    303d, 146, 162

292 • INDEX

Japanese army units: (cont.)
  312th, 146, 162
  351st, 146, 162
Joint Chiefs of Staff (JCS), xix, 37; Germany and, 51; and Luzon-Formosa issue, 55–56; meeting with president, 157–58; and Okinawa, 58; and OLYMPIC operation, 155; and Philippines, 129; strategy of, 1942, 38; treatment of emperor, 170–71

kamikaze, xii; detected by ULTRA, 158–59, 161; expected at Kyushu, 150, 156–57; at Okinawa, 58; at Philippines, 56; tactics for Kyushu, 158, 161. See also fight-to-the-death mentality; special attack tactics
Kawabe Torashirō: quoted on decisive battle, 152
Kaya Kuninori Prince: Yunnan operations, 201
Khalkhin-Gol, xiii, 1, 43, 139; Japanese assessment of, 5; Japanese casualties at, 3; Japanese lessons from, 11; Japanese lessons not applied at, 12–13; Soviet casualties at, 3; Twenty-third Division reaction to, 89
Kido Kōichi: at 6 September 1941 imperial conference, 181; at 8 June 1945 imperial conference, 208; and decisive victory, 199, 205; and Matsushirō issue, 206, 208; meets Anami, 208–9; personality of, 179; preserving kokutai, 205, 211; role at court, 178–79, 184, 187; and Soviet mediation, 201–2, 209; and Suzuki Kantarō, 202; vetoes Higashikuni as prime minister, 182; and war with West, 185, 186; and war termination, 201, 205
King, Ernest J., 46, 51; advocates central Pacific advance, 50; compromises on Pacific command, 51–52; favors Formosa plan, 55
Kobayashi Jun'ichirō, 13
kōhatsu (landing barge), description of, 18
Kohima, India, 53
Koiso Kuniaki: cabinet of, 194; decisive battle at Leyte, 197; Hirohito and, 194, 197; personality of, 194–95; relations with military, 195, 196, 197. See also Leyte, Philippine Islands: decisive battle at
kokutai: Anami Korechika and, 204; connection to decisive battle, 172, 194, 204, 209; definition of, 172; Hirohito and, 172, 211, 213; implications if defeated, 211–12; Kido Kōichi and, 205, 211; imperial princes and, 213; preservation of, 186, 193, 194, 201, 203, 204, 210; Tōjō Hideki and, 194; and unconditional surrender, 205; Yonai Mitsumasa and, 196
Komatsubara Michitarō, 2. See also Japanese army units, infantry divisions: Twenty-third
Konoe Fumimaro, 174; advises Hirohito to end war, 198; and imperial abdication, 198; and kokutai, 193; and Prince Higashikuni, 193; resignation of, 182; and war with West, 180; and war termination, 194, 198, 205
Konuma Haruo, 5, 13, 218 n.6
Krueger, Walter, xii, 67, 68; at Leyte, 136–39; and controversy at Leyte, 137, 143
Kuomintang, xi, 47
Kurile Islands, 49, 52
Kurita Takeo, 133; and controversial decision, 133–35, 143; at Leyte Gulf, 133–34
Kwantung Army, 2, 5, 6, 8, 10, 11, 13; Adachi Hatazo and, 97; mobilization of, 1945, 41,

57; redeployments of, 57; and Seventeenth Army issue, 207; special maneuvers of, 1941, 32. *See also* Khalkhin-Gol

Kyushu, Japan: advantages of defenders at, 153; and beach defenses, 149, 151; Hirohito and, 207; and Japanese defensive plans, 160, 161; military build up at, 1945, 58, 147–48, 154, 156; scope of, 153; and shortages, 148–49, 164–65; and U.S. estimates of reinforcements, 165, 210; ULTRA detects reinforcements, 155–60. *See also* Marshall, George C.: and Kyushu buildup; war termination: negotiations conflict with Kyushu buildup

Lae, North-East New Guinea, 103, 124; weather broadcasts from, 125–26

Leyte, Philippine Islands, x, xiii, xiv, 52, 65; campaign of, 68–69; decision to reinforce, 136; decisive battle at, 40, 195; Hirohito's evaluation of, 213; Japanese defenses at, 130; Japanese losses at, 137; MacArthur's estimates at, 136–37; signals intelligence at, 128–29; U.S. invasion of, 56, 127. *See also* under Halsey, William F.; Krueger, Walter; Shō operation; signals intelligence; ULTRA; Willoughby, Charles A.

Leyte Gulf, 128; and exaggerated victory claims, 134–35; Japanese losses at, 135; Kurita Takeo at, 134–35; as scene of Shō operation, 55–56; ULTRA available on, 131–32; U.S. losses at, 135. *See also* under decisive battle; Halsey, William F.; Leyte; Shō operation; signals intelligence; ULTRA

Liaotung Peninsula, China, Japanese landings on, 14,15

logistics, Japanese Army, 39; attitude toward, 11; evaluation of, 9–11; at Imphal, 53; in Malaya operation, 10–11; operational radius of, 3, 10; and shortages, 1945, 147, 148

Louisiana Maneuvers (1940), 65

Luzon, Philippine Islands: defenses, 40, 136; in Japanese war plans, 16, 28, 29; as MacArthur's objective, 128; as scene of decisive battle, 197; strategic debate on, 55–56; U.S. landing at, 56

MacArthur, Douglas, xi, xiv, 29, 37, 38, 46, 49, 91, 165; accelerates New Guinea offensives, 54–55; Adachi Hatazo's assessment of, 105; and divided command, 52; estimate at Leyte, 136; favors Soviet invasion of Manchuria, 58; Hirohito and, 170–71; ignores intelligence, 116, 128–30, 157–58, 166; and invasion of Japan, 58, 155; Japanese expect to capture, 196; and leapfrog operations, 104–5; and New Guinea operations, 104–6; objects to central Pacific drive, 51; objects to Formosa plan, 55; and Philippines as objective, 55–56, 71; regard for intelligence, 128, 166; as SCAP commander, 170. *See also* Willoughby, Charles, A.: and estimates at Leyte

Madang, North-East New Guinea, 104, 125

MAGIC, definition of, 128

Malaya operation (1941–42), 7, 10, 44, 48, 64; and invasion, 48; Japanese tactics in, 65. *See also* Singapore

Manchuria, 71, 97; as focus of Japanese army, 64, 65; mobilization in, 45; redeployments from, 40,

Manchuria (*cont.*)
  41, 57, 129; and Russo-Japanese War, 27, 71; Soviet invasion of, 58. *See also* Khalkhin-Gol; Kwantung Army
Mao tse tung, 43, 47, 54, 59
Mariana Islands, 33, 38, 55
Marshall, George C., 52, 67; concern about U.S. casualties, 157–58, 166; considers tactical atomic bombs, 163–64, 166, 167; Groves, Leslie, and, 163–64, 166–67; invasion of Japan, 58; and Kyushu buildup, 157–58, 162–66; Kyushu reinforcements, 158; MacArthur, Douglas and, 157–58, 165; meeting with president, 157–58; proposes alternate invasion sites, 165–66; warns of buildup in Philippines, 128, 129. *See also* atomic bomb
Marshall Islands, 33, 38, 52
Matsudaira Yasumasa, 199; and Umezu report, 208
Matsushirō, Japan: as alternate command post, 206, 208; Hirohito's objections to, 206, 261 n.188; significance of, 206–7
Mediterranean strategy, 48, 51
Meiji Emperor, 75, 250 n.15; as passive leader, 175
Midway, 34, 46, 131; operation, 36–37
Mikasa Takahito, Prince, and imperial abdication, 171
military academy, Japan. *See* officer education, Japan
MI operation, 36. *See also* Midway
mobilization, 20, 165; for homeland defense, 146, 147, 159, 165, 166
Mountbatten, Lord Louis, 49, 57
Mutaguchi Renya, 11, 91; defeated at Imphal, 54, reacts to Wingate, 53

Nagano Osami, 33; at 6 September 1941 imperial conference, 181; and Pearl Harbor plan, 184; and Midway operation, 187–88; and chief naval general staff, 174; decisive battle and, 179–80, 183; dismissal of, 192; Guadalcanal and, 188, 189; and imperial audiences, 184, 185; lack of strategy, 176, 180; personality of, 175–76; unable to guarantee victory, 180, 181. *See also* Imperial Japanese Navy
Nagasaki, Japan: atomic attack on, 59, 166, 167
Nakahara operation (China), 99
Nakamura Tadahisa, 199
Nanking, China, 30, 43; rape of 43
National Defense Policy (1918), 16
naval general staff: emperor and, 173, 175; functions of, 27, 33; Leyte and, 133–34; and oil embargo, 179. *See also* Imperial Japanese Navy; Nagano Osami; Oikawa Koshirō; Pearl Harbor; Shimada Shigetarō; strategy, Japan
navy ministry: emperor and, 173; favors attacking Australia, 36; functions of, 27. *See also* Imperial Japanese Navy; Midway; Nagano Osami; Oikawa Koshirō; Pearl Harbor; Shimada Shigetarō; strategy, Japan
Naval War College, U.S., 24
Nave, Eric, 111, 112, 113; trains cryptanalysts, 111–14
Netherlands East Indies, 30
New Britain, Bismarck Islands, 70, 102, 104. *See also* Rabaul, New Britain
New Guinea, 37, 65; Adachi Hatazo and, 102; Allied operations in, 49, 52–53, 55; Fifty-five Wireless and, 111, 114, 120; Hirohito's evaluation of, 188–90; and Japanese operations and strategy, 33, 102–9, 122, 124; and U.S. strategy, 37, 48. *See also* Adachi Hatazo: and

INDEX • 295

New Guinea campaign; Aitape, North-East New Guinea; Buna, Papua New Guinea; Hollandia, Netherlands New Guinea
Nimitz, Chester W., 38, 54, 55, 56, 129; use of ULTRA, 143–44
Nishimura Shōji, 132, 133
Nomonhan, 1, 2; lessons learned, 11. See also Khalkhin-Gol

officer education, Japan, xiv, 4, 70, 232–33 n.5; cadet education, 92–93; compared to U.S. system, 72–73, 95–96; curriculum of, 96; deficiencies of, 70, 72, 74, 95; and military academy, 93–94, 233 n.8; relationship to emperor, 92–93; and selection for war college, 95–96; and war college, 71–72, 73, 95–96
officer education, U.S., 72–73, 74; compared to Japanese system, 72–73, 95–96
Ogasawara Islands, 49, 52. See also Iwo Jima
Ogata Ken'ichi, 189
Oikawa Koshirō, 201; briefs Hirohito on Leyte, 196–97; and decisive battle, 198; Koiso Kuniaki and, 197; as navy minister, 174, 194; personality of, 176; *Yamato* and, 200
oil embargo, 32, 186; effect on Japanese, 179
Okinawa, 39, 56; campaign of, 40, 57–58; casualties at, 58; as decisive battle, 198, 199; Hirohito and, 199; and sacrifice of Okinawans, 57–58
OLYMPIC (invasion of Japan), 58; changing intelligence estimates, 154–55; date set for, 155; estimated U.S. casualties in, 157, 158, 167; and U.S. plan, 154–55. See also Truman, Harry S.: and OLYMPIC; ULTRA: role in OLYMPIC; Willoughby, Charles A.

Orange plan, 24, 50
Owen Stanley Range, Papua New Guinea, 114, 115, 117; Japanese advance through, 115–16; Hirohito and, 188, 256 n.94
Ozawa Jisaburō, xiii, 55; at Leyte Gulf, 56, 132

Palau Islands, 220 n.36; Japanese base, 122, 125
Papua New Guinea, 49, 103; See also Buna, Papua New Guinea; New Guinea; Port Moresby, Papua New Guinea
Pearl Harbor, Hawaii, Japanese attack on, 26, 43, 46; consequences of, 46; secrecy surrounding, 184–85, 254 n.70; planning of, 182–83; Hirohito's knowledge of, 183, 254 n.70, 255 n.73
Philippine Islands, 24, 28–29, 50, 51; bypassing debate on, 50–51; as decisive battle, 40; Japan, 1942 campaign in, 65; Japanese buildup in, 39–40, 128–29; Japanese defensive plans in, 19, 28–29, 48, 64; Shō operation in, 39, 55–56; as strategic objective, 50–51; U.S. defeat in, 46; U.S. defensive plans in, 29, 40, 44. See also Leyte, Philippine Islands; Leyte Gulf; Luzon, Philippine Islands; ULTRA
Port Arthur, China: Japanese landing, 1894, 14; Japanese landing, 1904, 15–16
Port Moresby, Papua New Guinea, 49; air raid alerts at, 117–19; and Fifty-five Wireless Section, 114–15, 117–19; Japan, overland advance on, 115–16; and Japanese navy plans, 34. See also Coral Sea Battle
Potsdam Declaration, 211, 213, 214

Quadrant conference (1944), 54

Rabaul, New Britain, 37, 103, 123, 125, 126; and Allied objective, 50; and Bismarck Sea battle, 125–26; isolation of, 54–55; as Japanese air and naval base, 34, 37, 120, 122, 123
Rangoon, Burma, 49; as Slim's objective, 57
Red Army (Soviet), 1, 2, 19, 64, 69. *See also* Khalkhin-Gol; Soviet Union
Roosevelt, Franklin D., 44; and China, 47
Royal Australian Air Force (RAAF), xix; trains intercept operators, 111–12
Royal Australian Navy, xix; cryptologic agency, 111
Russo-Japanese War (1904–1905), 14, 15, 21; amphibious operations, 15–16; consequences, 27; influence of, on cadet education, 93; influence of, on war college curriculum, 71, 75, 96; Hirohito's interpretation of, 175, 187–88, 189; as precedent for decisive battle, 171–72, 179
Ryukyu Islands, 55, 130. *See also* Okinawa

Saipan, Mariana Islands, 111; loss of 39; U.S. landing at, 55. *See also* Hirohito: and Marianas; Tōjō Hideki: resigns after Saipan
Sakai Kōji, 194; war termination, 205
samurai, 75, 91, 228 n.2; and new army, 75–76; values derived from, 75–76, 91, 92
Satsuma uprising (1877), 75
Second Tank Division (Japan), 9, 40, 130
Sextant Conference (1943), 38
Shanghai incident: 1932, 18; 1937, 20, 21, 30, 43; and Japanese operations, 98–99

Shantung Peninsula: Japanese landings on, 14, 15, 16, 20
Shigemitsu Mamoru, 194; and imperial house, 194
Shimada Shigetarō: attitude toward Germans, 185; evaluation by peers, 192; loyal to Tōjō, 177, 192; and Marianas operation, 192–93; as navy minister, 174; and Pearl Harbor, 185; personality of, 176–77; and inevitability of war, 177
shipping units, Japan, 119, 120, 238 n.34, 122, 124–26
Shō operation, 39; detected by ULTRA, 132; First Division and, 139; Koiso Kuniaki and, 196; Leyte, 131; variations, 39, 55–56. *See also* Leyte, Philippine Islands
Shōwa emperor. *See* Hirohito
signals intelligence: in Australia, 111–12; in Bismarck Sea battle, 125–26; in Buna and Guadalcanal operations, 119–20, 122–23; definition of, 128; and OLYMPIC operation, 154; training in, 111–13; shortcomings at Leyte, 137, 139. *See also* codebreaking; Fifty-five Wireless Section; ULTRA; "Y" intelligence
Singapore, Malaya, 45, 64; fall of, 48, 219 n.26; naval base 44. *See also* Malaya operation
Sino-Japanese War (1937) 17, 63
Slim, William, 48, 49; and advance on Rangoon, 57; assessment of Japanese soldier, 73, 89; tactics of, 53–54
Solomon Islands, 33, 37; Allied operations in, 49. *See also* Guadalcanal
Southwest Pacific Area (SWPA), 116, 137, 141, 143, 161–62
Soviet Red Army, 1, 2, 19, 64, 69. *See also* Khalkhin-Gol

Soviet Union, xi; as anticipated Japanese opponent, 12, 19, 25, 27, 28–30, 31, 42, 64, 65, 71, 96, 97; enters war against Japan, 58–59, 166, 210; and German invasion, 31, 45; as Japanese intermediary to end war, 202, 209; in 1942, 34; in 1945, 41, 207. *See also* Khalkhin-Gol; Manchuria

special attack (suicide) tactics, 40, 41; doctrine of, 151–52; Hirohito and, 200; at Kyushu, 150, 154, 156, 161; and Tokyo orders, 153; *Yamato* and, 200. *See also* fight-to-the-death mentality; kamikaze

Stark, Harold R., on winning and losing, 44–45

Stilwell, Joseph W., 48, 54; personality of, 49; and strategic goal, 48

Stimson, Henry, 58

strategy, Allied, xiii, 38, 61, 74; assessment in Pacific, 59; against Axis, 45; and British-U.S. disagreements, 48, 70–71; and competition for resources, 50–51; definition of, 26; and dual Pacific drives, 38, 48, 50–52, 55; global responsibilities defined, 47–48; and invasion of Japan, 58; and MacArthur, 52; planning of, 71; and submarine offensive, 50, 54; and U.S. navy, 52; and U.S. prewar Philippines, 44

strategy, Japanese, xiii, 42, 70, 74; in 1944, 40, 49–50; army and, 26, 27, 28, 30; assessment of, 41; and decisive battle of homeland, 58–59; and imperial conference, September 1943, 38, 52–53, 191; of Koiso Kuniaki, 196; and lack of strategic objective, 30, 33, 45–46, 190; at Leyte, 131–32; in March 1942, 47; navy and, 26, 27, 28, 33; at opening of war, 45; and protracted war, 33; underestimate West, 43, 45, 47. *See also* homeland defense; Imperial Japanese Army; Imperial Japanese Navy

submarines, Allied, 54; against Japanese merchant fleet, 50, 147; aided by ULTRA, 129–30, 140

Suematsu Taihei, 86

Sugiyama Hajime, 29, 33, 184, 192, 197, 201; advocates war with West, 181, 183; as army chief of staff, 174, 177; bearing of, 177; and Buna operations, 189–90; embarrassed over China, 180; at Guadalcanal, 189; and imperial audiences, 184, 190; personality of, 177–78; relationship with Hirohito, 177–78, 190; and September 1941 imperial conference, 181

suicide tactics. *See* special attack (suicide) tactics

Supreme Commander for the Allied Powers (SCAP), xix, 170, 171

Supreme Council for the Direction of the War, 195, 196; and surrender, 214

surrender policy, Japan: and atomic bomb consideration, 167; attitude toward, 147, 152, 153, 164; and IGHQ expectations for Kyushu, 150–51; mentality revealed in ULTRA, 154–55, 157; and reputation for fighting to death, 153; and unwillingness to surrender, 55, 165. *See also* fight-to-the-death mentality

Suzuki Kantarō, 194; Anami Korechika and, 203; and decisive battle, 202–3; Kido Kōichi and, 202; personality of, 202–3; and war termination, 202–3

tactics, Japan, xiv, 1, 3, 11–12; against Great Britain, 65; against Soviet Union, 64; at beginning of war, 46; emphasis on intangibles, 11–12; at Imphal, 53–54; shifts in, 12;

tactics, Japan (*cont.*)
  and lack of innovation, 25. *See also* infantry, Japan; special attack tactics
tactics, U.S., xiv; and anticipated opponent, 64; assessment of, 73; and infantry-artillery team, 61–62; and jungle warfare, 61–62, 63; pre–World War II, 61, 62
Takagi Sōkichi, 194; war termination, 205
Takamatsu Nobuhito, Prince: estimates success in war, 185; and imperial abdication, 198, 206; and November 1941 war games, 182–83; and preservation of *kokutai*, 194, 198; and war termination, 205
Takebashi Incident (1878), 75, 228 n.3
Tarawa, Gilbert Islands, 52, 177
Terada Masao, 11
Terasaki, Gwen, 169–70
Terasaki Hidenari: background of, 169–70; and imperial abdication, 171; transcribes *dokuhakuroku*, 169
Tōgō Heihachirō, 187, 192
Tōgō Shigenori, 203; told by Hirohito to end war, 209; and war termination, 201
Tōjō Hideki, 29, 176, 184; cabinet of, 192; compares self with Hitler, 192; ignores Hirohito's advice, 179; personality of, 178; and preservation of *kokutai*, 194; as prime minister, 174, 182; recommends war, 183; relations with Hirohito, 178, 183, 187; resigns after Saipan, 55, 193; responsibilities of, 174; and Shimada Shigetarō, 192
Toyoda Soemu, 201; *kokutai* and, 204; personality of, 203–4
training, Allied: for signals intelligence, 111–13

training, Japan, xiv; allegiance to emperor, 81–82, 90; assessment of, 71; barracks life, 83–85; and discipline, 84; emphasis on infantry, 64, 69; goal of, 83; NCOs' role, 81, 85; and recruit training, 76–77, 80–81; relation to combat, 76, 89–90; training cycle of, 86–87; and violence, 77, 82, 83–85, 87
training, U.S.: deficiencies of, 67; of infantry, 62–63; prewar, 61, 68
Tripartite Pact (1940), 44; Hirohito and, 188; Yonai Mitsumasa and, 195
Truk, Caroline Islands, 34, 38, 220 n.36; decision to bypass, 51; strategic location, 50
Truman, Harry S.: concern over U.S. casualties, 157; and Okinawa, 58; OLYMPIC, 157–58; reaction to atomic bomb, 164, 166–67. *See also* atomic bomb; war termination
Tsukada Ko, on prolonged war, 183

ULTRA: assessment of, 130; availability to MacArthur, 143–44; definition of, 128; detects Kyushu reinforcements, 158–61, 167; ignored by MacArthur, 166; limitations of, 137–38, 141, 143; role at Leyte, 128–30, 132, 133, 141, 143; role in OLYMPIC, 153, 158. *See also* codebreaking; signals intelligence; "Y" intelligence
Umezu Yoshijirō, 155, 194, 209; Anami Korechika and, 204–5; and decisive battle of homeland, 145, 195, 199, 200, 201, 207; demands conditional negotiations, 210; and Matsushiro project, 206; and Okinawa, 200; personality of, 195; pessimistic report to Hirohito, 208; and Yunnan issue, 201. *See also* war termination
unconditional surrender: army's attitude toward, 205, 210; Japanese

view of, 213; opposed by Hirohito, 205. *See also* surrender policy; war termination
United States military units:
armies:
  Sixth Army, 68, 136
corps:
  I, 65, 162
  V Amphibious, 162
  XI, 67, 162
  XXIV, 136
divisions:
  First Marine Division, 24; at Guadalcanal, 37
  Thirty-second Division, 65; at Buna, 66–67; at Leyte, 68
regiments:
  112th Cavalry Regimental Combat Team, 67, 68
U.S. Army Command & General Staff College, 72–73

Vasey, John, 117, 118
Versailles Treaty: Hirohito sees as cause of war, 174

war economy, Japan, 39, 53, 60, 246 n.26; equipment shortages at Kyushu, 148; shortages of raw materials, 147
War Guidance Section, 194; prepares Leyte victory communiqué, 196
war ministry, 79, 81; emperor and, 173; functions of, 27; and surrender, 213
war termination, 209; army's conditions of, 203, 205; Hirohito and, 187–88, 189, 201–2, 213; and lack of consensus, 58–59, 209, 210, 214; and lack of plan, 33, 194; linked to decisive battle, 187–90, 198, 203; linked to *kokutai*, 193; negotiations conflict with Kyushu buildup, 161, 205, 210; after Okinawa, 201; and possible imperial abdication, 198; and senior statesmen, 198
weather reports: intelligence value of, 116–17, 124, 125, 126
western divisions (Japanese), 18, 25. *See also* Japanese army units, infantry divisions: Fifth, Eleventh, Twelfth
Wewak, North-East New Guinea, 104, 106, 124, 125
Willoughby, Charles A., 118; and ambiguous assessments, 141–42; and changing Kyushu estimates, 155–56, 161, 162, 164; and estimates at Leyte, 133, 137
Wingate, Ord, 48, 53, 54
World War I, 16, 18, 61, 66; influence on Japanese army, 96

Yamamoto Isoroku: and Pearl Harbor plan, 184; on Yonai, 195
Yamashita Tomoyuki: and defense of Philippines, 39, 40, 56, 59; at Leyte, 136, 140, 197, 259 n.149; personality of, 102–3; at Singapore, 219–20 n.16
Yamato (battleship), 200
Yamato damashii (Japanese spirit), 13, 90
"Y" intelligence, 113, 114; Fifty-five Wireless Section, 119
Yonai Mitsumasa, 194, 208; and imperial abdication, 198; and Koiso Kuniaki, 197; personality of, 195–96; and preservation of *kokutai*, 196, 198, 201, 205; recognizes war is lost, 194; seeks Soviet mediation, 201–2, 209; and war termination, 201, 204, 210
Yoshiwara Kane, 105, 106, 108; quoted 109

Zhukov, Georgi, 3

IN *STUDIES IN WAR, SOCIETY, AND THE MILITARY*

Military Migration and State Formation
The British Military Community in Seventeenth-Century Sweden
Mary Elizabeth Ailes

The Rise of the National Guard
The Evolution of the American Militia, 1865–1920
Jerry Cooper

In the Service of the Emperor
Essays on the Imperial Japanese Army
Edward J. Drea

You Can't Fight Tanks with Bayonets
Psychological Warfare against the Japanese Army in the Southwest Pacific
Allison B. Gilmore

Civilians in the Path of War
Edited by Mark Grimsley and Clifford J. Rogers

Soldiers as Citizens
Former German Officers in the Federal Republic of Germany, 1945–1955
Jay Lockenour

Arabs at War
Military Effectiveness, 1948–1991
Kenneth M. Pollack

The Grand Illusion
The Prussianization of the Chilean Army
William F. Sater and Holger H. Herwig

The Paraguayan War: Volume 1, Causes and Early Conduct
Thomas L. Whigham

The Challenge of Change
Military Institutions and New Realities, 1918–1941
Edited by Harold R. Winton and David R. Mets

Printed in the United States
40879LVS00005B/91